T0215650

Transformational Resilience

How Building Human Resilience to Climate Disruption
Can Safeguard Society and Increase Wellbeing

TRANSFORMATIONAL
RESILIENCE

How Building Human Resilience to Climate Disruption Can
Safeguard Society and Increase Wellbeing

Bob Doppelt

Routledge
Taylor & Francis Group

LONDON AND NEW YORK

First published 2016 by Greenleaf Publishing Limited

Published 2017 by Routledge
4 Park Square, Milton Park, Abingdon, Oxon OX14 4RN
605 Third Avenue, New York, NY 10017

Routledge is an imprint of the Taylor & Francis Group, an informa business

British Library Cataloguing in Publication Data:
    A catalogue record for this book is available from the British Library.

        ISBN-13: 978-1-78353-526-2 [hbk]
        ISBN-13: 978-1-78353-528-6 [pbk]

This book is dedicated to all of the children of the world who will be forced to live under conditions that no other humans for thousands of years have had to endure. It is my hope that this book offers some assistance in helping to ease your pain and setting society on a more constructive and hopeful course.

Contents

List of figures, tables and boxes

Figures

Tables

Boxes

Acknowledgments

This is the fourth book I have written on different aspects of what's needed to shift society's thinking and behaviors to sustain and restore the natural environment and climate while enhancing human wellbeing. Every time I engage in a writing project I am humbled by the extensive work required to produce a good-quality manuscript. I am also awed by the efforts of those who came before me, and who are hard at work today, to create the knowledge, insights, and tools that this book is built on.

There are too many people to name here, but I want to thank all of the practitioners and researchers who over the years have developed the fields of neuroscience, trauma-informed care, post-traumatic growth, and other elements of the field of building human resilience. I also give special thanks to all of the mindfulness teachers I have studied under or taught with over the past 35 years.

The initial drafts of many of the chapters of this book were written at the Rockefeller Foundation's Bellagio Center on Lake Como, Italy, where I was given a Fellowship to write and interact with a number of incredibly talented and insightful people from around the world. I give a special thanks to Cristina Rumbaitis Del Rio, my program officer at the foundation, Pilar Palacia, Managing Director and Elena Ongania, Resident's Coordinator at the Bellagio Center. I also send hugs and cheers to the 20 odd members of the "Occupy Bellagio" group, as our close-knit assembly of residents came to call itself.

In addition, I send my deepest thanks to my friends and colleagues Glenn Schiraldi from the University of Maryland and Resilience Training International, who is also one of the co-founding members of the International Transformational Resilience Coalition (ITRC) which I coordinate, Sue

Kroger from the psychology department at Willamette University, and Ernie Niemi, Principal with Natural Resource Economics Inc., who is one of the top natural resource economists in the business, for taking their valuable time to review and offer important editorial advice on early drafts of the book.

I also send my deepest appreciation to Elaine Miller-Karas, Director of the Trauma Resource Institute, and the other co-founding member of the ITRC, who has helped people around the world use the incredibly potent skills she has developed to calm their nervous systems. In addition, I thank the 14 members of the ITRC Steering Committee, as well as many other ITRC members, who have completed research, developed practical skills, or devoted a great deal of time and effort to building personal and psycho-social-spiritual resilience in the U.S. and globally. This book would not have been possible without all of your work.

I send a special thanks Rebecca Marsh, Rhian Williams, Neil Walker, Dean Bargh, and others at Greenleaf Publishing. Your insights, editorial suggestions, continued encouragement, and ongoing assistance are deeply appreciated.

Finally, I wish to thank my wife Peggy Bloom for enduring a year's worth of my preoccupation with the book and for offering her usual insightful editorial suggestions. You are the best editor any writer could ask for. Most important, you are my best friend and the love of my life.

Introduction: Climate disruption can be humanity's greatest teacher

Hurricane Katrina was unlike any storm residents of New Orleans had ever experienced. It hit the Gulf Coast of the U.S. in August of 2005 with an unprecedented fury causing tremendous physical damage. By the next day, after a number of levees had been breached, 80% of the city was flooded. One of the key lessons Father Vien The Nguyen, a Vietnamese American priest, learned through his efforts to help the members of his Mary Queen of Vietnam Parish recover was the need to create "a sense of calmness and certainty."[1]

Most of his parishioners lived in Village de l'Est, an area more than 15 miles from downtown New Orleans. After the storm they were scattered in locations across the U.S., so Father Vien contacted as many as he could find and urged them to return home. As they came back he held regular masses and other events where they could reconnect with and obtain emotional support from their friends and neighbors, sit in silence, or share their feelings and thoughts with others when they felt like it.

Father Vien knew the importance of what I call "Presencing." When humans experience acute or chronic hardships, deliberately calming our emotions and thoughts and connecting with people who offer emotional support and practical assistance helps buffer us from stress, and reestablishes the sense of safety and security needed to think clearly and make good decisions.

After many of his parishioners had returned to the neighborhood, Father Vien took the next step. Through committees he organized and other actions, he focused everyone on rebuilding their neighborhood. But he knew returning to pre-Katrina conditions was not enough. He said, "Something like

Katrina could happen again and the same thing would happen again. So we decided to prevent that."[2] He and other leaders promoted a new social narrative emphasizing the responsibility to take care of each other and work together to rapidly rebuild their area better than it was before.[3] Their collective response allowed them to reach out and block a toxic waste dump proposed by government agencies for their neighborhood, and to build strong connections between different local social support networks.

Within two years over 90% of the Vietnamese American residents had returned to Village de l'Est, making it one of the areas of New Orleans that recovered most rapidly.[4]

Leaders of the Lower Ninth Ward in New Orleans took the notion of improving conditions beyond previous levels even further than Father Vien. They established a new social narrative focused on rebuilding "as nothing less than the nation's first carbon neutral neighborhood." Environmental sustainability became a centerpiece of the neighborhood's new purpose and vision.[5]

However, the surge of water that hit the Lower Ninth was so strong that it knocked many homes off their foundations, making it one of the most severely damaged neighborhoods in the city. In addition, the neighborhood lacked connections to outside agencies and authorities, which limited its ability to bring in needed resources. These factors have made rebuilding even more challenging than in other areas of the city. But it has been designed with future risks in mind. Today this includes repairing existing homes and building new ones with flood resistant construction techniques, vastly increased energy efficiency, the use of renewable building materials, and solar energy systems. Areas are being redesigned to reduce dependence on cars and increase walkability by clustering businesses near homes, improving bus services, and widening sidewalks.[6] Food security is being increased by supporting community gardens, local markets, and promoting urban agriculture. Restoring wetlands and other ecological systems is also a core element of the strategy.[7]

Both Father Vien and the leaders of the Lower Ninth Ward understood the deep need most people have for what I call "Purposing." When people experience acute traumas or chronic toxic stresses, new social narratives that shift their field of focus to something greater than themselves such as helping the broader community and/or improving the condition of the natural environment can provide invaluable sources of meaning, purpose, and hope in their lives.

Have you ever had a similar experience of using adversity to learn, grow, and increase your own level of functioning and that of others above previous levels? For example, did a serious illness ever cause you to choose to eat more nutritious food, get more sleep, or in other ways take better care of yourself? Has experiencing or witnessing a grave injustice ever led you to actively work for social change? Have you ever been affected by a significant trauma or stressful time and come out the other side stronger, wiser, and with a keener sense of purpose, direction and hope for the future?

Many people answer yes to these questions. This is powerful proof that most people have the capacity to do much more than "adapt" to adversity or "bounce back"—these are the common views of what it means to be resilient, and they are important. However, as demonstrated by Father Vien and leaders of New Orleans Lower Ninth Ward, the majority of humans also have the ability to alter the stories they tell about the world and themselves and make decisions that actually *increase* their sense of wellbeing above previous levels by caring for other people and/or improving the condition of the natural environment and climate. I call this the capacity for Transformational Resilience.

The imperative of making Transformational Resilience a top international priority

Climate disruption is the greatest threat to the health, safety, and wellbeing of humanity today. To prevent uncontrollable planetary warming, climate-disrupting greenhouse gas emissions must be rapidly slashed to levels deemed necessary by the best available science (which ultimately means to almost zero). In addition, forests and other ecosystems that absorb and hold carbon must be protected and restored. Doing what is possible to prepare human-built infrastructure, agriculture, water systems, and other natural systems to withstand and adapt to the physical impacts of climate disruption is also important.

These actions are necessary because a growing number of climate scientists say that a 1.5°C (2.5°F) rise in global average surface temperatures above pre-industrial levels will generate significant damage to society and the ecological systems that support it, and that anything above that level poses major risks of triggering civilization-altering runaway climate disruption. At the 2015 UN Climate Summit in Paris world leaders agreed to constrain the rise in global temperatures to "well below" 2°C (3.6°F). This is a positive step. However, the emission reduction pledges made at the UN

Summit do not come close to limiting temperature increases to even 2°C above pre-industrial levels, let alone below that target. Further, the pledges are not legally binding, and voluntary efforts to significantly cut emissions have continually failed. Unfortunately, given the current state of affairs, it seems difficult to see how the rise in global temperatures will be limited to the 1.5° threshold. To the contrary, as of now, temperatures seem likely to rise by at least 2°C, and possibly much higher.

Further, even though efforts to prepare society's infrastructure and natural resources for and adapt to climate impacts are new and will improve, few are likely to prevent much physical damage as temperatures heat up. Some might even cause more damage.

These realities mean that significant harm to society's physical infrastructure, natural resource base, and economies is now inevitable. The damages will be indisputably traumatic and exceedingly stressful, producing significant effects on the human mind and body. Without landmark efforts to enhance the capacity of individuals and groups for Transformational Resilience, the traumas and toxic stresses—meaning persistent overwhelming stresses—will generate unprecedented levels of anxiety, depression, post-traumatic stress disorder, suicides, and other mental health problems for individuals worldwide. These woes will, in turn, produce a boatload of psycho-social-spiritual maladies, such as increased interpersonal aggression, crime, violence, hopelessness, and more, that undermine the safety, security, and health of people all around the planet.

In addition, traumatized individuals and groups exist in a fear-based self-protective survival mode that turns their focus inward, inhibits their ability to learn, and can all but eliminate their concern for the welfare of others or the natural environment. This will make it even more difficult to motivate people to slash their greenhouse gas emissions, prepare for climate impacts, and do their part to reduce climate impacts to a manageable level.

However, ample research shows that when individuals and groups develop effective resilience skills, they are able to avoid personally or socially harmful reactions to adversity, recover more quickly when they happen, and use trauma and stress as catalysts to actually increase their wellbeing above previous levels. Thus, a third major focus must be added to the global response to climate disruption. It must become a top international priority to proactively build the capacity of individuals and groups for Transformational Resilience. This will help people use the traumas and stresses generated by climate disruption as stimulus to make the changes in thinking, practices, and policies required to increase personal and social wellbeing, as well as the condition of the natural environment, well above current levels and thrive.

To actualize this goal, practitioners and policy-makers in the climate, environmental management, disaster preparedness, and related fields must quickly expand their focus beyond external physical issues such as emission reductions and adapting infrastructure and natural systems to climate impacts and make major investments in *preventative* initiatives aimed at enhancing the capacity of *people* for Transformational Resilience. Similarly, mental and behavioral health practitioners and policy-makers must rapidly expand their focus beyond treating psychological and emotional problems, and invest as much or more in teaching people how to *prevent* these maladies in the first place.

As a starting point, building the capacity for Transformational Resilience will require that adults and youth alike learn how trauma and toxic stress can affect their minds and bodies. It will also involve teaching people simple skills they can use to calm their nervous system and find meaning, purpose, and hope through concrete actions in the midst of the many traumas and toxic stresses generated by climate disruption. It will require that organizations and communities worldwide adopt principles and practices that enhance the capacity of their members and stakeholders for Transformational Resilience. Integrated strategies will also be needed in every nation to build widespread capacity for Transformational Resilience. The strategies will need to link policies and programs at the national, state, and municipal government levels with grassroots efforts to ensure that learning Transformational Resilience skills become as common as learning to read and write.

An essential step to achieving these ends is the development of new social narratives that emphasize the deep sense of meaning, direction, and hope in life people will find when they use climate-enhanced traumas and toxic stresses as catalysts to deliberately increase the wellbeing of others and improve the condition of the Earth's natural environment substantially above current conditions as a way to enhance their own wellbeing.

The failure to acknowledge the need to build a culture of human resilience

Unfortunately, few people have recognized the urgency or benefits of building the capacity of individuals and groups worldwide for Transformational

Resilience.[8] To the extent that the need to address the negative personal mental health and psycho-social-spiritual impacts of climate disruption has even been acknowledged, the emphasis has been on better post-disaster mental health treatment.[9]

Improving the capacity of the mental health elements of emergency response systems is important. However, as temperatures rise, the mental health and emergency services infrastructure of both wealthy and poor nations will *never* be robust enough to help the growing number of people traumatized by more extreme weather disasters that are occurring more frequently as temperatures rise.

Further, even if the mental health elements of emergency response systems were dramatically improved, most people won't seek help because of the stigma associated with being perceived as "mentally weak."

It is also important to understand that the personal psychological distress and psycho-social-spiritual maladies generated by climate disruption go well beyond the traumatic effects of extreme weather events to include many types of chronic toxic stresses. These range from the distress generated from dealing with the unrelenting threat of physical damage and personal injury caused by big storms, floods, wildfires, and other uncontrollable impacts, to the psychological and emotional strains of dealing with ongoing shortages of water, food, and other basic goods, the loss of jobs and livelihoods, new illnesses and diseases, rising hopelessness and helplessness, and much more. Post-disaster mental health treatments do not help people deal with these types of chronic toxic stress.[10]

The bottom line is that in the U.S., Europe, and most other nations, little help is currently available and, without major changes, even less is likely in the future to help people deal constructively with the negative personal mental health or psycho-social-spiritual impacts of climate disruption.

Climate disruption is unlike any crisis modern society has faced

The lack of assistance is extremely alarming because few people grasp how different climate disruption is than any other adversity modern society has ever faced. As temperatures rise, it will become clear that it is not merely a series of discrete extreme weather events primarily affecting "vulnerable" communities and individuals separated by long periods of calm that allow for recovery. The cumulative effects of the direct and indirect impacts are already significant in many parts of the world, and they will become increasingly unyielding affecting the rich and poor alike, no matter where they live, with no clear end-point that allows people time to recover.

This points to why climate disruption is so different than previous crises that people in the U.S. and Europe, for instance, have overcome, such as the Great Depression and World War II. In those situations people believed that if they persevered the adversities would eventually end. Those hardships also did not undermine the ecological basis of life on the planet. In contrast, without dramatic changes, climate disruption will continue for centuries, drive millions of species to extinction, and threaten the very existence of human civilization.

Climate disruption will shatter many of our fundamental assumptions and beliefs

Deep inside, each of us holds basic views about how the world works, who we are as individuals, and the relationship between both. We use our core assumptions and beliefs to make sense of events, construct plans, forecast the future, and guide our actions. Although our conceptual framework defines who we are, many people go through life without ever closely examining their deep-seated guiding perspectives.

The psychological definition of trauma is that an experience seriously undermines or completely shatters at least some, if not all, of an individual's core assumptions and beliefs. When this happens, some people try to deny, ignore, or blame others in an attempt to put their views of the world and themselves back together exactly as they were before the adversity. The more they try to hang on to their old assumptions and beliefs, the more mired in denial, overwhelmed, and distressed they become.

In contrast, people who grasp that reality demands that they reconfigure their basic perspectives become much more capable of dealing constructively with adversity, and able to find new and often even more fulfilling ways to live.

The physical impacts of climate disruption will produce this type of trauma for many, if not most people worldwide. In fact, as global temperatures climb toward, or rise beyond 1.5°C above pre-industrial levels, it will become clear that the experience lies completely outside of the boundaries of the existing assumptions and beliefs most of us hold about the way the world works and the types of thinking, behavior, and lifestyle that can be sustained on the finite system that is Earth. This will create a profound shock to our systems.

As the impacts escalate, it will become evident that climate disruption will put an end to many eras, including the epochs of unconstrained fossil fuel use, material and energy consumption, degradation of forests, wetlands, and other ecological systems that sequester carbon, and other activities that today seem completely natural and normal. As it plays out, many long cherished personal beliefs, as well as economic, cultural, and political ideologies will be shattered, leaving more and more people frightened and in a self-protective survival mode, struggling or unable to find meaning, direction, or hope in life.

Further, climate disruption is caused by human activities, and on a cumulative historic basis primarily by the high levels of material and energy consumption and carbon emissions generated by industrialized nations, and the U.S. most of all. Many people in nonindustrialized nations know this and are angry and resentful. Humans generally can accept the harm caused by disasters resulting from natural phenomena such as earthquakes. They are much less able or willing to put up with injury, and instead frequently retaliate, when they believe other people have caused their suffering. This suggests tumultuous international problems could lie ahead for the U.S. and other high emitting industrialized nations as temperatures rise.

However, few governments, not-for-profit, faith, or private organizations around the world have grasped the tremendous mental health and psychosocial-spiritual perils that lie ahead.

An old tale aptly describes our current predicament.[11] A person walking down the street at night notices a drunk hunched over with a determined look searching for something under a lamppost. "What are you looking for?" asks the walker. "I lost my keys," replies the drunk. "Oh, that's too bad. I'll help you find them." "Thanks, but you can't help," replies the drunk. "Why not?" asks the walker. "Because I dropped them somewhere else." "Then why are you looking in this spot?" "Because the light is better here."

Like the drunk, most practitioners and policy-makers in the climate, environmental management, mental health, disaster preparedness, and related fields continue to do what they have always done because it is easier to quantify and show results, and does not require major adjustments to their existing mindset and approach. The prevailing mantra in the climate field is that reducing greenhouse gas emissions, hardening physical infrastructure, and adapting agriculture and other key natural assets to withstand climate impacts, mainly through better science and new technologies, are what matter most. In the mental health field the dominant ideology is that anxiety, depression, and post-traumatic stress disorder found primarily among "vulnerable" populations as a result of extreme weather events is the primary psychological risk and post-disaster treatment can ameliorate this problem. The disaster preparedness field seems to embrace both views.

The worldwide rise in mental illness, interpersonal aggression, crime, violence, and other psycho-social-spiritual maladies directly produced or indirectly aggravated by climate disruption demonstrate that these perspectives are fundamentally flawed.

In contrast, as I will discuss throughout the book, a growing body of evidence shows that building personal resilience skills, robust social support networks, and close collaborations among local organizations—the core elements of Transformational Resilience—not physical infrastructure, natural resource adaptation, or post-trauma treatment, are the keys to enhancing human resilience. Unless practitioners and policy-makers rapidly grasp this and launch initiatives to proactively build the capacity of humans across the planet for Transformational Resilience, climate disruption will create a bleak future for much of humanity.

Personal and collective transformation: the potential silver lining of climate disruption

The good news is that it *is* possible to increase the human capacity for Transformational Resilience. Ample experience, backed up by a robust body of research, shows that at any age people can learn Transformational Resilience skills. With effective knowledge, skills, and tools most people have the capacity to use adversity as a catalyst to alter their perceptions and attitudes and make choices that can actually increase their sense of wellbeing, as well as that of other people, and even the condition of the natural environment. Restoring the climate while increasing the sense of wellbeing of others can give many individuals and groups the higher calling in life that they are desperately searching for.

There is nothing new here. For centuries heroic tales and mythical stories have been written about people who discover previously unknown strengths and experience tremendous growth as a result of adversity. The core tenets of Buddhism, Christianity, Judaism, Islam and other spiritual and religious traditions are founded on the notion that suffering can result in beneficial outcomes.[12]

One of the most rapidly expanding areas of psychological research is post-traumatic growth—or what I call adversity-based growth. This is the study of individuals who use tragedy as a catalyst to not merely return to their previous levels of functioning—as mentioned, this is the conventional view of resilience—but instead to increase their functioning to a level higher than it was before the trauma.[13] The trauma itself does not produce this change. It is the struggle to make sense of the adversities and adjust their assumptions and beliefs about the world and themselves to the new realities that leads to growth.

The concept of hormesis offers a useful analogy to describe this process. This is a biological response that *improves* the ability of the human body to handle stress. When bodybuilders lift weights, for example, their muscles are damaged by overload. They do not immediately get stronger. To the contrary, the weight actually weakens the body in the short term. However, in the hours and days that follow, the body reacts to the stress by building stronger muscles and a healthier, more resilient body. Hormesis does not return the body to a preexisting state. It creates better-than-before levels of functioning.[14]

The mental and social capacities of individuals can grow as a result of adversity through a similar process. Psychological hormesis occurs when people view stress as vital sources of information to learn from, and then turn and face their troubles rather than denying, ignoring, or blaming others for them. This process allows people to honestly examine their core assumptions and beliefs and gain new insights about how the world works and who they are as humans.

This transformational process does not eliminate their pain or loss. People usually do not heal, recover, or find closure in the way we typically think about these concepts. Instead, as they struggle to make sense of a traumatic experience, they alter the story they tell about the world and themselves in ways that lead to a new sense of purpose, direction, and hope in their lives. For many people this involves reorienting their personal values and goals toward what is called "eudaimonic" wellbeing. This involves finding fulfillment and joy by rising above their personal self-interests and in some way assisting other people or caring for nature.

As the examples provided in the book will show, organizations and communities can engage in similar transformative experiences.[15]

If this type of hormesis—or what I call Transformational Resilience— becomes a central goal of policies and programs aimed at addressing the climate crisis, and enhancing all forms of life—including but not limited to human life—becomes the fundamental mission, the negative personal mental health and psycho-social-spiritual maladies generated by the climate crisis can be minimized and when they do occur they can be more easily resolved. Equally important, many individuals and groups will be able to use the traumas and toxic stresses associated with climate disruption as catalysts to find new sources of meaning and hope in their lives and thrive.

Please do not misinterpret what I am suggesting: There is nothing positive about human-caused climate disruption. I am in no way attempting to minimize the tremendous challenges that lie ahead. To the contrary, it is a profoundly distressing tragedy of epic proportions that is certain to generate significant suffering and harm to humans and the Earth's ecological systems and species for generations to come.

Ample experience, however, reinforced by a robust body of research, has demonstrated that most people can learn how to use negative events for beneficial purposes. Humans are intrinsically motivated to seek out and move in a growth-oriented direction. This quality can be utilized now to help individuals and groups find a silver lining in climate disruption by using it as a powerful catalyst to rethink how they live and find ways to increase personal, collective, and environmental wellbeing.[16]

Purpose and outline of the book

This book is a clarion call to people everywhere, and especially to practitioners and policy-makers in the climate, environmental management, corporate responsibility, mental health, disaster preparedness, faith, and related fields to promptly expand their focus and launch major initiatives to proactively build widespread capacity for Transformational Resilience across the planet. The central premise is that at this time in history our chief task is not to save the Earth. It is to save ourselves from ourselves. Only by helping people learn how to notice when their minds and bodies are dysregulated by traumas or toxic stress, and then use simple methods to calm their bodies, minds, and emotions can personally and socially destructive reactions to the adversities generated by climate disruption be minimized. Only by helping individuals and groups realize, in the era of ever-increasing traumas and toxic stresses enhanced by climate disruption, the only way to find meaning and thrive in life is by in some way helping others and improving the condition of the natural environment. And only by helping organizations and communities worldwide enhance the capacity of their members for Transformational Resilience can these changes be sustained while the economic, social, and political shifts required to reduce the climate crisis to manageable levels unfold.

Most of the information and core principles offered in the book are applicable worldwide. However, the skills and techniques that are described will need to be adapted for different age and demographic groups and cultures. Some are likely to be applicable mostly in the U.S., E.U. and other industrialized societies.

Part 1 describes how traumas and chronic toxic stresses enhanced by climate disruption are likely to adversely affect the mental health of individuals and the psycho-social-spiritual functioning of organizations, communities, and entire societies. Chapters 1 and 2 of this section of the book might be difficult for some readers because the impacts can seem overwhelming and depressing. If you have this reaction I urge you to move on to Chapter 3 where you will begin to learn about the tremendous benefits and opportunities to be had by learning Transformational Resilience skills. However, I urge you not to skip Chapters 1 and 2 completely because it is vital that you understand what is at stake. One way to do that might be to refer back to those chapters when you read different sections of the book to make sure you understand why specific skills and tools are needed.

Part I also describes the *Resilient Growth*™ model, which is a framework I developed that can be used to guide efforts to build widespread capacity for Transformational Resilience. This model can be applied to any type of traumatic or ongoing overwhelming stress. However, I've focused it specifically on the adversities generated by climate disruption because it is the most serious challenge to personal mental health and psycho-social-spiritual wellbeing that exists today. As I've said, the failure to build widespread levels of human resilience for these difficulties threatens to stall or completely block efforts to reduce greenhouse gas emissions and adapt to climate impacts. This reaction will make it even more difficult to reduce climate disruption to manageable levels.

Part 2 of the book goes into detail about the "Presencing" skills that form the first part of the *Resilient Growth*™ model. These skills help individuals stabilize their nervous system and calm their emotions and thoughts in the midst of ongoing adversity.

Part 3 of the book describes the "Purposing" skills that form the second focus of the *Resilient Growth*™. These skills help individuals learn how to find meaning, direction, and hope in life even in the midst of trauma and stress.

Part 4 moves beyond the individual level and offers suggestions on how to build the capacity for Transformational Resilience within organizations, communities, and entire societies.

How to use this book

Part 1 of the book describes the research on the mental health and psycho-social-spiritual impacts of climate disruption in a straightforward manner. However, I've written the other sections in workbook form to allow you, the reader, to personally learn and practice skills and use tools that can enhance your capacity for Transformational Resilience. I've taken that approach because in order to teach the information and skills to others, you need to be solidly grounded in them yourself. The workbook form also allows you to use the book as a training manual to lead groups through the process of building Transformational Resilience. Indeed, that is the origin of this book. It is based on the manual used in the Transformational Resilience programs I facilitate.

Let us now begin the journey toward Transformational Resilience.

Part 1:
The personal mental health and psycho-social-spiritual impacts of climate disruption

1
The psychological effects of climate disruption on individuals

As Superstorm Sandy roared through her town destroying buildings and flooding streets, Kathy Michaels and her family took refuge in the attic of their home. "We were holding hands. We thought it would maybe be our last night on Earth," she said. They survived, and since that time Michaels has tried antidepressants, psychotherapy, and weekly support groups to cope with the trauma she experienced. But the distress persists. "You don't like things like this to define your life, but I don't think I'll ever be the same," she concluded.[17]

A record drought in Queensland, Australia has dragged on since 2013, causing much more than financial loss to farmers. "I can say from personal experience, the effects of the drought will lead many to suffer depression and a number to commit suicide. The mental stress suffered by watching your stock die, your family's livelihood and in some cases generations of family work fail is crushing," said Brian Egan, founder of Aussie Helpers.[18]

These stories illustrate how the traumas and toxic stresses generated by fast-moving extreme weather events and slow-growing climate impacts can undermine the mental health of individuals. These psychological problems, and much more, will become widespread as global temperatures heat up. As more people become psychologically and emotionally distressed, psycho-social-spiritual maladies will also increase, including interpersonal aggression, crime, violence, extremism, terrorism, and more.

However, virtually no attention has been given to preparing individuals and groups for the psychological and psycho-social-spiritual woes generated by climate disruption. This is a monumental mistake. Unless efforts are rapidly launched to help people learn how these events might affect their minds and bodies as well as skills to respond constructively to these adversities, the negative reactions will undermine the health and wellbeing of individuals, families, organizations, communities, and entire societies. They also threaten to stall or completely sink efforts to cut emissions and prepare for climate impacts, making it even more difficult to reduce climate disruption to manageable levels. On the other hand, if people learn simple resilience skills, they will have a much greater likelihood of using adversities such as those generated by rising global temperatures to learn, grow, and thrive.

This underscores that today's two dominant responses to climate disruption—emission reductions (usually called mitigation) and preparing physical infrastructure and natural resources to adapt to impacts (called adaptation)—while essential, are by themselves woefully insufficient for the challenges that lie ahead. A third major focus is needed: building the capacity of individuals and groups of all types to cope with climate-disruption-related traumas as toxic stresses in ways that not only prevent personally and socially harmful reactions, but also increase individual and collective wellbeing and the condition of the natural environment and climate substantially above current levels. This is the capacity for Transformational Resilience.

No matter how fast emissions are reduced significant physical damage is now inevitable

To understand the need for building the capacity of individuals and groups for Transformational Resilience, it is important to have a solid understanding of the types of physical damage rising temperatures will produce, and how those impacts are likely to negatively affect human psychological, social, and spiritual wellbeing. Remember, reading the information that follows can be distressing. If it becomes too much to bear, I suggest you skip to Chapters 3 and beyond to learn about how building widespread capacity for Transformational Resilience can minimize some of the problems. But the information presented in this chapter and the next is too important to ignore, so when you are ready, circle back and read it.

In 2014, the UN-sponsored Intergovernmental Panel on Climate Change's (IPCC) Fifth Assessment Report released a report stating that that average global surface temperatures have already increased by 0.85°C (about 1.3°F) above the levels that existed in the late 1800s. In late 2015 the National Oceanic and Atmospheric Administration (NOAA), the National Aeronautics and Space Administration (NASA), and other global temperature monitoring organizations said that global temperatures have now risen by 1°C (1.8°F).[19] In order to avoid triggering runaway climate disruption, at the UN Climate Summit in Copenhagen in 2009, the international community agreed to limit the rise in global temperatures to 2°C above pre-industrial levels, and we are already halfway there. However, Dr. James Hansen, former head of NASA's Goddard Institute of Space Studies, who is considered the godfather of climate research, along with 16 colleagues, says that 2°C is too high. In a report released in July of 2015 they said that anything more than a 1.5°C temperature increase above pre-industrial levels would pose a significant chance of unleashing civilization-altering climate disruption.[20]

Hansen and his colleagues also said that it is still technically possible to keep temperatures from rising more than 1.5°C above pre-industrial levels. However, that means further temperature increases must be limited to 0.5°C. This will require a massive full-out global undertaking. Researchers at the International Institute for Applied Systems Analysis and the Potsdam Institute for Climate Impact, for instance, calculated in 2015 that enough greenhouse gasses are already concentrated in the atmosphere to lock in at least another 0.5°C temperature increase. This indicates that global temperatures will rise beyond 1.5°C to at least 2°C by mid-century. Reinforcing Hansen's statement, those researchers also calculate that, with big rapid cuts in emissions, it is possible to bring temperatures back down to 1.5°C by 2100.[21] But the rise in temperatures to 2°C indicates big trouble ahead.

Further, even though the UN Climate Summit held in Paris in December of 2015 led to a global agreement to limit global temperatures to "well below" 2°C, no legally binding targets were included in the accord and it was left to each nation to determine how to cut their emissions. Consequently, following the summit, Dr. Hansen called the process "a fraud really, a fake." He went on to say that "It's just worthless words. There is no action, just promises."[22] I dearly hope Dr. Hansen is wrong and that the Paris summit is the wakeup call political, business, and community leaders worldwide need to grasp the risks and make quick dramatic cuts in emissions. But, so far, very few have been willing to initiate the changes required to slash emissions to levels that the best science says are needed to prevent catastrophe.

The bottom line is that, even if the international community begins to rapidly cut emissions, temperatures will still rise to levels that guarantee a wide range of destructive physical impacts.

The physical impacts of climate disruption

What types of impact can be expected? For the sake of simplicity I've divided them into three categories: fast-moving direct physical impacts; slow-growing direct physical impacts; and Black Swan events.

Fast-moving direct physical impacts

The consequences that most people associate with climate disruption are the direct physical impacts generated by major windstorms, rainstorms, snowstorms, floods, heat waves, cold spells, and other quickly developing extreme weather events. Research in 2015 by the Commonwealth Scientific and Industrial Research Organization (CISRO), one of Australia's leading climate science organizations, projected that climate disruption would double the number of extreme weather events in coming years.[23]

Indeed, extreme weather is increasing across the planet. Since 2007 extraordinary floods have impacted Pakistan, China, England, Italy, and other nations on every continent on Earth. Major heat waves and wildfires have impacted Russia. Record heat waves, cold snaps, snowstorms, wildfires, floods and hurricanes have hammered the U.S.

Research by Georgia Tech University and the National Center for Atmospheric Research found that since the 1970s the number of Category 4 and 5 hurricanes, which are the most powerful, have increased by 20–35% around the world.[24] A few years after that study was released, research found that about twice as many Atlantic hurricanes form each year on average compared with a century ago. Both studies concluded that warmer sea surface temperatures and altered wind patterns associated with climate disruption are fueling much of the increase.[25]

Many more frequent and intense fast-moving extreme weather events can be expected in coming years as global temperatures rise.

Slow-growing direct physical impacts

Less obvious to some people but equally important are a wide variety of slowly developing destructive physical impacts produced by climate disruption. These include drought, desertification, glacial melting that contributes to sea-level rise, coastal erosion, acidification of the oceans and fresh water, land subsidence due to depleted water tables, decreased air quality, soil impairment, forest degradation, biodiversity loss, disease expansion, and other gradual changes with majorly detrimental effects.[26]

Record drought, for example, hit the U.S. state of California particularly hard in 2014 and 2015. January is usually San Francisco's wettest month, averaging four and a half inches of rain since 1850. However, the city saw no rain at all in January 2015—not a drop. In the previous 165 years, that had never happened. The closest the city came to a rainless January before that was when it got 0.06 inches—and that occurred the year before—in 2014.

Sea levels are rising slowly, though at a faster rate than climate scientists originally projected. Already in many locations around the world the result is flooded estuaries and lowlands, higher tides, larger and more destructive storm surges, increased coastal erosion, and the salinization of groundwater and soils.[27]

Conservative estimates suggest that about a 0.6 m (2 feet) sea-level rise is likely by the year 2100. New research suggests, however, that the high end might be a 6 m (20 feet) rise over the long term due to melting ice sheets and glaciers.[28] No matter what the actual increase turns out to be, by the end of the century—and maybe much sooner—densely populated coastal areas on every continent ranging from London to Mumbai and New York will be continually threatened by flooding or completely submerged. The physical safety as well the homes, businesses, and other assets of millions of people will be lost unless gargantuan amounts of money are spent to build dykes, install pumps, and implement other actions to prevent it. Even then, in many cases it will be impossible to prevent significant ongoing damage.

Black Swan events

Another type of damaging physical impact that will become increasingly common as climate disruption unfolds is a Black Swan event.[29] This term describes a change that occurs somewhere at the global or regional levels which, like one domino pushing over another, slowly cascades through multiple systems producing surprising harmful effects.

An example is the growing body of research that suggests that the contrasting weather extremes experienced in the U.S. in the winter of 2015, when the east coast was exceptionally cold and snowy and the west coast was unusually warm and dry, resulted at least in part from the accelerated warming taking place in the Arctic. Additional warmth in one part of the globe—the Arctic—appears to have weakened the polar jet stream and increased the frequency of periods where frigid Arctic air was pushed south into the eastern U.S. impacting people and ecosystems, while warmer air moved north into the western half of the country leading to drought and other impacts.[30] Many other surprising and often counterintuitive Black Swan events can be expected as the Earth's climate system heats up.

The physical impacts directly affect society

The physical damage caused by climate disruption will continually degrade or destroy human-built structures and systems as well as the natural resources society depends on. For example, residential and commercial buildings can be impaired or totally ruined by extreme weather events, as can transportation, water delivery, sewage, energy supply, and communications systems. Crop production and food supplies can be reduced or completely wiped out by extreme heat, drought, catastrophic storm, or new diseases and insects. Supply chains can be disrupted and businesses can be temporarily or permanently closed as a result of climate change. Structures in low-lying coastal areas are being physically damaged by higher storm surges and over time entire regions will be completely flooded by rising sea levels. Many other known and surprising physical impacts to human-built systems and structures are certain to occur as well (see Box 1.1).

Box 1.1: Examples of the physical impacts of climate disruption

Fast-moving physical impacts

- Record rainstorms
- Record snowstorms
- Record windstorms
- Record hot temperatures
- Record cold temperatures
- Record flooding
- Record wildfires
- Larger tides and storm surges
- Many other surprise fast-moving impacts

Slow-growing physical impacts

- Drought and water shortages
- Desertification
- Sea-level rise
- Ocean acidification
- Saltwater intrusion into groundwater
- Soil depletion
- Reduced air quality
- New illnesses and diseases
- Many other surprise slow-growing impacts

Black Swan Events

- Changes that occur in one part of an ecosystem that ricochet through multiple systems causing significant harm.

The Fukushima problem: limitations and risks of current approaches to adapting to climate impacts

In an attempt to minimize the damage, efforts to prepare key human-built infrastructure and natural resources to withstand and adapt to these physical impacts have been launched in many parts of the world. My organization was one of the first in the U.S. to engage in climate preparedness. For over a decade my staff organized and led adaptation programs across the country, from Florida to Oregon. My staff also established the American Society of Adaptation Professionals, the first professional society of climate preparedness specialists.[31] After carefully assessing our work and that of many others in the field, I concluded that, even though climate adaptation is new and will improve, with global temperatures now on a path to rise by at least 1.5°C above pre-industrial levels, and likely much higher, few interventions are likely to prevent much physical damage. Worse, some might lead to even more harm, a classic problem called iatrogenics, which means damage caused by the treatments of a healer.[32]

Many preparedness programs, for instance, base their plans on climate impact projections generated by the downscaling of global computer models to regional levels. Global climate models have been very accurate in projecting the rise in global average temperatures resulting from increased atmospheric concentrations of greenhouse gasses. However, when downscaled to the regional and local levels, they are much less accurate. Downscaled global climate models can at best project long-term trends, not the specific types, frequencies, intensities, or locations of impacts. When used at the local level to guide adaptation efforts, the result will frequently be massive wastes of time and money because the actual impacts will occur at different magnitudes, in different locations, or in different combinations than downscaled global computer models can project.[33] Not only will the public's safety fail to be enhanced, helplessness and hopelessness will grow as people see and experience failed efforts.

The theory of using downscaled global computer models to forecast impacts is based on the often unspoken supposition that the "vulnerabilities" of physical infrastructure and natural resources to climate impacts can be diagnosed, quantified, and "fixed," largely with better science and technologies. This approach is based on the medical model of health, where health is seen as the absence of pathology. Although few climate adaptation practitioners seem to be aware of it, this has become an ideology—and one filled with many unproven assumptions. Better science and technologies will, of course, be important. But focusing on vulnerability often becomes a self-fulfilling prophecy because it focuses attention on limitations and allocates resources to fixing weaknesses. From the perspective of physical infrastructure, after one type of vulnerability is identified another often appears in a never-ending process. From a social perspective this notion leads to the idea that income levels, age, and minority status usually determines vulnerability to the impacts of climate change. However, research has found that these and other similar "vulnerabilities" are not the primary factors that determine risk or resilience.[34] To the contrary, it is the lack of individual and group skills, robust social support networks, and other personal and psycho-social-spiritual factors that most determine risk. Further, building on strengths, not eliminating weaknesses, enhances resilience. Focusing on vulnerability is often the exact opposite of building resilience.

Still another problem is that most climate preparedness programs focus on direct shocks associated with extreme weather events and ignore longer-term persistent stresses. This has led to an emphasis on emergency planning and disaster response, which is primarily a reactive approach.

Many climate adaptation efforts are also based on the erroneous principle of needing to protect systems from volatility and minimize environmental change. In reality, these are the very factors that build strength and resilience. Wildfires, for example, are an essential element of the natural processes that create resilient forest ecosystems. However, forest management agencies in the U.S. spend millions of dollars trying to prevent wildfires or quickly put them out after they ignite. As a result, forests become less ecologically resilient and more prone to serious harm from human-caused and natural disturbances.

Many climate adaptation efforts also seek to protect systems that degrade or destroy ecological processes, such as the fossil fuel infrastructure.

In addition, few climate preparedness programs acknowledge the profound inequities produced by today's lopsided distribution of power and wealth. Although a few programs in the U.S. and elsewhere focus on preparing "vulnerable" communities for climate impacts, more often than not these are operated by not-for-profit organizations that have limited resources. Based on what I have seen, the vast majority of resources invested in climate adaptation continue to be spent on protecting physical infrastructure and natural resources used by mainstream wealthier populations, which leaves people that do not have economic or political power on their own.

These failures often occur because many climate preparedness professionals fail to grasp the limitations of coping and adapting. As they are often used today in the climate field, both coping and adaptation seek to maintain "homeostasis"—that is, the goal is to build the capacity to return to something close to pre-crisis or "normal" conditions and maintain the status quo after impacts occur.

In much of the world, however, it will be difficult, if not impossible, to maintain homeostasis as temperatures climb to 1.5°C above pre-industrial levels or higher because what is coming is at an altogether larger scale than people can comprehend and their capacity to prepare and adapt external physical systems will often be overwhelmed.[35] In fact, in many locations it has not even been possible to maintain homeostasis in the face of the 0.85 degree Celsius global temperature rise that has occurred so far, which is just half, and maybe far less than half, of what lies ahead.

For example, researchers at the United Nations University in 2012 assessed coping and adaptation efforts in five countries—Bangladesh, Bhutan, Gambia, Kenya, and Micronesia—representing three major regions. They concluded that existing adaptation strategies were not enough to avoid significant loss or damage, have considerable economic, social, cultural, health and other costs that are not regained, generate a number of negative long-term effects, and in many cases were not even possible to implement.[36]

In the near term, the outcomes of preparing and adapting might be more positive in wealthier nations that have greater resources and capacity, although I have seen little credible evidence supporting this conclusion. However, even if some programs are effective, there will never be enough money available to redesign and retrofit every road, building, water, and sewer system, and other elements of society's physical infrastructure or natural resource base to prevent significant damage as temperatures rise close to or beyond 1.5°C above pre-industrial levels. Further, financial investments in disaster preparedness have historically been embroiled in politics, which make them an unreliable source to deal with on-the-ground needs.[37]

Equally important, much of what is considered "normal" today is not very desirable. For many people, "normal" includes high levels of childhood abuse and trauma as well as racism, sexism, economic oppression, poverty, an ever-increasing pace of life driven by technologies that were supposed to make life easier, and other traumas and stressors. Further, in most industrial societies the massive amounts of fossil fuels and material resources that are consumed and the waste that is generated, including greenhouse gasses, are seen as completely normal and in fact essential to keep the economy from collapsing. Yet these are the root causes of the climate crisis.

In short, most existing efforts to prepare for the climate crisis are organized around goals and strategies that will do little to prevent harm or reduce the problem to manageable levels. And, by leaving existing systems and structures essentially unchanged, some will perpetuate existing ills or produce altogether new ones.

This is the Fukushima problem. Just as the designers of the Japanese nuclear plant erroneously thought the designs produced by their risk management protocols addressed every conceivable threat, in complex systems with numerous difficult-to-perceive feedback systems in play such as the Earth's climate, small and often imperceptible changes that occur in one part of the system can generate exponentially large, surprising, and sometimes irreversible impacts in many other parts.

Humanity will, of course, adapt as the planet's temperatures heat up. But it is important not to confuse adaptation with being personally or collectively safe and secure. In many cases the current approaches to adaptation will provide little relief.

How climate-enhanced traumas and stresses can affect the psychological health of individuals

If significant physical impacts are now inevitable, without significant efforts to build widespread capacity for Transformational Resilience, what are the likely consequences for personal mental health and psycho-social-spiritual wellbeing? To answer this, let's begin by understanding how the human capacity to cope with adversities can be undermined.

Through thousands of years of experience humans have developed the capacity to withstand a great deal of adversity. This is one of the reasons our species now dominates the planet. Even when they experience a major adversity, most people recover fairly rapidly. However, a number of factors can lengthen the time it takes to recover, or leave people permanently dysregulated by acute traumas or chronic toxic stresses. Let's examine some of these factors.

- **First, the sheer demands of a trauma or stress can be overwhelming.** In other words, the severity or significance of an event is too much or happens too fast for people to come to grips with, thereby disrupting their sense of safety, control, predictability, and trust.[38]

- **Fears about personal safety can produce significant psychological distress.** Closely linked with the first factor, overwhelming trauma and persistent toxic stress can shatter an individual's sense of safety, which is one of the most primal needs of humans. When feelings of safety disappear, such as when people fear for their lives, or the health and wellbeing of family or close friends, their ability to calm their emotions, think clearly, and make wise and skillful decisions diminishes.

- **Constant uncertainty is a major contributor of toxic stress, which makes irregular but persistent sequences of adversity particularly harmful.** Humans experience much less mental distress when they believe situations are fairly predictable, such as when they know that heat waves will occur in the summer rather than other times of the year, compared with when they perceive a situation to be unpredictable, such as when they have no way to know when a horrific storm might harm them. People are also less distressed when they believe they have the ability to control a situation, such as the ability to prevent a local stream from flooding by constructing revetments, compared with when they experience uncontrollable situations, such as the inability to prevent continually debilitating waves of hot or cold weather.[39]

- **The depletion or destruction of the physical, financial, and social resources people need to deal with adversity can produce great psychological distress.** Lack of resources can lead to anxiety, depression, and feelings of desperation and hopelessness. This is especially problematic when the resources available to individuals are already low due to prior traumatic stressors, poverty, joblessness, or other factors.

- **The loss of a sense of place can undermine psychological wellbeing.** This can occur, for example, when an individual is forced to leave their home and community and migrate to another region as a result of a traumatic situation. Think about the mental distress the Vietnamese community in New Orleans experienced after they were forced to leave their friends and neighborhood and relocate to other cities after Hurricane Katrina, as described above.

- **Traumatic events produce significant mental distress when they shatter an individual's sense of meaning, order, and justice in the world.** This is especially true when the person believes that other people have caused their suffering, or when they feel mistreated by others after a serious adversity. An example is the psychological distress experienced by many people of color in New Orleans after government agencies failed to build dikes strong enough to prevent massive flooding, and then failed to provide assistance after Hurricane Katrina destroyed their neighborhood.[40]

- **Traumatic events become more dysregulating when they aggravate past or ongoing stressors.** Often, a new trauma or chronic toxic stress can surface and intensify psychological distress that people experienced in their childhood, or in some other time in their past. It can also amplify existing emotionally distressing conditions such as racism, sexism, economic injustice, and other forms of systemic oppression.

Climate disruption is already exposing people to many if not all of these stresses, and they will become increasingly pronounced as temperatures rise.

Examples of the psychological effects of fast-moving direct climate impacts on individuals

With this information as background, let's investigate some of the specific adverse psychological impacts on individuals generated by fast-moving climate impacts.

- **Research has found that 25–50% of the people who experience an extreme weather disaster may experience negative mental health consequences.**[41] Most people affected by extreme weather events have short-term psychological reactions such as fear and anxiety and then recover. However, when an individual is seriously injured by an event, when a family member or friend is wounded or killed, or when their home or business is destroyed by a weather disaster, they are much more likely to experience acute stress disorders such as depression, incident-specific fears, phobias, separation-disorders, traumatic grief, anger, sleep disorders, or PTSD.

Other psychological problems, including family dysfunction, difficulties at work, increased misbehavior of children, and a sense of lost identity are also likely from exposure to destructive weather events.[42] Studies in a variety of cultures have found that these adverse post-trauma reactions tend to persist when people continue to perceive conditions as threatening or dangerous. As climate disruption grows in force, this will often be the case for many individuals.[43]

- **Children are particularly susceptible to adverse psychological impacts from climate-enhanced extreme weather events.** One study found, for example, that a year after Hurricane Katrina, children exposed to the event were four times more likely to be depressed or anxious and twice as likely to have behavioral problems compared with before the storm.[44] A study of child abuse following Hurricane Floyd that hit North Carolina in 1999 concluded that children were more susceptible to abuse by their parents following the disaster. The authors of that study concluded that the causes were likely related to decreased social support for parents, which results in increased distress.[45]

- **Hotter temperatures have been linked with increased alcohol and drug use, mental health problems, physical aggression, interpersonal conflict, crime, and violence.** The many types of stress generated by rising temperatures cause people to increase their use of drugs and alcohol. Researchers have also found that during heat waves more people will seek help for preexisting psychiatric problems.[46]

  In addition, tempers can flare and people are more likely to act in harmful ways toward others. This will be one of the most disturbing outcomes of rising global temperatures. Researchers have tested this correlation in multiple ways and it has been repeatedly confirmed. For example, hotter cities in the U.S. already experience significantly higher violence rates than cooler cities, even when factors such as poverty, unemployment, age distribution and other risk factors are statistically controlled.[47] Behavioral and environmental factors such as poverty and isolation contribute to this problem, while also increasing the number of deaths when temperatures soar.[48]

Researchers found that the risk of exposure to extreme heat could be as much as six times higher for the average U.S. citizen by the year 2070 compared with levels experienced in the last century, indicating serious problems ahead.[49]

- **Cold waves also cause dysregulation.** Heat waves are not the only problems. The abnormal cold periods generated by climate disruption also cause significant suffering. For instance, one study of deaths between 1985 and 2012 in 384 locations in 13 countries, including ten regions of the U.K. and 135 cities in the U.S., found that cold weather kills 20 times as many people as hot weather, and that premature deaths are more often caused by prolonged spells of moderate cold than short extreme bursts.[50] The emotional distress suffered by family and friends as a result of these deaths is certain to be high.

- **Randomly changing patterns of extreme weather are sporadic stressors that will become more common as temperatures rise.** The unpredictability of the timing and strength of storms, floods, heat waves, cold waves, and other extreme weather events will tax the psychological capacity of many people to cope.[51] Suicides increased in India, for example, as a result of climate-enhanced extreme weather events that combined with poverty to push farmers over the edge. A study completed in communities in northern Italy found more incidences of suicide as a result of significant climate variability.[52]

- **Research suggests that flooding is a major psychological stressor in itself, and the secondary stresses of rebuilding and returning to normal life can create substantial psychological problems.** The impacts of flooding can range from clinical depression and anxiety, to PTSD, substance abuse, and damaged relationships.[53] The flood event is frightening enough. One study found that the follow up phase of clean-up and rebuilding, which can take months to years, dealing with insurance companies, and other factors involved with recovery can be even more distressing.[54] Studies have also found large gender differences in the impacts of flooding. For example, in some locations of the world women, especially poor and disadvantaged females, are at greater risk than men of adverse psychological reactions because of their lower status and lack of power and resources.[55]

Examples of the psychological effects of slow-growing climate impacts on individuals

- **Droughts often produce a variety of psychological distresses. However, because they are slow-growing events, the impacts are different than fast-moving extreme weather disasters.**[56] For example, rather than acute distress disorders such as PTSD, the mental strain and financial devastation of a long-term drought can cause people to experience intense feelings of anxiety, grief, helplessness, and hopelessness, as well as a deep-seated sense of dislocation and loss due to the damage done to their local environment.[57]

  As the Australian story at the start of this chapter indicates, persistent droughts have also been found to generate higher rates of depression and suicide. For example, mirroring a pattern seen in Australia, during the droughts of the 1980s male farmers and ranchers in the U.S. states of Wisconsin, Minnesota, North and South Dakota, and Montana demonstrated twice the number of suicides as the national rate.[58]

- **Long periods of hotter temperatures increase mental distress.** For example, hotter temperatures exacerbate industrial air pollutants and research has found that people who live near major sources of pollution are likely to experience more anxiety and tension.[59] Warmer weather worsens vehicular pollution as well, which has been linked to higher rates of schizophrenia.[60] In addition, people who believe the quality of the air they breathe has deteriorated often feel more depressed.[61] Higher levels of ozone and air pollutants generated by hotter temperatures have also been associated with increased rates of family violence.[62]

- **The stress of maintaining a business during a drought, or restoring it afterwards can increase the risk of mental health problems.** This is especially true for parents and their children when the adult has less time to spend with their family or to engage in activities that help them relieve their own stress and anxiety.[63]

- **The spread of physical illnesses and diseases due to climate disruption increases the risk of mental health problems, especially in children.** Researchers have found that warmer temperatures increase asthma and children with asthma are at least two times more likely to have anxiety symptoms, almost twice as likely to be depressed, and report general psychological distress.[64] Research on the SARS epidemic found that children can experience intense, delayed anxiety in response to outbreaks of infectious disease, especially if they are anxious to begin with.[65] Many infectious diseases produce long-lasting psychological symptoms that reduce the thinking and expressive capacity of children, as well as their academic performance, attention and memory, and language skills.[66]

- **A strong relationship exists between low socioeconomic status and poor mental health.**[67] Many slow-growing climate impacts will add to the psychological strains experienced by low-income individuals, and these stresses will become even more pronounced if, over time, the economy suffers and jobs are lost as predicted by economists such as Sir Nicholas Stern and many others.[68] Drought-prone regions often suffer from low educational attainment as well as low economic status. This suggests that higher levels of mental distress can be expected in these regions compared with areas less affected by drought.[69]

- **Secondary trauma negatively effects psychological wellbeing.** The term secondary (also called vicarious) trauma is often used to describe the despair people feel when they see others in distress but feel helpless to do anything about it. It also refers to the slow-growing burnout people in the helping professions feel when their physical and emotional capacity to assist others is depleted. Many emergency responders, medical aids, mental health workers, child-care professionals, and faith leaders attend my Transformational Resilience workshops because they seek ways to deal with high levels of secondary trauma resulting from feeling helpless to assist people to cope with droughts, heat waves, and other slow-growing climate impacts.

Climate disruption also generates a wide range of chronic toxic stresses for individuals

The psychological effects of fast and slow-growing climate impacts extend well beyond acute traumas. They also produce a truckload of chronic toxic stresses for individuals. People might have a difficult time linking these adversities with rising global temperatures, but the connection exists none-theless. The stresses will create significant mental health challenges for individuals.

- **The mental distress of dealing with continually changing weather and related impacts.** Coping with constantly changing unpredict-able weather conditions can be extremely taxing. For example, research has found that the direct effects of extreme heat can cause physical and psychological changes in our bodies that produce a number of negative outcomes. This is especially problematic if high temperatures are accompanied by high humidity, as they often are in a summer heat wave. In extreme heat people have more trou-ble sleeping.[70] Less or poorer quality sleep over a long time-period causes many types of problem including lower concentration, less energy, depression, and lower moods.[71] Climate impacts can also affect infrastructure and can lead to power failures, breakdowns in public transportation, the loss of social support services, and other impacts that create more strain for people.

- **The mental strains of dealing with resource shortages and rising costs for basic goods and services can be significant.** Rising food prices due to drought, for example, as was seen in the Middle East before the Arab Spring, and that is occurring as I write this in mid-2015 in California, put added pressure on middle- and low-income families to decide whether to purchase food for their children or pay the rent. In some locations food availability is likely to be reduced due to disruptions in global and regional food supply chains resulting from extreme weather events and other climate-related impacts. In other locations food systems will completely collapse due to drought and water shortages. The availability of other essential goods and services such as energy, medical assistance, and insurance are also likely to be effected, and when they are available their costs will often rise.[72] All of these impacts place greater emotional strain on people.

- **Rising levels of economic insecurity.** Many people are likely to experience great psychological and emotional strains resulting from financial difficulties associated with climate disruption. Job losses and reduced income, for example, are already being seen in agriculture, forestry, tourism, and other climate-sensitive indus-tries, and research shows that unemployment impairs mental health.[73] Extreme weather events can lead to the loss of homes and other personal financial assets. The financial costs of rebuilding or relocation will also cause significant distress. In addition, the reorganization of emissions intensive industries such as coal mining, coal-fired power plants, agriculture, and heavy industry are likely to present significant psychological impacts due to the potential loss of employment, especially for low-skilled workforces and people with few other employment options.[74]

- **Reduced economic participation.** Diminished financial security will frequently be aggravated by the increased costs of basic goods and services. These factors are likely to prevent many individuals and households from actively participating in the economy while also exposing them to mental health impacts resulting from the irrecoverable loss of limited assets and significant financial stress, reduced personal autonomy, negative self-perception, insecurity, and social isolation.[75]

- **Increased social exclusion.** In addition to economic exclusion, climate disruption is likely to diminish many of the ways in which people connect with others in the community. In many parts of the world climate disruption is already fracturing family and community connections through increased involuntary displacement and forced migration. The psychological impacts of the erosion or loss of social support networks can be profound.[76]

- **Depression and hopelessness caused by rising levels of poverty.** It is extremely stressful living on the edge, and climate disruption will force many more people into poverty. In the U.S., a 2012 Gallop poll found that almost a third of the people living in poverty have been diagnosed with depression, compared with 16% of other Americans. From India to Australia, Africa, and Europe, similar patterns have been seen worldwide. The constant worry, depression, and sense of hopelessness that result are one of the reasons some people living in poverty adopt self-destructive coping behaviors such as drug and alcohol abuse.[77]

- **Psychological distress caused by rising illnesses and diseases.** Heat-related illnesses and deaths will increase, as will air-borne lung diseases, allergies, and asthma. In addition, food-borne diseases such as salmonella, water-borne diseases such as Cryptosporidium and *Giardia*, and animal-borne diseases such as West Nile

Virus and Lyme disease are expected to multiply as temperatures rise.[78] As they linger these illnesses and diseases will generate significant mental health problems for people.

- **Chronic toxic stress resulting from exposure to crime and violence.** In many locations people are likely to experience rising levels of psychological distress related to fears about for their physical safety due to increased crime and violence aggravated by climate disruption. Research indicates that this type of fear can generate a wide range of mental health impacts including anxiety, depression and post-traumatic stress disorder.[79]

- **Psychological distress and dissociation due to awareness of the long-term implications of climate disruption.** Hopelessness, helplessness, and a loss of meaning in life will escalate as people feel powerless to prevent temperatures from rising to levels that generate permanent harm to humans and the natural environment. Over the past few years, for instance, I have worked with a number of individuals who are experiencing significant existential distress as a result of knowing what the science says is happening to the Earth's climate system but feeling helpless to prevent it. Other

Box 1.2: Examples of the traumas and chronic toxic stresses generated by climate disruption

Acute traumas

- Anxiety, depression, incident-specific fears, PTSD from extreme weather events
- Grief, anger, and depression from the death of or serious injury to loved ones
- Anxiety, depression, and hopelessness due to damage or loss of home or valuables
- Separation disorders from fractured or lost social support networks
- Secondary trauma and compassion fatigue
- Many more acute traumas

Chronic toxic stresses

- Strain of hotter temperatures, drought, water shortages, food shortages, etc.
- Pressure of rising prices on household expenditures, e.g., food, water, energy
- Distress of job losses and income reductions
- Anxiety and depression from involuntary migration
- Impacts of illness and disease
- Persistent threat of crime or violence
- Distress from loss of sense of "place"
- Many more chronic toxic stresses

people will dissociate in response to the knowledge of what is happening to the Earth's climate, meaning they disconnect from what is occurring within and around them and function in a state of denial or anger at others for discussing the topic. Many more people can be expected to experience this type of distress or dissociation as they grasp what is happening to the Earth's climate and feel overwhelmed, depressed, or in despair about what the future holds.[80]

Box 1.2 summarizes these stresses.

The psychobiology of trauma and toxic stress

It is important to understand that these are completely natural human reactions to trauma and toxic stress. They are not signs of mental pathology, deviance, weakness, or moral failing. Nor do they appear in one type of culture or in certain nations and not in others. They can be found in all types of people and in every society, rich and poor alike. The psychobiology of trauma and stress explains why. To help you understand what this means, I'll first explain the process in scientific terms, and then I'll describe it in simple terms.

Let's start with the science. The word trauma is derived from the Greek word describing a physical wound. In the medical field it is used to describe a serious injury to a person's body. The mental health field also uses it this way. In this case trauma is the term used to describe experiences that puncture the conceptual framework—the deep-seated assumptions and beliefs—people hold that allow them to make sense of the world and define who they are. Acute traumas and chronic toxic stresses therefore result from the speed and size of an event *and* by the way we interpret the situation.

When we perceive an event to be threatening—whether it be an frightening demand from someone, a challenge to our self-esteem, or the sight of floodwater racing toward you—neuroscientists have found that information is instantaneously sent to the brain's locus coeruleus, which is the part of our brain stem involved with physiological responses to stress and panic. This immediately signals your limbic brain, and the amygdala in specific, which can be called the "Fear and Alarm Center," to sideline the prefrontal cortex, which is the "Executive Center" or thinking part of the brain, to enable your body to put all of its resources into protecting you from the threat.

In a process that occurs outside of your everyday consciousness, your brain's "Fear and Alarm Center" continuously scans the external environment for anything that might be a threat. When it senses danger it immediately transmits an "emergency alert signal" to the brain's hypothalamus to prepare you to fight back, flee the scene, or freeze and hope the threat passes you by. The hypothalamus communicates with the rest of your body through the autonomic nervous system, which controls the involuntary body functions such as breathing, blood pressure, heartbeat, and dilation or restriction of key blood vessels and small airways in the lungs called bronchioles.

The autonomic nervous system has two components, the sympathetic and parasympathetic nervous system. The sympathetic nervous system (SNS) operates much like a gas pedal in a car. It triggers the fight or flight response, providing the body with a burst of energy so that it can respond to a perceived threat. The parasympathetic nervous system (PNS) acts like a brake. It promotes the "rest and digest" response that calms the body down.

When your "Fear and Alarm Center" sends emergency alerts, the hypothalamus activates the SNS by releasing two chemicals. One tells the adrenal glands to instantaneously send a torrent of the hormone epinephrine, also known as adrenaline, into the bloodstream to get your heart, leg and arm muscles, and lungs ready to move. The other signals the pituitary gland to direct the outside layer of the adrenal glands to swiftly produce cortisol, which raises your blood pressure and releases glucose into your system.

The flush of adrenaline and cortisol happen so quickly that you are not aware of it. In fact, the wiring of the brain is so efficient that the amygdala and hypothalamus begin the process even before the "Executive Center" has had a chance to consider what is happening. That's why you are able to jump out of the path of a wall of water suddenly speeding toward you before you even realize you are doing it.

The hormones released into your body have instantaneously put it in a state of hyperarousal that produces both mental and physical reactions. Your body tenses as the chemicals cause your blood pressure and pulse rate to rise. When this happens you might find it difficult to breathe or experience cold sweats. Your muscles tense and you might get a head or stomachache. Some people experience sleep disorders or gastrointestinal problems when they are in a state of hyperarousal.

The condition affects much more than your body. Your mind will usually begin to race as you ruminate over and over again about every potential danger you might face. All of this is intended to focus the body's energy on keeping your mind, heart, and muscles on super-high alert.

Cortisol is the primary stress hormone. It lasts longer than adrenaline and keeps you going after the initial fight or flee reaction has dissipated. For example, you might find yourself running faster than you ever thought possible up an alley and then easily hopping over a fence to avoid the floodwater you see coming your way. The adrenaline mobilized your brain and body to accomplish these feats. But you then need to spend hours helping your family and friends to reach safer high ground, which the cortisol helps with.

This is a process that humans have in common with most other mammals, and it has allowed our species to survive for millions of years. Your brain's "Fear and Alarm Center" has undoubtedly transmitted millions of emergency alert signals to your body throughout your lifetime that have protected you from numerous real threats, and many more that turned out to be false.

The perception of an overwhelming trauma or a highly stressful event can trigger such intense emergency alert signals that the hyperarousal experienced by an individual becomes extreme. This is what can trigger the freeze response that leaves people immobilized, unable to respond in any way.

That's not the only outcome of traumatic stress. When the "Fear and Alarm Center" sends an emergency alert signal to the hippocampus to record a terrifying event it becomes embedded deep in the brain's memory system. A situation that is even remotely similar to the original event therefore can trigger the old memory and set off a whole new sequence of emergency alerts.

In addition, when people experience what they perceive to be a serious trauma such as being caught in a flood, the sensitivity of their brain's "Fear and Alarm Center" becomes much more elevated. In this condition, even the sound of rain on the roof or water filling a bathtub, for example, might trigger a full blown fight, flee, or freeze response in the person because they unconsciously associate it with the earlier trauma, such as the flood they once almost drowned in. Thus, the brain's "Fear and Alarm Center" gives emotional charge to the traumatic memories.

Individuals in this condition often become physiologically unable to learn because their brain's "Executive Center"—the thinking and learning part of their brain—has been sidelined. They might also adopt coping behaviors intended to relieve the mental distress and physical tension they experience when they are hyper- or hypo-aroused. They could, for instance, abuse alcohol, drugs, or tobacco, eat excessive amounts of food, seek out dangerous situations, or conversely hide away from the world. They can also overwork or obsess over an issue or activity in order to distract their minds from thinking about the past events.

At some point in our lives many of us utilize one or more of these types of coping behavior to temporarily ameliorate the distress we feel when we are dysregulated. Most of the time these behaviors are short-lived because we soon find ways to calm ourselves and release the hyperarousal. However, when an individual experiences a serious trauma, or is exposed to continual toxic stresses, and does not know how to dissipate their mental and physical hyperarousal, their repeated use of these unhealthy coping behaviors can become self-destructive.

Having a few extra alcoholic drinks for a night or two, for example, might temporarily relieve your distress, but it is not likely to turn you into an alcoholic. However, when you drink excessively for months on end, your coping strategy becomes self-destructive. The same is true with continual use of legal and illegal drugs, tobacco, overeating, overworking, and other practices that with repetition become self-destructive. Behaviors that were originally intended to relieve psychological and emotional distress end up becoming the source of even greater pain and suffering. When this occurs, your ability to deal with the issues that originally triggered the self-destructive coping patterns is diminished, your life becomes increasingly constrained, and you can easily get caught in a vicious downward spiral.

Because the body and brain are inextricably linked, if the self-destructive coping behaviors persist for months or years they can lead to a physical breakdown. Cardiovascular problems, for instance, including heart disease, high blood pressure, heart attacks, and stroke have all been linked to high levels of stress. The immune systems of people who experience chronic stress can be suppressed, making them more vulnerable to infections, allergies, and autoimmune diseases such as arthritis and multiple sclerosis. Skin problems such as psoriasis and eczema, backaches and other forms of muscular pain, diabetes, obesity and other eating disorders, gastrointestinal problems such as GERD, gastritis, ulcerated colitis, and irritable colon syndrome, and some cancers have also been linked to persistent stress.[81]

In addition, spiritual problems such as existential hopelessness and an inability to find meaning in life often grow when people experience continued trauma and stress, leading to depression, anxiety, and other harmful states.

Cognitive problems, including difficulty in remembering things, can rise as a result of acute trauma and chronic stress, and people might chronically dissociate. This term describes an individual that becomes disconnected from their memories, feelings, and reality in general. Dissociation also frequently shows up as fragmented memory functions.

FIGURE 1.1   The mental health and psychosocial impacts of climate-enhanced trauma and chronic toxic stress

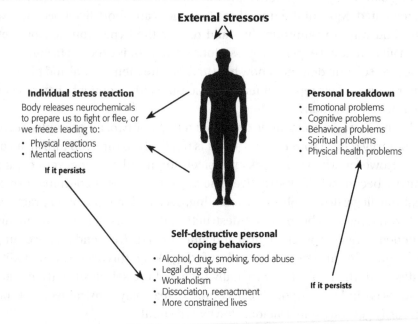

Numerous types of behavioral problem can result from acute traumas and chronic toxic stresses. If a person has not learned good communications skills or cannot regulate their emotions, for example, they can have a difficult time with their families, friends, employer, or community. The result is that they often feel overwhelmed, confused, or depressed, and have poor self-esteem. Anger, interpersonal aggression, and abuse are some of the typically seen outcomes.

Again, these reactions can precipitate a vicious downward cycle that can be very difficult to reverse.

In sum, the impacts of acute traumas and chronic toxic stress can be all-encompassing, affecting every aspect of an individual's life. To paraphrase Dr. Sandra Bloom, "they can turn the past into a nightmare, the present into a quagmire of repetitive harmful behaviors, and the future into a litany of mental and physical problems that might eventually even lead to death."[82] Figure 1.1 graphically describes these reactions.

It is important to remember that three decades of research has found that these reaction to trauma and toxic stress are shaped not only by what happens to us, but also by the way we interpret the events and how we deal with them as they happen and afterwards.[83] These issues will be described in more depth in the chapters to come.

Here is the simpler way I promised to understand the psychobiology of trauma and stress.

The human brain evolved to deal with threats that existed in the Stone Age. After all, for about 90% of human history people lived as hunter-gatherers in small groups of about 10–12 adults plus children. For the most part the threats our ancestors learned to deal with were predators and an occasional natural disaster such as an earthquake.

Today, however, people are forced to deal with a rising tide of increasingly complex problems generated by the Industrial and Information Ages. Just to name a few:

- A gigantic 250% increase in the human population in merely the past 100 years

- Mass urbanization that leaves people densely packed together in often-polluted cities with little to no open space or regular contact with greenery or nature

- Unprecedented amounts of resource extraction, material consumption, solid and molecular wastes including greenhouse gasses, and environmental degradation: more resource consumption has occurred in the past 50 years than in the entire history of humanity

- An economic system that, in order to prevent collapse, requires people to work harder and produce more with the same or fewer resources

- Cheap, readily available, and increasingly powerful weapons that make it easy for anyone to wound or kill others

- Email, smartphones, and other electronic gadgets that allow people to instantaneously communicate while also transmitting every piece of bad news and frightening information happening around the world

These and other stressors of modern society produce a constant flood of stimuli that our Stone Age brain interprets as threatening. Our brain's "Fear and Alarm Center" consequently continually sends emergency alert signals to our brain and body, which keeps many of us in a state of constant dysregulation. Most people have the capacity to eventually pull themselves out of this type of dysregulation. However, if they lack sufficient skills and resources, some people completely shut themselves off to the world and live in a rigid state of distraction and avoidance. Others react by adopting a chaotic pattern of self-destructive or socially harmful behaviors.

In short, we are suffering the consequences of living in a time that our brains are not well equipped to deal with.

The most important question is "What happened to you?" not "What's wrong with you?"

Again, it is important to remember that these reactions are completely natural. They are the human brain and body's built in way of defending itself from harm resulting from real or perceived threats. Thus, while not condoning or making excuses for their actions, when someone engages in personally or socially harmful behaviors, we should ask, "What happened to them?" rather than "What's wrong with them?" In other words, we need to understand what the individual or group experienced in the past, or is experiencing today, that causes their body's "Fear and Alarm System" to react with fear-based self-protective behaviors that produce personally or socially destructive conduct.

When you shift how you think about harmful behaviors in this way, entirely new insights and means of responding present themselves. In fact, ample research and experience shows that with effective knowledge, tools, and skills, individuals can avoid personally and socially damaging reactions to trauma and stress. The brain's "Executive Center"—the prefrontal cortex that is the meaning-making part of the brain—can learn how to regulate and deactivate the "Fear and Alarm Center"—the part of the brain that mobilizes our internal resources to deal with threats—when it is not needed in ways that avoid or minimize harmful reactions. Even more exciting is that people can learn to use adversity as a catalyst to actually increase their well-being above the levels that existed before the trauma. Research indicates that many people do so by rising above their own self-interests to improve the wellbeing of others in some way, or care for nature.

Before we dive into how people can use climate-enhanced adversity for constructive purposes we need to take one more step and understand that, left unaddressed, the adverse human reactions to climate-enhanced trauma and toxic stress will also profoundly affect organizations, communities, and entire societies.

2

The psycho-social-spiritual effects of climate disruption on organizations, communities, and societies

Customers often lined up out the door to buy the Italian ices and pizzas served at LaRocca's Family Restaurant. That came to an abrupt halt in 2012 when Superstorm Sandy walloped Staten Island, New York. The storm destroyed the restaurant's roof, freezers, cooking equipment, and electrical system. The LaRocca's had $100,000 in flood insurance but the damage totaled almost $400,000. After unsuccessfully searching for six months for financing to repair the facility, they gave up and permanently closed their 25-year-old business. "When that water came up, it destroyed us all," said Joe LaRocca.[84]

All told, more than 23,000 businesses and the 245,000 people they employed were impacted by Sandy. Of the firms in the Rockaways area of Queens shut down by the storm, most were small businesses and 30% had failed to reopen a year later, leaving many people without a job. Likewise, on Staten Island's hard-hit Midland Ave., almost a third of the impacted companies were still closed a year later.[85]

Severe depression was found in almost a quarter of the people living in the most impacted areas of the eastern seaboard after Sandy came onshore.[86] In addition, anxiety disorders, alcohol and substance abuse, as well as PTSD, rose dramatically.[87] In the 15 months following Sandy, the state of New Jersey's disaster mental health program served 500,000 people. Two years after the event, New York health officials estimate about 700,000 residents were still experiencing storm related mental health problems, including anxiety, depression, and hopelessness.[88]

Not only were many business owners, workers, and their families impacted by Sandy, the New York subway system and many other aspects of the area's infrastructure were also damaged. In addition, numerous government agencies, human service organizations, and religious institutions were physically damaged or closed. The storm traumatized the entire community.

In fact, researchers estimate that 15% of the entire U.S. population was affected by Sandy due to impacts on the economy, travel, and other factors.[89]

The impacts of Superstorm Sandy show how organizations, communities, and entire societies can be physically damaged and psychologically, socially, and spiritually dysregulated—meaning they feel a deep lack of meaning and hope in life—by the more frequent and intense extreme weather events that can be expected as climate disruption worsens.[90] One respected researcher said that if the world continues to emit greenhouse gasses at the current pace, the Jersey shore from Atlantic City to Cape May might experience Sandy-level storm surges on an annual basis by mid-century.[91] Similar risks exist throughout the world.

How climate disruption can physically impact organizations

The physical damage and resulting financial impacts that private firms experienced as a result of Sandy are not unique. Extreme weather events aggravated by climate disruption are impacting organizations worldwide.

Historic flooding in 2011, for example, affected more than 160 companies in Thailand's textile industry, undermining about a quarter of the country's garment production.

Bunge, a multinational firm in the agri-business and food industry sector, in 2010 reported a $56 million quarterly loss in its sugar and bio-energy units caused primarily by droughts in its main growing areas.

The electric power company Constellation Energy saw their quarterly earnings reduced by about $0.16 per share due to the record-setting 2011 heat wave in Texas that forced it to buy incremental power at peak prices.

The reinsurance firm Munich Re received claims totaling more than $350 million from the record flooding that occurred in Australia in 2010–11, which contributed to a 38% decline in quarterly profits.[92]

Private organizations will experience climate-related costs beyond direct physical damage as well. These costs will produce greater emotional strain for the members in the organizations. The U.S. Securities and Exchange Commission, for example, warned publicly traded firms that capital expenses will rise due to new public policies to control emissions, the costs of new emissions control technologies, higher prices for goods and services, and changing public perception about firms that emit large amounts of greenhouse gasses.[93]

In addition, worker output is likely to be reduced because hotter weather generates a number of chronic toxic stresses. Researchers in Japan, for instance, found that every degree increase in temperatures above 25°C (77°F) results in a 2% drop in productivity. Similar results were found in Germany as well.[94] Research completed on Central American and Caribbean nations found that once temperatures rise above 26°C (78°F), economic output in both agricultural and nonagricultural sectors of the economy drops about 2.4% for every additional degree Celsius increase in temperature.[95] Just like rising costs, reduced worker productivity will place greater financial stress on everyone in the organization.

The impacts of climate disruption also run the risk of injuring and killing workers, especially those who work outside. The Risky Business Project, for instance, projects that as global temperatures rise, extreme heat in some regions of the U.S. will surpass the threshold at which the human body can maintain a normal core temperature. They concluded that during these periods, people whose jobs require them to work outdoors or without air conditioning will face severe health risks and potential death.[96]

The negative impacts of climate disruption are already being acknowledged by the private sector. Almost a third of the businesses that responded to the 2015 Corporate Adaptation Report said that climate disruption is negatively affecting their profit margins. Almost 70% of respondents were concerned that climate change will have a material impact on their supply chain, distribution, customers, and markets. Two thirds of respondents also expressed concern over increased operational and capital costs. Despite these worries, the study found that only a small percentage of the firms were taking aggressive action to prepare for these impacts.[97]

Public agencies and not-for-profit organizations face climate-related threats that mirror those experienced by private firms. In addition, mental health, emergency response, child welfare, food security, and other organizations involved with disaster response will often experience skyrocketing demands for services that overwhelm them, thus diminishing their effectiveness.

In 2012, for example, heavy rain swamped over 350 communities in the Nigerian states of Delta and Bayelsa. About 1.3 million people were displaced and more than 500 died. Aid agencies were not prepared for the size and scope of the impacts and could not provide enough tents, healthcare services, cooking utensils, or food. These deficiencies contributed to the death of many people from starvation.[98] Similar patterns have been found, and much more can be expected in other nations worldwide, as extreme weather events increase in frequency and intensity.

Organizational dysregulation

Organizations are social systems. They are composed of individuals interacting with their physical, social, cultural, economic, and political environment. Much like with individuals, stress in a social system is a transactional issue. It results from the way people appraise their situations, interact with, and try to cope with changes occurring around them.

As described in the previous chapter, when an individual is traumatized or chronically stressed their "Fear and Alarm Center" continually emits emergency alert signals that dysregulates the nervous system. If it persists, the dysregulation frequently leads to fear-based coping behaviors that can become self-destructive.

Much like an individual, groups and organizations of all sizes and types frequently respond to trauma and toxic stresses with fear-based reactions that put them in a state of dysregulation. In excessive or prolonged states of distress, the dysregulation can become so pervasive that the organization becomes "trauma-organized." This term describes an organization that has reacted to adversity by adopting mechanisms intended to protect it from the threat, but which instead generates more distress for members and stakeholders. Dr. Sandra Bloom has completed some of the most thorough research on organizational trauma and much of the following discussion is based on her work.[99]

Sometimes a group or organization can become trauma-organized as a direct result of climate impacts. Other times, traumas and toxic stresses aggravate existing or expose previously hidden or unacknowledged problems.

I got a first-hand look at a climate-related trauma-organized organization a few years back when I received a phone call from a staff member of a large national organization focused on solutions to climate disruption. The staffer, a scientist, said the organization was in disarray and wondered if I could help.

Over the course of the next hour, the caller explained that employees were demoralized because they saw little progress being made in addressing the climate crisis. Many worked nonstop and were continuously stressed out. Tempers were short, people often harshly criticized each other, and many staff feared being humiliated in public. Managers did not grasp the problems. Instead, they called more and more meetings to discuss how to get work done, which only created additional stress for staff because they had less time available to do their work. Managers also issued decrees aimed at "improving" employee output that staff ignored or found ways to work around. This only angered the managers who issued more top-down directives. As a result, some key staff members had resigned and others were searching for new jobs.

The difficulties experienced by this group are not unique. Without significant preventative efforts to give organizations effective knowledge, tools, and skills, an increasing number will become trauma-organized as climate disruption worsens.

Common signs of trauma-organized organizations

The dysfunction I heard about from the caller described above, and the problems I saw first-hand when I began to work with the group, are indicative of the patterns seen in trauma-organized organizations. In her writings, Dr. Sandra Bloom has expertly described the symptoms of trauma-organized mental health and social service organizations.[100] My 25 years of experience in the field indicates that her analysis applies to all types of organization, not just those in the human services field. The following signs of hyperaroused trauma-organized organizations are adapted from Dr. Bloom's work, with addition information provided from my experience and research in the sustainability and climate fields.[101]

Confusion over their purpose, vision of success, and guiding values

The mission or purpose of an organization, and its vision of how to achieve that end provide the building blocks of success because they focus the attention of members on specific outcomes and methods. The purpose, vision, and ethical principles that are used to guide decision-making, and the social narratives that promote them, also frame group communication, self-talk, and type of learning that occurs focused on those goals. When clarity over these fundamental issues is absent, chaos often reigns. Organizations that are trauma-organized are usually confused about why they exist, what they are striving to accomplish, and the values they will use to guide their actions. This confusion often results from the inability to perceive with sufficient accuracy the nature of the real or perceived threats facing the organization or mistakes made when reacting to them. As problems mount, a crisis atmosphere takes over. In their state of panic members forget the reason their entity exists, what they are trying to achieve, and the values they have chosen to guide their efforts toward those ends.

Poor emotional management and communications

Emotions are contagious. Feelings of fear, anxiety, and dread often emerge when a crisis atmosphere exists and these powerful emotions tend to rub off on those around them. Unless they are handled well, people end up saying things that offend, infuriate, or harm others. When this happens, the capacity for members to manage their emotions and communicate effectively breaks down. Tension flairs, animosity grows, and people lash out at each other. Rather than working on ways to resolve organizational problems, people spend their time and energy engaged in or protecting themselves from emotional threats.

Lack of widely agreed-on acceptable behaviors and practices

Lack of clarity about the mission or purpose of the organization and poor emotional management and communications lead to lack of general agreement over the behaviors and activities that are acceptable for members to engage in or pursue. Dealing with crisis and dousing fires becomes the norm. People often get rewarded for their ability to put out fires as quickly as possible. Less and less concern is given to how the fires are suppressed. Because they exist in a reactive, survival mode, some people advocate that any method that quickly resolves a crisis is acceptable. Others say that only certain methods are acceptable because they are consistent with the (now disputed) organizational purpose and values. The lack of agreement over acceptable behaviors, practices, and policies creates conflicts and tensions that can affect many aspects of the organization.

Siloed, disconnected, and fragmented people and functions

Because they lack clarity over their purpose, vision, values, and acceptable behaviors, group members frequently operate as separate entities and pursue their own agendas with little interaction or cooperation with others in the organization. Gaps, overlaps, contradictions, conflicts, and fragmentation typically result. Poor performance and additional crises are the usual outcome.

Rigid and often punitive rules and regulations

Continual chaos and confusion, fragmentation, competing self-interests, and personal conflicts often cause organizations to enact excessive, rigid, and sometimes retaliatory rules and regulations in an attempt to reestablish order. If members do not understand or support the rules they will often resist or find ways to work around them. The result is that tensions continue to increase, which can lead to even more and tougher rules and regulations.

Constant groupthink, quick-fix thinking, and the inability to learn

Just as dysregulated individuals have difficultly learning because their brain's "Executive Center" has been shut off to concentrate all the body's energy on self-protective reactions, so organizations fail to learn when they become trauma-organized. This often takes the form of organization dissociation, meaning that members try to act as if the troubles don't exist or fail to comprehend the significance of information that affects them in the way they would when not dysregulated. Groupthink often results, which means that members fail to share opinions that differ from what appears to be the consensus view for fear of retaliation from people that are uncomfortable with tension, or executives seeking to prevent challenges to their authority. What seems like uniform agreement is therefore nothing more than a facade covering up important differences of opinion. Innovation and risk taking becomes frowned on because it might upset the status quo or expose mistakes made by higher-ups, which only adds to the organization's struggles. These problems leave the group unable to extract lessons from the past or plan effectively for the future. Just like a dysregulated individual, decision-making becomes focused on defensive short-term goals and simple quick-fix solutions. The organization as a whole becomes learning impaired.

Failure to acknowledge or correct injustices

Groupthink and the inability to identify or solve problems often prevent organizations that are trauma-organized from acknowledging or correcting inequities in power or distribution of resources, interpersonal or collective injustices, and abuses of power and authority. In addition, the inability to grasp the inherent interdependence between humans and the natural environment, and the self-protective focus that dominates organizations that are trauma-organized, often make them unable to see—much less care about—their impacts on the Earth's ecological systems or climate. Because the organization cannot learn or understand the adverse effects it generates, its actions typically become repetitive, leading to constant reenactment of poor decisions and harmful practices and activities. However, the damage is rarely acknowledged. The few negative impacts that might be recognized are dismissed as insignificant or justified as the inevitable cost of doing business. Individuals that raise concerns are ostracized, called extremists, or in other ways demonized and isolated.

Inability to mourn losses leading to reenactment and learned helplessness

When serious mistakes occur, valued employees leave, or someone is physically injured or dies, it is essential to mourn the loss. Yet trauma-organized groups don't know how or don't take the time to grieve. Unexpressed emotions appear as physical and emotional health symptoms. Tensions rise, communications become more problematic, and people repeat the same behaviors over and over again, leading to more problems and crisis. When this occurs, people no longer feel they can control what happens in the organization. Many conclude that nothing they do will affect the outcomes, so they simply give up. A pervasive and demoralizing sense of learned helplessness takes root.

Authoritarian leadership and abuses of power

When mistakes pile up, people often begin to believe that things are spinning out of control. Members with greater rank or power can react to these situations by exerting more control. Explicit or subtle messages are transmitted that establish lines that others must not cross without penalty. People that are distressed by the tension in the organization, or by their own feelings of dysregulation, throw their support behind people who promise simple solutions and quick relief. This allows individuals with authoritarian traits to obtain power. When this happens, dissent is often silenced as leaders try to mobilize people to move together in a single direction. As problems pile up, authoritarian leaders typically respond with increased aggression and punitive measures. This, in turn, often elicits blatant resistance or passive aggressive behaviors by those who oppose tighter control, all of which further increases the likelihood of increased authoritarianism, groupthink, and abuses of power.

Lack of trust, empathy, compassion, and social support

Dysregulated individuals typically adopt coping behaviors intended to relieve their distress that instead backfire and cause more harm. Similarly, the flawed perceptions, inability to manage emotions, poor communications, and short-term quick-fix thinking that dominate organizations that are trauma-organized often lead to decisions and actions that reduce trust among members and diminish their sense of empathy and compassion for each other, which diminishes the sense of camaraderie and mutual support among group members.

Fears about physical, psychological, and emotional safety

All of these issues combine to create a pervasive sense of fear among group members for their personal safety. This can result from trepidation about personal injury caused by external factors such as extreme weather events, or crime and violence where the organization is physically located. Threats from internal organizational factors such as physical assaults by managers or fellow workers can also be present. Just as prevalent in trauma-organized organizations, however, are worries about psychological and emotional injury that results from being subtly or overtly threatened, publicly chastised, humiliated, treated unfairly, or being forced to participate in or observe illegal or unethical conduct. When a large number of people in an organization believe that at a basic level they are physically, psychologically, or emotionally unsafe, a collective fear often begins to dominate. In this situation, the "Fear and Alarm Centers" of group members continually send out emergency alert signals, putting them in a continual state of dysregulation. People begin to see individuals or sub-groups within and outside of the organization, and all types of situation, as potentially danger-ous. As global temperatures rise, fear about personal safety will rise in many groups and organizations.

In sum, when organizations experience acute traumas or persistent toxic stressors, the mechanisms that govern how it operates can frequently become structured to protect members from the threats in ways that end up further harming many people, the entity as a whole, and the natural envi-ronment. Many of these traits can be seen in the climate-protection organi-zation that called me for help.

Unless organizational leaders learn how acute traumas and toxic stress can affect their members and stakeholders, along with how to construc-tively respond to these challenges, the adversities generated by climate dis-ruption will push many groups into a state of dysregulation and cause them to become trauma-organized.

The impacts of climate disruption on communities

Not surprisingly, the adverse psycho-social-spiritual impacts of climate dis-ruption go well beyond individuals and organizations to affect communi-ties. By community I mean a group of people of any size whose members reside in a specific local geographic area and share common government or governance systems. Both large urban cities and small rural towns fall into this category.

Just like organizations, communities are social systems—they are com-posed of people constantly interpreting and interacting with their physical, economic, social, cultural, and political environments. And, just as orga-nizations do, when a number of individual members, as well as numerous informal and formal groups within a community are in state of dysregula-tion, the entire community can become trauma-organized. Here are some examples of how communities can become trauma-organized due to cli-mate disruption.

Economic disruptions and job losses

One of the ways in which climate disruption can cause a community to become trauma-organized is through impacts on the local economy and jobs. As New York experienced as a result of Superstorm Sandy, climate-enhanced fast-moving extreme weather events are already damaging local economies and throwing many people out of work. The extreme heat wave and drought in 2003 across Europe is another example. In this case, a severe drought led to record low river levels, which disrupted the transport of raw materials and finished goods along inland waterways.[102] Supply chains were disrupted along with product distribution systems, leading many businesses to slow production or stop outright.

This problem extends beyond urban areas. As previously mentioned, as temperatures rise, communities that depend on forestry, tourism, recreation, agriculture, and other climate-sensitive industries will frequently experience increasing economic impacts and job losses.

The forest products sector in many parts of the world, for instance, will face increased wildfires, pests, and diseases. Reduced mountain snowpack due to warming will adversely affect communities that rely on winter sports as a major industry. Heat waves will deter people from recreating outside. Agriculture can be negatively affected by drought, disease, and insects, which will affect economic output. Reduced agricultural output will also raise concerns about the availability of food in communities around the world.[103]

As climate disruption worsens, these and other factors will increase the risk that residents in communities will see their incomes, jobs, or even entire livelihoods diminished or lost.[104] The impacts will push many people into a state of dysregulation.

Diminished physical health of community members

As previously mentioned, injury and deaths will increase as a result of more frequent and intense extreme weather events as well as slow-growing climate impacts such as sea-level rise. In the U.S. respiratory health problems such as asthma are also expected to swell because rising heat worsens smog and causes plants to produce more allergenic pollen. Heat waves will increase the risk of heatstroke and exhaustion and send thousands of people to emergency rooms. Hotter summers can make disease-carrying insects more active for longer time-periods. Illnesses such as dengue fever, West Nile virus, and Lyme disease are therefore likely to spread into new areas. Hotter days and nights, and shifting rainfall patterns including heavier downpours can reduce the quality of water supplies and increase the risk of contamination to domestic drinking water as well as food.[105]

European communities are expected to experience similar health impacts. Researchers forecast that temperature-related illness and death, physical injury and mortality resulting from extreme weather events, water- and food-borne diseases; vector-borne diseases; and food and water shortages are all likely to increase.[106]

The World Health Organization says many of the same health impacts expected to affect U.S. and European communities are likely on a global scale. In addition, the WHO states that rising temperatures and more frequent droughts and floods run the risk of compromising food security, leading to malnutrition that will be especially severe in communities that depend on rain-fed subsistence farming. Heat-related illnesses and deaths are also likely to increase. Outbreaks of diseases such as cholera are likely, especially when water and sanitation services are absent, damaged, or destroyed. Rising temperatures and altered rainfall patterns are also expected to alter the geographical distribution of insect vectors that spread infectious diseases such as malaria and dengue fever. Both water scarcities and excess water resulting from more frequent downpours will likely increase the burden of diarrheal disease, which is spread through contaminated food and water.[107]

Rising costs and the inability to provide basic services

Many municipal governments will face rising costs due to the burden of responding to these health impacts. It will also increase costs related to hardening physical infrastructure to prevent climate impacts from damaging transportation, communications, energy, sewage, drinking water, and other essential systems or relocate them to safer locations. Repair and maintenance costs will also rise.[108]

At the same time, in many communities tax revenues will plummet if their economies suffer, making it increasingly difficult for local governments to provide basic services to residents such as police, fire, emergency response, parks and recreation, road maintenance, and more.

The mental health systems of many communities will be one of the services that experience significant strain. Few communities around the world have robust mental health systems. The strong programs that do exist frequently already operate at capacity with staff and budgets stretched to the limit. This suggests that most mental health systems will be hard pressed to deal with the rising psycho-social-spiritual distress produced by climate disruption, and many will simply not be able to provide the level of services needed.[109] Physical health systems will also be increasingly strained.

Rising poverty and other disproportional impacts

At least in the near term, the impacts described above will not be evenly spread in neighborhoods or socioeconomic groups within a community. Instead, they will reinforce existing inequalities. This means that many community members that exist outside of the mainstream, including low-income individuals and families, minorities, the elderly, single women, children and others without rank and power in the community will initially suffer the most. Poverty is therefore likely to grow among these populations.[110]

One of the reasons is that transit, water, energy, and other infrastructure as well as buildings in many low-income neighborhoods and communities are often poorly constructed and located in high-risk zones such as low-lying coastal areas or floodplains. This makes them particularly susceptible to major storms, flooding, and other climate impacts. These localities also have fewer resources to devote to preparing for extreme weather events or recovering from them after they are damaged. In addition, government agencies often devote far fewer resources to help low-income neighborhoods and communities prepare for and recover after major events than they do to wealthier areas.

Don't assume, however, that the majority of climate impacts will fall on these at-risk groups, or that these populations should be the primary focus of human-resilience-building programs. While it is clearly important to provide assistance to these groups as early as possible, many people within at-risk populations are very resilient due to the knowledge and skills they possess, or the presence of robust social support networks. In addition, as seen in the northeast of the U.S. after Superstorm Sandy, in the U.K. during the record floods of 2007, and elsewhere around the world, many wealthier communities are also already being hard hit. Further, is it often the case that wealthier populations prey on vulnerable groups in the midst of adversity, suggesting that richer people can benefit from learning resilience skills as much as the poor. The bottom line is that *everyone* is at risk, not just people that might be deemed to be at greater risk.

Involuntary and voluntary migration

Millions of people voluntarily move each year, often within their own country but also across international borders. People relocate for numerous reasons including family ties, discrimination, the search for better jobs, and other economic factors. However, research has linked involuntary migration to the traumas and stresses generated by sea-level rise, drought, destruction of local economic resources, and other climate-related shifts in communities worldwide. For example, drought and land degradation have combined to contribute to the migration of nearly 8 million people in northwest Brazil since the 1960s. Flooding and severe storms have been linked to migration in the Philippines, Pakistan, and China.[111]

Large-scale migration undermines the social fabric of the communities people leave behind. It also frequently leads to tension, conflict, and violence in the communities migrants move to, while exposing immigrants to cultural, racial, or economic discrimination that produce negative mental health impacts.[112]

The adverse psycho-social-spiritual impacts on communities

When many individuals, informal groups, and formal organizations in a community experience this type of distress the entire community can become hyperaroused and trauma-organized. This leads to a wide range of destructive psycho-social-spiritual outcomes.

Increased interpersonal aggression, abuse, crime, and violence

One of the most distressing psycho-social-spiritual reactions to climate impacts will be more assaults, rapes, larcenies, robberies, and burglaries.[113] Studies that compare the violence rates of regions with different average temperatures, for example, have found that hotter regions have higher violent crime rates. As previously mentioned, time-period studies generally have also found higher violence rates in hot years, hot seasons, hot months, and hot days. In comparison, nonviolent crimes are not affected by temperature.[114]

One study examined cities across the U.S. in the early 1990s and discovered that crime rates went up during the summer regardless of the relative temperature increase as compared to winter temperatures. This means that comfort levels are not the likely cause of increased crime. Instead, the culprit seems likely to be some type of psychobiological reaction to increased heat.[115]

Another assessment looked at 30 years of monthly crime and weather data for 2,997 counties in the U.S. The conclusion was that temperature has a strong additive effect on criminal behavior. The study used the historical patterns to project that between 2010 and the end of the century in the U.S., climate disruption will cause an additional 22,000 murders, 180,000 cases of rape, 1.2 million aggravated assaults, 2.3 million simple assaults, 260,000 robberies, 1.3 million burglaries, 2.2 million cases of larceny, and 580,000 cases of vehicle theft.[116]

The authors of this study also determined that public gathering places tend to be more susceptible to crime in the hot summer months.[117] This is problematic because in many low-income neighborhoods and communities around the world, people do not have access to air conditioning and are thus more likely to be outside during hot weather to benefit from natural breezes.

This problem is not limited to the U.S. Research has consistently shown that violent crime increases in every city around the world as temperatures rise, no matter how hot they were previously. Summer months with warmer than average temperatures have tended to show greater crime levels than summer months with below-average temperatures.[118]

In some cases violence will rise due to greater alcohol and drug abuse, which has been found to increase during extreme weather events, including heat waves. Researchers found, for example, that in rural and semirural communities in Australia drug and alcohol abuse rose substantially in hotter weather.[119]

When a community member fears for their safety, their brain's "Fear and Alarm Center" continually sends out emergency alerts that triggers fight, flee, or freeze reactions. As a result, some people adopt coping mechanisms they believe will protect them from harm such as obtaining weapons and other actions that ironically heighten, rather than reduce, the sense of fear among many people. A vicious cycle can result whereby people continually elevate their efforts to protect themselves, causing others to do the same, precipitating ever-rising levels of tension, anxiety, and fear within the community.

Authoritarian leadership and hate-based extremism

Just as in organizations, when numerous community members remain chronically dysregulated, some become willing to follow anyone who explains the causes and solutions of the problems in simple terms and offers rapid relief. This frequently involves blaming others and creating scapegoats, which are usually people outside of their group or those who look, think, or act differently. This increases the likelihood that authoritarian leaders will gain influence.

Research on people with authoritarian traits has found that they rarely spend time examining evidence, thinking critically, reaching their own conclusions, or seeing whether one set of their ideas is consistent with other things they believe. Instead, authoritarians typically accept that what other authorities have told them is true, adopt the opinions of those people without careful evaluation, and have great difficulty identifying false ideas and beliefs. As a result they often believe a number of contradictory things but lack the capacity to grasp their incongruity. The inability of authoritarians to think critically, synthesize information, or deal with complexity leads them to prefer long-standing traditions and customs that maintain their existing beliefs.[120]

Authoritarian leaders typically believe that people who hold views that differ from what established authorities have proclaimed to be the truth are socially deviant and therefore pose a threat to the social order. This frequently leads them to conclude that aggression toward, or punishment of people who think, look, speak, or act differently is justified, especially when it is supported by their authority figures.[121]

As climate impacts grow in frequency and intensity communities will face increased risks that local officials or others with strong authoritarian traits will assume influential positions. These individuals will frequently promote and reward authoritarian leadership throughout the community. The result will typically be that little creative thinking and problem-solving occurs. Instead, more extremism, rigidity, polarization, discrimination, and inequality can be expected. All of this can threaten democratic processes within many communities.

The risks of authoritarianism go beyond individual leaders. Constant fears about personal safety, the distress caused by reduced incomes and job losses, the threats posed by migrants moving into an area, poverty, famine, and associated spiritual sense of hopelessness and helplessness frequently cause groups to form around the hatred of particular religious, racial, gender, or ethnic groups, or government authorities. Hate-based extremism on all sides of the political spectrum can be focused on a single issue, such as opposition to abortion, people of color, or immigrants, or it can extend to multiple issues.

Indeed, hate-based violence appears to be growing in many parts of the world, including the U.S., and climate disruption is likely to aggravate this trend. One research group, for example, found that since the 9/11 terrorist attacks in the U.S., hate groups affiliated with a variety of far-right wing ideologies, including white supremacists, antiabortion extremists, and antigovernment militants, have killed more people in the U.S. than groups associated with al Qaeda.[122] This is not just a problem with groups on the far right. Far-left hate-based extremism is also likely to become a problem as climate impacts increase.

Growing risks of deindividuation

A dynamic closely linked to increased authoritarianism and hate-based extremism is deindividuation. This is a term used to describe situations when people give up or lose their personal identity in a group they affiliate with. When this happens the person no longer sees themselves as a separate individual. Instead, they merge their identity into the group. This eliminates personal responsibility and accountability for their actions, which can allow them to act in horrific ways.[123]

Throughout history, for instance, warriors have often gone to battle wearing masks. By covering their faces they can no longer be seen as individuals, which leaves them free to do whatever is needed to defeat their enemy. Ku Klux Klan members in the U.S. wear white robes to conceal their identity, facilitating violent racist behavior. Members of the group calling themselves the Islamic State, also known as ISIS, wear ski masks covering their entire heads when they video themselves killing hostages. The anonymity eliminates personal accountability, which allows them to merge their identity with their group and perform hideous acts of hate-based violence.

As climate impacts grow worse and more and more people become dysregulated, the risk of deindividuation is likely to grow, leading to significant stress and suffering in many communities.

Diminished community health and wellbeing

As discussed in Chapter 1, the psychological distresses, losses, and displacements resulting from climate impacts have been associated with a wide range of adverse mental health impacts on individuals. When they are combined with rising crime, violence, authoritarianism, deindividuation and other risks, many public safety and mental health systems established to safeguard communities will be overwhelmed and become incapable of meeting the challenges.[124] Part of the reason is, as I just mentioned, the revenue reductions resulting from increased costs to repair damage to offices and infrastructure; reduced tax revenues if economies struggle will make it more difficult to maintain high levels of services.[125] This will occur at the same time that demand for services increase. Researchers have found, for example, that hospital admission rates for mental health problems rise as a result of increased extreme weather events as well as chronic stresses generated by climate disruption. In Adelaide, South Australia, higher temperatures have been associated with increased hospital admissions for dementia, mood disorders, neurotic, stress-related and somatoform disorders, senility, and other mental problems.[126] People with existing mental illnesses, in particular, are vulnerable to the adversities produced by climate disruption.

These are just a few of the many ways in which the psycho-social-spiritual health and wellbeing of communities will be adversely affected by climate disruption. It is important to note that as global temperatures rise, no community will be safe from these negative psycho-social-spiritual reactions. Every community on the planet is at risk, no matter if they are rich or poor, urban or rural, located on the high plains or on low-elevation coastal areas, in industrialized or nonindustrialized nations alike.

Unless community leaders of all types, as well as residents, gain effective knowledge, tools, and skills to respond in constructive ways to these adversities, more and more large cities and small towns will become trauma-organized. This will precipitate reactions that harm the health, safety, and wellbeing of everyone in the community as well as the natural environment and climate.

The psycho-social-spiritual impacts of climate disruption on entire societies

The negative psycho-social-spiritual reactions to climate impacts won't stop at the city limits. They will affect entire societies.

I won't repeat all of the likely psycho-social-spiritual impacts already described in the book. However, I do want to note a few likely consequences that will affect entire societies.

Rising impacts on world GDP and associated job losses

The entire global economy, not just local economies and jobs, will be affected by climate disruption. In 2006, The Stern Review on the Economics of Climate Change projected that by mid-century the overall costs of climate disruption will be equivalent to losing at least 5% of global gross domestic product (GDP) each year, now and forever.[127]

A number of assessments since that time have projected costs a bit higher and lower than Stern's estimate. For example, the costs of climate disruption were projected to be at least US$1.2 trillion, according to a 2012 study produced by more than 50 scientists, economists and policy experts commissioned by 20 governments. This report estimated that by 2030, the cost of climate disruption and air pollution combined will be about 3.2% of global GDP, with the world's least developed countries forecast to bear the brunt, suffering losses of up to 11% of their GDP.[128]

In 2010 the Obama Administration calculated that the social costs of carbon—the monetized damage to people, society and the environment of carbon released into the atmosphere—would be US$37 per ton.[129] However, in 2015 researchers at Stanford University calculated that the social costs of carbon are likely to be six times higher, or around $220 per ton of carbon.[130] Emissions from the U.S. energy sector in 2013 totaled 5,396 million metric tons. If the Stanford numbers are applied, the costs of the damage to individuals and society of generating power in the U.S. alone totals well over US$1 trillion annually. Although it is large, the energy sector is not the only source of emissions in the U.S. Its Gross Domestic Product that year was US$16.7 trillion, meaning that the social costs of the carbon generated by U.S. society are massive.

No matter what the actual number turns out to be, the high social costs of carbon will reduce global economic output. Public, private, and non-profit organizations of all types will face increased pressure to reduce costs and make other changes, including cutting jobs, to survive. These losses will place even more stress on working people in industrialized nations, the majority of whom have seen their incomes stagnate or decline in the past 30 years. The impacts are likely to take an even greater toll on the economies and jobs of nonindustrialized nations.

Impacts on food security

Climate disruption is also already affecting food supplies worldwide, and the impacts will only increase as droughts, heat waves, disease, insect infestations, soil salinization, coastal flooding, and other impacts associated with climate disruption increase. Not only does inadequate access to food affect physical health, it also reduces the capacity of people to cope psychologically, emotionally, and spiritually with trauma and toxic stress.[131] For example, research has found that the lack of access to sufficient food along with water shortages can traumatize many people, resulting in more anxiety and depression. In some nations where women have lower status, these impacts have also been found to increase violence toward females.[132]

In addition, studies suggest that inadequate nutrition is associated with an increase in developmental and behavioral problems as well as lower IQs in children.[133] This suggests that without significant preventative efforts, in some locations around the world future generations will have even greater challenges on their hands.

As previously noted, climate disruption will also exacerbate socio-economic disadvantage, which is one of the primary causes of malnutrition which, in turn, impacts mental health.[134]

Forced displacement and migration

Although communities are affected by forced migration, the impacts affect entire societies. Researchers have concluded that economic struggles, poverty, food and water shortages, and other impacts directly or indirectly associated with climate disruption are likely to displace millions of people around the world and force competition for scarce resources.[135] The International Organization for Migration, for example, estimates that climate disruption will displace between 25 million and 1 billion people by 2050, with a figure of 200 million being the most widely cited estimate.[136]

As previously mentioned, anxiety, anger, despair and other mental distresses are often seen in people who experience involuntary migration. These reactions will fan the flames of unrest as well as many other adverse psycho-social-spiritual consequences in societies worldwide.

Rising global conflict and violence

Just as rising levels of aggression, crime, and personal violence will affect personal mental health as well as the psycho-social-spiritual wellbeing of communities, researchers have concluded that rising temperatures will lead to more global conflict, violence, and political instability that run the risk of triggering more civil wars, riots, ethnic violence, and land invasions.

One study, for instance, examined 60 existing studies, including 27 focused on industrialized societies, and 45 different data sets to study the link between climate disruption and violence. The results were sobering. It found that no matter what region of the world they looked at, as extreme weather and droughts increased and temperatures warmed, similar patterns of increased social conflict and violence occurred.[137]

This assessment also found that institutional breakdowns such as abrupt and major changes in governing institutions are more likely to occur as temperatures rise and people experience more volatile and unpredictable climatic conditions.[138]

The study concluded that climate disruption is not the only or even the primary cause of most conflict and violence. Instead, it typically interacts with and aggravates other issues such as poverty, ongoing oppression and inequality, unstable political conditions, and other factors. But when these conditions exist, deteriorating climatic conditions makes conflict and violence more likely.[139]

These patterns are already playing out in parts of Africa. Fights over access to usable land already occur between pastoralists and farmers in the Oromia and Ogaden regions of Ethiopia due to changes in rainfall patterns and drought. Interclan fighting is under way in Somalia and fighting often increases during drought periods in northern Nigeria.[140] One group of researchers predicts a 54% increase in armed conflict in sub-Saharan nations by 2030 compared with the 1980–2000 period.

Increased global hate-based extremism and authoritarianism

Just as the traumas and stresses generated by climate disruption are likely to open the door to authoritarian leaders in communities, so are hate-based extremism and authoritarianism likely to grow on a global scale. Authoritarian leaders tend to pit their followers against others in order to create an enemy to blame for their group's problems and claim the moral high ground. Researchers have also found that authoritarian leaders are predisposed to use punishment and violence to control people and can easily resort to torturing or killing others who oppose their views or who are seen as impediments to their desires.[141] As more and more people feel hopeless and helpless as a result of the direct and indirect impacts of climate change, a growing number are likely to gravitate toward authoritarian leaders.

It is difficult to imagine a situation more detrimental to society and the natural environment than the expansion of totalitarian leadership around the world.

Escalating war and terrorism

The growth of hate-based violence and authoritarianism are likely to con-tribute to resource shortages and other climate-enhanced problems to increase the likelihood of war and terrorism. In 2015, for example, 40 scien-tists, policy analysts, financial, and military experts from 11 countries pro-duced the report titled *Climate Change, A Risk Assessment* that said conflict and terrorism are likely to rise as a result of food and water shortages gen-erated by climate disruption and trigger mass migration, competition for resources, and state failure.[142]

That report was preceded by the *Climate Change Adaptation Roadmap*, which was produced by the U.S. Department of Defense in 2014. That assessment concluded that climate disruption poses immediate threats to U.S. national security due to increased terrorism and war resulting from ris-ing food and water shortages, health impacts, and poverty. Other assess-ments have reached similar conclusions.

These problems are already evident in parts of the world. Water shortages due to drought, for example, are believed to have caused farmers to relocate to Syrian cities and made young people more susceptible to joining extrem-ist groups. The Islamic State has seized scarce water resources to enhance its power and influence.

Terrorism is also a growing problem in sub-Saharan Africa. NASA images show that Lake Chad, which straddles Nigeria, Niger, Cameroon and Chad and was once among the largest lakes in Africa, has shrunk nearly 90% in the past 30 years. Local and international experts alike have concluded that climate disruption, combined with increased demand for water, are the causes. The lack of water has devastated the region's economy and created a massive pool of unemployed people, especially youth, which has made it easier for Boko Haram, the radical Islamic terrorist group, to recruit new members.[143]

In sum, the fast-moving and slow-growing impacts of climate disruption will combine with persistent economic, cultural, ethnic, religious and polit-ical stressors to inflame situations and generate increasing risks of war and terrorism. Even when societies do not directly experience the violence, the fear and anxiety produced by the knowledge that these threats might impact them will undermine the mental health of individuals and psycho-social-spiritual wellbeing of organizations, communities, and whole societies.[144]

Without significant preventative efforts, climate-enhanced trauma and stress will make it increasingly difficult for people to live the "ordinary

FIGURE 2.1   The mental and physical health impacts of climate-enhanced trauma and chronic toxic stress

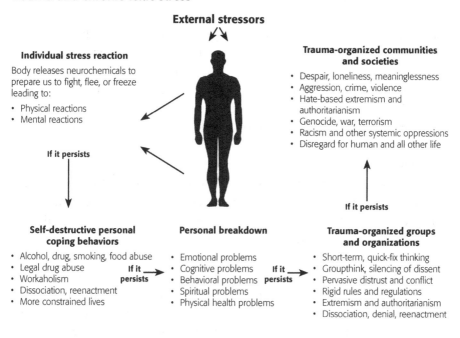

External stressors

Individual stress reaction

Body releases neurochemicals to prepare us to fight, flee, or freeze leading to:

- Physical reactions
- Mental reactions

If it persists

Trauma-organized communities and societies

- Despair, loneliness, meaninglessness
- Aggression, crime, violence
- Hate-based extremism and authoritarianism
- Genocide, war, terrorism
- Racism and other systemic oppressions
- Disregard for human and all other life

If it persists

Self-destructive personal coping behaviors

- Alcohol, drug, smoking, food abuse
- Legal drug abuse
- Workaholism
- Dissociation, reenactment
- More constrained lives

If it persists

Personal breakdown

- Emotional problems
- Cognitive problems
- Behavioral problems
- Spiritual problems
- Physical health problems

If it persists

Trauma-organized groups and organizations

- Short-term, quick-fix thinking
- Groupthink, silencing of dissent
- Pervasive distrust and conflict
- Rigid rules and regulations
- Extremism and authoritarianism
- Dissociation, denial, reenactment

life" most of us desire.[145] It will no longer be possible to pursue happiness through family and work without being constantly threatened by climate-enhanced adversities.

Figure 2.1 describes the cumulative effects of trauma and stress on individuals, organizations, communities and whole societies.

Won't climate disasters bring us together rather than pull us apart?

A common belief held by many people is that the traumas and toxic stresses I just described will bring individuals together and cause them to work for the common good. This notion was popularized by Rebecca Solnit's book, *A Paradise Built in Hell*.[146] After observing the social response to a number of earthquakes and other disasters, Solnit argued that social bonding increases—maybe due to—the difficult conditions that exist. Indeed, from the volunteerism offered by many New York residents in response to the

9/11 terrorist attacks, to the social bonding seen after many hurricanes, this pattern does often emerge after disasters.

However, numerous studies have empirically documented that a rational cooperative response is far from universal. To the contrary, dysfunctional behaviors such as looting, riots, and violence have been documented after many disasters. Many studies have found that disasters can cause some groups to unleash pent-up anger on individuals or groups they see as outsiders, threats, or the cause of their problems.[147]

Further, many studies have shown that any positive changes that do occur in the social fabric of neighborhoods are often short-lived. After the immediate impacts have passed and people turn their attention to rebuilding their homes, businesses, or personal lives, the increased social bonding that took place during and for a while after a disaster often quickly dissipates, leaving no long-lasting change in the make-up of the community.[148]

The key point is that a there is no standard way in which individuals and groups respond to major adversities. The response depends on the skills and perspectives held by the people affected and strength and extent of their social support networks. When one or more these attributes is lacking, people might not come together after a disaster and, even if in the short run they do bond and cooperate, the positive changes are often short-lived. I'll say more about these issues in the chapters that follow.

What can be learned from this information?

First, as stated in the introduction, it is essential to do as much as possible to reduce the physical damage generated by climate disruption by rapidly and definitively slashing greenhouse gas emissions and protecting and restoring ecological systems that sequester carbon to the levels deemed necessary by the best available science. It is also essential to prepare physical infrastructure such as flood control, transportation, and communications systems as well as local water and food systems and other natural assets as best as possible to withstand and adapt to the impacts of climate disruption.

However, even if significant progress is made in these two essential fronts, global average temperatures will still rise by at least 1.5°C above pre-industrial levels in coming decades, and likely much more, producing many types of acute traumas and chronic toxic stresses for humans.

When they are extreme or persistent, trauma and toxic stress produce fear-based dysregulation in many individuals and groups. Without effective knowledge and skills, when people are chronically dysregulated they will do almost anything to ameliorate their distress. Some will try to anesthetize themselves with drugs, alcohol, tobacco, food, sex, overwork, thrill seeking, or other coping behaviors that can quickly become self-destructive. Others will take out their frustrations on their children, spouses, friends, or neighbors. Still others will follow almost anyone who identifies outsiders, "liberals," "conservatives," or other scapegoats as the source of their problems and promises quick relief. This will sometimes cause small numbers of people to commit horrific acts of violence against people or nature.

As these trends grow, the brain's capacity to learn will be shut off and fewer and fewer people will be concerned about how they impact the natural environment or climate. It will consequently become even more difficult to slash greenhouse gasses, protect and restore forests and other ecological systems that sequester carbon, and reduce climate disruption to manageable levels.

No response to the climate crisis will therefore succeed unless individuals and groups of all types around the globe understand how trauma and toxic stress affects their minds and bodies, and use skills to calm their emotions and thoughts, learn from, and find meaning, direction, and hope in adversity. The use of these perspectives and skills can turn what appears to be a hopeless situation into one that helps people thrive. To bring about these changes a third major response to climate disruption must be rapidly implemented: an international movement to build widespread capacity for Transformational Resilience.

Thus, the three core elements of an effective approach to reduce climate disruption to manageable levels must include: emission reductions by slashing fossil fuel use and restoring ecosystems that sequester carbon; preparing and adapting essential physical infrastructure, natural resources, and other external assets to withstand climate impacts; and building the capacity of *people* to cope with the traumas and chronic toxic stresses generated by rising temperatures and use them as catalysts to learn, grow, and increase personal and collective wellbeing, and the condition of the natural environment.

Each of these three core elements will affect and be affected by each of the others. For example, if done well, increasing the capacity of forests to sequester carbon will increase their capacity to withstand climate impacts. Successfully reducing emissions can build hope and increase the capacity for people to learn, grow, and thrive in the midst of climate impacts. And building the capacity for Transformational Resilience can motivate people to reduce their emissions and prepare for climate impacts.

FIGURE 2.2   The three necessary interrelated elements of an effective response to climate disruption

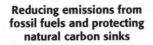

**Reducing emissions from
fossil fuels and protecting
natural carbon sinks**

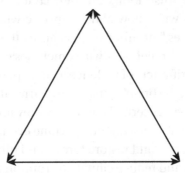

**Preparing and adapting
physical infrastructure
and natural resources**

**Building the capacity of individuals
and groups to cope with trauma,
learn, grow and thrive**

On the other hand, as mentioned, the failure to add this third major focus of building human capacity to cope with, learn, grow, and thrive in the midst on the climate-enhanced adversities is likely to delay or completely block efforts to reduce emissions and adapt to climate impacts, thus making the consequences of climate disruption even worse.

Figure 2.2 describes the three necessary elements of what is needed to respond effectively to climate disruption.[149]

If the third element of the global response to climate disruption is rapidly implemented worldwide, many negative personal mental health and psycho-social-spiritual maladies resulting from climate disruption can be prevented or minimized, and recovery can happen more quickly when problems do occur. Equally important, individuals and groups can use the climate crisis as a catalyst to learn what is needed to live fulfilling lives on a finite planet, grow as humans, and find important sources of meaning, purpose, and hope in their lives.

We will now turn our attention to how this transformational change can come about.

3
The imperative of building widespread capacity for Transformational Resilience

Psychiatrist and WWII concentration camp survivor Viktor Frankl once said, "Man is pushed by drives but pulled by meaning."[150] This quote shines a light on the two core elements of Transformational Resilience. Human behavior is driven in part by innate psychobiological drives. These drives cause many people to respond to acute traumas and chronic toxic stresses with fear-based self-protective behaviors that, left unresolved, can become harmful to others, the natural environment, or themselves. The first step in preventing this negative behavior is to become informed about how trauma and toxic stress affect us and to learn how to deactivate the fear-based reactions sparked by our psychobiological drives when they are not needed.

While essential, this alone is not enough.

Human behavior is also shaped by the instinctual desire to make sense of and find meaning in our experiences. To live a fulfilling life in the midst of rising ordeals associated with climate disruption, people must have a strong sense of purpose, direction, and hope to guide their actions.

I call the ability to deactivate and direct our psychobiological drives "Presencing" because it involves becoming aware of and regulating the physical sensations, emotions, and thoughts that are happening within us in the present moment. I call the capacity to intensify the pull of meaning, direction, and hope in our lives "Purposing" because it involves clarifying how we want to conduct ourselves in the midst of ever-present trauma and toxic stress.

The combination of Presencing and Purposing form the basis of Transformational Resilience. Both processes involve increasing the capacity of the brain's "Executive Center" to regulate the "Fear and Alarm Center" by noticing and naming what's going on within us, calming our emotions and thoughts, and then choosing the attitude and behaviors we will use to respond to other people, the natural environment, and ourselves in the midst of adversities aggravated by climate disruption.

Neither Presencing nor Purposing will eliminate the physical hardships generated by climate disruption. Nor will they make people into saints. Instead, Transformational Resilience is about minimizing the destructive human reactions that will magnify and prolong the harm caused by physical impacts, and learning how to use those adversities as catalysts to enhance personal and social wellbeing as well as the condition of the natural environment and climate.

Transformational Resilience is first and foremost preventative medicine. The knowledge and skills embedded within the processes can prevent harmful psycho-social-spiritual reactions before they occur. They also increase the likelihood of more rapid recovery after difficulties appear. Great peace of mind and a powerful sense of hope emerge when people know they can calm their emotions and thoughts and find meaning, direction, and hope in life even in the midst of climate-enhanced and other types of hardship.

Transformational Resilience skills can be learned by people of any age. They can also be utilized across the life-span. It is my firm belief that every individual, from childhood all the way through adulthood into their senior years, should have the opportunity to gain this knowledge and learn the skills.

This chapter describes the core principles and processes involved with Transformational Resilience using the *Resilient Growth*™ model as the framework. Subsequent chapters will explain how Presencing and Purposing can be applied in different settings.

What is mental health?

Most of us want to be psychologically healthy. But what does that actually mean? On the surface, the concept of mental health seems clear enough. However, when you scratch the surface, the definition becomes cloudier.

The view most commonly held in the field of psychology is that mental health is the absence of mental illness.[151] This perspective is based on the medical model of health that has dominated in the U.S. and Western Europe throughout the 20th century that sees humans as machines to be fixed when broken. This is a deficit model that assumes that health is the absence of disease. Once mental illness is eliminated, people are deemed to be healthy.

The medical model focuses on alleviating symptoms of mental illness through psychotherapy and drug therapy. Prevention is rarely emphasized. Few mental health programs today proactively help individuals and groups learn skills that can prevent psychological problems before they appear and promote mental and emotional wellbeing.

The World Health Organization (WHO) has adopted a more holistic definition. It says "Mental health is defined as a state of wellbeing in which every individual realizes his or her own potential, can cope with the normal stresses of life, can work productively and fruitfully, and is able to make a contribution to her or his community."[152] The WHO perspective alludes to a living systems, rather than mechanical view of humans. It emphasizes that mental health is about wellness that is fostered by positive attributes, not merely the absence of mental illness.

The distinction between eliminating pathology and fostering wellness is important because the ongoing traumas and toxic stresses generated by climate disruption will often make it difficult, if not impossible, for many people to be free of distress. Instead, individuals and groups will need to find ways to live principled and rewarding lives even in the midst of many ongoing painful or sad situations.

Researchers have found that when psychological health is defined as more than the elimination of pathology, the characterization typically follows two primary directions. The first is that mental health includes "hedonic" wellbeing. This term is associated with the pleasure principle. The second view is that psychological health concerns the development of what is called "eudaimonic" wellbeing, which is associated with qualities such as meaningfulness and purpose in life.[153] These qualities develop most often when people expand their focus beyond striving to meet their own personal needs and wants to finding meaning and fulfillment in life by helping others or caring for animals or the natural environment.

These two approaches complement each other. However, both research and experience underscore that the pursuit of pleasure by itself typically reduces mental wellbeing over the mid and long run, while the pursuit of meaning and purpose in life by helping others increases eudaimonic wellbeing, even in the absence of pleasurable feelings. *Thus, mental health—and increased resilience to adversity—is achieved most often through self-transcendence, meaning when people rise above their own self-interests to assist others or in other ways engage in a mission and purpose greater than themselves.*[154]

What is resilience?

If mental health includes factors that foster wellness, what does it mean to be psychologically and emotionally resilient?

As with mental health, the concept of resilience has often been viewed through the lens of the old medical model where health is the absence of illness.[155] For example, resilience has been defined as the absence of adverse symptoms following trauma.[156] Closely aligned with that perspective, and by far the most common understanding, is the American Psychological Association's definition which is that resilience is "bouncing back after difficult experiences."[157] This explanation suggests that an individual is resilient when distress is no longer evident and he or she has returned to their previous or normal conditions after adversity.

When considering the misfortunes generated by rising global temperatures, the concept of "bouncing back" is helpful. Avoiding long-term mental health and psycho-social-spiritual disabilities should be the baseline goal for responding to the many traumas and stresses people face with climate disruption. However, this definition can also give the wrong impression about the attributes required to respond constructively to ongoing climate-enhanced adversities.[158]

One concern is that bouncing back does not necessarily produce beneficial outcomes. History is filled with examples of destructive individuals, organizations, and governments that were able to bounce back from adversity and continue to harm or kill other people and often degrade the natural environment as well. As the sole goal, bouncing back is clearly insufficient.

Another problem is that the notion of bouncing back can easily lead to the conclusion that any factor that promotes health leads to the type of resilience needed to maintain personal mental health and psycho-social-spiritual wellbeing in the midst of rising harm associated with climate disruption. For instance, psychologists often say that eating moderate amounts of healthy food and getting regular physical exercise and a good night sleep help people bounce back to previous conditions after adversity. On one level this is a no brainer. The more physically healthy you are, the better off you will be. However, this perspective does not acknowledge what resilience involves for people that are not afforded such opportunities.

Nearly 20% of the U.S. population in 2013 lived in households with moderate to high levels of food insecurity, meaning food was not always readily available.[159] Globally, nearly one in eight people worldwide experience chronic undernourishment.

In addition, even when they do not live in poverty, many low and middle-income people today in industrialized nations must hold multiple jobs to make ends meet. This makes it difficult to get sufficient exercise or sleep.

As temperatures rise, it will become substantially more difficult for a large portion of the global population to obtain sufficient quantities of nutritious food, sleep, or exercise. However, with effective knowledge, tools, and skills these individuals still can remain calm and collected and live meaningful principled lives. Emphasizing the importance of good food, exercise, and sleep therefore runs the risk of misrepresenting what is needed for individual and psycho-social-spiritual resilience.

Still another problem with the idea that resilience involves bouncing back is that this is not a very desirable goal for a large portion of the world's population.

The Adverse Childhood Experiences study, first published in 1998, asked more than 17,000 members of Kaiser Permanente medical system in California if they had suffered adverse childhood experiences (ACEs) including physical or sexual abuse, emotional or physical neglect, domestic violence, family dysfunction including mental illness, substance abuse, or had a family member who was incarcerated.

The result was shocking. The number of people impacted by ACEs outnumbered those who were unaffected. And, adults that experienced these adversities in their childhood were often found to have a wide variety of physical health problems ranging from heart and lung diseases to diabetes and more. They also displayed more mental health problems such as suicide attempts as well as psycho-social-spiritual problems such as substance abuse, family violence, adolescent pregnancy, financial problems, and difficulty performing in the workplace than people who did not experience ACEs.

Since the original study, ACEs research has been completed in the majority of U.S. states and in the U.K., Eastern Europe, Norway, the Philippines, and Canada. Research that assessed similar but not identical issues has also been completed in five African nations as well as communities in China, Taiwan, Singapore and Malaysia. Each study produced comparable outcomes: half or more of the populations studied suffer at least one, and often multiple childhood traumas that in adulthood led to mental or physical health problems.[160]

Few people who have experienced ACEs want to return to their previous levels of mental and emotional distress following new adversities.

Finally, the goal of bouncing back suggests that people should rebound and reengage in today's cultural values and norms that emphasize the never-ending material and energy consumption that contribute to climate disruption.

Are these the conditions we want people to "bounce back" to? In an era of human-induced climate disruption, is this how resilience should be defined?

I think not. Something more expansive and constructive is required.

Resilience defined as coping and adapting

Embedded in the notion of bouncing back are the concepts of coping and adapting. Coping is typically thought of as the capacity of individuals and groups to use their existing resources to withstand and overcome immediate adversities. The goal is to rapidly restore present levels of functioning following an adversity.[161]

Adaption has the same goal but uses a slightly different approach. It can be described as the ability of individuals and groups to maintain existing levels of functioning by learning from the past, anticipating future threats, and then making incremental adjustments before new impacts occur in order to maintain present levels of functioning.[162]

The primary differences between coping and adapting are the methods and time-scales involved. Coping focuses primarily on tactical reactions with immediate or short-term benefits. Adaptation has a more strategic focus and includes more mid- and long-term planning.[163]

Just like bouncing back, both coping and adaptation seek to maintain homeostasis. The overriding goal is to make changes intended to sustain steady and relatively constant personal and psycho-social-spiritual conditions after adversity. These concepts are also helpful in some ways. The ability to adjust to changing conditions is a central attribute of wellness and will be vital as climate impacts worsen. However, the notions are also inadequate to explain what is needed to deal with the consequences of a global temperature rise of 1.5°C or more above pre-industrial levels.

One of the reasons is that as temperatures rise, the impacts of climate disruption will rarely be one-time disasters followed by long periods of stability that allow people time to return to previous conditions. Instead, as seen in many parts of the world already, the combination of acute traumatic events and chronic toxic stresses will grow in frequency, intensity, and length and frequently leave little time for people to recover to previous conditions.

In addition, reducing climate disruption to manageable levels requires major shifts in the way people think and act, and in social, economic, and political systems. These changes cannot be achieved by maintaining our existing ways of viewing the world and ourselves. They will necessitate new conceptual frameworks as well as new behaviors and practices.

My experience is that when asked to think deeply about these issues, a majority of people will say they do not want to cope or adapt in order to maintain homeostasis. Most people want more *equal, just, and healthier conditions* so they can increase their wellbeing *beyond* existing levels and *thrive*.

Resilience as hormesis

To flourish in the midst of rising climate-enhanced trauma and stress, individuals and groups must rise above their existing circumstances and adopt new ways to think about and respond to adversity that actually increase their sense of wellbeing, the welfare of others, and the condition of the natural environment well above previous levels. This type of transformational experience is not only possible, it is an innate capacity of human beings.

As discussed in the introduction, the concept of *hormesis* offers a useful analogy for this process. This is a biological response to stress that actually improves the capacity of the body to handle stress. While homeostasis maintains relatively stable conditions, hormesis creates better-than-before levels of functioning.[164]

The same dynamic builds our psychological and emotional capacity to deal with adversity. Stress often produces negative mental and physical reactions in the short term. However, used correctly it can increase our personal strengths and capacities in the mid and long term. The pressure of knowing that you are going to take a test, for instance, stimulates you to study and learn. The stress that results from failing at a task or making a serious mistake can lead to new insights into what could be done differently to perform better next time. With a proper mindset, stress can be viewed as an important source of information and a beneficial motivator of learning and growth.[165]

The rapidly growing field of neuroscience explains how this works. Neuroscientists have discovered that the human brain is malleable and can reorganize itself throughout a person's lifetime, a capacity they call neuroplasticity. They have also discovered something even more exciting: neurogenesis. This is the capacity of the brain to grow new cells and networks in response to stress, much like muscles grow in response to exercise.

Research has found that deliberately pausing when you are in the midst of stress, and nonjudgmentally focusing your attention on what is occurring within you in the present moment enhances neuroplasticity and neurogenesis. This can also occur through a process called cognitive reappraisal in which you challenge the accuracy of thoughts such as "My situation is completely hopeless." This directly engages the Executive Center of the brain, resulting in decreased power and control by the Fear and Alarm Center.[166] Both of these processes are core elements of Transformational Resilience.

The concept of hormesis typically has been used in reference to low doses of mild stressors that make cells and organisms more robust. Psychologists have found, however, that many people use extremely difficult situations as catalysts to learn, grow, and make beneficial changes. The quote by German philosopher Friedrich Nietzsche gets to the heart of the process, "What does not kill me makes me stronger."[167]

The main differences between coping, adapting, and the transformational process of hormesis is the degree of change and the intended outcomes. Transformation is focused on deep-seated change where the goal is

	Bouncing back	**Coping**	**Adapting**	**Transformation through hormesis**
Response to climate threats	After impacts	After impacts	Before impacts	Before, during, and after impacts
Time-horizon	Immediate/ short-term	Immediate/ short-term	Medium-term	Immediate, medium- and long-term
Degree of change	Low/status quo	Low/status quo	Medium/ incremental	High/deep-seated fundamental change
Outcome	Restoration of prior level of functioning	Restoration of prior level of functioning	Restoration of prior level of functioning and security of future	Increased wellbeing for present and future generations and ecological systems

TABLE 3.1   Comparisons of methods for building human resilience

Source: Adapted from Keck, M., & Sakdapolrak, P. (2013). What is social resilience? Lessons learned and ways forward. *Erdkunde*, 67(1), 5-19.

not to return to or maintain existing levels of functioning, but to use trauma and stress as catalysts to increase wellbeing beyond previous conditions. It thus incorporates, but goes well beyond coping and adaption.[168]

Table 3.1 describes the differences among bouncing back, coping, adapting, and the transformational process of hormesis.

The transformational process of hormesis is learnable

Individuals and groups *can* learn information and skills that enable them to use trauma and toxic stress as catalysts to increase their personal as well as collective wellbeing and improve the condition of the natural environment.[169] The potential for this type of transformational experience will prove much greater if efforts begin *now*, before global temperatures rise by 1.5°C above pre-industrial levels, because the impacts at that point will likely be relentless and severe.

However, if the transformational process of hormesis, rather than homeostasis, quickly becomes the central goal of initiatives aimed at reducing the climate crisis to manageable levels, and explicit efforts are made to build the attributes and processes that help individuals and groups engage in this type of transformational experience, significant pain and suffering can be avoided. Done well, a major worldwide focus on enhancing the capacity for transformation through hormesis might stimulate the next great spurt of human development.

Transformational Resilience

With these definitions as background, what does Transformational Resilience mean? I define it as the capacity of individuals and groups to use their existing strengths and resources to deliberately regulate their body, emotions, and thoughts, and use adversity as a catalyst to find new meaning, direction, and hope in life by making decisions that enhance personal, social, and environmental wellbeing.[170]

This definition emphasizes that Transformational Resilience is a preventative, strength-based, growth-oriented approach for dealing with adversity. It combines the common view of resilience as the ability to bounce back, with post-traumatic or adversity-based growth, meaning the capacity to achieve new levels of functioning as a result of adversity.[171]

The concept of Transformational Resilience highlights the importance of the biology of the nervous system as well as the critical transactional role that assumptions, beliefs, and perceptions play in shaping the capacity of people to find purpose and fulfillment in life. It is thus both a process and an outcome. This fits the notion of resilience held by most people. Even if all of the symptoms of psychological distress disappear, the majority of people don't feel resilient if they lack a sense of meaning, direction, and hope in life.

Because it focuses on prevention, in addition to climate disruption, Transformational Resilience can be used to prepare people to deal with all types of human-caused adversity such as family troubles, financial difficulties, school shootings, and terrorist attacks as well as natural disasters such as earthquakes or tsunamis. It is not a problem-solving or post-trauma treatment technique *per se*, although with these skills people can recover move rapidly when they are traumatized. Nor is it psychotherapy. However, it can be very therapeutic.

With practice, the skills and tools included in the process can be self-administered at a moment's notice. They are also dose-based, meaning the more they are practiced the greater the effects.

Transformational Resilience is a bottom-up self-organizing approach to building personal mental health and psycho-social-spiritual resilience that can be developed person-by-person and group-by-group. It is not a top-down expert led psychological treatment that seeks to attain specific therapeutic goals and objectives.

Presencing: the first building block of Transformational Resilience

The initial focus of Transformational Resilience is to gain the capacity to moderate the "push" of our innate psychobiological drives and regulate the body's Fear and Alarm Center. This can occur through the use of a number of skills that activate the Parasympathetic Nervous System (PNS), which is the body's brake system, and moderate the Sympathetic Nervous System (SNS), which is the body's accelerator. I call this process "Presencing" because it involves becoming aware of what is occurring within and around us in the present moment.

When we deactivate the body's Fear and Alarm System when it is not needed and calm the nervous system we have much greater potential to stay within our "Resilient Growth Zone."[172] This is a concept developed by Elaine Miller-Karas and Laurie Leitch. Our "Resilient Growth Zone" is created through the combination of the biology of our nervous system and by the way we perceive and think about the adversities we experience. When we are in this zone we are much more capable of effectively regulating our body, emotions, and thoughts. We are also able to learn from the past, incorporate new information into our views of the world and ourselves, and grow as people. These attributes are essential to making wise and skillful decisions in the midst of adversity.

When we are in our Resilient Growth Zone our nervous system has a natural rhythm and flow to it. Sometimes we become a bit hyped up and find ourselves at the upper end of our Resilient Growth Zone. At other times we get a little down and move to the lower end of our Resilient Growth Zone. This type of up and down movement is completely natural as we deal with daily life.

Most of us occasionally get pushed outside of our Resilient Growth Zone by some type of triggering event. This is also completely natural. It might be a personal injury or the serious illness of a loved one, the memory of a previous traumatic event that we can't stop thinking about, or an image in our head of some type of frightening future hardship. When we are pushed outside of our Resilient Growth Zone we are no longer living in the present moment. Instead, we are usually caught up in memories of the past or images of the future as if they are happening now.

This occurs when the emergency alert signals sent by our brain's "Fear and Alarm Center" have thrown the natural rhythm of our nervous system out of balance and put us in a state of dysregulation. This can leave us feeling constantly on edge, amped up, hyperactive, anxious, enraged, or in pain. The dysregulation might also cause us to feel sad, depressed, exhausted, disconnected, or numb. We experience these feelings in our body as well as in our minds. When we are dysregulated in this way we have a difficult time dealing with everyday events in the way we would do when we are within our Resilient Growth Zone. We also cannot learn and grow.

Most of the time when we are pushed outside of our Resilient Growth Zone we are able to bring ourselves back into the zone in relatively short order, with little harm done. Serious problems tend to occur only when we get stuck in a high state or a low state outside the zone for long periods of time. Figure 3.1 depicts this process.[173]

FIGURE 3.1   Transformational Resilience skills help you widen and easily return to your Resilient Growth Zone

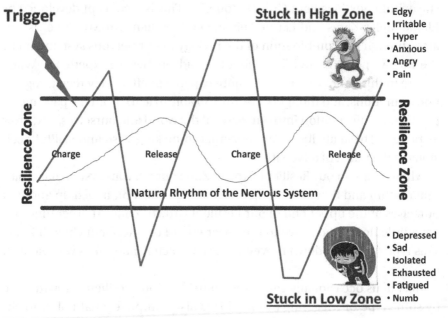

Source: Adapted from Community Resiliency Model, adapted by Elaine Miller-Karas from the original work of Elaine Miller-Karas and Laurie Leitch.

As discussed in Chapter 1, in a misguided attempt to relieve this distress we might adopt self-destructive coping behaviors. Long periods of dysregulation can also cause us to direct our fear-based reactions outward and harm other people or the natural environment. Presencing skills help us recognize when we are dysregulated and enable us to take steps to deactivate our fear-based reactions and bring ourselves back into our Resilient Growth Zone.

Three basic skills included in the *Resilient Growth*™ model describe the fundamentals of Presencing: first, deliberately take steps to stabilize the nervous system. Second, remember to call on our personal skills, resources, and social support networks that can help calm our emotions and thoughts. Third, observe and modify thought patterns that trigger or reinforce dysregulation.

With practice, these skills expand our Resilient Growth Zone so that increasingly powerful traumas or toxic stresses are required to shove us outside. The process also helps us become more aware of when we are dysregulated, and allows us to more rapidly move back into our Resilient Growth

Zone where we have greater ability to rationally assess our situation and make wise and skillful decisions about how to respond.

Purposing: the second building block of Transformational Resilience

Moderating the push of our psychobiological drives by regulating the body's fear-based reactions when they are not needed is essential to respond effectively to the traumas and stresses generated by climate disruption. However, this is just the first step needed to deal with ongoing adversities generated by rising global temperatures. We must also realize that how we respond is our responsibility, and that only by making decisions that increase not only our own wellbeing, but the welfare of others, and the condition of the natural environment can we find meaning and fulfillment in our own lives. In other words, we must intensify the pull of meaning in our lives.[174] This is a fundamental step in the recovery from trauma. I call it "Purposing," and it is the second core building block of Transformational Resilience.

Human beings naturally seek to find meaning in their lives. This is how we navigate our way through life's trails and tribulations. The drive becomes especially keen when adversity strikes because we are much more able to tolerate suffering if we find meaning in it. Without meaning, serious adversity can often lead to self-destructive behaviors and despair. However, when we find meaning, direction, and hope in the midst of hardship we can more easily bear it and even find benefits in the situation.

In addition, no matter how distressing or painful the experience, or what is damaged or taken from us, humans always have the capacity to choose their attitude about their situation. Although many people believe freedom is autonomy from externally imposed constraints, Viktor Frankl, the WWII concentration camp survivor who went on to be an internationally renowned psychiatrist and whose quote began this chapter, called the ability to choose our attitude toward any life circumstance a human's "ultimate freedom."[175]

Just as Father Vien and the leaders of the Lower Ninth Ward in New Orleans did after Hurricane Katrina, these two dynamics—the innate human drive to find meaning in tragedy, and the capacity to choose our attitude in any situation—help people use misfortune as a catalyst to "re-author" the stories they tell about the world and themselves and transform their lives.[176]

This process widens our Resilient Growth Zone, makes it more difficult for adversity to push us outside, and allows us to return more quickly when we are dysregulated.

Our personal narratives define who we are. Each individual develops a story about the way the world works and their role in it as a way to understand and make sense of their life experiences. Our personal narrative shapes our sense of "Self"—our ideas and beliefs about who we are as human beings—and it includes a set of assumptions and beliefs that largely determine how we interpret events, interact with others and the natural environment, and treat ourselves.

Major trauma and unrelenting toxic stress can shatter these foundational assumptions and beliefs, and awaken us to the finite and transitory nature of life. People find that the assumptions and beliefs they hold about living in an orderly, safe, and understandable world are mere fantasies.[177] But if an individual can sufficiently calm their body, thoughts, and emotions and grieve their losses, they can engage in deep-seated self-reflection to find meaning in what happened. A silver lining of a new sense of purpose in life often emerges from the negative events. Learning and growth arise from the struggle to find meaning, not from the traumatic event itself.[178]

The reevaluation process for most people typically involves much more than merely seeing things in a new light. It leads to more realistic assumptions and beliefs about the world and their role in it, and a deep-seated understanding that they are responsible for how they handle themselves in the midst of adversity. The result is an altered sense of Self that includes greater clarity about what's truly important in life, who they want to spend time with, and where they want to focus their energy now and in the future.

This new sense of Self also commonly includes the knowledge that only by assisting other people in some way can they achieve happiness and well-being. Self-transcendence, which I call a shift "From Me to We" and is also sometimes termed altruism, is thus as much about people helping themselves as it is about assisting others.

By accepting this responsibility people can transform their sense of Self from "victim" or "survivor" to "thriver" or "flourisher." This opens the door to new ways of viewing the world that allow them to rise above misfortune to levels of functioning that are beyond what they previously experienced. The process also dramatically increases an individual's wherewithal to tolerate future adversities and thrive.[179]

It is important to remember that meaning-making occurs not only at the individual level. Groups also engage in the process. This can be seen after a major trauma such as a destructive storm that destroys an entire neighbor-hood, a mass shooting, or an outbreak of collective violence, when people come together, abandon long-standing prejudices, and together care for complete strangers. Even when an individual is not directly impacted by a collective trauma, people that know others who are affected, or who even just witness the event from afar, often go through the same psychological search for meaning as the people that are directly impacted.[180] This turns what appears to be an individual event into one with shared implications.

The *Resilient Growth*™ model

A simple way to keep the elements of Transformational Resilience in mind is through the use of the *Resilient Growth*™ model. The word Growth is pur-posely employed to emphasize that individuals and groups benefit when they use adversities generated by climate disruption as catalysts to grow as humans.

Each letter of the word signifies a different element of the growth process. The first three letters—G, R, O—address the core elements of Presencing. The last three letters—W, T, H—describe the central aspects of Purposing.

To repeat, using the traumas and toxic stresses generated by climate dis-ruption as catalysts to learn, grow, and thrive requires that you first Ground and center yourself by stabilizing your nervous system. As you do so, it helps to Remember that you have personal skills, resources, and a social support network that you can call on to help you constructively deal with the adversity. Throughout both steps, it is helpful to deliberately Observe your thoughts about the situation nonjudgmentally with self-compassion.

After your body, emotions, and thoughts are sufficiently calmed, you need to decide your course of action. Before you choose a path, you will benefit when you Watch for new insights about the world and yourself and find meaning in the adversity. You can then Tap into the core values you want to live by in the midst of the hardships. Finally, you pull it all together by Harvesting hope for new possibilities by making choices that enhance the wellbeing of others, the condition of the natural environment, and thus yourself.

A variety of age- and culturally appropriate techniques can be used within each of the focal areas of the *Resilient Growth*™ model. Each individual and

FIGURE 3.2   The Resilient Growth™ model of Transformational Resilience

---

**Focus: *Presencing* skills to regulate the
body's fear-based reactions**

Ground—and center yourself by stabilizing your nervous system

Remember—your personal strengths, resources, and social support network

Observe—your reactions to and thoughts about the situation nonjudgmentally with self-compassion

**Focus: *Purposing* skills to find meaning,
direction and hope in adversity**

Watch—for new insights and meaning in life in climate-enhanced hardships

Tap—into the values you want to live by in the midst of climate adversity

Harvest—hope for new possibilities by making choices that increase personal, social, and environmental wellbeing

---

group will benefit by using methods that resonate with and work best for them. Figure 3.2 describes the model.

In the chapters that follow I will describe each of the elements of the model in more detail.[181] Parts 2 and 3 describe the application of the model to individual resilience. Part 4 outlines how to apply Presencing and Purposing skills in the organizational and community context.

Theoretical underpinnings of Transformational Resilience

Three primary areas of research and practice have influenced the development of Transformational Resilience and the *Resilient Growth*™ model.

The first is the rapidly growing field of neuroscience, also called neurobiology, which is the scientific study of the human nervous system. The research on interpersonal neurobiology by Dan Siegel and others has had a particularly strong influence on the development of my approach. Within individuals, interpersonal neurobiology focuses on the integration of internal emotions, thoughts, and physical sensations. In relationships the focus on integration involves respect for each individual's autonomy as well as the inherent links they have with other people and their environment.[182]

A related aspect of neuroscience research that influenced my approach is trauma theory. This is the study of the psychological traumatization that occurs when the internal and external resources of an individual or group are overwhelmed or inadequate to deal with real or perceived threats. The work of Judith Herman,[183] Ronnie-Janoff-Bulman,[184] John Briere[185] and Bessel van de Kolk[186] influenced my work. The research and methods developed by Elaine Miller-Karas and Dr. Sandra Bloom in particular have been exceedingly helpful in the development of the model.

The rapidly growing field of Post-Traumatic Growth, or what I call Adversity-Based Growth, is the second area of research and practice that has shaped the development of Transformational Resilience and the *Resilient Growth*™ model. This field of study focuses on the beneficial psychological changes people experience as a result of their struggle with distressing events. Adversity-based Growth is not about returning to the same level of functioning or way of living that existed prior to a traumatic event. Rather, it is about undergoing profound life-changing shifts in the way we view and think about the world and ourselves that lead to increased functioning beyond previous levels. The work of Stephen Joseph,[187] Richard Tedeschi, Laurence Calhoun,[188] and a number of other researchers have been particularly influential to my thinking.[189]

Embedded within post-traumatic or adversity-based growth is the transactional view of trauma and resilience developed by Richard Lazarus and Susan Folkman.[190] This perspective emphasizes that psychological trauma does not result solely from changes in the external environment or from the characteristics of the individual or group. Rather, it results from a dynamic relationship between the individual and their environment and how they perceive their capacity to meet the demands posed by the events. The constructive narrative perspective developed by Michael Murray and others[191] is also embedded within the *Resilient Growth*™ model. It views individuals and groups as storytellers that craft narratives about the world, themselves, and the future in order to make sense of and find meaning in events. The stories people construct influence how they respond to adversity.[192]

The third area of research and practice that has influenced the development of Transformational Resilience and the *Resilient Growth*™ model is mindfulness. This is an age-old practice derived from traditional Buddhist practice, although the *Resilient Growth*™ does not involve any religious or metaphysical concepts or customs. The term mindfulness as it is used here means nonjudgmentally and deliberately observing what is happening within and around us in the present moment when we are distressed.

A robust body of empirical research has demonstrated that developing this capacity generates greater ability to tolerate distress and also increase personal wellbeing. In particular, Vipassana meditation (I am a mindfulness teacher) and Mindfulness-Based Stress Reduction (MBSR) developed by Jon Kabat-Zinn (I am also an MBSR instructor) have influenced my approach.[193] Wellbeing Therapy, which is based on Carol Ryff's multi-dimensional model of psychological wellbeing,[194] Acceptance and Commitment Therapy developed by Stephen Hayes and others,[195] and Dialectic Behavioral Therapy developed by Marsha Linehan[196] have also influenced the creation of Transformational Resilience and the *Resilient Growth*™ model. Each of these approaches use mindfulness in combination with other techniques to help people use adversities as catalysts to gain new insights, grow, and thrive.

Summary

Deep-seated change is required to prevent global temperatures from rising to levels that unleash uncontrollable civilization-altering climate disruption. All social change begins at the individual level, and this is where the process of Transformational Resilience starts.

I am not suggesting, however, that the responsibility for personal psychological health or psycho-social-spiritual wellbeing rests solely with the individual. To the contrary, the capacity of any individual to use adversity as a catalyst to gain new insights, grow, and thrive is heavily influenced by the people, culture, institutions, and systems of power in which they are enmeshed.

The goal of Transformational Resilience is not to help people accept or adjust to injustice, racism, or any other form of systemic oppression, violence, or poverty, or to the negative outcomes of climate disruption. Instead, the purpose is to help people become more effective in dealing with and alleviating these and other adversities by learning how to care for themselves and find meaning, direction, and hope in their lives by helping other people, and improving the condition of the natural environment and climate.

In other words, to use the hardships generated by climate disruption as catalysis to gain insight, grow, and thrive it will be essential to rise above a sole focus on "Me" to find meaning and fulfillment in life by enhancing the "We" which includes other people and the climate that make all life possible on planet Earth.[197]

Part 2:
Presencing—the first building block of Transformational Resilience

The first building block of Transformational Resilience is Presencing. It has two goals. The first is to calm the body, mind, and emotions in the midst of acute trauma or toxic stress. This involves releasing the hyperarousal that dysregulates your nervous system and deactivating your fight, flee, and freeze reactions when they are not needed. The second goal is to create psychological flexibility. This means nonjudgmentally noticing, but not becoming caught up in, the thoughts going through your mind that trigger or sustain dysregulation.

Presencing stabilizes your nervous system and allows you to achieve cognitive and behavioral control. When confronted by adversity, it is important to actively search for strategies to regulate your body, emotions, and thoughts and ease your distress. This widens your Resilient Growth Zone, which makes it less likely that you will get pushed outside it when stressed. It also makes it easier to return to your Resilient Growth Zone when you are pushed out of it.

As previously mentioned, three interrelated skills form the approach to Presencing included in the *Resilient Growth™* model of Transformational Resilience. Each skill can be carried out using a variety of tools and techniques. The three skills correspond with the first three letters of the word "growth." In this section I will describe each of these skills and offer tools and techniques that can be used to carry them out.

A fundamental process that applies to all three skills is to deliberately observe your body's sensations, emotions, and thoughts without judgment. This involves noticing what's going on within and around you and giving it a name. Noticing and naming how trauma and stress affect the mind and body helps calm the nervous system. It also increases your capacity to become aware of the role your perceptions and thoughts play in triggering dysregulation. In addition, it creates space between the thoughts that pop into your mind and your reactions to them. Even a tiny space between your thoughts and reactions can provide the psychological flexibility needed to make wise and skillful decisions in the midst of hardship. "To name it is to tame it" is a phrase neurological researchers use to describe the benefits of this type of nonjudgmental self-observation.

4
Ground and center yourself by stabilizing your nervous system

"During Hurricane Katrina, my son and I were trapped in a building in downtown New Orleans," recalled Whitney Stewart. "We had to wait five days for helicopters to rescue us. During that time, I used meditation as a means of staying calm, alleviating fear, and being mindful. When I returned to New Orleans, I volunteered as a creative writing teacher in a public school. I discovered that students were very often stressed, unhappy, and frightened every time the weather turned stormy. They could not concentrate on their work. I taught them to meditate before we did our creative writing exercises. Many of them told me how much they loved to meditate at the beginning of class."[198]

Stewart's experience underscores that the first skill involved with Presencing is to Ground and center yourself by stabilizing your nervous system. Remember, the nervous system regulates the activities of your body and mind. When you experience a traumatic event or persistent toxic stress such as that generated by climate disruption, the brain's "Fear and Alarm Center" sends out emergency alert signals that put you in a state of dysregulation and throws the natural rhythm and flow of your nervous system out of balance.

When you are dysregulated you can easily be shoved outside of your Resilient Growth Zone. If it persists, you can get stuck in an elevated state of agitation, anxiety, anger, or irritability. Conversely, you can bottom out and continually feel sad, depressed, fatigued, or numb. Sometimes you might find yourself ricocheting back and forth between these high and low states. Both conditions block the executive functions of the brain and reduce your ability to think things through clearly and objectively.

If these conditions persist you might go on autopilot, attending to everyday details while ignoring or suppressing your internal distress, or isolating yourself from others. You might also try to sedate yourself with drugs, alcohol, overeating, or other behaviors that, without great care, can easily become self-destructive. Conversely, you could become prone to bursts of anger, interpersonal aggression, or violence, or in other ways inappropriately focusing your distress on other people. You might also attempt to soothe yourself with mindless shopping, obsessive use of smartphones, computers, and other technologies, or other high resource and energy consumption patterns that damage the natural environment and climate and ultimately come back to harm other people—and you.[199]

To prevent these negative reactions, or to quickly reduce them when they appear, it is important to actively search for ways to activate your parasympathetic nervous system (PNS)—which is the body's break system—and allow it to deactivate your sympathetic nervous system (SNS), which is the body's accelerator.[200]

If you recall from Chapter 2, the PNS stimulates the vagus nerve, which runs from the base of the brain to the abdomen and is responsible for moderating the responses of the SNS. The vagus nerve does this by releasing a neurotransmitter called acetylcholine that immediately reduces your heart rate and blood pressure and increases your focus and calmness. A direct benefit of more acetylcholine is decreased anxiety and stress.

Techniques for stabilizing the nervous system

A variety of techniques can be used to stabilize your nervous system. The overarching goal of all of the techniques is simple: become attentive to your internal processes, including physical sensations, emotions, and thoughts. This is important because focusing your attention inward—especially when not focused on something distressing—activates the PNS which can rapidly reduce your blood pressure, lower your sense of stress, lift your mood, and produce a sense of calm. These changes strengthen the capacity of the brain's "Executive Center" to calmly assess your external conditions and make prudent decisions about how to respond, rather than allowing the "Fear and Alarm Center" to automatically and habitually control your reactions.[201]

Body-based techniques

Your body and mind are a unified system. This means your body reacts to the world just as your mind does. It automatically contracts and directs its energy toward preparing you to fight back, flee the threat, or freeze. Learning to become aware of troubling physical sensations—which activate the SNS—as well as sensations that are comforting—which are associated with the PNS—helps calm and stabilize your nervous system and allows you to remain within your Resilient Growth Zone or more easily return to it when you are pushed outside. Two body-based skills are particularly helpful in activating the PNS.

Tracking[202]

Tracking is a body-based skill developed by Elaine Miller-Karas and Laurie Leitch and the discussion that follows is adapted from the Community Resilience Model Handbook developed by the Trauma Resource Institute.[203] Tracking means noticing the physical sensations in your body. The sensations might be felt in your skin, or they might be experienced in your muscles or internal organs. These sensations tell you what is happening within your nervous system.

One of the goals of tracking is to learn to tell the difference between sensations that are pleasant and those that are neutral or unpleasant. The more you place your attention on neutral or positive sensations, the more you will stimulate the PNS, which puts the brake on the revved up sensations generated by your SNS.

The exercise described in Box 4.1 walks you through the tracking process.

Tracking physical sensations, even ones that are pleasant, can initially be difficult. Go slow and try it for a minute or so the first time. Then, try tracking your sensations again a few hours or a day later for 2–3 minutes. Slowly increase the length of time you practice Tracking to 5–10 minutes at a time. Slowly but surely you will build your capacity to notice the physical sensations in your body.

Often when you first begin to track your physical sensations, your attention will be quickly drawn to unpleasant sensations such as muscle tension, rapid heartbeat, burning, or painful areas. This can be uncomfortable and cause you to stop tracking. However, the more you make a conscious effort to search your body for neutral or pleasant sensations such as relaxed muscles, agreeable tingling, slower heart rate, deeper breathing, or soothing warmth, the easier tracking will become. When you notice an unpleasant sensation you can then shift your attention back and forth between a

Box 4.1: How to track physical sensations

- Begin by turning your attention inward, and place it on physical sensations occurring within your body.

- Examine your feet, legs, torso, arms, hand, neck and head for sensations that feel pleasant, neutral, or unpleasant.

- Spend a few moments noticing different sensations in various parts of your body. When you notice a sensation just accept it for what it is. Don't try to change it in any way or judge it as good or bad. Just notice the sensations occurring within you in the present moment.

- You might find your attention drawn to an unpleasant sensation. This is completely natural. If this happens, gently move your attention to a pleasant or neutral sensation.

- Then, without judgment or trying to change anything, gently move your attention back and forth from the unpleasant to the pleasant or neutral sensations.

- If the unpleasant sensations become too much to bear, place all of your attention on areas of your body that feel pleasant or neutral.

- Continue to track your physical sensations for as long as you are comfortable. When you are ready to end the exercise, take a few deep breaths and reorient your focus to the external world.

neutral or pleasant sensation and the unpleasant sensation. The more you do this the greater the likelihood that the unpleasant sensations will begin to fade into the background. As you continue to track your physical sensations, it will become easier to move back within your Resilient Growth Zone when you are pushed outside.

When learning to track it often helps to have some words to use to describe the sensations you notice. Box 4.2 includes words that might be helpful.

When your body begins to move back into balance by tracking your physical sensations you might notice what Miller-Karas and Leitch call Nervous System Release. This is a biological process that occurs automatically when hyperarousal is released and your body moves back into balance. When you first experience Nervous System Release it can be unsettling because the sensations can include extensive heat or cooling down, tingling in different parts of the body, trembling or shaking, crying, laughing, burping or stomach gurgling, yawning, itching, rapid hand movement, or deep breathing (see Table 4.1 for a summary). If these sensations become too strong, you can make a conscious decision to stop the process for a while. You can also slow it down by noticing the urge to release without allowing your nervous system to release the energy all at once.

Box 4.2: Sensation words

- Twitch
- Frozen
- Smooth
- Solid
- Congested
- Tingling

- Dull
- Airy
- Chills
- Numb
- Expanding
- Shaky

- Sharp
- Thick
- Vibrating
- Empty
- Tight
- Paralyzed

- Achy
- Trembling
- Itchy
- Blocked
- Puffy
- Sweaty

- Jagged
- Shivery
- Pulsating
- Moving
- Bubbly
- Hard

Source: Elaine Miller-Karas, "From Community Resilience Model Workbook." Trauma Resource Institute, p. 15.

Trauma/stress	Release
Constricted breathing	Shaking
Rapid heartbeat	Trembling
Tense muscles	Burping/yawning
Pain	Heat/warmth
Numbness	Vibrating/tingling

TABLE 4.1   Sensations associated with trauma/stress and release

Source: Adapted from Elaine Miller-Karas, "From Community Resilience Model Workbook." Trauma Resource Institute, p. 15.

Grounding[204]

Another body-based technique developed by Miller-Karas and Leitch that helps stabilize the nervous system is called grounding. It involves noticing where your body is physically supported by something. For example, if you are sitting you can ground by focusing your attention on where your body touches a chair. If you are standing you can focus on where your feet are supported by the floor or earth, if you are leaning against a wall you can focus on where your back is supported by the wall.

Traumatic events and stressful situations can literally knock you off your feet. They can also push you so far out of your Resilient Growth Zone that you become detached from reality. When you practice grounding on a regular basis and notice where and how your body is supported by something solid, it is much easier to come back into the present moment. This activates the PNS, which helps move you back toward your Resilient Growth Zone.

Box 4.3 describes how to practice grounding.

Box 4.3: How to ground

- You can ground while sitting, standing, lying down, or walking.

- Begin by finding a comfortable position.

- Now, notice where your body makes contact with the chair, floor, wall, bed, earth, or other substance.

- If you are sitting, focus your attention on how you body is making contact with the chair, sofa, etc. Notice the sensations in your legs, thighs, and then your feet where they make contact with something solid.

- Notice which sensations are more pleasant or neutral, which means you might not sense any sensations in that area of your body.

- If you become aware of uncomfortable sensations, consciously move your attention to places in your body that feel pleasant or neutral.

- As you bring your attention to where your body is contacting the floor, chair, wall, etc. notice your breathing, heart rate, muscle relaxation, and other physical sensations.

- As you get ready to close the exercise, look over your entire body and bring your attention to all of the sensations that are pleasant or neutral.

Source: Adapted from Elaine Miller-Karas, "From Community Resilience Model Workbook." Trauma Resource Institute.

Amp down/ramp up Help Now[205]

The Trauma Resource Institute developed these skills to enable you to move back within your Resilient Growth Zone when you are stuck outside in a "high" or "low" zone. Try one or more of the actions below and see which work best for you. You can also ask a family members or friend to help you with them:

- Drink a glass of water, tea, or juice.

- Look around the room or wherever you are, paying attention to anything that catches your attention.

- Name six colors you see in the room (or outside).

- Open your eyes if they have a tendency to shut.

- Slowly count backwards from 20 as you walk around the room.

- If you're inside, notice the furniture, and touch the surface, sensing if it is hard, soft, rough, etc. …

- Notice the temperature in the room.

- Notice the sounds within the room and outside.

- If you're outside or inside, walk and pay attention to the movement in your arms and legs and how your feet are making contact with the ground.

- Push your hands against the wall or door slowly and notice your muscles pushing. You can also push your back and lower torso against the wall facing forward.

Other body-based calming techniques can be used as well to stabilize your nervous system. A great resource is the Trauma Resource Institute, which offers a variety of these skills. Their website is: http:// traumaresourceinstitute.com.

Catherine's story

After Typhoon Yolanda devastated her nation, Catherine participated in a Community Resilience Model training program offered by The Trauma Resource Institute in Cebu, the Philippines. After another participant gave her additional information about the Grounding skill that was taught, she responded by writing: "Thank you very much for this resource ... it has strengthened my resolve about the health benefits of grounding. I am also happy to tell everyone how I was able to help a co-worker through Help Now (pushing against the wall) get back to her resilient zone when she faced a stressful situation. I pushed the wall with her and used Tracking to let her be aware of what's happening to her body. The quick exercise helped her calm down and get her breathing and heartbeat steady. The amazing sensation of warmth inside after knowing that the skills can really help us and other people has become a great reason to continue teaching the skills to others. God bless you all!"[206]

Breath-Based techniques

Some people are uncomfortable using body-based techniques to calm their nervous system because focusing on physical sensations can sometimes be overwhelming or seem awkward. If this is the case, you might try breath-based techniques.

Our breathing patterns typically reflect our emotional states. When you are calm and relaxed the breath normally proceeds in three stages. It begins with relaxed stomach muscles that allow your diaphragm to move downwards, which draws air into your lungs. This allows your abdomen to expand before your chest moves as the air fills the lower portion of your lungs. The in-breath then expands your chest muscles, which causes your rib cage to enlarge and allows the air to fill the middle portion of your lungs. At the peak of the in-breath your collarbones move upward and your shoulders relax, which allows the upper part of your lungs to fill with air. In other words, relaxed breathing starts at the bottom of the abdomen and moves upward filling your entire lungs.

In contrast, when you experience trauma and stress you can easily fall into "Fear and Alarm Breathing" which is the exact opposite of relaxed breathing. Rather than breathing deeply into the bottom of the lungs with relaxed stomach muscles, you contract and hold your stomach muscles very tightly, which prevents the lungs from expanding and forces you to breath into the top of your chest.

"Fear and Alarm Breathing" mirrors the breathing patterns that occur when you wear a tight girdle around the middle part of your body. The girdle constrains your lower lung and prevents your stomach from expanding. Your breath is forced up into your chest, which becomes inflated to accommodate the added load. In addition to breathing into your upper chest, you are forced to take short shallow breaths at a faster rate.

Fortunately, unlike most other bodily functions such as digestion and blood flow that we cannot consciously control, we can deliberately alter the way we breathe. This makes the breath especially important in stabilizing the nervous system because how we breathe affects our mind and body. When you practice intentional breathing you can quickly dismiss the hyperarousal generated by the brain's "Fear and Alarm Center" and stabilize your nervous system.

Six-second breath counting

When you experience overwhelming emotions it can be very helpful to deliberately focus on counting the breath. This distracts your mind from the stressful situation for a moment and provides time to gain some distance, become more objective, and let your emotions dissipate. Six-second breath counting is a simple and safe calming method. With practice it can be used at any time when emotions overpower you. It can also become a sanctuary that you can retreat to in times of distress in order to regain control of your body and mind. Box 4.4 explains how to engage in six-second breath counting.

Box 4.4: Exercise in six-second breath counting

Count your breath as you do each step in this exercise and aim for a six-second breathing cycle:

1. Inhale for two seconds

2. Hold for one second

3. Exhale for two seconds

4. Hold for one second

5. Repeat the process 5–10 times or more until sufficiently calmed

Controlled breathing

Controlled breathing is also known as "paced respiration," "diaphragmatic breathing" and "deep breathing." In the mid-1970s Dr. Herbert Benson wrote a book titled *The Relaxation Response* which highlighted its benefits. Benson argued that controlled breathing works to counter the fight, flee, and freeze responses of the SNS. Research has confirmed this conclusion.

The dynamic that helps to stabilize the nervous system is full oxygen exchange, which means that you strive to get more oxygen entering the body and more carbon dioxide exiting it. Box 4.5 describes the core elements of controlled breathing.

Box 4.5: Basic elements of controlled breathing

1. Inhale deeply through the mouth or nose for a count of five or so, making sure that the abdomen expands

2. Hold the breath for a moment

3. Then, exhale completely through the mouth for a count longer than the inhalation

For best results repeat this process for 5–10 minutes.

Like six-second breath counting, controlled breathing is one of the most potent tools available to quickly stabilize the nervous system because it can be activated at a moment's notice and the effects can manifest quickly. Research shows that, when it is regularly practiced, controlled breathing can lower your blood pressure and heart rate and produce a state of calm. In additional to releasing hyperarousal, this puts less wear and tear on your blood vessels and reduces the stress that contributes to physical health problems. Another important outcome of controlled breathing is that it can alter the expression of genes involved in immune function, energy metabolism, and insulin secretion and improve your physical health. Herbert Benson was involved in the original research 40 years ago that discovered this, and it has been reconfirmed since that time.[207]

Mindful breathing

While controlled breathing focuses on consciously changing the way you breathe, the intent of mindful breathing is to watch the breath flow in and out of your body in whatever way it naturally occurs.

Like each of the previous techniques, mindful breathing increases awareness of your internal processes. In this case the focus is awareness of physical sensations associated with breathing in and out through the nostrils or mouth. This activates the PNS and tempers the fear-based reactions produced by the SNS. In addition, mindful breathing emphasizes nonjudgmental awareness of thoughts, which creates psychological flexibility. This occurs by watching your thoughts come and go, but not becoming engaged in them.

Mindful breathing is a secular form of meditation. Research shows that when you intentionally focus your attention on your breath, a state of brain activation is induced. With repetition, this intentional internal state can produce long-term changes in brain function and structure. This is a basic property of neuroplasticity: how the brain changes in response to experience.

Specific studies have found that with regular practice, mindful breathing is associated with changes in specific brain areas that are essential for body awareness, attention regulation, regulation of emotions, self-perception and learning. On the molecular level, dopamine and melatonin are found to increase, serotonin activity is modulated, and cortisol as well as norepinephrine have been documented to decrease.[208]

Even more encouraging is the finding that these types of biochemical change—along with associated reductions in stress reactions, depression, and anxiety, as well as increased self-control and greater optimism—can be achieved after only eight weeks of practice in a Mindfulness-Based Stress Reduction program.[209]

Box 4.6 describes the basic process of Mindful Breathing.

You can practice mindful breathing anywhere, at any time, for just a few minutes or for longer periods when you are in the midst of trauma or stress. Practicing mindful breathing on a regular basis builds your capacity to

Box 4.6: Mindful breathing instructions

- Sit or lie in a relaxed position. You may choose to close your eyes or keep them open. If you keep your eyes open you might want to focus your attention on the floor or a blank wall to reduce distractions.

- Begin by gently placing your attention on the process of breathing. Simply watch yourself breathe.

- Observe each of your breaths as they happen nonjudgmentally without trying to change anything. Watch as the breath enters your mouth or nostrils, fills your lungs and abdomen, and then leaves your body and your abdomen and lungs contract.

- Try to feel the sensations of the breath as it enters and leaves the mouth or nostrils. Feel what it is like to breathe, without trying to alter your breath or judging it in any way. Just observe the breath entering and leaving your body.

- As you follow your breath your mind will likely wander and you might find yourself thinking about the past or future, noises in the room, or bodily sensations. This is completely natural. When you notice your mind wandering, tell yourself it is OK, and very gently bring your attention back to the breath. Follow your breath for 5–10 minutes or as long as you feel comfortable.

- When you are ready to end the exercise, take a few moments to be fully present in the moment. Expand your awareness from the breath into your location and notice everything that surrounds you. When you are comfortable, open your eyes, and bring your attention back to the external world.

- Before moving on, however, take a few moments to reflect on your experience and how you feel at this time.

stabilize your nervous system and create psychological flexibility prior to adversity. When used in the midst of trauma and stress it also helps activate the PNS and moderate the SNS.

The intent of mindful breathing is to be continually aware of the breath. As you practice, however, you will quickly notice that your mind can be very unfocused and continually wander away from the breath. In fact, when you begin the process you might find your mind regularly drifting off into thought for 5–10 minutes at a time. This is completely natural. You are not doing anything wrong. It merely shows that thoughts come and go in our minds all the time. However, we run the risk of becoming dysregulated when we get caught up in thoughts about the past or the future as if they are happening today. Instead of becoming involved with the contents of your thoughts, just notice when your mind wanders away from the breath, maybe acknowledge it with a chuckle ("There goes my wild mind again!") and then gently being your attention back to your breath.

Combo techniques

The Reset Button[210]

Another helpful technique I call the Reset Button combines body-based and breath-based methods to stabilize your nervous system. The purpose of the Reset Button is to take a brief time out, turn inward, and observe all that is happening within you at the present moment. It is not about stopping to think. It is about stopping to observe yourself. Like the other methods, this activates your PNS, calms your SNS, releases hyperarousal, and produces a sense of grounding, centeredness, and calm.

Box 4.7 describes the Reset Button.

Box 4.7: Reset Button exercise

- Begin by taking 3–5 long deep breaths. Don't worry about the shape of the breath. Just allow your body to breathe in whatever way feels comfortable.

- After you have taken a number of breaths bring your awareness to your inner experience.

- Begin by spending about a minute or so noticing your body sensations. Examine your body for sensations that are pleasant, neutral, or unpleasant. Once again, do not judge them or try to change them in any way. Just notice the physical sensations that exist in your body in the present moment.

- Now, keep your attention focused inward and turn your attention to any emotions that are present. Are you feeling happy, sad, excited, or depressed? As with your thoughts, don't become engaged in the emotions, judge them, or try to change them in any way. For a minute or so just notice the emotions that exist at this moment in time.

- When you are ready, shift your attention to the thoughts that are going through your mind at this present moment. Are you thinking about something that happened in the past such as a regret, disappointment, or traumatizing event? Are you planning something in the future or imagining a difficult or frightening situation? Are you thinking about an existing noise, pain somewhere in your body, or how to do this exercise? Spend a minute noticing the types of thought going through your mind.

- Strive to notice the *types* of thought going through your mind without getting caught up in the content of those thoughts. As best as possible acknowledge the thoughts as temporary mental events that come and go, much like clouds moving across the sky. Don't try to change them and don't judge them in any way. Just notice the types of thought that are popping into your mind at the present time.

- After noticing your thoughts, bring your attention back to your breath and inhale and exhale slowly 3–5 times. When you are ready bring your attention back to the external world.

If you experience adversities directly or indirectly associated with climate disruption, or other type of traumatic or stressful situation, you can use the Reset Button to determine how best to respond. You can do so by spending a few minutes completing the exercise and then, after you feel sufficiently calmed, ask yourself what a wise and skillful response would be to your situation. Then, tune in and see what type of answer emerges from within you.

Sometimes the best answer to that question might be "I don't yet know how to respond." If this occurs you might want to take another few minutes to drop into awareness, reengage in the Reset Button, and notice your thoughts, emotions, and physical sensations. Then ask the question again. Rather than automatically reacting, by pausing and turning inward for a few more moments and then asking for direction, your innate wisdom is more likely to emerge.

Janice's story

Janice is a counselor who works with the homeless. She signed up for a Transformational Resilience workshop I facilitated because she was distressed and experiencing intestinal and sleep problems. The root cause was that she felt increasingly powerless to protect the homeless people she worked with in her community. Then, in the dead of winter, a major freeze occurred that quickly killed one of her clients and threatened others. She told me afterwards, "I needed to stay calm and think straight to help as many people as I could. Instead of just holding the tension, as I would normally do, I continually practiced the Reset Button and six-second breathing. They made a huge difference. I found myself much calmer and was able to figure out how to get all of my clients into a shelter."[211]

Other techniques for grounding and centering yourself by stabilizing your nervous system

Below are other techniques that can be used to ground and center yourself by stabilizing your nervous system. You can learn each on your own, though it is usually very helpful to get instructions from an expert, listen to a tape, or watch the process on a video when you begin. Select one or more that are appropriate for the age group and the culture you are working with, or that resonate with you.[212]

- **Body Scan.** This is a more extensive version of tracking. It was developed by Jon Kabat-Zinn and is used in Mindfulness-Based Stress Reduction courses. Rather than briefly examining your body for physical sensations, a Body Scan is a guided meditation that methodically focuses your attention on each part of the body sequentially starting with the toes and moving in a stepwise fashion to the legs, arms, hands, torso, shoulders, neck, forehead and scalp. Tracking emphasizes searching for pleasant, neutral, or unpleasant sensations and then focusing your attention on those that are pleasant or neutral. In contrast, a Body Scan simply asks you to experience whatever sensations are present, without trying to focus your attention on any particular type or changing them in any way.[213]

When practiced with regularity, the Body Scan is a very powerful method for stabilizing the nervous system and increasing the capacity for self-regulation.

- **Zombie Walking.** This is a meditation technique that promotes calming the nervous system by focusing on the physical sensations that occur in your feet, legs, and body as a whole as you walk very slowly. The goal is to notice every movement as you very slowly lift one foot, straighten it, place the heel, then the ball of the foot, then the toes on the ground, then slowly raise the other foot and place the heel, ball of the foot, and then the toes on the ground. People often think they look like a zombie when they walk mindfully. Even though it can look odd, this practice can be a powerful way to calm and stabilize the nervous system. Mindful walking can also serve as a bridge to other mindfulness practices.[214]

- **Mindful Eating.** This technique promotes calmness by focusing attention on the entire process of eating. You can begin by carefully observing the color and texture of the food in front of you. In addition, smell the food to discover its aromas. Then, notice each aspect of your body movement as you place a small bit of food on your utensil and raise it in your hands toward your mouth. Place the food on your lips and feel the sensations that result. Then slowly place the food on your tongue, but don't chew or swallow yet. Instead, become aware of the physical sensations, smells, and flavors it produces. Spend a few moments savoring the sensations, aromas, and flavors before chewing. When you begin to chew, focus your awareness on the physical sensations, aromas, and texture. How might they differ from before you began chewing? Continue this process while chewing. Then mindfully swallow the food and try to follow the sensations as it travels down your throat into your stomach. Slowly repeat the process until the meal is completed.

- **Gentle Standing and Lying Yoga.** These techniques bring your attention to moment-by-moment sensations in your body as you gently move from one yoga pose to another. Awareness can also include your self-talk about engaging in the movements. As with other mindfulness practices it is important to practice yoga non-judgmentally. There is no perfect pose or "right way" to engage. Choose poses that can be done without harming yourself.[215]

- **Hatha Yoga and Tai Chi.** These are more physical versions of gentle yoga. They combine mindfulness, self-awareness, breathing control, and mental and physical stretching.[216]

- **Yawning.** Yawning is sometimes thought of as negative because we often yawn when we are bored or sleepy or don't understand something. But yawning is a positive means of releasing energy and calming the nervous system. The key is to yawn consciously—not to wait until the body yawns on its own—and to yawn totally, generously, with maximum stretch and sound.[217]

- **Gesturing and Spontaneous Movement.** This is another technique developed by Miller-Karas. It involves paying attention to movements you make that feel calming or protective. Gestures can include movements of the body or limbs that express or emphasize an idea or sentiment, or that use motions as a means of expression. They typically happen without thinking about them. When you are feeling stressed or are pushed outside of your Resilient Growth Zone purposefully make movements and gestures that give you a sense of calm, protection, or connection with others. Repeat them slowly. Slowing down via comforting movements will often strengthen your sense of wellbeing and help you return to your Resilient Growth Zone.[218]

- **Dancing, Singing, and Other Calming Techniques.** In many African nations, dancing is seen as an important way to release tension and integrate physical, emotional, and spiritual aspects of one's being.[219] From ancient times to today, almost every culture on Earth has used singing in groups as a powerful way to calm the nervous system. In Russia people go to the Banya, a hot sauna, to calm themselves. In Sweden taking a *fika*, a coffee break with friends, has been a part of the culture since the 1700s. In China, women often do a foot soak called *zuyu* before bed. Many other culturally unique calming techniques exist as well.

Lessons from 9/11

More than 1,000 New Yorkers received free yoga breathing courses beginning two weeks after the September 11, 2001 World Trade Center terrorist attack that continued for six months. The following are three stories that describe the results:[220]

- Case 1: Ms. P, aged 28, suffered constant panic attacks after witnessing the twin towers' collapse and having her apartment engulfed in the toxic cloud. She was afraid to be alone, afraid to go out, and felt "numb, depressed, and paralyzed." Twelve weeks after the terrorist attack, she took the yoga breathing course on the advice of her therapist. The first one gave her a feeling of lightness and clarity. During the second, she felt happy and peaceful, as though "purified." The course relieved her symptoms and helped her get on with life.

  Ms. P is a recovering alcoholic who was sober for two years before 9/11. When interviewed in 2005, she said the yoga programs helped her stay sober and quit smoking. She still practices SKY and is taking advanced courses. She has no post-traumatic stress disorder (PTSD) or depression symptoms.

- Case 2: Ms. M, aged 48, did not sleep more than one hour a night for two weeks after 9/11. She was so groggy that she could not return to work as a waitress. During the first yoga breathing course she cried with fear every time she got to the fast breath cycles because they reminded her of how she was breathing while running from the dust cloud, terrified that she would die. The next day, however, she felt peaceful during the yoga breathing course and finished it feeling happy. That night she slept 12 hours.

- Case 3: Ms. L was so nauseated after 9/11 that she could not eat. For three weeks, she vomited every time she tried to eat. The night after her first yoga breathing course she was able to hold down a meal. After the second yoga breath session, she felt hungry for the first time in weeks.

It is clear that breath-based techniques can be very effective in calming the body and mind in the midst of trauma and stress.

Numerous Presencing options are available

This example illustrates just one of many different techniques individuals and groups can utilize to become more present by activating their PNS and moderate the read-based reactions of their SNS even in the most difficult situations. Choose techniques that resonate with you and that you can easily engage in. The important point is that, when traumatized or feeling stressed, make the effort to use techniques that allow you to become grounded and centered by stabilizing your nervous system.

Teaching these skills to adults and children worldwide can help them learn to deliberately ground and center themselves by stabilizing their nervous system when they are dysregulated. Once sufficiently calmed, they can decide if the threats they are reacting to are real or perceived. If they are real, the calm state can allow them to decide the wisest and most skillful way to respond while avoiding harm to themselves, other people, or the natural environment. If they determine that the threats are not real, people can use the experience to improve their ability distinguish between real and false threats and reduce the number of times they become dysregulated.

Learning skills to stabilize the nervous system when we are distressed by the traumas and stresses associated with rising global temperatures, however, is just a first step in calming our body and mind. It is also important to connect with people that can provide unconditional emotional support and practical assistance.

5
Remember your personal strengths, skills, resources, and social support network

During the worst moment of Superstorm Sandy, Jack Buzzi looked out the window of his parents' Jersey Shore home and saw something horrifying: His neighbor's house was floating. Part of the top floor had broken off, and the other parts of the house were destroyed. When he witnessed this, Buzzi was on the phone with his friend Jack, whose sister Kathey owned the house. Both were concerned that Kathey was in deep danger.

When the winds calmed a bit, Buzzi waded through knee-high water toward what remained of Kathey's house and yelled to her. But she didn't respond. So he returned home and called Jack again, who said he had just talked with his sister on the phone. She was trapped but uninjured. Buzzi went into the storm again and found her standing on a slab of wood that had been part of a doorway on the second floor of her home. Kathey appeared amazingly calm. "I knew you would come," she said. Buzzi brought her back to his house unharmed.

The next morning, Buzzi and Kathey used a kayak to rescue Kathey's sister Mary and her boyfriend Dave, who'd been trapped in the attic of Mary's flooded abode. On the way back from Mary's house, Buzzi rescued local carpenter Nick Spino, who had spent the night on his neighbor's roof. All told, six neighbors stayed with Buzzi at his house until they evacuated five days later.

"It's human nature, right?" he said. "We protect each other."[221]

This story demonstrates that in the midst of trauma and stress, it is our family, friends, neighbors, and other members of our personal social support network who are most likely to provide the practical assistance and emotional sustenance needed to stabilize our nervous system. In addition, our ability to stay psychologically and emotionally calm in the midst of climate-enhanced or other types of adversity is closely connected to our personal strengths, skills, and the resources available to us.[222]

When experiencing adversity it is therefore of great benefit to consciously Remember that you have personal strengths, skills, resources, and a social support network that can help you stay grounded, centered, and calm. This is the second core skill of Presencing.

Your strengths, skills, resources, and social support network are the key protective factors of resilience.[223] Taking the time to deliberately remember and call on them is sometimes all that is needed to overcome a stressful situation. The process can buffer you from stress and give you the energy required to persevere.[224] Noticing and naming them can boost your spirits and shore up your courage even when things seem hopeless.

Most importantly, when you acknowledge your strengths, skills, resources, and social support network, your PNS becomes activated which helps calm your body, thoughts, and emotions. The "Executive Center" of the brain can then kick in, which enables you to thoughtfully analyze the situation and choose wise and skillful responses rather than allowing the "Fear and Alarm Center" to automatically dictate your reactions.

Most of us have strengths, skills, resources, and people we can call on in difficult times. When we are in the midst of extreme hardship, however, we often fail to remember this. To minimize this likelihood, it is helpful to explicitly identify what and who they are.[225]

Identify your Circles of Support™

A powerful way to remember your strengths, skills, resources, and social support network is to map your Circles of Support™.[226] This is a tool I developed that can be used in almost any setting. When people complete the exercise for the first time they are often surprised by the number and types of strengths, skills, resources, and True Allies they list. First timers also frequently become aware of gaps and weaknesses in their Circles of Support. When people repeat the exercise a few months later they are frequently able to identify even more personal capacities and allies they can count in tough times.

Step 1: Identify your personal strengths and skills

Put your name in the middle of a blank piece of paper. Then, draw a circle around it and within the circle note all of your personal strengths and skills you can identify that help you deal with adversity. Take your time, dig deep, and note all of your strengths.

Box 5.1 offers examples of personal strengths and skills. Figure 5.1 provides an example of how to develop your first circle of support based on how Ted, a participant in one of my Transformational Resilience workshops, filled out his first circle.

Box 5.1: Example of personal strengths and skills

These include qualities that help you deal with trauma and stress such as physical and mental strength, problem-solving skills, ability to make friends, determination, perseverance, courage, creativity, openness, assertiveness, optimism, compassion, honesty, patience, respect, confidence, kindness, empathy, self-discipline, good communications skills, kindness, humor, and physical abilities.

FIGURE 5.1 Ted's personal strengths and skills

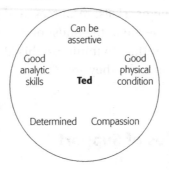

Step 2: Identify your internal mental resources

Draw a second circle around the first and within this one note the internal mental resources you have to center and calm yourself when dealing with adversity. These include mental images that make you feel safe and calm as well as personal values and beliefs you can bring to mind to create a sense of internal tranquility and help you make wise and skillful decisions in the midst of adversity.

Box 5.2 provides examples of internal resources. Figure 5.2 offers an example of how Ted filled out his second circle of support.

Box 5.2: Examples of internal mental resources

These include mental images your can access to calm and stabilize your nervous system such as a mental picture of holding a beloved pet, the image of a room or other place where you feel safe and secure, hugging a loved one, recalling a time when you had a particularly peaceful experience. They also include personal sources of meaning, spiritual or religious sayings or practices, values, and attitudes you can call on in times of distress.

FIGURE 5.2   Ted's Internal Resources

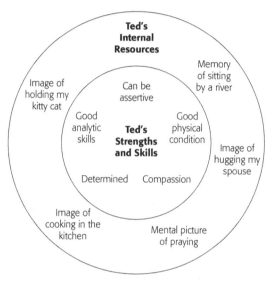

Step 3: Identify your bonding social support network

Draw a third circle and within this one note the people that are your "True Allies"—the family members, close friends, neighbors, and others you bond with and can count on to help and support you through thick or thin. Most of us have a number of friends and acquaintances, but only a limited number of people we truly bond with. Your True Allies are people who will stand by you, provide emotional support, allow you to freely express your feelings, and give you practical advice or provide assistance without telling you what to do or trying to control you. This group of people can be called your "bonding" social support network.[227]

Box 5.3 includes examples of people to consider as part of your social support network. Figure 5.3 provides an example of how Ted developed his third circle of support during a Transformational Resilience workshop.

Box 5.3: Examples of people in your bonding social support network

This can include a spouse or significant other, family members, neighbors, a mentor, coach, work colleague, minister, or spiritual leader, and others who you can unconditionally count on to provide emotional support, give honest advice, provide practical assistance, or link you with key resources in difficult times without telling you what to do when you do not desire it.

FIGURE 5.3   Ted's Bonding Social Support Network

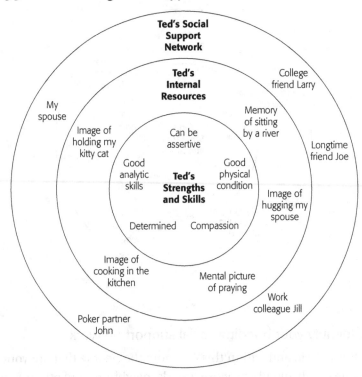

Step 4: Identify your external physical resources

Draw one last circle and within it note the external physical resources at your disposal for dealing with trauma and stress associated with climate disruption, and other types of adversity. These are actual places you can go and things you can use to create a sense of safety and calm. See Box 5.4 for examples of external physical resources. Figure 5.4 offers an example of how Ted developed his fourth circle of support.

Box 5.4: Examples of external physical resources

External physical resources can include a room in your home you can go to and feel safe, a garden spot you can sit in, a local organization such as a YMCA you can visit, a place of worship, or material resources such as a rainy day pot of money or an emergency preparedness kit with food, water and temporary shelter.

FIGURE 5.4   Ted's External Physical Resources

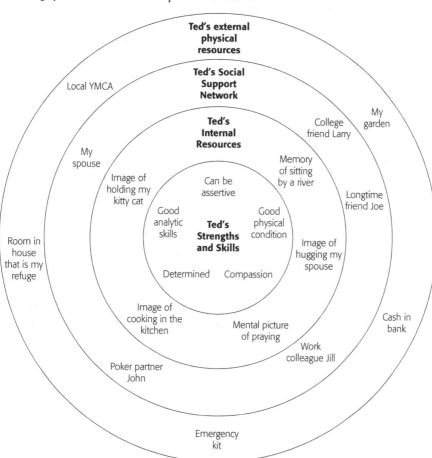

Step 5: Observe your strengths, skills, resources, and bonding social support network

Take a few minutes now to look over your Circles of Support. What do you notice? Are any personal strengths, skills, resources, or members of your social support network missing? If so, add them now.

Your personal strengths, skills, resources, and social support network can help keep you afloat and make wise and skillful decisions in the midst of stressful situations. The more these resources overlap—for example, stowing an emergency preparedness kit in a room in your home that also serves as a personal refuge from adversity—the more confident you are likely to be when faced with stressful climate-enhanced conditions.

Step 6: Notice how it feels to remember your strengths, skills, resources, and bonding social support network

Continue to look at your Circles of Support. As you do so, turn your attention inward and focus on the physical sensations in your body. Notice pleasant, neutral, and unpleasant sensations. As you Track the sensations keep examining your Circles of Support. Observe the personal strengths, skills, resources, and the people included in your social support network. Go deep into them and bring to mind specific examples of how your strengths or skills helped you during difficult situations in the past. Remember a specific time when one of your True Allies helped you out. Think about what the person did and how you felt. Revisit the situation in your mind and note how it felt. Try to recall as many details as possible. As you deepen your remembrances about your Circles of Support, notice your breathing patterns, heart rate, and areas of warmth, tingling, or muscle relaxation in your body.

If you find your attention captured by unpleasant sensations, purposely move your focus to neutral or pleasant sensations. Savor those sensations for a few moments as you observe your Circles of Support.[228] This step deactivates the brain's fear-based reactions and allows your thinking mind to take over.[229]

Sandra's story

In West Islip on New York's Long Island … health insurance executive Sandra Galian has drawn on her experiences during Sandy to find more ways for neighbor to help neighbor. Galian's home was flooded with three feet of water during the storm, forcing her family to flee. She, her two kids and husband spent 12 weeks living with friends before finding temporary housing. She used her contacts as part of a civic association and created an email chain sharing information and giving updates on recovery resources. "I felt obligated to help my family, friends, and neighbors as much as I could."[230]

Step 7: Fill in any missing supports

After attending to the physical sensations that appear as you examine your Circles of Support, look at your map one more time and see if any strengths, skills, resources, or key members of your social support network are missing that you would like to include. Also, identify weaker areas you would like to strengthen, such as a relationship that is not as supportive as you would like. Think about ways you can fill the gaps and strengthen the weaker areas.

Identify how your bonding social support network connects with other bonding networks

Take one more step now and determine how your bonding social support network might be connected to the bonding social support networks of other people. For example, do the family, friends, and neighbors that you feel a close bond with regularly communicate with a similarly close-knit group of family, friends, or neighbors that you know or live somewhere near you? The more connections your bonding personal social support network has with other similar bonding networks the more likely it is that you and your True Allies will have access to information, resources, and assistance that can prove very important in the midst of a traumatic event or stressful situation. These connections can be called "bridging" social support networks.[231]

In addition, see if you can identify the ways in which your bonding and bridging social support networks are linked with organizations in your community that can provide essential resources, information, or in other ways provide critical assistance in the midst of adversity. You might also note any links your networks have with elected officials, public staff, or others with social, economic, or political influence that can assist when hardships persist. These can be considered your "linking" social support networks.[232]

Ted described two social support networks that his network had ongoing communications with: Joe and Anne's, who live down the block, and the one that work colleagues Beth and Sue belong to. Figure 5.5 describes the social support networks Ted's personal network is connected to. He did not identify any "linking" social support networks.

FIGURE 5.5   Ted's Bridging Social Support Networks

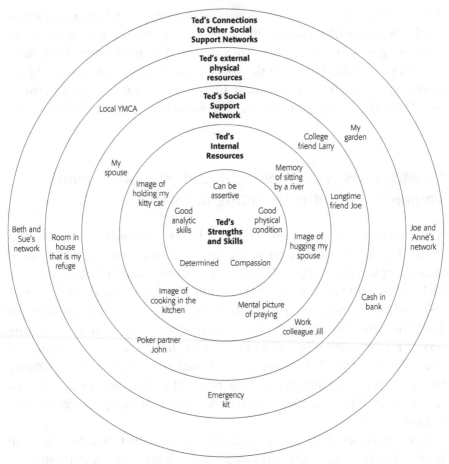

Identify your ecological Circles of Support

Finally, now that you have identified your personal strengths, skills, resources, and social support network, it is important to also remember what makes it all possible: the Earth's ecological systems and climate. Draw one final circle around yourself and within it list all of the ecological systems, structures, organisms you can think of that make life possible for you and the members of your social support network.

In Ted's case, he listed the sun, which provides the solar radiation that keeps the Earth warm enough to support his life, the soil from which he obtains his food, the oceans that influence the planet's temperatures, the rain, which is linked to the oceans and nurtures the soil he uses to grow his food, and plants, animals and other forms of biological diversity that interact with everything and are an essential element of the Earth's ecological support systems.

Figure 5.6 describes the ecological systems that Ted noted in his Circles of Support.

Ted listed only a small number of ecological systems and structures that make his and all other life on Earth possible. He could have also listed all of the Earth's organisms—from bacteria, worms and insects to large mammals and birds—as well as its forests, wetlands, water bodies, ice sheets and glaciers, and much more. The presence and health of each of these

FIGURE 5.6   Ted's Ecological Circles of Support

systems and organisms is determined by the Earth's climate system. This is a complex system involving continual interactions between incoming solar radiation from the sun, some of which is absorbed by the oceans, forests, soils, human-built structures, and other processes, and some of which is reflected back out into the atmosphere by those same systems and structures, as well as the planet's ice sheets and glaciers. The greenhouse gasses that naturally surround the Earth serve as a heat-trapping blanket that captures just enough of the solar radiation that is reflected back from the Earth to make life possible on Earth.

However, since the start of the industrial revolution the concentration of greenhouse gasses in the atmosphere has dramatically increased due to the human use of coal, oil, gas and other fossil fuels, as well as the degradation and loss of forests, wetlands, and other ecosystems that naturally sequester carbon. Between 1990 and 2013 there was a 34% increase in "radiative forcing," the warming effect of greenhouse gasses on our climate. In addition, the oceans have been accumulating carbon dioxide that would otherwise increase in the atmosphere. This also has far-reaching implications. The current rate of ocean acidification appears to be happening at a pace not seen for at least the last 300 million years.[233] It is imperative to rapidly and dramatically reduce our impact on the climate and oceans so that the impacts on people and the planet can remain manageable in the future.

The point is that by always remembering that your most important circle of support is the Earth's climate, it is possible to alter the story you and others tell about the attitudes and behaviors required for life as we know it to continue to exist into perpetuity.

Enhance your personal strengths and skills

Our personal strengths and skills go a long way in defining who we are as individuals. They help us survive, and thrive. We use them to achieve our goals. They also help us respond to trauma and stress of all types, including those generated by climate disruption.

No one is perfect, however, and we all have qualities that are not as positive as we would like. If you had a difficult time listing personal strengths or skills when you completed that section of your Circles of Support, you might consider explicitly working to enhance and expand them.

Like the other processes involved with Presencing, nonjudgmental self-observation is important here. Spend time observing your thinking and behaviors and take note of your positive qualities. Affirm your strengths and skills by looking deeply to see which positive qualities make you unique. Are they your sense of humor, persistence, or creativity? Perhaps they are your capacity for empathy, compassion, spiritual beliefs, or love for the natural environment?

Ted, for example, realized that his analytical skills and determination were special.

One of the best ways to enhance your strengths and skills is to focus on your passions. Spend some time determining the activities or functions that make you truly happy; the things that bring a natural smile to your face or that energize you. As you do this, adopt a positive outlook by viewing this as a wonderful opportunity to learn about yourself and grow as a person! Be patient and focus on enhancing your strengths, but don't push too hard or too fast. Be grateful for the strengths you already have. Gratitude is a strength that can get you through the most difficult of times. I'll return to this point in the next chapter.

At the same time, note qualities and skills you would like to strengthen and make an agreement with yourself to improve them. For example, you might want to become more patient with other people. If this is the case, you might turn this into a written agreement with yourself and keep the document in a place where you can review it on a regular basis. After a week or so evaluate your progress.

Most importantly, accept and appreciate who you are, from your positive qualities to your warts, and everything in between. We are all shaped by events that happened in our early childhood, many of which we were too young to remember, as well as experiences that occurred later in life. Have compassion for yourself. Very few of us behave as well as we would like all the time.

It might benefit you to repeat this statement to yourself: "It's not my fault. I did the best I could given the information and skills I had at my disposal at the time." This testimonial shines light on the reality that you have done the best you could in your life. When you repeat it to yourself, you can also make a commitment to use troubling situations, mistakes, and actions you are not proud of to learn and grow as a person, rather than beating yourself up.

It is important to understand that I am not excusing or condoning harmful or destructive behavior. We must all take responsibility for how we treat ourselves, other people and the natural environment. However, it often helps to recognize how events in our lives can trigger reactions that cause us to behave poorly. Acknowledging the negative events can be a powerful step toward understanding what triggers powerful emotions and thoughts within us and how we can choose more constructive responses in the future. We will return to this issue again in Chapter 7.

The importance of robust social support networks for Transformational Resilience

Humans are social animals. From birth onward we depend on other people to survive. In difficult times, few things are more harmful to our mental and physical health than feeling that we are alone or are isolated from others. At the same time, like other animals, we are hard wired for survival. When we experience traumatic or extremely stressful situations we naturally prioritize our own safety and wellbeing. However, a large body of research shows that, rather than being a sign of weakness, interacting with and obtaining emotional support as well as practical assistance from others during hard times strengthens your capacity to care for yourself.

Low levels of social support and high levels of isolation, for example, have been linked to higher levels of stress, generalized anxiety disorder, depression, and social phobia.[234] Poor social support is also associated with physical health problems such as cardiac problems, coronary artery disease, and some cancers.[235] In fact, some researchers believe that the negative outcomes of low social support on life expectancy might be as significant as the effects of smoking, obesity, hypertension or low levels of physical activity.[236]

Conversely, you benefit in numerous ways when you know that other people care about you and will be there to support you in difficult times. Higher perceived social support, for instance, has been found to reduce the potential for traumatic events to produce mental illness.[237] It has also been found to have beneficial effects on the cardiovascular, endocrine, and immune systems.[238]

It is important to know that not all forms of social support are beneficial. When we are pushed outside of our Resilient Growth Zone into a high or low state of dysregulation, what we often need most is to be able to share our feelings and grieve with people who will listen to us attentively, offer appropriate advice when asked, and provide practical assistance when necessary. When members of your social support network meet these needs in ways that nurture your ability to take responsibility for your life, they are extremely valuable. When, even if they have good intentions, they urge you to talk when what you need is silent time, explicitly or implicitly urge you to repress rather than share your feelings, offer advice when you do not want it, or in other ways judge you when what you really need is to feel accepted and supported, the relationship can delay recovery or keep you in a state of dysregulation.[239]

Thus, it is the quality of your relationships that matters, not the number of people you are connected with. Strong, consistent empathetic support from just a few people is much more valuable than modest or superficial support from a larger group.[240]

Nurturing relationships reduce distress and help protect you during hardship. They also reduce the possibility of developing depression and increase the chances of improved mental health after significant adversity. In short, a robust social support network enhances your resilience and improves your mental and physical health.

Receiving support from others is not the only way to benefit from fulfilling relationships. Giving support to other people is also extremely helpful for your mental and physical health and wellbeing. In fact, a growing body of research indicates that bonding with and giving support to others can be more beneficial for your health than receiving it. Thus, you increase your capacity for Transformational Resilience when you have a strong bonding social support network *and* when you contribute to others by being a member of someone else's social support network.[241] I will say more about the importance of bonding, bridging, and linking social support networks in Chapter 11 when I discuss building the capacity for Transformational Resilience in communities.

One reason receiving and giving support is so important is that these processes release the hormone oxytocin into our body. Oxytocin enhances our ability to recognize other people, remember their qualities, develop trust, and form friendships. It also deactivates the SNS, which protects us against harmful chemicals such as cortisol that are released into our system when we are stressed.[242]

Fortify your bonding and bridging social support networks

If you found it difficult to identify people to include in your bonding social support network or to note connections between your group of True Allies and other bonding networks when you completed those steps in the Circles of Support exercise, you might consider strengthening them. This will require taking the initiative to boost your existing network and reaching out to other people you know that have a different group of close supportive relationships. I'm not suggesting that you become dependent on others. Your goal should be to improve the quality of the relationships that already exist and add new people to your group that you can count on in times of hardship. You can also develop relationships with other close-knit groups of family, friends, and neighbors that you can exchange information and resources with.

Expanding your bonding and bridging social support networks won't necessarily be easy. It takes time, effort, and persistence. But no matter how limited or feeble your existing network might be, you can expand and strengthen it. For example, you might call a family member or friend who you have not spoken with recently, ask how they are doing, and offer your help. You could also strike up a conversation with a fellow worker or someone from your church or synagogue, or a civic or recreational group you belong to and after conversing for a while, ask them to join you for tea, coffee, or lunch.

If you are shy or have weak communications skills you might attend assertiveness or social skills training programs. After you feel more confident with your skills, you can start to attend social functions such as dances, hiking, biking, or other outdoor trips, concerts, classes, book clubs, Rotary meetings, or talks by various speakers. Events at a place of worship are often one of the best places to meet people. Gather your courage and strike up conservations with people.

You might also consider joining a support group. The web or local newspapers often list local women and men's groups or groups focused on issues such as child raising, dealing with trauma, helping seniors, the homeless, and children, or joining a women's or men's group. Many conservation groups such as the Audubon Society also have regular meetings you can attend where you can meet like-minded people.

No matter how you approach it, remember that strengthening and expanding your bonding and bridging social support networks will require genuine two-way communication and sharing, not superficial dialogue. This requires the honest exchange of personal feelings and thoughts as well as meaningful assistance and encouragement. It also requires minimizing competition, overprotectiveness, or the desire to control others.[243] As you increase your capacity to meaningfully connect with and support other people, more often than not you will find that you receive as much or more in return.

The knowledge that you have a robust bonding and bridging social support networks to call on in times of distress helps calm your body, emotions, and thoughts.

Pete's story

Pete had a number of buddies he hung out with. He went boating with them, went out to eat, and attended concerts with his group of friends. But after mapping his Circles of Support in a Transformational Resilience workshop, Pete realized there was only one person that he could count on to support him through thick or thin: his father. This was a real eye-opener. He now understood that most of the relationships he had were superficial. So he decided to do something about it. He told me that over the course of the following year he asked six of his buddies out for lunch or dinner, one at a time. He shared details of his life with them, shared personal feelings, and asked about their lives and feelings. Through this process he found that he did not connect with half of the group. They never called him again, and he never pursued a relationship either. But he became much closer to his other three friends. He said he now feels his Circles of Support are larger and more stout. He has also learned how to become a true ally for his three friends.[244]

The Wiser Self

A very special resource that is available to you on a moment's notice is the Wiser Self.[245] We all have a Wiser Self, even if we don't call it by that name. It is an image we keep in our mind of a judicious, resourceful, capable embodiment of our truest self that we can instantly call on to advise us how to act wisely and skillfully in the midst of adversity and stress. In other words, the Wiser Self is our own intuitive wisdom.

It often helps to establish an image of a person who is your Wiser Self in order to have a picture you can bring to mind in difficult times. This could be an image of someone you actually know or have met, such as a family member, friend, role model, coach, mentor, or spiritual leader. It could be a composite of several people you know, or the embodiment of a spiritual guide such as Jesus, Buddha, or the Prophet Muhammad. It might even be an image of yourself when you are in your calmest and wisest moments.

No matter what mental image you adopt, by following the exercise described in Box 5.5 you should always be able to ask your Wiser Self for candid feedback or seek their advice on how to respond to climate-aggravated stress and adversity.

You have now learned two of the core skills involved with calming your body, emotions, and thoughts by Presencing yourself. You first want to take steps to stabilize your nervous system. As you do so, it helps to remember that you have personal strengths, skills, resources, and a social support network you can call on to help when you are in the midst of climate-enhanced trauma and stress or other adversities. One additional practice goes a long way in helping to establish a sense of calm: minimizing Thinking Distortions that cause or reinforce dysregulation.

Box 5.5: Instructions for developing your Wiser Self

- Sit comfortably and take several slow deep breaths to ground, center, and calm yourself.

- Now imagine that you are taking a walk in a beautiful forest. Birds are singing, there are lush fields of colorful flowers everywhere you look. Deer and other animals graze peacefully in the distance. You feel completely at ease.

- Now, envisage yourself approaching the home of your Wiser Self. Picture yourself walking toward the entrance. Notice how your Wiser Self greets you. Do they step outside to meet you? Does she invite you in? Does he shake hands, bow, or hug you? Notice how old the Wiser Self is, how she is dressed, and how he moves.

- Imagine yourself sitting and talking with your Wiser Self. Notice her presence, her energy, and how it affects you.

- Ask your Wiser Self how she or he came to be who he is? Ask her what helped her most along the way? What did he have to let go of to become who she is? Can she share a few examples of how they dealt with stress and trauma in her life, and how they triumphed over adversity?

- Now ask him about a specific traumatic or stressful situation you are facing in your life. Notice what advice she offers that you can take with you. Listen carefully to what he has to say.

- Imagine what it would be like to embody your Wiser Self. Invite him to become part of you. Notice how it feels to inhabit your Wiser Self from the inside out and to experience the Wiser Self within you.

- When you are ready, imagine your Wiser Self becoming separate again from you.

- Now imagine that your Wiser Self offers you a gift—an object, a symbol, a word, or a phrase—that you can carry with you at all times to remind you of him or her. Receive the object in your hand and place it somewhere in your clothing or on your body for safe keeping. Your Wiser Self then tells you her or his name. Remember it well.

- As you prepare to leave, take a few deep breaths to anchor your connection with your Wiser Self. Know that you can evoke this experience of meeting her at any time, under any condition.

- Imagine thanking him or her for the time you have spent together, and them imagine saying goodbye. Then, imagine yourself walking back out into the forest and slowly taking the same path through the forest home.

- Gradually, become aware of your surroundings, and when you are ready slowly open your eyes.

- Take a few moments to write down your experience with your Wiser Self to help you integrate it into your conscious memory. You can use it at any time you need honest feedback or guidance from within about how to calm your emotions and thoughts and be more resilient. As with all calming skills, the more you practice calling on your Wiser Self, the more reliably you will be able to embody her or him and call on their wisdom, insights, and skills.

6
<u>O</u>bserve your reactions to and thoughts about the situation nonjudgmentally with self-compassion

Stress was never a major issue for Sam. That is, until the heat wave enveloped his town for six weeks, which was followed by a huge windstorm that toppled a number of trees on his block, which was followed by weeks of more extreme heat. After the big storm he began to worry about when the next big disaster would occur. As the heat persisted and pressure built, Sam would begin to think in a "What if" manner. "What if a big storm destroys my house?" "What if I can't get food and water for my family?" "What if a storm shuts my company and I lose my job?"

"I was having a difficult time sleeping," he said. "Sometimes I could not go to sleep, other time I would wake up after only a few hours and not be able to go back to sleep. I became edgy, and constantly barked at my wife and kids. I was a mess."[246]

As he told this story to the other participants in a Transformational Resilience workshop, he then broke into a wide smile. "My wife finally told me to snap out of it. She said it was my way of thinking that caused my problems, not anything happening in the real world. I realized I was catastrophizing about almost everything. This awareness helped me calm down and sleep better again."

If it is not possible to calm your body, emotions, and thoughts by using the skills explained in the previous chapters, it might help to examine the way you are thinking about the situation. Observing your reactions to and thoughts about your situation nonjudgmentally with self-compassion is the third core practice of Presencing.

How you think determines how you act

People who use adversity as a catalyst to gain new insight, grow, and increase their wellbeing realize that how they see—or don't see—the world largely determines how they act. To respond constructively to traumas and stresses directly caused or aggravated by climate disruption, it helps to continually observe your experiences, as well as your physical and emotional reactions to and thoughts about them, with clear eyes, even if it is painful, frightening, or embarrassing. The process involves separating the events you see or conditions you experience from distorted ways of thinking.

In the short term, denial, avoidance, and other forms of dissociation—meaning detachment from your physical and emotional experience—can sometimes help you cope with overwhelming adversity by giving you time to process the events. But if this approach is used for a long period of time, it will cause you to react not to reality, but to mental fantasies about people and events. This leads to perceptions, thoughts, and behaviors that can harm other people, the natural environment, or you. Continual use of these patterns also blocks deep-seated emotions from coming to the surface and being dealt with, which causes them to emerge down the road instead as troubling mental or physical health problems.

Observing your perceptions and thoughts with honesty and clarity is especially important given the acute and chronic adversities climate disruption is already producing and will increasingly generate. If we ignore, deny, or distort the profound changes that are under way, our families, friends, communities, and ourselves, along with all future generations, will end up much worse off.

The ABC model of observing your thoughts

Recognizing the links between the adversities you experience, your beliefs about them, and the consequences of them is key to avoiding harmful reactions. The ABC model of observing your thoughts can help you accomplish this goal. The approach I describe here is based largely on the adaptations of the cognitive-behavioral approach to change as described by my colleague Dr. Glenn Schiraldi of Resilience Training International.[247]

We often see the events that produce distress in our lives fairly clearly. Call this A, the Activating event. We also are fairly cognizant of the consequences

FIGURE 6.1   The ABC Model of honestly observing the situation and your views about it

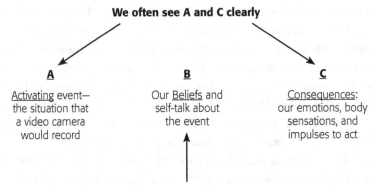

We often see A and C clearly

A
Activating event—
the situation that
a video camera
would record

B
Our Beliefs and
self-talk about
the event

C
Consequences:
our emotions, body
sensations, and
impulses to act

But we are often not aware of B: our beliefs and automatic self-talk

We think the event caused our reaction, when it was our interpretation of it that
did, which usually includes some true and many false beliefs and stories.

of these events, such as the physical changes or emotions we feel in our body. Call this C, the Consequences of the Activating Event. What we are often not aware of, however, is that A does not actually cause C: the Activating event does not cause the Consequences. The beliefs we hold about the Activating event, and how we interpret the situation, is actually what led to the Consequences. Call this B—our Beliefs and self-talk.

Figure 6.1 depicts how B, our beliefs, determines C, the consequences of A, the activating event.

Our internal beliefs about the world and ourselves are shaped by the experiences we've had in childhood and possibly even in the womb, all the way though to the present day. Our parents, social support network, the culture in which we live, the organizations where we work, our spiritual or religious institutions and practices, the media, and likely even our genetic make-up, influence our internal beliefs and self-talk. Rather than truly reflecting reality, our internal beliefs and self-talk often include many false ideas and beliefs. Thus, what we see happening around us is always viewed through lenses tinted by inaccurate or skewed beliefs and assumptions about the world and ourselves.

Through this process we can easily end up with numerous Thinking Distortions. These are ways of thinking that lead us to misinterpret, exaggerate, catastrophize, inaccurately assign blame, or in other ways fail to see Activating events clearly and accurately. Thinking Distortions lead to erroneous judgments and flawed conclusions. In turn, our mistaken assessments can

FIGURE 6.2   Ten common "Thinking Distortions"

1. Fixated on flaws: zooming in on what goes wrong and ignoring positive aspects ("I can't enjoy myself given my mistake" rather than "I made a mistake but will improve" or "I made mistakes and some good")

2. Dismissing the positive: negating positives that might lift lour mood and self-esteem ("Oh, anyone could have done that" rather than "I did a good job under the circumstances")

3. Assuming: mind-reading ("I know the boss hates me") or fortune telling ("I know I won't enjoy the party" or "I know I'll do poorly")

4. Labeling: giving yourself or another a name or label as if a single word described humans ("He is a loser" or "I am a dud")

5. Overgeneralizing: concluding that a negative experience applies to all situations ("I always mess up" or "Everyone hates me—no one likes me")

6. All-or-nothing thinking: evaluating yourself or a situation in extremes—with no middle ground ("I am a hero or a failure," or "She is brave or a coward")

7. Catastrophizing: making things much worse than they really are ("This is awful and horrible" or "This can't possibly be any worse")

8. "Should" statements: rigid, unchallenging expectations about self, others, or the world ("He should know better" or "I ought not to tire, or make mistakes, or be afraid, or be depressed")

9. Personalizing: seeing yourself more responsible or involved than you are ("It's all my fault that my son has problems" or "Only I can save this person, solve the climate crisis, make this work")

10. Blaming: putting all responsibility on externals makes us feel helpless ("I am this way because of my crummy childhood" or "Government has to do it—I can't do anything to reduce climate change")

Source: Adapted with permission from Schiraldi, G.R. (2011). Definitions and examples of Aaron Beck's thinking distortions. In: *The Complete Guide to Resilience*.

cause us to act in personally or socially harmful ways. Thinking Distortions consequently lead to mental and physical health problems, and can generate destructive psychosocial behaviors such as aggression, crime, and violence as well.

Figure 6.2 lists ten common Thinking Distortions. Go through the list and see if you recognize any that you commonly practice.[248]

The ABC Thought and Emotion model

The ABC Thought and Emotion Record found in Figure 6.3 is a tool that can be used to learn if and how your internal beliefs and self-talk might skew your reactions to the external events you experience.

FIGURE 6.3   ABC thought and emotion record: Sally's example

Event (Describe)	Consequence (For you, others or the environment)	Belief (Self-talk)	Is it really true? (Yes/No)	Possible Thinking Distortion	Write an alternative Belief/self-talk	What would you be like with the alternative?
Example Sally worked in rush mode long after regular work hours ended to complete a project	Sally: bought fast food for dinner, was tense and irritable when got home, yelled at kids, ate and drank too much, felt bad about self afterwards	I am the only one in the organization that can do this work	No	Personalizing	Others are skilled–next time I'm running late I'll ask for help	More calm, thoughtful, and effective at work A more caring parent
	Kids: Felt like second priority, angry for being yelled at	If I don't do it, climate change will grow worse	No	Over-generalization	I alone can't prevent CC and I'll be more effective if I care for myself and my family	More at ease with myself and the world
	Environment: needless consumption of packaging, chemicals, energy	I'm too tired and stressed to cook	No	Catastrophizing	I can cook a simple meal and it might relax me	Feel good abut less impact on the environment

Start by describing in the first column on the left a recent stressful Activating event. In the example cited in Figure 6.3, when Sally, who works for a climate advocacy organization, attended one of my Transformational Resilience workshops she chose: "I worked late after hours in a rush mode to complete a project."

In the next column to the right describe the consequences of that event, including your emotional reactions, your behaviors, the consequences of your actions for other people, and even the consequences for the natural environment. In the Figure 6.3 example, because she was running late and stressed, Sally said she brought fast food home for the family dinner, got home tense and irritable, ended up yelling at her children, drank too much alcohol, then felt bad about the entire situation afterwards. She was embarrassed to say it, but her kids ended up feeling like a second priority and were angry and confused about why their mom yelled at them for no reason. In addition, Sally admitted that the fast food she purchased harmed the environment through the needless use of the plastic packaging it was wrapped in (most plastic is derived from fossil fuels), the use of chemicals and fossil fuel energy required to make it, and the solid and molecular waste, including greenhouse gases that resulted. Sally acknowledged that these impacts were undoubtedly much greater than those that a fresh home cooked meal would have generated.

In the third column, record the beliefs or self-talk that went through your mind when you experienced the activating event. Sally said she stayed late and worked in a rush because she believed she was the only person who could do the work, she believed that if she did not stay late and complete the project climate change would grow worse, and she purchased fast food because she told herself that she was too tired and stressed to cook even a simple healthy meal at home.

Now, ask yourself if the beliefs you held at the time are really true, and record your answer in the next column with a simple yes or no. On reflection, Sally said she realized she was not the only person in the organization that could do the work, the status of climate change was not dependent on this project, and she was actually not too exhausted to go home and cook a good simple meal with fresh food.

In the next column to the right list the possible Thinking Distortion you might have made that led to the Beliefs and self-talk you recorded in the previous column. A number of the Thinking Distortions might be relevant, so list all that seem to apply. In the example in Figure 6.3, Sally said she realized that her belief that "I am the only one in the organization that can do the work" is a form of personalizing the situation. Sally's belief that "If I don't do the work climate change will worsen" was overgeneralization. Her self-talk that said, "I'm too tired and stressed to cook" was a form of catastrophizing.

Don't be surprised if you identify multiple Thinking Distortions when you complete this exercise. During a Transformational Resilience workshop I once facilitated for a large mental health organization one of the participants suddenly blurted out "What if I practice all of these Thinking Distortions?" as she completed this exercise. Everyone in the room broke into laughter when she said it, and many nodded their heads acknowledging that they felt the same way. This is not uncommon. When under constant stress it is easy to fall into unhealthy thought patterns. However, the situation can be corrected if you become aware of your internal beliefs and self-talk.

In the sixth column to the right, write an alternative belief you can adopt or self-talk you can use if and when a similar situation comes up again. Think hard and write an alternative that is based on reality, not a Thinking Distortion. Rather than adopting the belief that "I am the only person in the organization that can do this work" Sally decided she could say to herself, "Others in the organization are skilled. Next time I'm running late I'll ask for help." Rather than using self-talk that says, "If I don't do the work climate change will worsen" Sally decided she could say to herself, "I alone cannot prevent climate change and I will be more effective in the work I can do if I care for myself and my family." As an alternative to the self-talk that says, "I'm too tired and stressed to cook" Sally decided she could say, "I can cook a simple meal and it might even relax me."

In the column on the far right of the chart describe how you would feel if you adopted the alternative beliefs and self-talk. In Sally's case she realized that she would be more calm, thoughtful, and effective at work. She would feel better about herself as a more caring parent. She would feel more at ease with herself in the world. In addition, she would feel good that she was generating less impact on the natural environment that she had devoted her life to protect.

Now it's your turn to use the ABC Thought and Emotion Record. Identify a recent distressing situation and use the ABC Thought and Emotion Record provided in Figure 6.4 to assess if you might be unknowingly practicing any Thinking Distortions. Start with a relatively minor event—one you would rate 4–5 on a scale of 1–10. Then, walk through each of the columns in the chart in a stepwise fashion.

After you complete your own ABC Thought and Emotion Record, take a moment to turn your attention inward and once again focus on the physical

FIGURE 6.4   ABC thought and emotion record

Event (Describe)	Consequence (For you, others or the environment)	Belief (Self-talk)	Is it really true? (Yes/No)	Possible Thinking Distortion	Write an alternative Belief/self-talk	What would you be like with the alternative?

sensations in your body. Notice pleasant, neutral, and unpleasant sensations. Pay attention to your breathing patterns, heart rate, areas of warmth, tingling, or muscle tension and relaxation. If you find your attention captured by unpleasant sensations, purposely move your focus to neutral or pleasant sensations. See what it feels like to become aware that your emotional reactions and resulting behaviors to adverse events actually result from your internal beliefs about them and your self-talk, not the activating event itself. Savor those sensations for a few moments.[249]

Kurt Hoelting's story

Kurt works as a mindfulness teacher and offers mindfulness retreats and Mindfulness-Based Stress Reduction (MBSR) classes in the Seattle, Washington area. He wrote this story titled *Walking the Tightrope Between Joy and Fear* on his blog:

"I have been doing a lot of soul searching lately … I'm seeing more clearly how the toxicity of negative thinking in particular, especially of future catastrophizing, has too often led me into emotional exile. I'm really genuinely tired of that …

There are more good reasons now for catastrophizing than at any point in human history. The news is rampant with reasons for pessimism and despair. Every one of us has a front row seat on the most alarming developments around the planet on any given day and hour, constantly, without cease. Some of it is the usual natural disaster stuff. We get to be up close and personal, up to the minute, with human suffering that is in the "act of God" category. But the biggest stuff is our own doing. The climate isn't changing. We are changing the climate, with consequences that dwarf the worst natural disasters. We are the architects of most social unrest, political extremism, human brutality, and ecological collapse.

How to be with all of that, without losing heart, without sacrificing our aliveness in the moment, and at the same time without turning away from the difficult truths? That is the Big Question I ponder these days …

This inquiry happens best, I'm finding, within the absolute nuts and bolts of daily life, on the very ground I tread—the smallest daily encounters, the most intimate choices that are continually being offered—to either be present to what is, with a full and open heart, or to turn away in fear and despair. That is never a choice that is bound to circumstances, or that depends on a particular outcome. It is a choice freely offered, freely taken (or not), in the deepest heart of our experience, here and now. Therefore I will continue to live and fight for what I love in that spirit. I will not allow the great losses of this moment in history to rob me of my joy, compassion, and expansiveness of heart, that is as real and accessible now as it ever has been.

And when I am able to do that, in those moments of actual presence, I have learned to expect surprises, possibilities I hadn't imagined, aliveness in unexpected forms, immense beauty emerging all around, endless reasons for gratitude."[250]

Takeaways

One of the most important lessons from this exercise is that we all occasionally get tangled up in Thinking Distortions. It is not a sign of mental weakness or pathology. We are all susceptible at times, especially when our "Fear and Alarm Center" has sensed a threat, issued emergency alert signals to our body, and pushes us outside of our Resilient Growth Zone. It is especially difficult to avoid this trap because few of us have been taught how to separate our beliefs and self-talk from the external events we experience.

Another important takeaway is that our thoughts are not facts and do not necessarily correspond with reality. In fact, many times our FEAR is nothing more than "False Evidence Appearing Real!"[251] If you can remember this the next time you are distressed it might prevent a great deal of self-imposed suffering.

The third takeaway is the most important: You *can* change the way you view and respond to the world. It is possible to use the ABC Thought and Emotion Record on a regular basis to notice and correct Thinking Distortions. When you make these changes you can calm your body and mind, improve your mental and physical health, and become much more capable of using traumas and toxic stresses associated with climate disruption as catalysts to gain new insights, grow, and thrive rather than react in harmful ways.

Making these changes requires regular practice, and a good deal of self-compassion and self-acceptance.

Self-compassion and self-acceptance

As you begin to notice Thinking Distortions, it is important to cultivate self-compassion and self-acceptance. This is a crucial step in Presencing. Here are some ways you can use to become more accepting of and compassionate toward yourself.

Acknowledge that you did the best you could

It can be distressing to see how we create pain and suffering for ourselves, other people, and the natural environment by the way we think about and react to external events. You might feel shame, inadequacy, or self-loathing for doing harmful or thoughtless things as a result of holding erroneous assumptions and beliefs. You also might criticize yourself for failing to act differently. If this is the case, step back and think about the statement I offered earlier in this chapter: *"You did the best you could given the information you had and the resources that were available to you at the time."* Keep repeating this to yourself. It describes the reality of all of our lives. You are doing the best you can; in fact, we are all doing the best we can given what we know and the resources we believe are available to us. This awareness opens the door to responding to climate-enhanced adversity in healthier and more effective ways in the future.

Treat yourself as a good friend[252]

Here is another exercise you can use to become more self-compassionate.

1. Think about a time when a close friend felt really bad about themselves or was having a very difficult time with something. Write down how you would respond to your friend. What would you typically do, say, and how would you communicate your concern?

    _____

2. Switch gears and recall times when you feel bad about yourself or are having a very difficult time. How do you usually respond to *yourself* in these situations? Write down what you typically do and say and how you talk to yourself:

    _____

3. Examine the two responses and note any differences. Ask yourself why these differences exist? Try to identify why you treat yourself and other people you care about in different ways:

_____

4. Now, note how you might feel and think if you responded to yourself in the same way you typically respond to a close friend when you're suffering:

_____

Can you imagine treating yourself like a good friend when you realize that you made a mistake or are having a difficult time in the midst of trauma and stress? If you can be compassionate toward yourself, you will have much greater ability to calm your emotions and thoughts in the midst of an adversity aggravated by climate disruption and any other type of difficult situation.

Keep a self-compassion journal

Another way to increase your self-compassion is to keep a daily self-compassion journal for a week or longer. In the journal, note things you feel

Betty's story

Betty worked for a philanthropic foundation that funded organizations working to reduce climate disruption. She attended a Transformational Resilience workshop after she realized she was depressed about climate disruption, but the largest part was anger and disappointment in herself for not personally doing more solve the problem. She told the group that when, during one of the exercises, she repeated to herself the phrase, "You did the best you could with the information and skills you had at the time," she immediately burst into tears because she realized it was true. She felt like a huge weight was taken off her shoulders.

With this awareness fresh in her mind Betty decided to take ten minutes at the end of each day for two weeks to write down compassionate thoughts to remind her that she did her best to reduce her family's energy use. A number of months later during a follow up workshop she told me that the journaling had relieved her distress and actually helped her become more active in finding ways to reduce energy use.[253]

bad about, times when you judged or were critical of yourself, and difficult situations that caused distress. For example, perhaps you were rude to someone, or yelled at your kids. Afterwards, you felt guilt, shame, or humiliation. After each event you note, write down words, phrases, or sentences that allow you to see and think about the situation in a compassionate manner. For example, after describing how you were rude to someone, you might write down, "I was tired and in a rush. Next time I'll do my best to notice that I feel harried and be kinder." Journaling is a very effective way to express emotions, and has been found to enhance both mental and physical wellbeing.[254]

Develop your own "Presencing Safety Plan"

Take a few moments now to create a *Presencing Safety Plan* for yourself. This is a short document with two primary focuses. First, it describes the signs you will watch for indicating you are dysregulated and outside of your Resilient Growth Zone. For example, you might watch for a rapid heartbeat,

FIGURE 6.5   My personal Presencing Safety Plan

I will watch for these signs that I'm outside of my resilient zone	When I see these signs I will take these actions
(Physical examples: rapid heartbeat, high pulse rate, constricted breathing, head or stomach ache, muscle tension, sleep troubles. Mental examples: racing mind, excessive worry, anxiety, or fear)	(Examples: Practice the Reset Button, Tracking, Grounding, Mindful Breathing, Walking or Eating, Circles of Support, Wiser Self, ABC Thinking Distortions, Self-compassion)
1.	1.
2.	2.
3.	3.
4.	4.
5.	5.

constricted breathing, muscle tension, problems going to or staying asleep, and other symptoms of stress. Second, the Safety Plan notes the specific actions you will take when you are dysregulated to calm your emotions and thoughts and bring you back into your Resilient Growth Zone. For example, you might decide to practice tracking your physical body sensations, use practice breath-based techniques, or look to see if you are practicing any Thinking Distortions. Choose the practices that resonate best with your personality and work well in your situation.

The form in Figure 6.5 can be used to develop your personal Presencing Safety Plan.

Keep your Presencing Safety Plan with you at all times. You might want to put it on a small note card and keep it in your wallet or purse so you can pull it out and look at it whenever you are feeling stressed. You can also stick a copy on your bathroom mirror or on your desk at work so that it is visible whenever you experience trauma or stress.

Every adult and child would benefit from a personal Presencing Safety Plan

Many people who develop a personal Presencing Safety Plan during a Transformational Resilience workshop report that it is a tremendously helpful tool to remind them how to regulate the nervous system and stay calm and collected in the midst of adversity.

Imagine the benefits if every adult and child around the world had the opportunity to understand how trauma and toxic stress affect them, learn the skills described in this section—or others that accomplish the goal of calming their minds and bodies—and then developed their own Personal Presencing Safety Plan. It seems likely that many would greatly increase their ability to calm themselves when they experience trauma or toxic stress, increase their ability to make wise and skillful decisions about how to respond, and therefore avoid or minimize personally and socially harmful behaviors. This capacity will be particularly important as global temperatures rise toward 1.5°C or more or beyond.

I therefore urge every individual, family, organization and community to learn and practice Presencing skills and develop a personal Presencing Safety Plan.

Part 3:
Purposing—the second building block of Transformational Resilience

Philosopher Friedrich Nietzsche once said, "He who has a why to live can bear almost any how."[255] This statement underscores the importance of Purposing.

Deactivating the push of our psychobiological drives when they are not needed is essential to deal with the ongoing adversities generated by climate disruption. This, however, only gets you part of the way. There is another uniquely human trait that must also be addressed. This is the innate need to reflect on and make sense of our experiences and find meaning in life. Intensifying the pull of meaning is the focus of Purposing, which is the second building block of Transformational Resilience.

Purposing has two interrelated goals. The first is to help individuals and groups understand the importance of finding a sense of meaning and direction in their lives that can be sustained even in the midst of adversities generated by climate disruption. The second goal is to help people realize that how they conduct themselves is of utmost importance because in an era of unending turmoil amplified by climate disruption, a meaningful and fulfilling life can only be achieved by enhancing not only their own wellbeing, but also the health and welfare of other people and the condition of the natural environment.

Acute traumas and persistent toxic stresses are never desirable. The fewer people experience, the better. But if they happen, research shows that people benefit by viewing them as the beginning of the story, not the end. This is how we must approach climate disruption; as information we take in, gain insight and learn from, and craft constructive new stories for each of us individually, our families, organizations, communities, and for humanity as a whole.

The new story will require most of us to revise our internal conceptual framework. We will need to let go of many deep-seated assumptions and beliefs about how the world works and our role in it, as well as numerous long-standing habits. Many revered economic, cultural, and political ideologies will also need to be discarded. These concepts must be replaced with a clear understanding that in this era of continually rising adversities associated with climate disruption, no individual or group will be able to care for themselves or their immediate family unless they find ways to care for other people and improve the conditions of the natural environment. This will require a clear understanding of how the planet functions, along with new social narratives focused on the imperative to increase the functioning of *all* life on Earth; including but not limited to human life. As we make these changes we will also need to deal with the ongoing physical harm caused by a disrupted climate and the personal mental health and psycho-social-spiritual traumas and toxic stresses that result.

These changes will not be easy because who we are as people is the sum total of our assumptions, beliefs, and ways of perceiving the world. Humans are by nature cognitively conservative. Some people will get bogged down trying to maintain their old stories of themselves and the world by denying what is occurring or blaming others for it. When this behavior persists, these people will remain dysregulated and often display many of the personally or socially destructive behaviors discussed in this book.

However, a large body of research shows that when people acknowledge rather than deny reality, accept that tragedy has occurred, learn from it, and recognize that they are responsible for how they act, they are much more likely to be able to re-author their lives in positive ways. For many people the natural direction of this growth is toward "eudaimonic" wellbeing, meaning a reprioritization of personal goals and values to focus on something greater than themselves. If done well this can include finding ways to increase the wellbeing of others and/or care for nature as a way to find meaning and fulfillment in their own lives.[256]

For people who take this path, some of the common outcomes include a more positive attitude, better mental health, better physical health, extended life expectancy, and greater capacity to deal with future hardships.[257] In addition, research indicates that people who use misfortune as a catalyst to adopt a mission in life beyond merely meeting their personal needs exhibit increased honesty, kindness, love, gratitude, fairness, forgiveness, modesty, and prudence. They also exhibit greater leadership skills, teamwork, social intelligence, bravery, creativity, and judgment.[258] These qualities will be extremely important as we strive to live meaningful lives while also doing what is needed to reduce climate disruption to manageable levels.

In short, when combined with the capacity to regulate our fear-based psychobiological reactions, the development of new meaning, direction, and hope in life increases the capacity of individuals to thrive in the midst of ongoing climate-enhanced adversities.

These skills can be learned across the life-span, from childhood through our senior years, and the benefits can be expanded to include the natural environment, if teaching the purposing skills described in the following chapters becomes a top priority in the U.S., EU, and nations worldwide.

Three interrelated skills form the approach to Purposing included in the *Resilient Growth*™ model of Transformational Resilience. The titles used for these skills correspond to the last three letters of the word Growth. Just like Presencing, each skill can be carried out using a variety of tools and techniques.

7
Watch for new insight and meaning in life as a result of climate-enhanced hardships

For months after returning to New Orleans following Hurricane Katrina, Denise Thornton felt "listless and depressed" as she and her husband lived in the top floor of their home and cooked on a portable electric stove while they renovated the downstairs that was severely damaged. Then she realized that her house was one of the few places with running water, air conditioning, and comfortable places for people to sit. So Thornton decided to turn her home into a resource center for her neighbors. Not only did she help many people, the idea spread and what became known as "Beacon of Light Resource Centers" were opened throughout the city.

"The only way to survive here and to battle this depression is to start helping people," she said. "Once you start helping people, you get focused off of your own problems, you get so darn busy, and at the end of the day you're ten feet off the ground."[259]

Thornton used the adversities she experienced to gain new insights, re-author her personal story, and find new meaning in her life by transcending her own needs and helping others. Her journey illustrates the first skill involved with Purposing, which is to Watch for new insight and meaning in life from hardships directly or indirectly generated by climate disruption.

When have you experienced significant insight and growth?

In the space below quickly note three of the greatest moments of insight and growth in your life:

1. _____

2. _____

3. _____

Review your answers and see if the moments you listed occurred during periods of relaxation and tranquility or in the midst of, or immediately after, challenging or stressful situations.

I frequently ask this question when facilitating a Transformational Resilience workshop. The vast majority of the responses people give are associated with difficult or stressful periods in their lives. Few people say that taking a peaceful vacation or relaxing with friends produced their greatest insight and growth. Instead, they almost always point to demanding situations such as starting a new job, leaving home for the first time, having a child, dealing with a serious personal illness, or coping with the death of a loved one as the times of greatest insight and growth.

This underscores the fact that adversity and stress can be powerful engines of personal transformation. The traumas and stresses generated by climate disruption are no exception. The lessons they offer can help us gain insight into the importance of relating to other people, the natural environment, and ourselves with much greater care and compassion.

How did you decide to gain insight and grow?

Look at the times of great insight and growth you just listed and answer these questions:[260]

- How did you decide to use the experience to gain new insights about the world or yourself?

_____

- How did you identify your goal?

_____

- How did you motivate yourself, and sustain this motivation?

  _____

- How did you know you were making progress?

  _____

If you are able to answer any of these questions you likely already know the basics of using stressful situations as catalysts to gain new insights and grow! You might not have realized you were doing so or described it that way, but you intuitively understand what's involved with this transformational process.

The choices you make during adversity determine your pathway

Whether you were conscious of it or not, the choices you made in the midst of the experiences you just described determined whether or not they led to new insights and growth.

After a short time, following a serious traumatic event, most people recover and return to prior levels of functioning, although some people can remain impaired for long periods of time. However, in their struggle to make sense of major adversities, certain people make choices that allow them to use their experience as a stimulant to increase their functioning above pre-trauma levels. Much as Denise Thornton did after Hurricane Katrina, these people make the decision—sometimes after much thought and in other cases rather quickly—to reframe their perceptions and attitude and move beyond their struggles in a beneficial way.

This process can be thought of as the difference between seeing the glass as half full or half empty.[261] It is sometimes called "Benefit Finding,"[262] "Stress-Related Growth," "Adversarial Growth," "Altruism Born of Suffering," and "Post-traumatic Growth."[263] I call it Adversity-Based Growth. Figure 7.1 graphically describes the process.

When people gain new insights about the world and themselves and grow as a result of adversity it does not mean the experience was positive in the way we normally think of the term. Most of the time they wish the ordeal had never happened. Only rarely does the distress they experienced completely disappear. Adversity-Based Growth means that when people

FIGURE 7.1   The choices we make in the midst of adversity determine our pathway

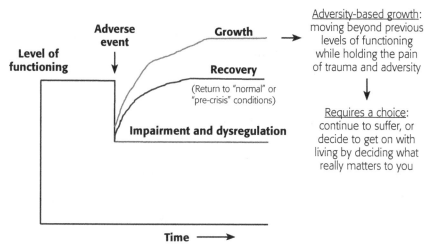

Source: Adapted from Joseph, S. (2011). *What Doesn't Kill Us: The New Psychology of Posttraumatic Growth.* New York, NY: Basic Books, p. 69.

do experience acute traumas or toxic stresses, they use the pain as motivation to reevaluate and alter their perceptions about how the world operates along with their beliefs about themselves—that is, they re-author their lives—and grow in ways that lead to new beneficial forms of meaning and purpose in their life.

Nelson Mandela's story

The life of Nelson Mandela illustrates this process. He was born in 1918 in the village of Mvezo in Umata, which was at that time part of South Africa's Cape Province. His teacher later named him Nelson as part of a custom of giving all schoolchildren Christian names. His father died when he was nine, and the local tribal chief took him in and educated him. He briefly attended University College of Fort Hare but was expelled after taking part in a protest. He then got involved in civil disobedience and made a lifelong commitment to opposing apartheid in South Africa. In 1962, Mandela secretly received military training in Morocco and Ethiopia, which indicated his belief at the time in the need for armed conflict to end apartheid.

In June 1964 Mandela and seven other members of his group were sentenced to life imprisonment by the South African apartheid government for their political views and activism. He ended up spending 27 years in prison. An international campaign grew over time and exerted pressure for his release, which finally occurred in 1990 amid escalating civil strife in his country.

Mandela could have come out of prison an embittered man bent on revenge against those who stole so many years of his life, and oppressed him and his people. Instead, his message was reconciliation, not vengeance. He ended up inspiring the entire world after he negotiated a peaceful end to apartheid and urged forgiveness for the white government that imprisoned him. He was elected South Africa's first black President and led his government's National Unity program, established a new constitution, created the Truth and Reconciliation Commission as a way to investigate past human rights abuses without sending the nation into violent civil war, and accomplished much more.

Mandela said in his autobiography, "The policy of apartheid created a deep and lasting wound in my country and people. All of us will spend many years, if not generations, recovering from that profound hurt. But the decades of oppression and brutality had another, unintended effect, and that was that it produced the Oliver Tambos, the Walter Sisulus, the Chief Luthulis, the Yusuf Dadoos, the Bram Fischers, the Robert Sobukewes or our time—men of extra-ordinary courage, wisdom and generosity that their like may never be known again. Perhaps it requires such depths of oppression to create such heights of character."

Nelson Mandela re-authored his life during his incarceration and made the choice to find meaning and fulfillment by offering an olive branch to his oppressors. In doing so, he changed the lives of millions of people for the better.[264]

What occurs when we gain new insight, grow and find new meaning in life?

You might not be able to change the fate of an entire nation through the choices you make, but you can make a difference in small and large ways if you use adversity to re-author your life. Re-authoring involves changing the narrative you have developed—the stories you tell ourselves—that you have you are used to define who you. You make these changes through an active process of observing and experiencing phenomena, comparing them to the assumptions and beliefs you currently use to make sense of things, and then deciding if and how to adjust your perspectives and construct new personal narratives.

To explore this process I invite you to think back to an experience that was particularly traumatic or stressful for you. In the space below describe the situation in as much detail as possible. Then, explain how you reacted, including what you did and said and the way in which you communicated. After you have completed that section, describe the effects on yourself (including your body, emotions, and thoughts), other people (including your family, friends, fellow workers), and the natural environment (including any changes in your material or energy consumption or waste generation).

- Description of stressful event:

- Your reaction:

- How your reaction affected you:

- How your reaction affected other people:

- How your reaction affected the natural environment:

Reflect for a moment on what you just described and then answer these questions:

- What story did you tell yourself about how the world, other people, and yourself that led you to react the way you did? For example, did you tell yourself that this was yet another situation in which you need to protect yourself from people who wanted to do you harm? Conversely, did you tell yourself that everything would work out for the best? What story popped into your head in the midst of this situation?

- Did you focus only on your own needs and wants throughout the process?

- Looking back, was the way you reacted really necessary?

  _____

- Are you satisfied with the consequences or on reflection would you have liked to react in different ways?

  _____

- Does the way you reacted and the effects seem familiar; is this part of a pattern?

  _____

It was natural to focus only on your own needs when you experienced the adversity. Remember, as I have explained throughout the book, when you perceive yourself to be under threat your "Fear and Alarm Center" issues emergency alert signals that quickly trigger fight, flee, or freeze reactions. But if your reaction is part of a long-term pattern and you would like to respond in different ways and generate more positive outcomes the next time something similar occurs, your answers to the following questions might help:

- Was there a way you could have responded to the situation that met your needs and also the needs of the other people involved?

  _____

- Was there a way you could have respond to the situation that met your needs and benefited others, while reducing your environmental impacts or even restoring nature?

  _____

- Was there a way to respond to the experience that would have allowed you to become a more caring or compassionate person?

  _____

- Was there a way to respond to the experience that would enhance your strengths, skills, wisdom, or sense of personal responsibility?

  _____

- In sum, are there lessons that can be learned from the way you reacted to this situation that would help you gain new insights and grow as a person?

These questions offer a way to actively search for new insight about the world and yourself, grow, and find meaning in your life in the midst of adversity by assisting others or caring for nature. Ask them the next time you experience trauma or stress. Write your answers on a piece of paper and reflect on what they mean about the stories you normally tell yourself in the midst of hardship. How would your personal narrative change if you pursued the different approach suggested by your answers to the last five questions?

Carole's story

Carole is a senior manager in the public works department of a city government. She told the breakout group she joined during a Transformational Resilience workshop that her moods were bouncing back and forth between anger and depression because of problems she was having with an employee.

Carole said the problem was that the employee had an important job but would not perform it the way Carole thought was best. She had sat down and discussed the problems with the employee a number of times. When that did not work she sent a formal memo to the employee outlining the changes the individual needed to make. When that failed to produce the desired results, Carole put the employee on notice that if the person did not adhere to the requirements Carole laid out their contract would be terminated. However, the employee did not change, and news of Carole's actions quickly spread and elicited strong negative reactions from other employees.

With Carole's permission, the small group then brainstormed what might be happening along with potential solutions. People asked Carole questions such as why she considered the employee's behaviors problematic, how the employee saw the situation, why Carole took the approach she did, and if other responses might be possible? As the questions and dialogue proceeded, Carole suddenly realized that the employee had actually found more cost-effective and environmentally beneficial ways to do their job and did not want to abandon them. However, Carole had discounted the new approaches because she felt the individual was challenging her authority. The employee had picked up on Carole's decision and reacted defiantly, which only reinforced Carole's belief that the individual was flouting her command.

At the close of the discussion, Carole told the group that said she now realized that it was her choices, not the employee's actions that had precipitated the problem and led to her emotional distress. She said she now realized she could make different choices that hopefully would resolve the problem and restore the trust of the employee and other staff members. Carole also said that this was a very powerful lesson for her about how she approached life.[265]

What are you changing from?

In order to understand how the traumas and toxic stresses directly or indirectly generated by climate disruption might change you, it is helpful to have a basic understanding of who you are today and how you came to be that person. Pause for a moment and look back at your life. Use the spaces provided in Table 7.1 to develop a simple timetable describing what significant positive and negative events taught you during your life.[266]

Age periods	Significant positive events	Significant negative events	Lessons the significant events taught me
Early childhood (ages 1–10)			
Adolescence (ages 11–19)			
Young adulthood (ages 20–29)			
Mature adulthood (ages 30–44)			
Middle age (ages 45–65)			
Senior years (age 66 and up)			

TABLE 7.1   Your life-events timetable

Start by trying to remember childhood experiences that taught you about the world and yourself. If you have trouble recalling childhood experiences, this exercise might help. Close your eyes and imagine yourself as a young child standing at the front door of a house you grew up in. Your mother, father, or primary caretaker(s) are standing there and say to you, "Whatever you do in life you must always ..." Finish their sentence in your mind by stating whatever comes to mind.[267]

This exercise often yields surprising results. Many people finish their caretakers' sentences with statements such as "do as you are told," "be nice to others," "trust other people," "say your prayers," "don't count on anyone but yourself," "never let other people see your fears," "never give up," or other such statements.[268] Write down whatever comes to mind as you complete your caretakers' sentences. Then, write down any other significant events you can remember that influenced how you saw the world and yourself during early childhood.

After you have noted what you can about your early childhood, complete the other sections of the timetable by trying to identify other significant events and what they taught you in different periods of your life. For example, during adolescence your parents might have given you extra love and care during a serious illness, which taught you that the people close to you could be counted on. Or, perhaps you were neglected or abused and learned not to trust people, or that you were unlovable. Add more lines as needed.

After the timetable is completed, spend a few moments reviewing the entire flow of your life and reflect on how different events influenced the assumptions and beliefs you hold today about the world and yourself. Consider questions such as:

- How did your life change after each event you listed?

- How did your reactions to the negative events in your life compare to your reactions to the positive events?

- Did you learn anything of value from the negative events?

- How might your life have been different had you not experienced the events?

- Did you adopt different identities or rely on different personal qualities in various periods of your life?[269]

After completing the timetable you might set it aside for a while. Then, after a few days review, it again to determine if additions or revisions are needed.

Describe your current life narrative

After you have developed a life-events timetable that feels complete, write a short narrative summarizing who you are today and how you came to be that person. This is an important part of the exercise so take your time. Here are some key issues to cover:

- **Summarize how you now see the world and other people.** For example, do you believe the world is a benevolent, predictable, and just place, or do you see it as cruel, chaotic, and inequitable? Do you see the majority of people as honest and worthy or as dishonest and unworthy?

- **Describe the various aspects of your personality as seen in the different eras of your life.** For example, do you have vulnerabilities that appear during some periods in your life and strengths that surface in others? Do you have some likable and other less likable qualities? How might these characteristics have come about? How have they helped you navigate through life?

- **When one aspect of your identity is weakened or threatened, note how you rely on others that remain intact.** For example, when one of your vulnerabilities has been exposed does a different quality appear in its place? If so, how did you develop this type of flexibility, and what are the upsides and downsides?

- **Finally, describe your views about the natural environment.** For example, do you think it is finite and fragile or inexhaustible and indestructible? Can your actions negatively affect the environment, or do they have little to no effect? Do you regularly think about how your behaviors might affect nature and the climate, or never give it much thought? Again, point out how significant events in your life might have influenced these views.

This exercise is likely to illuminate how different people and experiences have influenced your views of the world and yourself. It might also shine light on the fact that your assumptions and beliefs are not set in stone: it is likely that you have altered them a number of times as you gained new insight from different events in your life. This could lead to the realization that you are more flexible and more multi-dimensional than you might believe, and have relied on a variety of personal qualities during different times in your life.

The many different capacities and qualities you possess can be called on to help you gain insight, grow, and find new meaning in life in the midst of adversities aggravated or directly caused by climate disruption. If a climate-enhanced hardship thwarts or entirely blocks the expression of one characteristic, you can rely on others to respond constructively to the situation.

Now that you know who you are today, how you came to be that person, and what you would be changing from, let's examine how climate disruption might change you if you use the adversities as catalysts to gain new insights into the world and yourself, grow, and find meaning in life.

What does it actually mean to find new meaning in life?

Meaning is a personally created construct that influences our choice of goals and activities, and gives our lives a sense of purpose, self-worth, and fulfillment.[270] Because new meaning is derived through the process of gaining new insights and growing as a human, it is inherently a very personal process. Although the cultural narratives that dominate the groups we associate with influence what we see and experience and how it should be interpreted (factors I will discuss in Part 4 of the book), who you are as an individual—your basic assumptions and beliefs, personal qualities, and aspirations—shape your capacity to gain insight, grow, and find new meaning in life through adversity.

Most people can tolerate distress and disappointment if they can find meaning in it. The search for meaning provides purpose and direction in the midst of traumatic or persistent adversity. Without it, misfortune often leads to anger or despair. Meaning is thus a powerful driver of both healing and growth. In fact, finding meaning is an essential element of recovery from any traumatic experience, climate-related or not.

This is what psychiatrist Viktor Frankl realized when he was imprisoned in a WWII concentration camp. While there, he saw that people who found some type of deeper meaning in their suffering were much better able to handle the situation than those who felt hopeless and helpless. He described this dynamic in his seminal book *Man's Search for Meaning*.[271] Here is a summary of what he discovered:

- **The will to meaning.** Human behavior is motivated by the need to find meaning in our existence. Meaning-making is a defining characteristic of all humans.

- **Life has meaning.** The possibility to create or experience meaning is present from birth until the last minutes of life. If trauma or toxic stresses lead us to believe that life has no meaning, it is not because meaning does not exist. Rather, it is because we have failed to seek out meaning in those adversities. The necessity is therefore to constantly search for meaning and meaningful moments even in the midst of suffering.

- **Freedom of will.** Humans are always free to choose their attitudes toward any type of suffering. While there are many aspects of life that we cannot personally control, this is our ultimate "freedom." No matter how terrible the situation might be, we humans always have the freedom to choose our attitude toward it.

Although climate disruption cannot be compared to Frankl's experience of being in a concentration camp, as the Earth heats up we will all experience increasingly significant limitations, uncertainty, and suffering over which we will have little or no control. Freedom of will suggests that even in the midst of these difficulties, you still control your attitude. You can adopt an outlook that causes more suffering for other people, the Earth's climate, and ourselves, or you can adopt an attitude that allows you to learn, grow, and increase personal, collective, and environmental wellbeing.

Sources of meaning

How do we humans find meaning in life? There are at least four basic sources of meaning.[272]

- The first source is **historical meaning**. It results from a deep sense of satisfaction derived from something you did in the past or are doing today that generates future benefits. For instance, you might have gained a compelling sense of meaning by helping disabled people, caring for abandoned animals, or from the lasting positive effects you had on the next generation through your role as a youth mentor or coach.

- **Attitudinal meaning** refers to the outlook you adopted that allowed you to surmount a personal adversity over which you had little control. For example, you might have found meaning in the way you handled a serious medical problem without complaint, or when you took the high road rather than retaliating when someone maligned you.

- A third source of meaning results from **creative pursuits**. Writing, painting, drawing, music, and other artistic endeavors or hobbies often provide a powerful source of meaning.

- A fourth source of meaning is **experiential**. This involves being intimately connected with loved ones or friends, lovingly caring for pets or other animals, being absorbed in the beauty and mystery of nature, or other experiences where we are fully present and engaged.

These primary sources of meaning illuminate the fact that when boiled down to the basics, meaning in life is obtained by engaging in a purpose greater than yourself, that you perceive to have significant value, and that increases your sense of self-worth.[273] These attributes most commonly emerge through the underlying processes of connection, caring, and contribution. You find meaning in life when you fully *connect* with other people or the natural environment by being totally present and engaged. It is only when we truly *care* about a relationship with others or the natural environment that connection flourishes. For connection and caring to thrive we need to unselfishly *contribute* to the wellbeing of other people or the natural environment by nurturing, sharing, rebuilding, or restoring.[274]

Identify how you find meaning in your life

Let's examine how you currently find meaning in life. If you believe your life has meaning, and can identify how that powerful feeling comes about, it is more likely that you can continue to find meaning even in the midst of ongoing climate-enhanced traumas and stresses.

In the spaces below, list past or current experiences or moments you have had in each of the four primary categories that have been found to generate meaning for people. It does not matter whether the feeling was extremely powerful or mundane. Just note meaningful moments or experiences that made an impact on your life. Then, determine why they were meaningful by assessing if in some way they involved connecting, caring, or contributing.

- Historical sources of meaning (feeling good about something you did in the past or are currently engaged in that leaves a positive legacy):

  _____

  Underlying processes that made it meaningful (e.g., connection, caring, contribution):

  _____

- Attitudinal sources of meaning (an outlook you adopted that allowed you to rise above a difficult situation):

  _____

  Underlying processes that made it meaningful (e.g., connection, caring, contribution):

  _____

- Creative sources of meaning (fulfillment you derive from artistic pursuits or hobbies):

  _____

  Underlying processes that made it meaningful (e.g., connection, caring, contribution):

  _____

- Experiential sources of meaning (connecting with life through close and loving relationships and becoming deeply immersed in nature):

  _____

  Underlying processes that made it meaningful (e.g., connection, caring, contribution):

  _____

Review all of the ways in which you find meaning in life, and their underlying sources, and in the space provided write a short summary of how you currently find meaning in your life. The summary can provide a reminder about how you can meaning in life when you experience future adversities, including those aggravated by climate disruption.

Common changes resulting from gaining insight, growing, and finding new meaning in life through adversity[275]

If you are able to gain new insight, grow as a person, and find meaning in life in the mist of hardships associated with climate disruption, you are likely to experience changes in one or more of five areas of your life.[276] It is important to watch for these changes because they indicate positive growth and change.

- **Greater appreciation of life.** Climate-aggravated trauma and stress is likely to increase your sense of vulnerability. You might realize that you can no longer predict, prevent, or control distressing events. This awareness might cause you to recognize that every moment you are alive is precious. As a result you might pay more attention to small things that you have previously ignored or viewed as insignificant, such as the sound of birds singing or a brief hug from a loved one.[277]

- **Closer relationships.** People who use adversity to gain new insights, grow, and find new meaning in life often develop closer and more satisfying relationships. You might cherish your loved ones even more and spend additional time with them. You might also become closer to certain friends. At the same time your desire for more nourishing relationships might cause you to distance yourself from people you once considered friends that you do not connect with in a satisfying way.[278]

- **Greater awareness of your capabilities.** When you use hardships to gain new insight, grow, and find meaning in life you are likely to discover that you have more capabilities and a much greater capacity to deal with adversity than you previously thought. In fact, you might come to see yourself as two different people—the one that existed prior to the trauma and the more confident and capable person that emerged afterward.[279]

- **Enhanced spiritual development.** Increased spirituality is another common trait seen in people who find new meaning in life through misfortune. If you are religious, your faith in a higher entity might increase as you search for ways to deal with the difficult experience. Research shows that many nonreligious people also experience some type of secular spiritual development as a result of traumatic events.[280]

- **A new philosophy of life.** Finding new meaning in climate-aggravated adversity might also lead you to develop an entirely new way of viewing life. Your basic assumptions and beliefs about the way the world works and your role in it might be altered in important ways. You might begin to see entirely new ways of living, as well as new opportunities in areas such as work, relationships, or creative endeavors.[281]

The changes described above might combine to produce important benefits for you such as:

- **Improved mental and physical health.** Research has found that people experience significant improvements in mental and physical health when they have a strong sense of meaning in life, including reduced rates of depression and increased stamina, executive functioning, and memory.[282] A number of studies have also found that using adversity to find new meaning in life promotes creativity and flexibility in thinking and problem-solving.[283]

- **Self-transcendence: focusing on something greater than yourself by making the shift "From Me to We."** Often, the only way to regain our footing in times of hardship and find meaning in the experience is to focus on something greater than yourself. Indeed, as Denise Thornton found, self-transcendence, or what I call a shift "From Me to We," is one of the most important outcomes of gaining insights, growing, and finding new meaning in life as a result of adversity.[284] Given the precarious condition of the Earth's climate today, it is vital to realize that doing whatever is possible to significantly reduce your greenhouse gas emissions and protect and restore ecological systems that sequester carbon are two of the most important ways you can adopt a mission greater than yourself. This can include behavioral and technological changes in your home, workplace, and community. Today, self-transcendence also requires supporting public policies and programs that facilitate these changes and electing political leaders who will enact them.

In addition, focusing on something greater than yourself will be essential to deal with racism, sexism, economic discrimination, and other forms of systemic oppression that might become more pronounced as a result of the fear-based reactions of individuals and groups to the adversities associated with climate disruption. The key to responding constructively to these types of trauma and toxic stress will be to use the principles and practices discussed in this book to increase your personal skills and resources, and connect with other people committed to similar social change goals. I will say more about responding to injustice, oppression, and other systemic ills in Chapter 11 when I discuss how to build the capacity for Transformational Resilience within communities.

Ample experience, backed up by a significant amount of research, has found that people who constantly seek pleasure, whether through drugs, alcohol, sex, thrill seeking, material consumption, or other practices, rarely achieve a solid or steady sense of meaning or wellbeing. That is because this type of pleasure is always fleeting. It vanishes as quickly as it appears. However, because pleasure is so intoxicating people can easily become hooked and continually seek more. This can quickly become self-destructive. It is also a major contributor to the excessive material and fossil fuel energy consumption, production of toxic waste, and generation of greenhouse gasses that are disrupting the Earth's climate.

In addition, research has revealed that, after a certain basic level of income and wealth, continually grasping for more money and affluence does not increase meaning or satisfaction with life. Neither do attempts to climb to the top of the ladder or acquire more power and authority. To the contrary, more often than not these pursuits lead to feelings of emptiness and disillusion. In fact, many of today's social ills, including the addiction to rampant consumerism, social media, alcohol, drugs, food, gambling, sex, exercise, and work can all be seen as attempts by people to escape deep feelings of meaninglessness.

In contrast, the psychological, emotional, and spiritual wellbeing generated by focusing on something greater than ourselves such as helping other people, or your community, and restoring the Earth's ecological systems and climate—that is, by shifting from a dominant focus on "Me" to an equal or greater focus on "We"—is powerful and long lasting.[285] Research has found that helping others in the aftermath of a major trauma is associated with increased wellbeing, self-esteem, and positivity and enhances an individual's psychological resources.[286]

César Chávez's story

The struggles of César Estrada Chávez aptly illustrate how people can use adversity to learn, grow, and find meaning in life by helping others. Chávez was the grandson of a runaway Mexican slave. During the Depression, the Chávez family lost their farm and most of their belongings. When César completed eighth grade, he worked in the fields. He asked for safer working conditions but was ignored. So he began speaking to migrant workers about their rights and eventually organized the United Farm Workers (UFW) of America. The landowners denied the UFW's requests for raises and safer working environments, so they organized peaceful strikes and grape boycotts that quickly spread across America. Chávez and the other strikers suffered many hardships but never abandoned their convictions and soon the laws began to change.

Rising out of poverty and overcoming obstacle after obstacle, Chávez found meaning in his life by helping others. Mexico eventually awarded him their highest civilian honor, the Aguila Azteca award. In 1973, he received the Jefferson Award for Greatest Public Service Benefiting the Disadvantaged. And, in 1994, he was presented posthumously with the Presidential Medal of Freedom by U.S. President Bill Clinton.

Grieving is often essential to find new meaning in life through adversity

We frequently have to give up something that we deem important when we make significant changes in our life. This will be especially true when we gain new insight, grow, and find meaning in life in the midst of ongoing climate-aggravated impacts. Sometimes we will need to mourn an injury that alters our lives, grieve the death of a loved one, or the destruction of parts of our community. Other times, many of the basic assumptions and beliefs we hold that define who we are will be severely challenged or completely shattered. In both cases, before we can regain a meaningful and lasting sense of self, we will need to find ways to mourn our losses.

Deep inside, many of us believe that the world is benevolent and that we are invulnerable.[287] These assumptions and beliefs can be torn apart if our home is destroyed in a major storm amplified by human-caused climate disruption, we develop a serious illnesses linked to warmer temperatures, or we lose an important job due to climate-driven shifts in the economy. In addition, many people in Western nations will find their sense of self-worth shattered by the realization that their belief in the righteousness of accumulating more and more financial wealth and material possessions has contributed to the destabilization of the Earth's climate system and consequent death and destruction across the planet.

Coming to grips with these changes will be difficult and painful. Many people are likely to ignore, deny, or suppress their emotional distress rather than acknowledging it and mourning the loss. This can lead to a general sense of spiritual emptiness, including helplessness and hopelessness, psychological and emotional distress, and physical health problems. The inability or unwillingness to take time to grieve also causes emotions to build up in ways that can lead some people to repeat problematic behaviors over and over again. Reenactment of personally or socially harmful behaviors thus is often a symptom of unresolved trauma.[288] As global temperatures rise we will all need to find ways to mourn our loss before we can rebuild our basic assumptions and beliefs and find new sources of meaning, direction, and hope in life.

Experts have described the feelings and symptoms of grief in various ways. In general, they can include: shock, denial, anger, guilt, anxiety, sleep disorders, exhaustion, overwhelming sadness, and difficulties concentrating. Some people experience a number of these emotions at the same time.

Contrary to the common notion that grieving takes place in well-defined stages, research indicates there is no set course for normal mourning. It is usually a spontaneous process in which we can continually ruminate about the losses, even in our dreams. As the mourning proceeds, the obsession eventually passes, leaving behind a much more realistic assessment of life and the ability to move forward.

To be successful, mourning requires that you take the time needed to ponder your place in the world and your relationship with what has been lost. After sufficient time—which for each of us varies depending on the type of loss, our present situation, our personal skills and strength of our social support networks, and other issues—we can reengage in life while having adjusted to living with loss. When we do not take the time to mourn, we can suffer for the rest of our lives.

Here are some suggestions for that might help your grieving process:

- **Take extra care of yourself.** Grieving can take a toll on your mind and body so place extra emphasis on self-care.

- **Stay closely connected with your social support network.** Your True Allies are likely best able to support you through the process.

- **Join a support group.** Being with people who are going through similar processes can often be very helpful.

- **Don't make big changes.** You are not likely to be thinking straight when you are grieving so don't make any big decisions or big changes right away.

- **Remember, many people around you might be grieving as well.** As climate disruption grows worse many people will be mourning. Remembering this might offer the opportunity to connect with new people to relate to and find new ways to mourn.

- **Acknowledge that mourning takes time.** Don't rush the process or deny, distract yourself, or ignore the feelings—take the time you need to develop a new sense of self.

Who might you become as a result of climate-enhanced adversity?

Let's tie all of this information together and explore how you can gain insight, grow, and find new meaning in life in the midst of climate-aggravated traumas and stresses. Step out of your current situation and imagine yourself in this scenario:[289]

> Life has been particularly stressful for your community and family for quite some time. Three years ago the largest employer in town laid off most of its workforce, including two of your good friends who have struggled to find steady decent paying work since then. They have tried to keep a positive attitude, but nevertheless have

struggled with anxiety and depression ever since. The closure of the plant and other recent economic problems reduced local government tax revenue, which led the City to cut the summer program your kids attended, and to close the senior center your elderly parents visited daily to interact with friends.

In addition, summer is fast approaching and the past few have been unusually hot. Extreme heat waves scorched the area for weeks on end, and the TV weather gurus say more of the same can be expected this summer. Local planning and construction gave little concern to the natural environment, leaving few trees or natural areas and miles of hard surfaces that retain heat. This made the scorching temperatures even more difficult to deal with. Your family struggled with the heat last summer, and a number of deaths and numerous incidences of heatstroke and heat exhaustion were reported in the community. In addition, petty crimes and burglaries rose during the heat wave, as did gun violence. These events make you nervous about allowing your kids to move about town or even play outside, especially during the evening.

Then, three months ago a horrific wind and rainstorm hammered your community, which quickly turned into a major flood. Climate scientists say the storm mirrors what can be expected as global temperatures rise due to the emission of human generated greenhouse gasses. The home of one of your friends was severely damaged and a number of other friends had their vehicles flooded and destroyed. Fortunately, your family came through unharmed, but many other people did not. Your best friend was caught in the flood trying to save his pet dog and now has PTSD. Portions of the ground floor of your home were flooded. Your family is now staying across town in your parents' small apartment until your home is fixed.

Immediately after the storm, people in your community pulled together to help you and others in need and to plan recovery efforts. This created a sense of bonding and helped people feel safe and more secure. Now that the immediate crisis has passed, however, people have turned their attention to their personal situations. You need to figure out what to do.

This is an all too real scenario faced by people around the world today. It was adapted from the situation many people experienced in New Orleans prior to, during, and after Hurricane Katrina. Let's explore how you might respond in this situation and how you could use it as a catalyst to gain new insight into the world and yourself, grow, and find meaning in life. As you imagine yourself in the midst of that situation, answer these questions:

Describe how you would likely normally react in this scenario

- What words or phrases would you use to describe yourself during the difficult times before the big storm? For example, would you be calm and collected or tense, happy or sad?

  _____

- How would you likely describe yourself after the big storm? How would your body, emotions, and thoughts differ from those before the storm?

  _____

- How you would normally react to this situation? For example, what would you likely try to accomplish, how would you communicate, how would you treat other people and the natural environment, and how would you treat yourself?

  _____

- Describe the likely consequences of your normal response for other people, the natural environment, and you, and where that would leave you:

  _____

- In sum, describe how the events would affect the person you are today as depicted earlier in this chapter:

  _____

Now reimagine your reaction and consider alternative responses by answering these questions

- Who are you responsible to in this situation—just yourself and your family, or are you responsible to other people as well?

  _____

- What are you responsible for—your family and you alone, or also for helping friends and others in the community and protecting the natural environment?

- Is there a way to meet your own needs by helping other people *and* conserving the natural environment?

- Are there any new activities that you can pursue or opportunities that might now be open to you as a result of this experience?

- Have any previously unknown personal strengths, skills, or qualities become evident that you can utilize for beneficial purposes?

- Building on your previous patterns, are there ways to find historical, attitudinal, creative, or experiential sources of meaning in life for you?

- Are there any other new ways to find meaning in your life by connecting, caring, or contributing to other people or the natural environment?

Jenny's story

Jenny experienced something similar to this scenario after Superstorm Sandy. After attending a Transformational Resilience workshop she wrote me a note stating: "I was struggling before the storm. I was not happy with my job or with where I was living. The storm was the last straw. It completely knocked me off my feet. My home was badly damaged and I was left with just the clothes I quickly threw into a suitcase. I was depressed and kept asking, "What did I do to deserve all this?

"After a while the answer appeared. It was big wakeup call. The storm forced me to think hard about what I really cared about. It forced me to reconsider my desire for more material things. I realized I was trying to make more and more money and then I was spending it just as fast. But when I was buying stuff I felt empty. So I quit my job and took one for much less pay in the arts field that I truly love. The house I now live in is much smaller than the one before the storm but meets all my needs and is in a neighborhood filled with people I like. I no longer have a car, but that's not a problem. I rent one whenever I need it. I no longer watch TV—in fact I don't even have one. I realized it just traumatized me by broadcasting all the bad things happening in the world. I'm much more frugal now and spend money only on things that are really necessary—with an occasional splurge for a good meal with friends.

"I'm now more compassionate toward others because of my experience, and more engaged with people. I used to be a loner, focused on my career. Now I help children learn art. I have time for family and friends and we have fun learning and doing different things. I used to be on the internet all the time but now I do it just once a day and sometimes not at all. I feel better and it minimizes my use of electricity. I'm looking for new opportunities all the time. The storm caused me to reevaluate what I was doing and I now much happier and feel more fulfilled."[290]

Although the specifics will differ, much as Jenny did, can you imagine yourself altering your perspectives, behaviors, and lifestyle as a result of climate-aggravated adversity? A positive, growth-oriented mindset and life metaphor can help facilitate this type of change.

Adopt a growth mindset and positive metaphor for your life

Embedded in the stories we tell about the nature of the world, other people, and ourselves are certain mindsets and metaphors.[291] To find benefits in the midst of adversity similar to those described by Jenny, it can help to examine and alter these mental models.

For example, in one form or another some people see themselves as "victims" in life. People who hold this mindset have often been mistreated, neglected, persecuted, or abused by others, or for other reasons feel that life has not treated them fairly. As a result they see themselves as defeated and helpless. Others adopt a victim mindset even when they have not experienced this type of adversity. No matter what the cause, people who think of themselves as victims usually adopt a passive role in altering their life because they think nothing they do can make a difference.

Other people see themselves as "survivors." They might not use this exact term, but people with this mindset usually see themselves as tough enough to do what is needed to bounce back from adversity and persevere. Survivors, however, usually struggle to find true joy and fulfillment.

Even if you don't use these words, deep inside, do you envision yourself as a "victim" or "survivor?" If so, how does that mindset influence the way you see the world and yourself, and the way you live your life? How does it affect how you respond to adversity?

Now, look deeply and see if you can bring to mind a word or phrase that describes you as a "thriver" or "flourisher." These are growth mindsets that imply action, mastery, and hope. If you think of yourself this way, when you experience a climate-related or other type of adversity you might respond in new ways. Can you find a word or phrase that describes you as a thriver or flourisher? Is that possible?

To enhance your capacity to adopt a growth mindset you can also examine the metaphor you hold about your life. Life-metaphors link your past with your future. For example, people who hold a mindset of a "victim" or "survivor" often hold a metaphor that, in one way or another, describe their lives as tragedies or constant struggles with no end in sight. This often creates a self-fulfilling prophecy. People fail to accept responsibility for their attitude and actions because they expect bad things to happen anyway.

Other people, however, adopt positive life-metaphors that acknowledge pain and suffering while also explaining their life journey as moving toward new adventures or better things. For example, George worked as a river guide during the summer months. He told a group during one of my workshops: "After thinking about it today, I can now see my life as an otter swimming down a river. I get bumped around, there are twists and turns, and I sometimes end up stuck in a side eddy. But when I make the effort I am always able to get back into the main current and I look forward to swimming the next big wave."

What metaphor do you hold about your life? Can you identify a positive metaphor that incorporates tough times while also describing your journey toward growth, meaning, and greater fulfillment in life?

Here are some other metaphors people have come up with during Transformational Resilience workshops:

- "My life is like fruit on a tree—sometimes it is ripe and I eat and savor it, and other times I don't realize it is ripe and miss the opportunity, but more fruit will always grow."

- "My life is like a tree. When I forget to give it water it does not grow much. It grows when I water it."

- "My life is like a sailing adventure on the ocean. I get hit with big winds and waves sometimes that send me off course, but I always get back on course and on to the next great adventure."

Take a few moments and in the space provided identify a positive metaphor for your life:

_____

_____

When in some form you can see yourself as a "thriver" or "flourisher" and adopt a positive metaphor for your life, you will likely be much more able to take control of your life, despite the adversities you experience. This can initiate a positive spiral that allows you to sustain the new perspective through any new hardships you might experience.

Laughter facilitates learning, growth, and meaning in adversity

When you experience scenarios such as the one described above about the heat wave intermixed with the big storm—and many of us are unfortunately likely to experience something similar as global temperatures rise—it can improve your state of mind to find humor in life.

Laughter is a very powerful force with both short- and long-term benefits. Laughter enhances your intake of oxygen-rich air and stimulates the heart, lungs, and muscles. Your body releases endorphins and dopamine, which are nature's feel-good chemicals. They activate the PNS and calm the SNS. The result is that your fear-based stress reactions are reduced and you are better able to remain within your Resilient Growth Zone. This allows you to think clearly and see problems as opportunities to gain new insight, grow, and find new meaning in life rather than reacting by fighting, fleeing or freezing.

Laughter provides many long-term benefits as well. It improves your immune system. Negative thoughts activate the SNS and trigger the release of hormones that create more stress in your system and decrease your immunity. Laughter, on the other hand, activates the PNS and releases neuropeptides that help fight stress and potentially more-serious illnesses.[292]

The sound of laughter is contagious. When people laugh and play together, it creates bonds and increases intimacy as well as calmness.

Best of all, laughter is free, readily available, and easy to use.

It is important to note that not all forms of laughter are beneficial. When it is used to put down, demean, bully others, or express hostility, it can be harmful. The type of laughter and humor I'm talking about is positive, appreciative, enlightening, or psychologically and emotionally easing in nature.

Although the scenario described in the exercise we just completed is no laughing matter, could you imagine ways to use humor to lighten the load for you and others if you were in that situation?

Here are a few simple tips to help you laugh more often when you experience those types of hard times:

- **Alter your perspective.** As I have emphasized throughout this chapter, one suggestion is to change the way you look at the situation. Mark Twain once said, "Humor is tragedy plus time." When something unpleasant or stressful happens, ask yourself, "Will any part of this seem funny months or years in the future?" For example, maybe you can laugh about the fact that you always wanted a new garage and the storm has given you the opportunity to get one! Or maybe you can find humor in the way you scurried around in your underwear and boots collecting valuables from your home before the storm arrived. However you do it, step back and take a big picture look at the situation. See the absurdities in the situation. This often allows you to see humor even in difficult situations.

- **Smile—even when you don't feel like it.** Another way to find humor in the darkest of times is to "put on a smiley face." I know this might seem fake, but it works. The Zen Buddhist meditation teacher Thich Nhat Hahn advises us to deliberately smile before we get out of bed in the morning, even if it is the last thing we feel like doing. Smiling produces real benefits. One research study found that when people were asked to smile regardless of their mood, they saw more humor in their surroundings than those who were asked to frown.[293]

- **Explicitly seek out laughter.** You can also cultivate a sense of humor in the midst of difficulties by purposely doing more of what you usually do to find humor and laugh. For example, if you like to listen to or tell jokes, watch funny movies, sing in the shower, or read comic strips, deliberately increase your engagement with these activities. You might also consider playing more often with your significant other, children, or pets, or intentionally engaging in humorous banter with friends, or with fellow employees, clients, or customers at work.

The more you can make humor an integral part of your life, the easier it will be to gain new insight, grow, and find meaning in adversity.

Mark's story

Researchers studying family resilience point to the comments from "Mark" after Hurricane Katrina had blown his house apart as an indication of the power of humor in stress management. "He chuckled wryly as he talked to researchers outside his temporary quarters, a tiny Federal Emergency Management Agency trailer, "My wife had been nagging me to replace the cabinets in the kitchen. I guess she'll get her wish now!" Mark's use of sarcasm aimed at himself was helpful to him in turning a bad situation into a "silver lining."[294]

Pursue your own path to gain new insight and meaning in adversity

The techniques offered in this chapter represent merely one way to learn about the world and yourself from the traumas and toxic stresses generated by climate disruption—or any other type of adversity. Other methods are available as well. Choose one that makes sense for you in your situation. The important point is: rather than denying or attempting to flee hardships, gather the courage to turn toward them and use them to learn about the external world as well as your internal assumptions, beliefs and way of seeing and reacting to events. The more that you use the difficulties associated with a warming planet as opportunities to learn, the greater the likelihood that you can find the type of meaning in the experiences that allows you to improve your own wellbeing by helping other people and enhancing the condition of the natural environment and climate.

8
Tap into the core values you want to live by in the midst of adversity

She was very young when it happened. Shana told the group that she never thought the memories would pass. She was a rape victim at 14 years old. It was difficult to live with. She was depressed for many years and at times saw no purpose in life. She could not understand why her uncle would do such a thing. However, she eventually came to realize that she could "live in a positive way and make a difference in the lives of others, or she could continue to wallow in anger and regret."

Ever since she was a little girl Shana said she had felt that helping other people was the most important thing a person could do in life. It was a value she probably adopted by watching her mother volunteer in the community. But she did not feel that way for many years after her trauma. Nevertheless, the feeling "kept pushing on me." At age 24 she finally decided that she either needed to "get her act together and begin to help people" or she would slowly wither away. So, she enrolled in graduate school and eventually got a job working as a counselor assisting rape victims. "Now, with each person I help, I feel better," she said.[295]

As Shana demonstrated, how we respond to hardships in our life emerges out of what we stand for as human beings and the values we have or want to realize. The second practice involved with Purposing is to Tap into the core values you want to live by in the midst of adversities enhanced by climate disruption and other types of hardship.

Living your core values gives your life purpose

What gives your life purpose and direction? It is living your values. What are values? This term refers to what is truly important to you—what you really value in life. Values are your deepest desires for how you want to act during your journey through life. They are the qualities you want to infuse into your everyday behaviors.

Values refer to actions, not beliefs or moral philosophies. We create our life through our actions, not intentions. Values reflect who you are through how you behave on a daily basis at home, work, and during time with family, friends, and strangers.

Values are not goals or rules

Values are not the same as goals. This is often confusing to people. Goals are something you want to achieve—things you can complete. Making a good living, finding love, and having good friends are goals. They are needs or wants you strive to obtain. Values, on the other hand, can never be attained. They are how you behave as you seek your goals—and how you act even when you cannot obtain your desires. This is important because a principled and meaningful life results from how you travel the path, not through the attainment of any particular set of goals.

Values are also not the same as rules. By rules I mean ideas and beliefs that tell you in absolute terms right and wrong ways to live your life. Rules are usually described by words such as "must," "should," "ought," or "good and bad." These directives tend to be restrictive and burdensome. In contrast, values tend to provide a sense of freedom. Values are energizing because there are many ways to act on them.

For instance, imagine that you decide to help your community in some way by volunteering at a local non-profit organization three hours a week. If you set this goal because you are feel obligated by rigid rules ("I should do this" or "Not contributing is wrong") you are likely to occasionally feel beleaguered by the time and energy you invest. If you decide to contribute to your community because of deeply held values such as wanting to help others, the experience will likely feel energizing and freeing and you will be less concerned about the amount of time you spend.

Values, goals, and rules can all be helpful in our lives, but it is important to recognize the differences because they generate very different types of internal experience and external outcome. You can set goals as stepping-stones for living your values. Society can use rules to establish laws and ethical codes of conduct such as "stealing is wrong." But the values that underlie your personal goals and rules are the key to living a principled and meaningfully life in the midst of adversity.

Values are profoundly important in responding to climate disruption

Your deeply held values will determine the choices about how to act that you make in the midst of traumas and stresses associated with climate disruption. Dealing with the impacts of rising global temperatures will be much easier when you recognize this. Living out your values is what will infuse your life with purpose. It will give you something to live for.

Unlike your emotions and thoughts that constantly change, your values tend to remain relatively constant. They might vary during different eras in your life. For example, the values you held as an adolescent are likely to be different than the ones you hold dear in adulthood. But your core values—the ones that are truly important to you because they depict who you are or want to be as a human—are likely to persist over long periods of time. This makes them particularly helpful as a beacon of light to help you find your way in the midst of rising adversities directly or indirectly generated by climate disruption.

Who are you and who do you want to be?

The starting point for clarifying your core values is to answer some important questions about who you are or who you want to be as a human being. Your answers to these questions might mirror the personal narrative you wrote in the previous chapter. However, that narrative described how you see the world and yourself today as a result of past life experiences. This exercise offers an opportunity to describe deeply held values related to who you really are, and how you would like to be in the world, that might remain unrealized. Write down the answers that come to mind here:[296]

- How do you ideally want to treat other people during your life?

  _____

- How do you ideally want to treat the natural environment and climate during your life?

  _____

- What personal qualities do you want to cultivate during your life?

  _____

- How do you want to be remembered after your time on the planet ends?

  _____

- In short, what type of person do you really want to be?

  _____

The answers you provide to these questions provide an initial look at what you see as truly important in life. Let's go further and clarify your values.

Surfacing your core values

It is often not easy to identify what truly matters to us. This exercise can help you think deeply about the question.

Step 1: Ask yourself what truly matters deep in your heart

A list of values is provided in Box 8.1. Go through the list and put a "V" next to those that are Very important to you, an "S" next to those that are Somewhat important to you, and an "N" next to those that are Not important to you. If you value something that is not included in the list, add it. Remember, there are no right or wrong values and each person is different. Your values will be unique to you.

Box 8.1: Identify the core values that will guide your responses to adversity

Go through the list below and write a letter next to each value:

<u>V</u> = Very important   <u>S</u> = Somewhat important   <u>N</u> = Not important.

Personal responsibility	Personal safety
Honesty	Rank and power
Fairness	Self-awareness
Patience	Diligence
Compassion	Public recognition
Simplicity	Love
Protection of nature/climate	Social equity
Generosity	Integrity
Gratitude	Charity
Independence	Mercy
Family	Respect for others
Community	Status
Professional achievement	Brotherhood
God	Selflessness
Reverence for human life	Wealth
Honor	Forgiveness
Loyalty	Open-mindedness
Social justice	Success
Respect for authority	Insert other
Humility	_____
Self-sufficiency	_____
Kindness	

Step 2: Look at all of the items that now have a "V" or "S" next to them and separate values from goals

Again, the difference is that values are how you want to act in all circumstances, while goals are something you want to attain or achieve. Take a moment to scratch off your list anything that from your perspective is actually a goal rather than a value.

Step 3: Identify your most important values

Now examine all of the values that are <u>V</u>ery Important to you, and circle the ten *most* important. This can take time and is often not easy to do. Stick with it. What are your ten most important values?

By becoming aware of the values that stand out as the most important, you will have a greater sense of who you are and how you want to live your life. Events or situations that violate your top ten values are more likely to trigger your "Fear and Alarm Center" and cause you to become dysregulated. Knowing this offers insight that can help you skillfully and wisely manage your response.

You don't need to rank them yet. Just list your ten most important values here:

1. _____   6. _____

2. _____   7. _____

3. _____   8. _____

4. _____   9. _____

5. _____   10. _____

Step 4: Go deeper still and prioritize your values

Go through your list again and prioritize them on a scale of 1–10, with 1 being your absolute most important value. You might decide that many of your top ten values have equal significance. This is valid in that different values are likely to float to the top in various stages of your life and in different situations you face. But if you are willing to honestly examine how you act in difficult times, you can identify the values that are actually at the top of your list.

If prioritizing remains difficult you can use a process called Paired Comparison Analysis.[297] This involves placing two values side by side, and then assigning a score to each based on which you think is more important. You then take the value with the highest score and compare it to the next value, and continue until you have compared all of the values to each other. Taking time to complete this process can be very valuable.

I want to emphasize that it is not always helpful to live by only a few values because your flexibility and openness to new experiences can become limited. But when push comes to shove, your top "1" or "2" values are likely be the ones that have the most influence over how you act. Your top "1" or "2" values are also likely to be the ones that are most sensitive to violation, and thus to dysregulation when they are breached. Increasing your awareness of the values that are most significant to you offers guidance on when and how to devote extra effort to regulating your reactions so you can live your values.

Prioritize your list of top ten values here:

1. _____   6. _____

2. _____   7. _____

3. _____   8. _____

4. _____   9. _____

5. _____   10. _____

Step 5: Reevaluate your top values

Take a few moments to think about the priority list you just developed. Are you happy with what it means for your life? If they are your true values—if you really live by them now—you can expect the same outcomes in your life as you are already getting. Are you satisfied with that? Is there anything gnawing away inside suggesting that you would feel better about yourself if you lived by different values and consequently achieved different outcomes?

You can answer this by determining if your top values help you live and act in ways that allow you to be the person you want to be. Recall your description of who you are and how you want to live your life earlier in the chapter. As a reminder, the questions you answered were:[298]

- How do you ideally want to treat other people?

- How do you ideally want to treat the natural environment?

- What personal qualities do you want to cultivate?

- How do you want to be remembered after your time on the planet ends?

- In sum, what type of person do you really want to be?

For example, if you want to be a caring and compassionate person but personal safety is one of your top values, are you concerned that fear-based reactions might prevent you from reaching out and helping other people? If after you die you want to be remembered as someone who worked to improve the common good, but accumulating financial wealth is a top value, might this lead you to do things that harm the natural environment that is the source of all life on Earth?

Make sure you are comfortable with what your top values indicate about your ability to live out what is truly important to you.

Step 6: Change your values

If, on reflection, you decide that some of the values that have shaped your life so far are not the ones you want to live by in the future, especially as climate disruption grows worse, you can change them. New values will lead to new behaviors and produce more fulfilling outcomes.

How can you alter your values? By going through a similar process of listing and prioritizing values, only this time do it by determining the values that can help you attain the things that are most important to you in life. This is important because many of us are influenced early in life by values pressed on us by our parents, religious beliefs and practices, or the culture in which we live, that become so deep-seated that we don't even realize what they are or how they continue to shape our perceptions and behaviors. We consequently go about life without understanding—or questioning—the values that drive our thinking and behaviors.

As Shana's story at the beginning of this chapter illustrates, the values you adopted early in life might still be extremely important to you. However, by surfacing and examining your values you can decide if they reflect what you truly value and how you want to live your life *now* rather than merely being legacies of your past. This is particularly important because values that promote unlimited material and energy consumption and waste are often legacies of the values held by people that lived through or grew up right after the Great Depression and World War II. Those values made sense to those people at that time as a way to lift millions of people out of poverty and get the economy moving. But conditions today are fundamentally different.

Similarly, in the U.S. the values of extreme individualism and complete autonomy grew out of an era long since passed when people had to make it on their own in the frontier. Americans no longer live on the frontier. In fact, humans have left no part of the planet untouched and climate disruption threatens all life on Earth. For any single person to survive a great deal of cooperation and collaboration will be needed.

The bottom line is that it is important to clarify what is truly important to *you* as your own person today.

To clarify and alter your values, go back through your answers to the five questions listed above about who you are as a human being and determine the values needed to live in ways that allow you to achieve those outcomes. Use the spaces below to complete the process:

- How do you want to treat other people during your life?
  Your answer:

  _____

  Values required to meet these outcomes:

  _____

- How do you want to treat the natural environment during your life?
  Your answer:

  _____

  Values required to meet these outcomes:

  _____

- What personal qualities do you want to cultivate during your life?
  Your answer:

  _____

  Values required to meet these outcomes:

  _____

- How do you want to be remembered after your time on the planet ends?
  Your answer:

  _____

  Values required to meet these outcomes:

  _____

- In short, what type of human being do you want to be?
  Your answer:

  _____

  Values required to meet these outcomes:

  _____

List all of the values you identified here:

_____

_____

_____

_____

Now, once again go though and prioritize the values you just listed with #1 being the most important:

1. _____   6. _____

2. _____   7. _____

3. _____   8. _____

4. _____   9. _____

5. _____   10. _____

Take a moment to ponder your new priority list. Is it different than your initial list of top values? If so, can you imagine how living out these top values might alter the way you act in the midst of climate-enhanced trauma and stress?

Apply your top values

To determine how your updated list of top values might change the way you think and act, let's return to the scenario presented at the end of the previous chapter describing the stress produced by economic problems and heat waves followed by the traumatic storm that damaged your home and community.

1. Brainstorm every possible way you could respond to that situation if you based your actions on your new list of priority values. Don't think about whether a different approach won't work. Just write down as many alternative ways you can imagine if you lived out your new list of top values:

   _____

   _____

2. Now, go through the list of possible alternative ways you could respond one by one and determine what you would *need to give up* if you were going to adopt that different approach. This requires honesty. Often the reason we continually respond to troubling situations in the same way is that to do otherwise requires that we give up something of importance. For example, would you need to swallow your pride to pursue an alternative approach? Would you need to accept less power and authority, or less money or wealth? Would you need to change your circle of friends and find people who are more supportive of your new beliefs or behaviors? Whatever the issues may be, write down what you would need to give up to respond to adversities by living out your core values. Then, take the time to mourn the losses:

    _____

    _____

3. Finally, envision yourself acting on the values-based alternative responses. Imagine what you would do and say on a step-by-step basis. As you do this notice the physical sensations in your body, your emotions, and the thoughts running through your mind. Notice your breathing patterns, your pulse, and you heart rate. Please understand that you are not being asked to choose a different approach. The point is to become aware of how you would feel physically, emotionally, and psychologically if you acted in ways that allowed you to live your core values. After you do so you can decide if you want to pursue a different approach in the future.

The process you just completed offers a method to go inside and become aware of what's truly important to you, based on who you are or want to be as a human being. Constant awareness of the deeply held values you want to live by will be extremely important as the impacts of climate disruption increase in frequency, intensity, and length. That's because research has found that even just thinking about and affirming one's most cherished values can diminish perceptions of threats, reduce fear-based reactions, and decrease Thinking Distortions such as constant ruminations after mistakes are made.[299] In addition, continually asking "Am I living my top values?" and then doing what you believe to be right solidifies your ethical compass, helps you grow stronger, and increases your capacity to gain new insights, grow, and find meaning in life in the midst of adversity.[300]

Gratitude is a powerful value

One of the most powerful yet often overlooked values that generates tremendous mental and physical health benefits is gratitude.[302] Throughout time, religious and spiritual leaders as well as philosophers have talked about the benefits of gratitude. The benefits have now been quantified through research.

Gratitude has been found to help people moderate their fear-based reactions by activating the PNS and moderating the reactions of the SNS. This happens because thankfulness enhances empathy, and reduces negative emotions of all types. Grateful people are also more likely to act in a constructive manner toward others, even when other people are unkind to them. In addition, people who deliberately think about things that they appreciate in life tend have more adaptive ways of responding to adversity.[303]

Research has also found that gratitude improves relationships. According to one study, showing appreciation to others can help you gain new friends. Thanking a new acquaintance also makes them more likely to seek an ongoing relationship.[304]

People who consider gratitude an important value rather than as something to practice on an occasional basis tend to be more optimistic, which is a characteristic that research shows boosts the immune system. They take better care of themselves and engage in more protective health behaviors such as regular exercise, eating a healthy diet, and getting regular physical examinations. This reduces a number of toxic emotions, causes fewer aches and pains, and leads to feelings of health.[305]

And, like humor, cultivating gratitude is free and doesn't require much time.

Here are a few tips for being thankful on a regular basis:

- **Keep a gratitude journal.** If you do not regularly give thanks for the opportunity to be alive, for things other people do for you, and for small things in your life, writing a journal can help alter this. Take a few minutes to give thanks in writing for both large and small things that happened to you during the day. Studies have found that spending just 15 minutes writing down a few grateful thoughts before bed improves the quality and length of sleep.[306]

- **Play Selma's Game.** One of my first meditation teachers more than 30 years ago, James Baraz, produced a hilarious and extremely touching video of his 89-year-old mother Selma giving a talk about how James "ruined her life" by helping her become more grateful.[307] After visiting his mother for a week and hearing her complain about almost everything, they decided to play a game they developed together. James tells the story:

> "At the end of each complaint that rolled so easily off her tongue, I would simply say "and …," to which she would respond, "And I'm really very blessed." Although it was a fun game, it started to have some real impact (She was saying that line very often!). We had a wonderful time as our week became filled with gratitude. To my delight, she's still keeping up with the experiment. You can teach an elder human new tricks!"

This turned out to be merely the beginning. His mother continued to practice gratitude until she died at age 94, despite losing her eyesight not long after she and James developed their gratitude game. James was a founding co-teacher at Spirit Rock Mediation Center. He also created the wonderful Awakening Joy course in 2003[308] and authored a book by the same name.[309] He chronicled

Fred's story

Fred worked for a major financial investment company. He attended a Transformational Resilience workshop because he felt something was missing in his life. He took his current job because he thought making a lot of money was the right thing to do. But the longer he stayed on the job, the more he questioned what he was doing.

As he worked through the process of identifying his values during the workshop the root of the problem finally hit him. He told the group that he now realized he was living by his father's values, not his own. From as far back as he could remember, he heard the message that making a lot of money was the best way to demonstrate your worth. He had adopted those values and organized his life around making a lot of money. But now, in his mid-30s, he came to realize that he no longer believed making a bundle of money was a good measure of who he was as a person. As he looked at his new list of top values he said he realized that what he really cared about was helping unwanted and injured animals. He wanted to be a veterinarian or work at an animal sanctuary.

Three months after the workshop Fred called me to say he had applied to veterinarian school.[301]

Selma's progress in a passage of his book, which included a poem she'd written on her 90th birthday: "Though my eyesight has been dimmed I see clearer than before/The glass is not half empty, it's overflowing to be sure."

You can play Selma's game to cultivate gratitude and awaken joy in your life. Keep notes for a day or two, or ask someone to monitor you in order to notice how often you complain about something. The complaint can be small—"It's cold outside"—or large—"I really dislike that person." After you begin to notice your pattern, make a conscious effort to add "and I'm grateful for___ (fill in the blank)" to the end of each statement ("Its cold outside ... and I'm grateful for having a home where I can stay warm"). Don't try to eliminate complaints—merely add something you are grateful for at the end of each statement. Keep at it and see what happens.

Participants watch the video of James and his mother during our Transformational Resilience Workshops and then play Selma's game. Most find it a powerful experience. The video is available on YouTube.

Tom Steyer's story

Billionaire climate campaigner Tom Steyer, founder and president of NextGen Climate, published a heartfelt opinion piece in Politico Magazine in July 2015 responding to news reports on the fossil fuel investments he made while he led San Francisco-based Farallon Capital Management. "I left the firm and committed myself to addressing global climate change because—based on the scientific evidence—I could not reconcile my personal values with managing a fund that by mandate is invested in all sectors of the global economy, including fossil fuels," he wrote.

Steyer has since separated his personal funds from Farallon and dropped his fossil fuel investments, although he has endorsed the use of natural gas.[310]

9
<u>H</u>arvest hope for new possibilities by making choices that increase personal, social, and environmental wellbeing

Rural western North Carolina has been hard hit by the offshoring of manufacturing plants and the resulting loss jobs in the textile industry. Between 1992 and 2012 the number of workers employed in the industry dropped by almost 88%. Opportunity Threads is a seven-year-old worker-owned cut-and-sew co-op that emerged as part of a movement to revive the region.[311]

Molly Hemstreet, who wears the multiple hats of founder, general manager, and a worker-owner of Opportunity Threads, was intrigued by the idea of creating a new way to generate jobs and increase the dignity of workers while conserving the natural environment. So in 2008 she founded Opportunity Threads, which is built on a three-part ethical platform: social, environmental, and economic benefits for the local community.

The co-op employs a "holistic approach." It uses organic cotton and reusable materials and strives to be a zero-waste facility as it manufactures high-quality textiles for a rapidly growing fair-trade, green market. This has helped them attract eco-conscious clients such as Maggie's Organics, Project Repat, and the toy company Eco-Bonk.

"We hit profitability five years ago and now fund our own growth," she told me. The co-op now employs over 20 people. In addition to receiving paid holidays, vacation, and sick and maternity leave, full members earn a share in the company's profits. This is a key motivator for many people, according to Hemstreet. Opening the door for people to become worker-owners allows them to contribute to the business' growth and strategy.

"This is not a panacea and it's not for everyone," Hemstreet told me. "But people who 'catch the cooperative fire' don't leave. They become deeply committed." Walter Vincent, one the worker-owners at the co-op, aptly summarized the hopefulness felt by many at the firm by stating, "I have dreams, and the hope is that we can grow the plant from 23 employees to 60 or more."[312]

"This is a big part of resilience to me," Hemstreet said. "When people have a job that provides 'enough'—it is not about being wealthy but having enough—and they can go work every day and are able to use their brains and be creative and connect with other people, and also focus on protecting the environment, its all part of resilience. They are better able to weather economic storms, family storms, and any other type of storm including the kind related to climate change."

The efforts of Hemstreet and her co-workers offer a shining example of how the lives of many people, along with the natural environment, can be improved by offering hope through concrete action. The third skill involved with Purposing is to Harvest hope for new possibilities by making choices that increase personal, social, and environmental wellbeing.[313]

Hope is the antidote to despair in the midst of ongoing climate impacts

The knowledge that human-induced rising global temperatures will adversely affect all life on Earth for centuries can leave many people feeling deeply discouraged and helpless. To live principled and fulfilling lives in the midst of rising climate impacts it will be essential to foster a great deal of hope.

Never underestimate the power of hope. It is an essential element of good mental and physical health. Hope is also a powerful motivator generating increased resilience for adversities.[314] This is basic knowledge within the fields of psychology and medicine. Research shows that children, adolescents, and adults who are hopeful about the future are better adjusted psychologically, have better physical health, and are better problem solvers.[315] Harvesting hope will be a key to finding meaning in life, living our values, and thriving in the midst of adversities generated by climate disruption.

There is no better way to harvest hope than establishing concrete alternatives that provide a glimpse of what a meaningful and purposeful life can look and feel like when we take action to assist other people while improving the condition of the natural environment.

What is hope?

Hope is a state of mind grounded in the belief that the future can be better and that we can play a role in bringing that change about. Hope is a psychological resource that inspires us to look to the future by establishing both a destination and the motivation to begin the journey. Hope is a mental frame that helps us navigate life's ups and downs and motivates us to persist even when times get tough.

Hope is not wishful thinking. Believing that you will be immune from the impacts of climate disruption is illusion, not hope. In contrast, hope is the belief that you can find ways to live a meaningful and fulfilling life even in the midst of climate-aggravated adversities. That's not to say a little pessimism isn't helpful at times. Pessimism can allow people to confront reality and see their world and themselves without blinders. But hopeful people don't become mired in pessimism. They use it as information to clarify the obstacles they must overcome to achieve their vision.

Hopefulness also does not indicate that you no longer care about what happened in the past, or have forgotten those who are no longer here. It means that you are deepening your devotion by getting in touch with how your loved ones would have wanted you to live your life after they are gone.[316]

Hope always involves a degree of uncertainty. After all, if things were certain there would be no need for hope. But hopeful people believe that if they persevere they can overcome whatever uncertainties arise.[317]

Hope can be deeply personal, such as the belief that if you do the right things during rehabilitation you can recover from a serious accident. Hope can also be interactive and require the involvement of others, such as when we have confidence that if everyone participates, personal mental health and psycho-social-spiritual wellbeing within your community can improve. The relational aspects of hope make it contagious. If a sufficient number of people feel hopeful, many others will follow, leaving the pessimists with no choice but to join in.

Hannah Baird's story

Hannah is a middle school student from Homer, Alaska. Along with one high school student and two other middle school students, Hannah received recognition for their environmental EcoLogical project. Her journey is described below. It demonstrates how youth can harvest hope for new possibilities through small actions:

"When we started our project … we had no possible notion of what we were actually getting ourselves into. We were simply four young teenage girls truly wanting to alter the way our town was living. We wanted to see change, both in family homes and the general public.

"We got our local middle school lunchroom to switch from using polystyrene trays to reusable plastic trays. We also introduced a 'Tin Bin' to our local landfill, and we held a community-wide 'Trash into Fashion' show.

"Then we won the President's Environmental Youth Award and suddenly we were going to Washington, DC, to accept our award. Before the awards ceremony, we got to talk with Lisa Jackson, the Administrator of EPA. She was authentically interested in what we did, and what we had to say. The award ceremony itself blew my mind. All of the winners stood in front of the White House on risers. President Obama simply walked around the corner. He was sincere, talking to us as one completely normal person might talk to another, as if he had forgotten that he was the President, and was simply a friend. He talked of how great our accomplishments were, and also of how important it was that we didn't stop here, that we kept going, because 'we are the future.' Each and every winner shook his hand, and got to look him in the eye. I wanted to talk, to thank him for his hard work, to chat about the world, and to ask what being the president of the United States is like, but even if I had the chance, I don't know if I would have been able to get the words out. I was in awe."[318]

What creates and renews hope?

Harvesting hope requires taking concrete action to become your own healer. I'm not talking about healing in the traditional way we think of it as recovering from a disease. *Real* healing is about using climate-aggravated adversities of all types to create *better* conditions for other people, the natural environment, and yourself. This requires going beyond the treatment of symptoms to address the root of the problems.

Making choices with awareness is the key to harvesting hope.[319] Life demands that we make continual choices in a variety of circumstances. You harvest the greatest hope in life when you recognize this and accept that much of what you experience is the result of decisions you and other people have made. For instance, your predecessors made decisions that led to climate disruption, and you have undoubtedly made choices that contribute to the problem as well. But if you and others make different choices today regarding the amount and type of material and energy you consume and greenhouse gasses you emit, the climate can eventually be stabilized and over time returned to healthy conditions.

Researchers have found that hope emerges most readily when three closely related factors are present: people have a vision of a place they want to arrive at or condition they want to achieve, a sense of how to get to their destination, and the commitment to work toward that end even when obstacles block their way.[320]

Let me clarify these three keys. Just as Molly Hemstreet and the other members of Opportunity Threads did, hopeful people have:

- A vision of a better place they want to arrive at in the future, along with goals that indicate they are moving in that direction

- An image of how they can attain their vision and goals—a strategy or set of strategies outlining different pathways they can use to move toward their destination

- Confidence in their capacity to solve problems and overcome whatever obstacles arise as they travel the path toward their vision and goals[321]

Let's explore these three core elements of harnessing hope as they relate to responding constructively to the traumas and stresses generated by climate disruption.

I. Create a positive vision of the future and goals to indicate progress

Step 1: Acknowledge your reality

The starting point for fostering hope that you can achieve better conditions even as global temperatures rise is an honest assessment of the current situation. This includes your own internal conditions—how your body, emotions, and thoughts are reacting to the hardships—as well as the external circumstances you face—including the physical, economic, and social conditions that surround you.

- **As a starting point, acknowledge your personal situation.** For example, is your body tense, are you having trouble sleeping, are you experiencing digestive problems, heart palpitations, or other physical symptoms of stress and anxiety? Do you feel anxious, depressed, confused, or in other ways feel overwhelmed? Are you unable to manage your emotions? Are you eating, smoking, or drinking too much, taking drugs, or using some other avoidance mechanisms that could become self-destructive?

- **Review how you are caring for yourself.** Are you taking the time to practice body-based, breath-based, or thought-based skills as we described in Chapter 4 to stabilize your nervous system and observe what's happening within you without judgment, as described in Chapter 4? Are you remembering your personal skills and resources and reaching out and receiving the nurturing and practical help from your social support network, as we discussed in Chapter 5? Are you examining your thought patterns to see if you are engaged in Thinking Distortions as we illustrated in Chapter 6?

- **Accurately describe your external circumstances.** Do any physical threats exist such as ongoing risks posed by a major flood? Does violence in your neighborhood remain a possibility or are you physically safe? Situating yourself in a place that affords as much personal safety as possible will be important to help deactivate and regulate your brain's "Fear and Alarm Center" and reestablish the capacity to think clearly.

- **Finally, look around at your community and region and acknowledge current and likely future conditions.** What traumas and stresses are people in your area already dealing with, and how are they reacting? Is your area likely to experience more extreme weather events, floods, wildfires, drought, or a heat wave in the future? How are your family members and people in the community responding to the acute and chronic impacts associated with rising global temperatures? If the economy is struggling, are conditions likely to significantly change anytime soon? To what degree are local people actively reducing their material consumption and use of fossil fuels and restoring ecological systems that sequester carbon? Is the community preparing to withstand the physical impacts of climate disruption?

Just as understanding the current assumptions and beliefs you hold about the world and yourself helps clarify how climate disruption might effect you, acknowledging where things stand within and around you provides a starting point for harvesting hope.

Step 2: Construct different scenarios[322]

The next step in creating a vision of hope is to use your imagination to see possible negative and positive outcomes of your current situation. This step can be accomplished by answering the following questions:

- **How could the situation be worse?** Envision ways in which your current situation could be worse than it is. For example, if you are drinking too much to deal with your distress, it would be worse if you were also using drugs and putting your physical health at risk. If friends are anxious or depressed, it could be worse if they had PTSD. If few people in your community are reducing their impacts on the climate, it would be even worse if the local utility began to purchase its electrical power from a coal-fired power plant. The key to this step is to identify what could be worse for you than the present situation.

- **How could the situation be better?** Now identify ways in which your situation could be much better than it is. How could it actually lead to new insights, growth, and meaning in life for you and other people? How could it stimulate serious efforts to reduce greenhouse gas emissions and restore the natural environment? For example, if you are drinking too much to deal with your distress, you could use the situation to begin practicing the Presencing skills described in Part 2 of the book. If friends are anxious or depressed, it could be better if they got involved with a group of people doing positive activities. If few people are reducing emissions, it could be better if civic, faith, business, and government leaders came together to urge community members to become vastly more energy efficient and disinvest from fossil fuels. Try to identify as many specific changes as possible that would make the existing situation much better.

- **Make up a story about how the worse version of the situation could actually come true.** Imagine that you are a novelist writing about your own life. For the worse version of the adverse situation to happen, describe what would need to change. Would you need to do something to make things worse? If so, what would that be? Would other people need to alter their behavior or the roles they are playing for the worse situation to come true? If so, in what way would they need to change? Then imagine other people or yourself actually taking the steps that make the situation worse. Can you see how bad things could be?

  After you have completed this story, determine the chances of the worst case coming true. On a scale of 1–10 is it extremely likely—say a 10—somewhat likely—a 5—or not likely at all—say a 1? If you think the worst case is not likely to come true, that's good news. But don't get complacent. Many improbable things happen. If the worst case seems very likely to happen, it means you need to redouble your efforts to make sure the best case happens.

- **Now, describe how the best version of the situation could come true.** Again, use your creativity and write a second story about what would need to change to bring about the better version of your situation. Would you or others need to adopt new ways of thinking or new behaviors to bring about the best case? If so, what would the changes entail? Do the roles you play, the tasks you are involved with, or the way you perceive things need to change? If so, how? Imagine actually making these changes to grasp how the better conditions can come about.

  As before, after you have completed this story, estimate how likely it is to come true. If you think the positive changes are not likely to happen—a 1–2 on a scale of 1–10—you need to think of ways to alter the situation so that they do. If the positive changes seem very likely to happen—such as a 9–10 on a scale of 1–10—that's good, but again don't get complacent. It is easy for things that seem obviously beneficial to never come to pass.

- **Add anything more you can do to bring about the better version of the situation and prevent the worse from happening.** Take a moment now to look at the stories you developed and identify anything that is missing. Are there other ways you have not thought about to bring about the positive and minimize the possibility that the negative situation will occur? Do you need different types of information, to engage with different people, to take a tougher stance, or in other ways to expand your thinking about how you can make the best case come true? This question offers the opportunity to reconsider each of the possibilities one more time.

Step 3: Create a future vision of hope

The scenarios you just crafted provide a platform from which a hopeful vision of the future can be developed. Do you have a vision of your hope for the future? What do you want to do in the near, mid, and long term to increase your wellbeing beyond current levels? Do you have a vision of how you can help increase the wellbeing of other people and the natural environment? Do you have a sense of what success would look and feel like? How will you know when you have achieved those ends?

You might not have answers to these questions right now. But hope depends on visualizing what you want the future to look like. Two steps can help you establish that vision:

- **Engage in magical thinking.**[323] Often the struggles we experience in life become so pressing that we become unable to see opportunities. When this is the case magical thinking can help. This exercise allows you to rise above your current situation and identify new possibilities. To foster magical thinking answer this "miracle question:"

  "Imagine that when you go to bed tonight, a miracle occurs. You suddenly have the capacity to gain new insights, grow, and increase your wellbeing above your existing levels even as you deal with many types of adversity, including those generated by climate disruption. You also have developed the capacity to increase the wellbeing of other people and the condition of the natural environment above current levels. When you awake tomorrow, how would your life be different? What would you begin to do on a daily basis? What would be different in one year? What would be different in three years?"

  Write your answer here:

  _____

  _____

The "miracle question" can promote personal optimism and self-transcendence or what I termed a shift "From Me to We."[324] As described throughout the book, these terms describe the ability of humans to transform their mental model from one that focuses only on satisfying their own needs, to one that sees caring for others and the natural environment as essential elements of self-care.

Self-transcendence also helps you see your role as the agent of change in the process. When you shift your focus to helping others or restoring the natural environment, existing problems often fade into the background or become easier to resolve.

If you are unsure about how to answer this question you might try a train-of-thought exercise. Have a friend ask you the "miracle question." You respond by talking for three minutes without stopping, stating whatever emerges from your mind. If you hit a blank spot where nothing comes to mind, repeat something you have already said and see if that elicits new ideas. The important point is to keep talking for the entire three minutes. This process often brings forth some very interesting ideas.

In addition, you can ask members of your social support network if they have any suggestions on how you could answer the question, or you could search the web for ideas based on what other people are doing.

- **Write a vision statement.** Turn your answers to the "miracle question" into a short vision statement. The advantage of writing a vision statement is that it helps you see yourself in a situation that has not yet occurred. Here is an example of a vision statement written by Mary, a high-tech manager, during a Transformational Resilience workshop:

  "My personal vision is that I will practice calming skills on a daily basis so that I remain calm in any stressful situation. I will use every adversity as a chance to learn more about how I become defensive and withdrawn in stressful situations. I will also practice self-compassion and use the experience to learn how I can help other people in need. I will also reduce my impacts on the climate by making my home carbon neutral and planting trees in our yard and in town to sequester carbon."[325]

Step 4: Set goals

After formulating your vision statement, the next step in building a pathway toward hopefulness is to establish solid short- and long-term goals. The goals should address big, important issues such as finding peace in your life, helping your community prepare for traumas and toxic stresses aggravated by climate disruption, or redesigning your lifestyle to be environmentally restorative. They should also address routine everyday goals such as setting up a daily schedule to practice Tracking your physical sensations, or getting the recycling out on time.

To establish near- and long-term goals answer these questions:

- What do you want to do within the next 30 days and within one year to increase your personal psychological health and wellbeing knowing that climate-enhanced impacts will continue to grow? Write your answer here:

_____

_____

- What do you want to do to within the next 30 days and within one year to increase the health and wellbeing of your family, friends, neighbors, and others knowing that climate-enhanced hardships will continue to grow? Write your answer here:

_____

_____

- What do you want to do within the next 30 days and within one year to increase the health of the natural environment and reduce the risks of runaway climate change? Write your answers here:

_____

_____

The 1 Million Women Initiative story

Two women in Australia were chatting over a cup of tea about the way they live and spend their money, and asked, "What if the choices we make everyday could help the planet and future generations?" They found out that in their nation, women determine about 85% of household purchases. They realized that if a million women all make one better choice, however small, it would lead to significant change. This was the start of the 1 Million Women Initiative.

The organization seeks to get a million women to pledge to take small steps in their daily lives that save energy, reduce waste, cut pollution and lead change. "I believe a million women will tell a million more and lead a million communities," said Natalie Isaacs, 1 Million Women Founder.

Since its creation in 2009, the organization has become the largest women's environmental organization in Australia, with almost 140,000 members as of 2014, who have committed to cut almost 150,000 tonnes of carbon pollution. The organization has identified over 50 different ways for members to cut carbon pollution. When they reach their ultimate target of a million women as members and over a million tonnes of CO_2 pollution saved, this will be equivalent to taking 240,000 cars off the road for a year.

In 2011, 1 Million Women launched its SAVE program, which sought to help its members conserve energy, cut waste and pollution while saving money at the same time. The program revolved around a series of monthly themes— Food, Drive, Power, Wear, Shop, Build and Invest. SAVE summit events in metropolitan and regional cities attracted more than 1,500 participants. SAVE included a practical guide to shrink household bills by $1,000 a year simply by cutting waste.

The organization has also launched a 100,000 Girls Project that seeks to get 100,000 girls under 18 years old to be leaders of change in their generation.

1 Million Women is an inspiring example of how to harvest hope for new possibilities by making choices that help other people and improve the condition of the natural environment and climate through.[326]

II. Describe pathways or strategies to achieve your vision and goals

The word "strategy" comes from the Greek word "generalship." It means to provide overall direction for a project or initiative. Strategy helps you determine how you will realize your vision and goals. It also helps to determine when and how to apply tactics, which are the specific actions you will take to implement your strategy.

A good strategy is always consistent with the vision of what you want to achieve as well as your top personal values. You will often need a variety of different strategies to deal with different challenges. For example, you might use one strategy to provide emotional support for people, and a different strategy to overcome financial constraints. Here are suggestions for developing your strategies.

Step 1: Identify likely challenges as well as your unique capabilities

Look at the information and ideas generated in the previous step and make a list of the different issues, needs, and challenges you will likely face as you strive to achieve your vision and goals. For example, there might be personal challenges such as your ability to stay focused or lack of knowledge and skills, social challenges such as resistance from others or fears about change, and external physical challenges such as lack of financial resources. You will need pathways or strategies that can address all of the issues you identify.

At the same time, look back at the Circles of Support you developed in Chapter 4 and identify the unique strengths, skills, and resources you have and determine how you can use them to your advantage to address the challenges. Your unique capabilities can help you identify which strategies are likely to be the right ones for you.

Step 2: Brainstorm strategy options

Use the information and ideas generated in the previous step to brainstorm as many pathways as you can think of to move toward your vision and goals. Brainstorming means to describe as many possibilities as you can without judging their feasibility or thinking about all of the obstacles that might make block their implementation.

Step 3: Evaluate strategic options

Now that you have identified a wide range of possible strategies, go through them one by one and evaluate their potential to help you address the issues and challenges you identified and achieve your vision and goals. Don't make final judgments until you have assessed all of the options. Evaluate each of them based on their potential to deal with real world contextual factors, and your personal capacity to implement them.

Step 4: Choose the best strategies

After you have completed your assessment, choose the pathways that seem to hold the most potential. Check to make sure the strategies you choose are consistent with your vision and values. It is easy to forget these critical elements when you start your journey toward harvesting hope. But they are essential to keep you moving in a direction that is right for you.

Adeline Tiffanie Suwana's story

This story was found on Earth911. It was published in 2009 and is a very poignant example of how to harvest hope for new possibilities:

"Twelve-year-old Indonesian student Adeline Tiffanie Suwana had great care and concern for the environment after seeing the effects of natural disasters and flooding on her country. She learned about the importance of mangroves in preventing damage during natural disasters and decided to do something to improve mangrove conditions.

She began by forming a community of young people called Sahabat Alam, which means "Friends of Nature." The community is now comprised of 1,700 members throughout Indonesia. Adeline organizes students to plant coral reefs, help with fish breeding and turtle protection, plant mangrove trees, and engage in environmental clean-ups and education activities.

Adeline and Sahabat Alam also operate the Electric Generator Water Reel project where they connect remote villages to an electric grid, providing potential economic growth to villagers and improving health and education facilities. They utilize clean renewable energy (hydro) to power these villages. Her ideas have been presented in schools, with the cooperation of governmental agencies and have led to the production of a television program on the subject.

For her efforts, Adeline was invited by the United Nations Environment Programme as a delegate to the 2009 Tunza International Children's Conference and awarded the 2009 Action for Nature International Young Eco-Hero award."[327]

III. Practice hope by making a commitment to persevere despite the obstacles

Implementing your strategies to achieve your vision and goals can often seem like a daunting challenge. It will require time, energy, and persistence. You are certain to bump into many obstacles and find numerous reasons to stop. To practice hope and perseverance you will need continual inspiration. Here are some suggestions:

- **Take small steps.** You can't achieve your vision and goals overnight. To harvest hope you need start small by taking one or two tiny steps in the areas where success is likely, review the results, and reflect on what you have learned and achieved. By having some early small successes your confidence will grow. A series of small successes is likely to change your self-talk from a pessimistic or uncertain tone to a positive "I can do this" attitude.

- **Develop problem-solving skills and contingency.** Some of the obstacles you face as you move down your pathway will be external. Many others will likely be self-imposed. It will be helpful to have a sense of what the barriers might be, and a toolbox of problem-solving skills you can use to surmount them. Here are some suggestions:

  - **Identify and keep track of self-limiting beliefs.** Often it is your own thoughts and emotions that are the greatest barriers to hope and change. Beware of what triggers a sense within you of inadequacy, resentment, perfectionism, greed, boredom, insecurity, shame, and other feelings of not being good enough. Also, pay attention to feelings of helplessness, compassion fatigue, burnout and other emotions sparked by secondary trauma. When these personal stories present themselves, your capacity to persevere will be challenged. Try to notice when these narratives are present without judgment and give them a name ("There is my insecurity again"). As with other issues discussed throughout the book, noticing and naming self-limiting beliefs and emotions often diminishes the power they hold over you and allows your brain's "Executive Center" to kick in and make wise and skillful decisions.

  - **Identify and enhance skills that may be lacking.** Sometimes we lose hope because we don't know how to resolve conflicts with other people, we communicate poorly, are not assertive enough, or conversely are too demanding. Take an honest look at yourself and determine if any of these obstacles are sometimes present. If they are, consider reading books, taking classes, or in other ways learning how to resolve conflicts peacefully, communicate openly and fairly, be assertive and ask for what you want without imposing your will or making people feel attacked or inadequate.

  - **Develop options to deal with external challenges.** You have already brainstormed a list of likely challenges you will face as you strive to achieve your vision. This list can be helpful because it gives you a sense of what might lie ahead. You can also look for ways to increase your knowledge and develop skills that increase your capacity to respond to the challenges. At the same time, surprises should be expected. One type of surprise that you can plan for is a traumatic storm or other event that requires you to take care of yourself and your family for quite some time without external assistance. Many people believe that government agencies will respond to their needs following a major climate disaster. Hurricane Katrina and many other recent major events, however, show that this assumption is false. With mass urbanization, reduced tax revenues, and diminished public resources, the capacity of governments to respond to crisis is greatly diminished. The more you, your family, and social support network prepare to take care of yourselves for extended periods of time—while also continuing to move toward your vision and goals—the better off you will be.

Developing a list of the likely obstacles you might face on the path toward your vision is a vital step in preparing to deal with them. Then, taking steps such as growing your own food and developing connections with neighbors or local farmers who produce food, securing a 72-hour emergency kit, having enough extra water on hand to cover your needs for a number of weeks, and other steps can help you prepare for emergencies. It can also be helpful to identify which organizations in your community provide different types of goods and services such as emergency healthcare, fuel, food, tools, or other important supplies.

- **Continually note signs of success.** Harvesting hope becomes easier, and you can more easily keep yourself motivated, when you see visible signs of success. Keeping a daily journal is one way to do this. Just as I suggested with practicing gratitude, it can be very inspiring to take a few moments at the end of each day to make a note to yourself when you used an adversity as a catalyst to make a choice that enhanced your own wellbeing, the welfare or others or the natural environment. You can also note successes in the Purposing Action Plan found at the end of this chapter.

- **Look for inspiring stories of learning, growth, and thriving.** A helpful way to practice hope is to continually read books and articles about people who have overcome significant adversities and emerged better off. You can also watch movies, attend talks, and in other ways help yourself stay hopeful about the future by immersing yourself in inspiring stories of people that overcame adversity.

- **Stay connected with family, friends, and others that support you.**
As discussed in Chapter 5 and continually mentioned throughout the book, staying connected to people who love or support
you improves your mental and physical wellbeing, and helps you
successfully navigate your way through hardships. To deal with
climate-enhanced adversities in constructive ways you might have
to reconfigure your support network and find people who will help
and encourage you to persevere. If that is not possible, consider
organizing or joining support groups where you can meet and
talk with people engaged in similar efforts to deal with climate-
enhanced adversity.

Muhammad Yunus's story

One of my favorite examples of how to harvest hope for new possibilities is
the story of Bangladeshi economist Muhammad Yunus, who pioneered the
idea of using tiny loans to lift millions of people out of extreme poverty. I had
the opportunity to attend a Social Business conference organized by his group
where I heard Yunus tell the story of his "eureka moment" that led to the
beginning of the microcredit financing movement.[328]

He was a young economics professor when he met a shy young woman with
calloused fingers weaving bamboo and asked her how much she earned. She
told him that she borrowed about five taka (nine cents in U.S. dollars) from
a middleman for the bamboo for each stool, and paid all but two cents back
to the lender. He realized that the weaver had become a slave to the lender
for all of five takas. This triggered a powerful emotional reaction that led him
to loan her and other members of her village about $27 to buy their own
materials and eliminate the money lender. He told them to repay him when
they could. Slowly but surely they paid him back over a year, while also using
the money to greatly improve their economic condition. From this experience
Yunus grasped that a small step—a tiny loan—could generate hope and
improve the lives of many people.

This awareness led Yunus to found Grameen Bank in 1993. Through careful
planning and a great deal of experimentation, failures, and recoveries the bank
continued to grow. It has now loaned billions of dollars to more than 8 million
borrowers, 97% of whom are women. Grameen Bank's success inspired the
growth of the microcredit financing movement that has now spread throughout
the world. For this work, in 2006 Yunus and the bank won a Nobel Peace Prize.

You might not be able to launch a bank like Grameen. But as Yunus's story illustrates, a tiny action can sometimes lead to big changes that benefit many people. Taking small steps to help others, as Yunus did, will be one of the most important things you can take to find meaning, direction, and hope in your life—and help other people find hope as well—as the planet heats up and the physical impacts of climate disruption intensify.

Put it all together by developing your own "Purposing Action Plan"

It is now time to use the information you developed in this section to create your own "Purposing Action Plan." The plan can help you remain clear about how you will find meaning, direction, and hope in the midst of climate-aggravated impacts by enhancing personal, social, and environmental wellbeing.

To develop your Purposing Action Plan found on the next page (Fig. 9.1), begin by listing your vision of the future as well as your top 3–5 values. Then, describe the goals you have adopted for increasing your personal wellbeing, the wellbeing of other people, and the condition of the natural environment. In each of these sections describe the immediate and longer-term actions you will take to achieve your goals, along with barriers you will likely face, strategies for overcoming them, and the date when you will begin.

You might need to revise and tweak your plan a number of times before it feels complete. Take your time and carefully think through how you will find meaning, direction and hope in the midst of ongoing climate impacts.

Just as you did with your "Presencing Action Plan," make a copy of your Purposing Action Plan and keep it in a visible place at home and where you work. Check it regularly to see how you are progressing. In addition, consider updating it every few months. You will learn a great deal as you complete each step. The new knowledge can provide valuable information to help you improve and expand your action plan.

FIGURE 9.1   My Purposing Action Plan

My vision:			
My values:			
Goals for increasing my *personal* wellbeing: 1. 2. 3.			
Immediate actions (within one month) I will take: 1. 2. 3.	**Barriers I will face:** 1. 2. 3.	**Strategies for overcoming barriers:** 1. 2. 3.	**Start date:** 1. 2. 3.
Immediate actions (within one year) I will take: 1. 2. 3.	**Barriers I will face:** 1. 2. 3.	**Strategies for overcoming barriers:** 1. 2. 3.	**Start date:** 1. 2. 3.
Goals for increasing the wellbeing of *other people*: 1. 2. 3.			
Immediate actions (within one month) I will take: 1. 2. 3.	**Barriers I will face:** 1. 2. 3.	**Strategies for overcoming barriers:** 1. 2. 3.	**Start date:** 1. 2. 3.
Immediate actions (within one year) I will take: 1. 2. 3.	**Barriers I will face:** 1. 2. 3.	**Strategies for overcoming barriers:** 1. 2. 3.	**Start date:** 1. 2. 3.
Goals for increasing the condition of *the natural environment and climate*: 1. 2. 3.			
Immediate actions (within one month) I will take: 1. 2. 3.	**Barriers I will face:** 1. 2. 3.	**Strategies for overcoming barriers:** 1. 2. 3.	**Start date:** 1. 2. 3.
Immediate actions (within one year) I will take: 1. 2. 3.	**Barriers I will face:** 1. 2. 3.	**Strategies for overcoming barriers:** 1. 2. 3.	**Start date:** 1. 2. 3.

People everywhere would benefit by developing a "Purposing Action Plan"

If you find it beneficial to create a Purposing Action Plan to help you find meaning, direction, and hope in the midst of adversities associated with climate disruption, imagine the benefits if millions of people around the world develop such a plan. Multitudes of people would likely adopt a new mission and purpose in life focused on caring for others while restoring the natural environment and reducing the climate crisis to manageable levels.

If almost everyone developed this type of action plan, it seems likely that many personally and socially harmful reactions to the adversities generated by climate disruption can be avoided, when maladies occur they could be more easily resolved, and untold numbers of people will be able to use the adversities of climate disruption as catalysts to gain new insight, grow, and thrive.

Part 4:
Building Transformational Resilience
in organizations and communities

When individuals and groups have sufficient knowledge and can use simple effective Presencing and Purposing skills, most have the potential to move in a growth-oriented direction following a traumatic or overwhelming stressful experience. However, the process can be enhanced—or thwarted—by the groups with which individuals engage. That's because humans are social creatures. We cannot survive without other people. Personal, organizational, and community wellbeing and resilience are therefore interrelated. Each influences and is influenced by the others. To foster widespread levels of Transformational Resilience within individuals, the need, methods, and benefits of doing so must become prominent within organizations and communities as well. Building a sound understanding of how to foster this capacity must become a top priority of organizations and communities worldwide.

Through their rituals, cultural myths, and associated social narratives every group—whether it is a civic, faith, not-for-profit, private business, or government organization—develops and transmits ideas, values, and practices describing the proper way to deal with adversity. These beliefs and practices are usually passed down over time and often exist as tacit understandings rather than explicit agreements. The basic assumptions and beliefs each of us hold about the world and ourselves are therefore significantly influenced by and typically incorporate some or all of the traditions, values, cultural myths, and social narratives of the groups we have been or are currently involved with.

In this section I highlight some of the key issues that must be addressed, as well as methods for, building the capacity for Transformational Resilience within two of the most influential group settings: organizations and communities.

Before you begin this part of the book it is important to know that few organizations or communities have made the transition to trauma-informed human resilience-enhancing entities for any purpose, let alone the need to respond effectively to the adversities generated by climate disruption. In fact, most have not even considered the issue.

As you will soon learn, a few private-sector firms have begun to teach their employees Presencing skills. However, their goal is not to prepare for the traumas of climate disruption. They are almost exclusively focused on increasing the productivity of workers by offering ways to help them deal with stress. In addition, a growing number of firms understand that climate disruption poses significant risks to their operations and financial welfare. However, few have done anything to prepare for climate impacts, and none of the companies that have begun to prepare have focused on building the capacity of their employees, clients, or stakeholders to deal with the adverse personal mental health or psycho-social-spiritual impacts of climate disruption.

The same is true for non-profit and public organizations. Few, if any, understand the risks posed by climate disruption or have acted to increase the capacity of their employees, clients, or stakeholders for Transformational Resilience.

Similarly, a growing number of coastal communities understand the threats posed by rising sea levels and more frequent and extreme weather events. In some communities, pumps have been installed and sea walls have been built or expanded to prevent swelling sea levels and larger storm surges from damaging buildings and infrastructure. However, little has been done to prepare the humans that live behind those revetments to deal with the acute traumas and chronic toxic stresses that are likely if those structures fail to do the job as planned.

In a few communities experiencing extended drought, more dams and holding ponds are being constructed to store water, and efforts are occasionally being made to increase water use efficiency or shift to more drought, heat, and disease resistant crops. However, little has been done to address the personal mental health issues such as debilitating anxiety, depression, and suicides, or the psycho-social-spiritual maladies including rising crime, violence, and intergroup conflict that are likely if and when water resources are depleted and food production as well as economic well-being are diminished.

In short, most organizations and communities have focused on preparing external physical factors for climate impacts and failed to grasp the urgency of building the capacity of people to calm their emotions and thoughts and use the adversities generated by climate disruption to learn, grow, and find new sources of meaning, direction, and hope in life.

Even though few examples exist of organizations or communities that have explicitly chosen to build the capacity of their members for Transformational Resilience, some are responding to the consequences of adverse childhood experiences (ACEs), and a select number are preparing for the external physical impacts produced by rising temperatures. In the next two chapters I will describe some of these efforts. I will then give examples of how some groups have implemented Presencing and Purposing to address non-climate-related adversities. I will close by explaining how organizations and communities can expand their efforts and make a transition to trauma-informed human resilience-enhancing entities to address climate-enhanced adversities. In the last chapter I will offer some policy recommendations and other final thoughts on how society can build the capacity of humans to respond constructively to the adversities generated by climate disruption.

10
Building Transformational Resilience in organizations

She had just recently been hired as superintendent of the school district, so Jenny Jones wanted to be on-site when the new school year began to get to know the system. But as Jones visited different schools on orientation day she became concerned as she noticed that many people failed to effectively manage their emotions and act appropriately.[329]

The most obvious sign of trouble appeared when she walked into the high-school administration office and found the office secretary standing in front of a group of freshman girls shaking her finger and telling them there will be no violations of the school dress code. The girls were clearly frightened and confused. Orientation day was intended, in part, to set the tone and help students get comfortable in their new setting. This behavior was obviously not what Jones hoped to see. Even worse, however, was the fact that sitting near the girls was the Athletic Department secretary who was scantily dressed. The administration office secretary never saw the incongruity in her behavior, nor did she seem concerned about its impacts on the girls.

As she looked more deeply over the next few months, Jenny saw that administrators and teachers operated in a crisis mode. One knee-jerk policy after another was adopted to deal with the next emergency. Teachers and staff often lashed out at others in public. Communications were poor, important issues went unaddressed, and problems remained unresolved. Teachers adopted a self-protective attitude and few tried to coordinate their efforts with other instructors.

Jones realized that these were the root causes of the overall poor performance that had plagued the district for years, including the 40% student drop-out rate. Although she did not use these terms, she understood that people lacked good Presencing and Purposing skills, and that the school district was consequently trauma-organized.

Organizational trauma is pervasive

The capacity for Transformational Resilience begins with the aptitude of the individual. However, the ability of any single person to use adversities such as those generated by climate disruption as catalysts to learn, grow, and increase their wellbeing above previous levels is heavily influenced by their surroundings, and their social settings in particular.[330] Among the most important social settings are the organizations people are employed by, are served by, or engage with. By the same token, the attitude and abilities of those individuals also influences the organization's capacity for resilience. Thus, Transformational Resilience is a transactional issue arising through the interplay of internal individual and group, and external social and environmental factors.

This again underscores the need to build the capacity for Transformational Resilience early on *before* major adversities arise. In the midst of hardships, members with good knowledge and skills can move their organizations in the right direction. For instance, if some of the teachers and staff in Jenny Jones's school district had good Presencing and Purposing skills, many of the problems she identified might have been avoided. In addition, when an organization as a whole prioritizes enhancing the capacity of its employees for Transformational Resilience, distressed members can get help to constructively navigate difficult times without harming the larger group. However, when a significant number of members lack these skills, the organization they are part of is at great risk of becoming trauma-organized.

Unfortunately, few organizations understand the grave risks posed by any type of significant trauma and persistent toxic stress, let along those generated by climate disruption. Nor do many take concrete steps to structure themselves as human resilience-enhancing entities. As a result, numerous private businesses, not-for-profit organizations, and government agencies today are dysregulated. Rather than enhancing the wellbeing of their employees, stakeholders, and the communities in which they operate, they diminish it and often harm the natural environment and climate as well.

There is nothing new here. Over 15 years ago the World Health Organization described "workplace stress" as a "worldwide epidemic." In 2014, workplace stress was responsible for an estimated $190 billion in U.S. healthcare costs alone. When poor performance and absenteeism are added, the impact of an unhealthy workplace is estimated to cost U.S. companies $300 billion annually.[331]

This is not just a U.S. problem. One study completed in 2012 assessed the resilience of 32,000 full-time employees in large and mid-sized organizations covering a range of industries in 29 different sectors around the world. It found that only 35% of employees were deeply engaged in achieving their organization's purpose and 38% felt significant stress and anxiety about the future. In addition, less than half said that senior executives were sincerely interested in their wellbeing. This suggests that 50–65% of employees were either notably stressed, felt uncared for by organizational leaders, or were not psychologically engaged.[332]

The authors of the study concluded that these conditions not only undermined the mental and physical health of the individuals, they strained workplace relationships, caused high turnover, increased healthcare costs, and reduced problem-solving, innovation, and productivity among employees.[333] This again underscores that for many organizations "bouncing back" after a crisis to pre-trauma levels is not very desirable. Organizations benefit most when they use adversity to substantially increase their functioning, and that of their clients and stakeholders, above previous levels.

In contrast, the study found that resilient employees had lower healthcare costs, reduced turnover, more optimism and creative abilities, and greater productivity.[334]

Few organizations are preparing for climate impacts and even less are addressing the personal mental health and psycho-social-spiritual consequences

Not only do most organizations fail to grasp the downsides of workplace stress and adversity, few are building the capacity of their employees or stakeholders to respond constructively to the harmful personal mental health and psycho-social-spiritual impacts of climate disruption.

A 2010 survey commissioned by the consulting firm Ernst & Young interviewed 300 executives from companies in 16 countries and 18 industry sectors with revenues of more than US$1 billion annually.[335] It found that investing in energy efficiency, developing new products and services, and improving transparency in corporate reporting topped the list of the actions they plan to undertake to respond to climate disruption. No executive mentioned building the capacity of their employees to deal with the traumas and stresses posed by climate disruption.

In 2012, the Carbon Disclosure Project (CDP) was commissioned by the U.K. Department for Environment, Food and Rural Affairs (Defra) to gather evidence of climate-resilience-building efforts among 89 U.K. companies that provide data to the CDP. The assessment found that 80% of the firms acknowledged that climate change poses physical risks to their business. Of these organizations, 37% identified these risks as posing real and present danger. Less than half, however, had incorporated climate adaptation into their business strategies. Among those that did, the main focus was on protecting assets, logistics, and their financial condition.[336] No firm mentioned building the psychological or emotional resilience of their employees or stakeholders.

At the international level, a survey of S&P Global 100 companies by the Center for Climate and Energy Solutions found that only 28% said they had done climate risk assessments, and an even smaller number—18%—said they use climate-specific tools or models to assess their risks.[337] None mentioned assessing the possible impacts on personal mental health or psychosocial-spiritual wellbeing.

Fast-forward to a 2015 report released by the Carbon Trust that found that 76% of the executives they surveyed said they perceived bottom line risks from direct impacts of climate change. Some 50% believed they would have to fundamentally change their products, services, or business models. However, few were making any substantial changes, and no executive mentioned efforts to prepare their employees for the traumas and toxic stresses posed by climate disruption.[338]

Small and mid-sized businesses are even less prepared than large corporations for the physical, psychological, and social impacts of climate disruption. According to the Institute for Business and Home Safety, a quarter of small to mid-sized businesses in the U.S. fail to reopen following a major disaster.[339] Yet the majority of small businesses have not analyzed the potential economic losses from extreme weather events or other climate-related risks.[340] In fact, 57% of small businesses have no disaster recovery plan whatsoever.[341] I found no evidence that any of the plans that do exist address the need to build the capacity of their employees or stakeholders to deal with climate impacts.

The lack of attention to preparing for the consequences of climate disruption is not limited to private firms. It can be seen in public agencies as well, although some are further along than the private sector. For instance, a 2015 report to Congress by the U.S. Congressional Research Service found that, "Almost 40 federal departments and agencies had, to varying degrees, produced climate change adaptation plans, climate change vulnerability assessments, adaptation milestones, and/or metrics to evaluate adaptation performance." However, "CRS identified few on-the-ground adaptations and few evaluations, as yet, of the effectiveness and efficiency of alternative adaptation approaches and actions."[342] Even among the few departments and agencies that were implementing climate adaptation plans, no evidence was found of efforts to enhance the capacity of employees or the people they serve to psychologically or emotionally deal with the adversities generated by climate impacts. I will return to this issue later in the chapter when I examine the Climate Adaptation Plan developed by the U.S. Department of Veterans Affairs.

The situation is similar in the U.K. where the responsibility for preparing and adapting to climate disruption is split between the national governments in Northern Ireland, Wales, Scotland, and England. Although priorities, metrics, and reporting requirements have been established, no evidence exists of efforts to prepare government employees or the people they serve for the personal mental health or psycho-social-spiritual impacts of climate disruption.[343]

Although a number of not-for-profit organizations in the U.S., EU, and worldwide are engaged in climate preparedness and adaptation, their focus is almost exclusively on assisting other organizations to assess vulnerabilities, harden physical infrastructure, strengthen economies, adapt natural resources, or address physical health issues. Other than my organization, I was unable to find any not-for-profits in the climate field focused on building human capacity for Transformational Resilience. Further, other than a few public health organizations, I found almost no not-for-profits in the education, social services, mental health, or related fields that are actively adapting to climate disruption, and none that had focused on building the capacity of their employees, clients, customers, or stakeholders to constructively deal with the acute traumas and toxic stresses generated by climate disruption.

Organizations must prioritize building Transformational Resilience for climate disruption

The lack of action to prepare their members for climate impacts is frightening because organizations of all types are certain to experience significant traumatic events and persistent toxic stresses as global temperatures rise. Sometimes this will occur as a result of physical damage from extreme weather events or other types of disruption due to climate impacts. Other times, the chronic toxic stresses generated by climate disruption will expose and magnify previously unacknowledged or dormant problems related to lack of trust, safety, an inability to learn, or other issues. In both cases, the impacts will diminish the personal mental health and psycho-social-spiritual wellbeing of their members, stakeholders, and the community in which they are embedded. As I have noted, dysregulated individuals and groups are likely, in turn, to give little attention to their impacts on other people or the natural environment and climate. This will impede efforts to slash greenhouse gas emissions and reduce the climate crisis to manageable levels.

Organizations react to threats just like individuals

As discussed in Chapter 2, organizations are social systems. They are composed of individuals interacting with their physical, social, economic, and political environments. When a number of members of an organization, and especially the leaders, directly experience or believe themselves to be under severe or persistent threats, the system as a whole can become dysregulated. If this persists, the group can become trauma-organized. This means it adopts sometimes explicit but oftentimes unspoken practices and policies intended to protect it from the threats. Rather than diminishing the fears, all too often these actions increase the distress felt by many people.

Despite these problems, after more than two decades of assisting organizations to design and implement change strategies, I have concluded that they can increase their capacity for Transformational Resilience, just as individuals can. Organizations can adopt mechanisms that buffer their members, clients, and stakeholders from trauma and stress. Organizations can also build the capacity of the people associated with it to use adversities as catalysts to increase their wellbeing well above previous levels—and increase the wellbeing of the organization. In short, they can become what

I call thriving, resilience-enhancing, "Safe Havens" for both members and stakeholders.[344]

Just like individuals, achieving these ends requires organizations to re-author the stories they tell about why they exist, what they seek to achieve, and how they will accomplish their goals. To learn, grow, and thrive in the midst of rising climate-enhanced adversities, the majority of organizations will need to adopt new social narratives—new stories—focused on the needs and benefits of increasing the mental health and psycho-social-spiritual wellbeing of everyone involved, as well as the condition of the natural environment that makes their entire operation possible. Put another way, they will need to restructure themselves to ensure that they enhance all forms of life, not just the economic condition of the organization.

Recap of common traits seen in organizations that are trauma-organized

Although the specifics differ based on the history, size, location, and sector in which the organization operates, trauma-organized organizations typically exhibit a number of similar characteristics. These were described in Chapter 2 and a brief summary is provided here. Organizations that are trauma-organized:

- **Are confused about their purpose, vision of success, and guiding values.** Organizations that are trauma-organized have usually lost sight of why they exist, what they seek to achieve, and the ethical principles they will use to guide their activities. Real or perceived adversities consequently can easily knock them off course and produce a crisis management atmosphere.

- **Lack good emotional regulation.** Members and stakeholders lack knowledge about how trauma and stress affect their bodies and minds along with skills to regulate their emotions. People thus do not know how, or do not take steps to deactivate their "Fear and Alarm Centers" and frequently say or do things that frighten, insult, embarrass, inflame, or harm others.

- **Lack agreement about shared norms and practices.** No organization can enhance the resilience of its members unless it is undergirded by certain behaviors and practices that are seen as acceptable by the majority. This is not about surface trivialities such as manners. It addresses fundamental issues such as whether it is acceptable to violate the rights of people within or outside the organization, or engage in activities that harm the climate. Organizations that are trauma-organized lack this type of agreement.

- **Include siloed and fragmented units and functions.** Because they lack clarity over their purpose, vision, values, and acceptable behaviors, individuals and sub-groups frequently operate as separate entities and pursue their own agendas, leading to gaps, overlaps, contradictions, conflicts, and overall poor performance.

- **Have rigid and often punitive rules and regulations.** Continual chaos and confusion, and personal conflicts often cause the organization to enact excessive, rigid, and sometimes punitive rules and regulations to keep people in line, which rarely resolves problems and instead causes more fear and anxiety among members.

- **Experience constant groupthink, quick-fix thinking, and the inability to learn.** When tensions are high and people feel overwhelmed, they frequently seek simple quick fixes to make problems rapidly disappear. People are discouraged from sharing ideas or information that challenges what appears to be the consensus, and are often punished when they fail to conform. Mistakes cannot be seen or corrected and the entity becomes learning impaired.

- **Fail to acknowledge or correct injustices.** Groupthink and the inability to identify or resolve problems often prevent trauma-organized organizations from acknowledging or correcting inequities, interpersonal or collective injustices, and abuses of power and authority.

- **Display an inability to grieve losses leading to reenactment.** When serious mistakes occur, valued employees leave, or someone is physically injured or dies, it is essential to mourn the loss. Yet trauma-organized organizations don't know how or don't take the time to grieve. Unexpressed emotions build up and spill out in ways that cause people to repeat the same problem behaviors over and over again.

- **Are susceptible to authoritarian leadership and decision-making.** Constant crisis and chaos cause some leaders to exert their authority in order to get people marching in the same direction or consolidate their status and power. A few people become willing to follow anyone that promises quick, easy fixes. As authoritarianism grows, certain people get left out of decision-making, triggering resistance that often sparks even stronger authoritarian reactions.

- **Lack interpersonal trust, empathy, compassion, and social support.** When people exhibit poor emotional management, are frightened about sharing contrasting views, or are left out of decision-making, trust, compassion for, and feelings of mutual support are diminished. Social trust and support are important buffers against trauma and stress, and when they are absent, people are at much greater risk of exhibiting self or socially harmful reactions.

- **Experience widespread fears over personal safety.** These factors combine to leave many people associated with the organization feeling frightened for their personal safety. Sometimes the fears relate to physical safety. More often than not, however, they relate to concerns about psychological and emotional safety.

To this list, add the failure to recognize or reduce environmental impacts

It is important to recognize that in addition to the traits described here, organizations that are trauma-organized typically fail to acknowledge or reduce their impacts on the natural environment and climate. One reason for this is that the attention of group members is usually directed exclusively toward meeting internally focused needs and goals. Individual members of the organization also adopt a defensive self-protective perspective that blocks their ability to learn. The result is that people have little focus on, or concern about, how their activities affect the external environment. Rather than enhancing life, the organization often ends up degrading it.

As climate disruption worsens, the organization's negative impacts on the Earth's ecological systems and climate will eventually circle back and generate more trauma and stress for everyone in the group—and even threaten its very existence. For these reasons I include lack of concern for impacts on the natural environment and climate as a central characteristic of organizations that are trauma-organized (see Fig. 10.1).

FIGURE 10.1   Common traits of trauma-organized organizations

Source: Adapted from Bloom, S. (2013). *Destroying Sanctuary & Restoring Sanctuary*. Oxford: Oxford University Press; Doppelt, B. (2003). *Leading Change Toward Sustainability*. Sheffield, U.K.: Greenleaf Publishing.

Examples of trauma-organized private- and public-sector organizations

The Amazon.com story

The story of online economic giant Amazon.com provides a classic example of what an organization that is severely trauma-organized looks and functions like.

The *New York Times* in 2015 interviewed more than 100 current and former Amazon employees, including managers, marketers, and engineers, who described the firm as a "soulless, dystopian workplace" driven by relentless pressure to generate more profit. For example, the *Times* found that, "Workers are encouraged to tear apart one another's ideas in meetings, toil long and late (emails arrive past midnight, followed by text messages asking why they were not answered), and held to standards that the company boasts are "unreasonably high." The internal phone directory instructs colleagues on how to send secret feedback to one another's bosses. Employees say it is frequently used to sabotage others."[345]

Within days after this story was published, the newspaper received more than 4,000 comments posted on its website, including many from

Amazon employees, who complained of 75-hour work weeks and verbal abuse from managers and fellow employees. The American Civil Liberties Union responded to the story by taking out a full page add in the Seattle Times soliciting Amazon employees who believe they have been "unlawfully penalized because of their decision to have children, or because they were caring for a sick relative or recovering from an illness of their own."[346]

Amazon clearly does not prioritize enhancing the resilience and well-being of its employees. Imagine the suffering that would be inflicted on its staff if the firm's profitability were significantly reduced by extreme weather events, long-term droughts, severe heat waves, or other climate impacts that damage its warehouses, disrupt its supply chain, or in other ways undermine its business model!

But the problems at Amazon go well beyond how the company treats its employees. It also appears to have little concern about its environmental or climate impacts. In 2014 Greenpeace wrote a scathing report that called Amazon one of the most egregious companies when it comes to dirty energy to run its massive computer and electronics centers. In the report Greenpeace also gave the company an "F" grade for transparency for its failure to openly report its energy and environmental footprint.[347] In addition, its business model of rapidly delivering every product purchased online directly to the customer requires massive amounts of fossil fuels for transportation and produces significant amounts of climate-damaging greenhouse gasses.

The result is that Amazon's purpose, methods, and structure compromise the personal mental health and psycho-social-wellbeing of employees, while degrading the condition of the natural environment and climate.

The U.S. Veteran Affairs Administration story[348]

Public agencies can also become trauma-organized, as illustrated by the problems reported in 2014 in the U.S. Veteran Affairs Administration. CNN reported that at least 40 Armed Forces Veterans died while waiting for care at the VA's Phoenix, Arizona facilities. A blistering 119-page report then described a culture of crime, cover up, incompetence, and coercion at the VA. Managers apparently trained and instructed staff to cook the books by using false scheduling and appointment logs. The problem was systemic and continued despite numerous attempts by a whistle-blower to disclosure the problems.

FIGURE 10.2   To what extent is your group or organization trauma-organized?"

Put a ✓ check to mark the trauma-organized factors that exist in your organization:

✓ Check or 1–5 rating	Employees	✓ Check or 1–5 rating	Clients, customers or stakeholders	✓ Check or 1–5 rating	Entire group, department, or organization
	Are chronically hyperaroused		Are chronically hyperaroused		Crisis-driven, constant hyperarousal, managing like hair is on fire
	Uncertain of role and future in group		Uncertain of role and future in group		Confusion over mission or purpose, vision of future, goals, and guiding values
	Inability to manage emotions		Inability to manage emotions		Harsh or inappropriate interactions; psychological or emotional abuses
	Poor communication skills		Poor communication skills		Poor and inappropriate communications, many unstated expectations, silencing of dissent
	Self-focused with little interaction with others		Self-focused with little interaction with others		Siloed and fragmented units and functions with little cooperation or integration among them
	Fear of sharing alternative views or information		Fear of sharing alternative views or information		Constant Groupthink: inability to allow contrasting ideas, leading to disconnect from reality
	Constant search for quick simple fixes; limited learning		Constant search for quick simple fixes; limited learning		Inability or unwillingness to look for, acknowledge, and learn from mistakes and resolve problems
	Lack of empathy, trust, compassion, and social support		Lack of empathy, trust, compassion, and social support		Widespread distrust and conflicts, lack of trust, empathy, compassion; sense that one is on one's own
	Constant resistance and problems with authority		Constant resistance and problems with authority		Authoritarian leadership and lack of inclusive participatory decision-making
	Arrested grief, reenactment of problem actions		Arrested grief, reenactment of problem actions		Inability to allow for mourning, resistance to change, leading to reenactment of problematic actions

✓ Check or 1–5 rating	Employees	✓ Check or 1–5 rating	Clients, customers or stakeholders	✓ Check or 1–5 rating	Entire group, department, or organization
	Constant reenactment of problem behaviors		Constant reenactment of problem behaviors		Repetition of failed policies, programs, and strategies
	Joyless existence		Joyless existence		No fun, deadening environment
	Chronic hopelessness and helplessness		Chronic hopelessness and helplessness		Chronic hopelessness, helplessness, just going through the motions, high staff turnover, legal challenges
	Inability to self-protect, feel victimized		Inability to self-protect, feel victimized		Inability to self-protect–revictimization, no collective action to address problems
	No awareness of, or concern for, impact on the environment		No awareness of, or concern for, impact on the environment		Little awareness of, or concern for, environmental impacts—the few that are acknowledged are downplayed
	Feel physically, psychologically, or emotionally unsafe		Feel physically, psychologically, or emotionally unsafe		Fears about physical, psychological, and emotional safety among employees, clients, or stakeholders

Source: Assessment adapted from tool developed by Dr. Sandra Bloom in 2007. Community Works.

One of the reasons for the problems was that the bureaucracy had been taught, over time, to hide its problems from headquarters in Washington. William Schoenhard, who was a former deputy undersecretary for health for operations and management, said, "There's no feedback loop. The agency was not getting credible data to assess its success and improve its practices and procedures."[349]

But the biggest problem, according to the investigations, was that a culture of fear existed in the agency. Few employees had the courage to speak up because the culture of fear was so strong at both the leadership and management levels that it merely resulted in more false audits and zero actions to correct the illegal and deceitful practices.

The VA's story illustrates the grave harm that can result when an organization becomes driven by fear—and the fear within the VA had nothing to do with climate disruption. One can only imagine the negative fear-based reaction of VA employees that will occur, and the consequences for them, their patients, and stakeholders when the acute traumas and toxic stresses generated by climate disruption accelerate. This once again underscores how essential it is to proactively transition organizations to human resilience-enhancing entities before global temperatures rise by 1.5°C or more above pre-industrial levels. It will be much more difficult to make this type of change when a majority of organizational members are dysregulated and in a defensive self-protective mode.

Is your organization trauma-organized?

Use Figure 10.2 to determine the degree to which your group or organization might be trauma-organized. You can either put a check mark besides each characteristic that seems present within your social system, or you can rate it on a scale of 1–5, with 5 signifying it is strongly present and 1 signifying it is not.

Where is your organization on the continuum between trauma-organized and resilience-enhancing?

If you checked more than a third of the boxes in Figure 10.2, or gave them a rating of 4 or 5, it is likely that your organization is to some degree trauma-organized. If you checked more than half of the boxes, or gave them ratings of 4 or 5, it seems certain that your organization is trauma-organized. This information should be a sign of ongoing or pending trouble. However, unless you checked all of the boxes or gave them all high scores, it indicates that your organization has some constructive and some less than constructive traits. This underscores that most organizations exist on a continuum between being trauma-organized and resilience-enhancing. Rarely is it an all or nothing proposition.

Common characteristics of a trauma-informed resilience-enhancing organization

Now that you have a sense of the degree to which your organization might be trauma-organized, compare it to the traits of resilience-enhancing entities. Presencing and Purposing lie at the heart of almost all of these characteristics. As described by Dr. Sandra Bloom with slight modifications based on my experience, human resilience-enhancing entities have:

- **A clear sense of purpose, backed up by an inspiring vision of success and explicit ethical principles to guide decision-making.** The purpose or mission of an organization is critically important because it focuses the attention and energy of its members in a certain direction while ignoring other issues. In a human resilience-enhancing organization most employees and stakeholders are clear about why it exists, what it seeks to achieve, and the ethical principles and values that will guide decision-making. This clarity leads to wise and skillful decisions that increase personal, collective, and environmental wellbeing.

- **Good emotional regulation.** Most members have a basic understanding of how trauma and stress can affect them and others, know how to use simple Presencing skills to regulate their fear-based reactions, and, rather than using defense mechanisms to protect themselves from adversities, utilize Purposing skills to turn hardships into opportunities to learn, grow, and increase personal and organizational wellbeing well above previous levels.

- **Widespread agreement over acceptable behaviors and practices consistent with their purpose.** Members have discussed and widespread agreement exists about the behaviors and practices that are acceptable to engage in and pursue. This is not about trivial activities such as customs or manners. It relates to more fundamental practices such as if it is permissible to do things that violate the rights of people within or outside the organization, or use products or employ practices that damage the natural environment or climate.

- **Integrated units and functions.** Again, consistent with the Purpose, each of the individuals and sub-groups within the organization understand the roles and responsibilities of others and work together cooperatively to produce benefits that are greater than any one unit or function could achieve on their own.

- **Rules, regulations, and procedures that foster safety and trust.** Group members support the organization's rules, regulations, and procedures because they believe they are reasonable and aimed solely at ensuring the safety and wellbeing of all members and stakeholders.

- **Embrace and utilize criticism and contrasting information to continually learn and improve.** People are openly encouraged to respectfully ask questions, share information, and state views that differ from the dominant perspectives because it improves understanding and leads to better outcomes. The entity prioritizes and rewards continual learning, innovation, and improvement.

- **Commitment to social responsibility and social justice.** Inequities, injustices, and abuses of power and authority are viewed as totally unacceptable and when they appear, members take immediate action to correct the situation and make amends to those who have been harmed.

- **Openly acknowledge and mourn losses.** Rituals, ceremonies, pauses in ongoing workflow, and other methods are used to allow group members to grieve and share their feelings when serious mistakes occur, valued employees leave, or someone is physically injured or dies.

- **Value diversity, participation, democratic decision-making, and open communications.** All group members are actively encouraged to share their views and participate in decision-making. Decisions that affect everyone are thoroughly discussed and vetted by everyone before they are finalized.

- **Strong levels of trust, empathy, compassion, and social support.** Group members trust that others will strive to do and say things that are consistent with the purpose, vision, and values of the organization. Empathy and compassion for those who experience problems, make mistakes, or in other ways are struggling is strong. People feel supported by others, which increases confidence in their ability to deal with stress and adversity.

- **Firm commitment to protect and restore the natural environment and climate.** Members are concerned about and constantly seek to identify and eliminate ways in which the organization negatively affects the natural environment and climate, including how the raw materials it uses are extracted and processed, the amount and type of material and energy it consumes, and the toxic materials, solid waste, and greenhouse gas emissions it generates.

- **Robust sense of safety among members.** All of these traits combine to build a strong sense of physical, psychological, and emotional safety among organizational members.

These are summarized in Figure 10.3.

FIGURE 10.3   Common traits of resilience-enhancing organizations

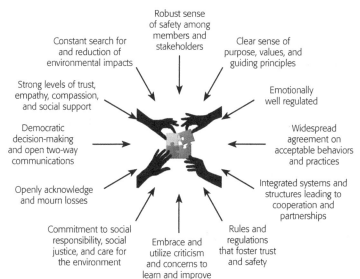

Source: Adapted from Bloom, S. (2013). *Destroying Sanctuary and Restoring Sanctuary*. Oxford: Oxford University Press; Doppelt, B. (2003). *Leading Change Toward Sustainability*. Sheffield, U.K.: Greenleaf Publishing.

Which of these traits exist in your organization?

Even when an organization exhibits numerous characteristics of being trauma-organized, most also display at least some of the positive traits seen in trauma-informed human resilience-enhancing entities. In the space below, describe any of the traits of a human resilience-enhancing entity you see in your organization:

- Clear sense of mission or purpose, an inspiring vision of success, and explicit principles to guide decision-making:

  _____

- Good emotional regulation:

  _____

- Widespread agreement over acceptable behaviors and practices:

  _____

- Integrated units and functions:

  _____

- Reasonable rules, regulations, and procedures that foster safety and trust:

  _____

- Embrace and utilize criticism and contrasting information to continually learn and improve:

  _____

- Commitment to social responsibility and social justice:

  _____

- Openly acknowledge and mourn losses:

  _____

- Value diversity, participation, democratic decision-making, and open communications:

  _____

- Strong levels of trust, empathy, compassion, and social support:

  _____

- Firm commitment to protect and restore the natural environment and climate:

  _____

- Robust sense of safety among members:

  _____

Examples of how private firms have implemented Presencing and Purposing to address non-climate-related stresses

The IBM and Aetna stories[350]

The multinational technology and consulting firm IBM, and Aetna, a U.S.-based health insurer, have embraced the importance of using Presencing skills to build the resilience of employees. However, the firms are not focused on preparing their employees for the impacts of climate disruption. They seek to reduce costs and enhance productivity by helping their employees manage workplace stress.

As reported by Business Insurance, in the early 2000s IBM shifted from "the more traditional [tactic of] dealing with risks" to building "resilience, capacity, energy and well-being," according to Stewart Sill, Raleigh, North Carolina-based manager of global health and vitality. "We think about resilience in a pretty broad way because [it] relies on a lot of things," Mr. Sill said, including "daily habits to build energy" and "other actions to promote well-being."

Among IBM's strategies are virtual programs to teach mindfulness skills to help people become more present by calming their emotions and thoughts, and nature-related programs that, according to Mr. Sill, "can clear your thinking [and] help reduce brain fatigue" along with other "restorative benefits." IBM has found that these skills have helped improve the health of participants, while reducing their healthcare costs.

Aetna teaches its employees Presencing skills to "become aware of the stress and its triggers, to allow people to control it," according to Paul

Coppola, Hartford, Connecticut-based head of care management strategy, innovation and design. "We can't make stress go away. Unfortunately, that magic pill doesn't exist," he said.

Aetna encourages this through its Mindfulness at Work program, which includes 12 one-hour virtual sessions for employees. "What's often a big driver of stress is the anticipation of other things that are going on," said Coppola. Mindfulness techniques help Aetna employees "stay present in the moment" and remain calm when dealing with distractions.

Since implementing the Mindfulness program in 2012, along with yoga classes, 13,000 of Aetna's 48,000 employees have participated. By analyzing work volume, employee turnover, presenteeism and benefit usage, Aetna determined that program participants' productivity rose by 62 minutes a week, resulting in a dollar return of $3,000 per employee.

In 2014, Aetna found that workers who participated in the Mindfulness program reduced their stress levels by an average of 28%. Aetna also has seen improvements in the health of its workers and a reduction in medical costs among high-stress individuals.

It is heartening to know that IBM and Aetna have documented the benefits of mindfulness, yoga, and other skills. With this knowledge, these and many other Presencing techniques could form one of the building blocks of Transformational Resilience programs to build the capacity of their employees, clients, and stakeholders to gain new insights, grow, and thrive in the midst of rising climate traumas and stresses.

The Sandler O'Neill & Partners story[351]

The experience of investment banking and broker firm Sandler O'Neill & Partners, L.P. goes well beyond the IBM and Aetna examples to offer a very poignant illustration of how Presencing and Purposing can be utilized to help an organization cope with, grow, and eventually thrive in the midst of a major trauma. In this case the adversity was the September 11, 2001 terrorist attack on the World Trade Center in New York City.

The offices of Sandler O'Neill were located on the 104th floor of the World Trade Center's South Tower. Of the 171 people employed by the firm at the time, 62 were killed in the attack including two-thirds of their management committee as well as Herman Sandler, one of the founders, and Chris Quackenbush, who started their investment banking practice. In addition, 24 more employees witnessed the attacks from a nearby concourse, 46 people become widows or widowers, and 71 children under the age of 18 lost a parent.[352]

On top of the loss of life and family, the firm lost nearly all of its physical assets and corporate records.[353]

Given the breath of devastation it would have seemed natural for the remaining members of the firm to be so emotionally distraught that they give up and abandon the enterprise. In fact, that is what the news media assumed would happen. Even though Sandler O'Neill informed the media that they would continue in business, CNBC misunderstood the message and broadcast just the opposite because that is what made sense to them given the circumstances.

Fortunately, the company had a number of individuals that understood the imperative of regulating their fear-based reactions, clarifying their purpose, and making values-based decisions that offered meaning, direction and hope to the remaining employees and the families of those who were lost. By utilizing Presencing and Purposing they helped their organization use the painful process as a catalyst not only to survive, but to come back stronger than before.

The day after the attack, Jimmy Dunne, one of the surviving members of the management team, and his remaining partners decided that the firm must continue to exist. They immediately clarified their purpose, which was defined as "not letting terrorists win and undermine America." This led researchers to describe the process of recovery after the 9/11 attacks as "resilience led by moral purpose."[354] The firm recovered by adopting a clear set of values focused on a mission greater than itself that included honoring their dead colleagues and a rejection of terrorism. This moral purpose is described as the key to the company's resilience.[355]

After establishing its purpose, the remaining Sandler O'Neill employees quickly reached out to their social support network of friends, clients, experts, and families to provide emotional sustenance as well as practical assistance to survivors and their families. This was consistent with the history of the company and way it operated, where friendships mattered and teamwork as well as self-management were emphasized. According to researchers, Sandler O'Neill's culture had built the social capital that was one of the seeds from which their capacity for Transformational Resilience grew.[356]

The recovery process was difficult. Overwhelming pain co-existed with a powerful will to move forward and thrive. But events after the 9/11 attacks opened the door for personal growth as well as changes in the organizational and business model. For instance, the burden of the tasks involved with rebuilding helped many employees and volunteers identify strengths and skills they previously did not know existed. These qualities allowed them to overcome adversity even as they lived with the often-confusing combination of anguish and purpose.[357] The firm also enhanced its participatory decision-making process focused on both financial and human resources. The organization knew how to sustain personal and collective growth in the midst of adversity.

Good leadership was a key to the company's capacity for Transformational Resilience. Jimmy Dunne in particular was a role model of Presencing and Purposing. Researchers said that he constantly acknowledged everyone's feelings of pain while role-modeling the process and allowing people to grieve. He also understood the support people needed from the firm and their need to find purpose, direction, and hope in the tragedy.[358]

The result was that even while dealing with their own deep emotional suffering, Dunne and his remaining colleagues established a social narrative that helped employees reframe their situation into one with positive meaning for the future. The story was rooted in hope because it convinced people that by continuing to work hard, focusing on restoring the business, and helping the families of the deceased, they would not only get through the difficult times, they would eventually see even better days and defeat the terrorists.

In 2015, 14 years after the horrific events of 9/11, Sandler O'Neill employed about 300 financial professionals and described itself as a company that has overcome tremendous challenges and losses. It recognizes the loss of its partners and employees, but it also acknowledges the tremendous contribution made by those who survived and rebuilt the firm into one that is larger and more diverse than before the tragedy struck. It fully recognizes both the pain and the opportunity posed by the crisis.

The Sandler O'Neill story offers a textbook example of how organizations can use Presencing and Purposing skills to learn, grow, and thrive in the midst of acute traumas and persistent toxic stresses. Imagine the benefits if a majority of organizations worldwide developed this capacity as a way to respond constructively to the adversities generated by climate disruption.

Even more, imagine if private, not-for-profit, and government organizations of all types around the world make these types of commitment and adopt these types of practice to slash their greenhouse gas emissions and other environmental impacts. The climate crisis might soon be reduced to manageable levels!

Shifting to a trauma-informed human resilience-enhancing organization requires new social narratives

How can an organization prevent itself from becoming trauma-organized, or make the transition to a trauma-informed resilience-enhancing entity, so that it is prepared to respond in positive ways to adversities such as those generated by climate disruption? As illustrated by Sandler O'Neill, one of the keys is to establish new social narratives that alter the culture of the organization.[359] This type of change requires that almost everyone—and especially group leaders—have a solid grasp of how trauma and stress affect individuals and groups, how the members of their organization perceive and respond to the world, and how to push the right levers to foster transformational change.

As previously stated, organizations are composed of people and thus are *living systems*, not machines. By system I mean that the numerous people that make up the organization interact in ways that produce specific outcomes. The human body is a living system.[360] The heart is a system of numerous valves and vessels that work together to distribute blood throughout the body. The heart system is part of a much larger circulatory system that distributes oxygen and other key nutrients throughout the body. The entire circulatory system works with all of the organs, muscles, nerves, and other components to keep the body functioning smoothly.

Similarly, organizations are composed of people that interact with each other and their physical environment to produce specific outcomes. The buildings, equipment, and raw materials that an organization uses are concrete items. However, the most important elements of a living system such as an organization tend to be non-substantive and hard to see or touch, such as the core assumptions and beliefs people hold about the world and their place in it, unstated but accepted norms and values, communication styles, the patterns of power and control, and more. These dynamics are created and reinforced by the social narratives that dominate the organization about why it exists, what it is striving to achieve, how it will achieve those goals, and who will benefit by achieving those outcomes.

To unpack this, it might help to think of living social systems as being defined by five key traits:[361]

1. **They have specific purposes.** Every social system has a central purpose that defines it as a discrete entity in relationship to the larger systems in which it is embedded. For example, the purpose

of a private company is usually to generate and distribute specific goods and services for a profit. The purpose of a government agency is also to provide goods such as drinking and irrigation water, power, or services such as education, police and fire protection deemed important to society. The purpose of an informal group of friends might be to provide a supportive environment for relaxation, fun, or personal sharing. In short, the purpose of a social system is defined by the system as a whole, not by any one of its parts. For instance, the manufacturing, human resources, marketing, or any other part of a private firm alone cannot accomplish its overall purpose of generating goods and services at a profit.

2. **All of the elements must be present and functioning well to achieve their purpose.** If key people or sub-groups within an organization can be removed or continually operate at very low levels without undermining the entity's overall performance, they constitute a collection, not a social system. For example, the manufacturing, distribution, human resources, marketing, and other units of an organization are all essential for a firm to achieve its purpose of providing specific types of goods or services. If even one of these subsystems is absent or performing poorly, the organization will not function well.

3. **The way the parts of a social system are arranged determines its performance.** If the individuals or sub-groups with an organization can be arranged in any arbitrary order, they constitute a fragmented collection, not a social system. In contrast, the ways the parts of a living social system such as an organization are arranged determine its capacity to accomplish its mission. For instance, if the manufacturing department reports solely to Division of Environmental Health and Safety rather than to the sales and distribution departments, the organization will fail to deliver its goods and services in a timely manner. If a technology wizard who has poor management and planning skills is placed in the role of a group leader, the group will suffer. All of the key subsystems (individuals and units) of an organization must be arranged in ways that effectively and efficiently maximize its performance.

4. **Each of the core elements of a social system is dependent on the others.** The core components of a social system form an interlinked set that influences, and is influenced by, all of the other elements.

For example, the effectiveness of the marketing and sales departments in an organization depends on the performance of the purchasing, production, and transportation units. The interactions
among these different subsystems are controlled by explicit and
implicit *rules* that determine how the system operates.

5. **Social systems seek to maintain stability through feedback.** Left
on its own, a living system will seek to maintain equilibrium by
retrieving and incorporating information from its external environment about how it is functioning that enables it to make
adjustments required to achieve its purpose. When the human
body becomes overheated, for example, the body's feedback systems kick in and cause the sweat glands to produce perspiration to
cool the system back down to a safe temperature. Information on
sales and market demand provide critical feedback to the production unit of an organization about the quantity and types of product to make. Without this feedback, the organization may over or
under produce, or generate poor quality products, leading to the
loss of customers, profits, or both.

In sum, just as every organ of the human body is inextricably connected
to every other, the individuals and sub-groups within a social system affect,
and are affected by, all others. It is almost impossible in most organizations
for changes to occur in one core element without generating ripple effects
throughout many, if not all of the others. The key point is that how an organization functions is the result of the interactions among its parts.[362]

Describe your social system

In the spaces provided, describe how your social system functions:

- Explain your organization's mission or purpose:

_____

- To what extent do the members of your organization understand
and agree on its mission and purpose? (It often is a real eye-opener
to ask people in different units and levels of the organization what
they think the purpose is):

_____

- To what extend are all of the individuals and sub-groups within your organization working together effectively to achieve its mission or purpose?

  _____

- To what extent are the various individuals and sub-groups in your organization arranged effectively to maximize effectiveness?

  _____

- To what extent are the individuals and sub-groups within your organization working cooperatively as interdependent parts of the whole?

  _____

- To what extent are your organization's feedback systems helping to identify and correct problems and improve performance?

  _____

The essence of culture in a social system

Because organizations are living social systems, as people respond over time to changes in their environment, feedback is received that establishes and continually reinforces a dominant set of beliefs, assumptions, values, decision-making, problem-solving, and behavioral patterns that are unique to the group. These traits constitute the culture of an organization. Just as individuals hold basic assumptions and beliefs about the way the world works and their role in it, the culture of every organization reflects widely held beliefs about the external world and the role of the organization in that reality. These shared perspectives hold a culture together. Culture synchronizes thought patterns, perspectives, and behaviors within a social system.

A culture can best be understood by its values and norms. As discussed in Chapter 8, values reflect beliefs about what is truly important—what people see as extremely valuable. Norms are the widely held and shared expectations about appropriate behaviors. Conformity with the values and norms of an organization is expected while noncompliance is frowned on and often punished. They are consistently reinforced by the feedback systems at play within the group or organization that signal when people are not in compliance.

The values and norms that make up the culture of an organization can assist or thwart efforts to shift from a trauma-organized to a resilience-enhancing entity. That's because values and norms provide the cognitive framework through which people interpret what they observe and experience, and shape the way people communicate and interact with each other.[363] The explicit and implicit feedback systems embedded in the organization almost always reinforce the existing values and norms.

Since culture is a product of, and embedded within, a social system, it is often invisible to the naked eye and hard to describe. Because culture is difficult to recognize, it can go unchallenged for years. Many times the only time people recognize the culture of their organization is when they describe, "The way things are around here."

The fact that cultures are so hard to discern and deeply rooted means that the successful shift from a trauma-organized to human resilience-enhancing entity requires that the norms and values of the social system be explicitly surfaced, discussed, and altered when needed. Change is achieved when the individuals that make up the organization begin to value new things—such as ensuring that all members have the skills to calm their body, emotions, and thoughts, and use adversities as catalysts to increase personal, collective, and environmental wellbeing—and believe that behaviors and practices that are inconsistent with those values are no longer appropriate.

True change from a trauma-organized to a human resilience-enhancing organization, therefore involves much more than sending out memos, hosting a few speakers, or adopting resilience-focused policies. Real change comes about only when values and norms that are fundamentally different than those that support the status quo are embraced by the vast majority of organizational members. This requires that the organization adopt and continually promote a new narrative describing its updated or new purpose, vision of success, and how it will make decisions to achieve those ends.

Describe your organization's culture

In the spaces below describe the culture of your organization:

- What written and explicitly stated values drive the thinking and actions of people in your organization?

  _____

- What unwritten and rarely discussed values drive the thinking and actions of people in your organization?

  _____

- What important norms are written down and openly discussed within your organization?

  _____

- What important norms are unwritten and rarely discussed within your organization?

  _____

- Write a summary of the narratives that dominate your organization that describe the values and norms that truly control the thinking and behaviors of people in your organization, i.e., "the way things actually work:"

  _____

Resistance to change

Because they are living systems seeking to maintain homeostasis, resistance can be expected in any social system whenever a change in culture is proposed. Just as the brain's "Fear and Alarm Center" triggers fight, flee, or freeze reactions to protect an individual from a threat, resistance to change in a social system is a natural outcome of the organization's feedback mechanisms that seek to maintain the status quo. A new social narrative that changes norms and values threatens to profoundly alter the way people view and respond to the world around them and thus upset the status quo—or homeostasis. Resistance is therefore a natural reaction, a safety response, to this type of interruption to business-as-usual.

Resistance to cultural change in a social system can appear in numerous ways. When a proposal for change first appears, resistance often arises due to perceived threats to current beliefs, behaviors, and practices. This frequently involves fear that the influence or position people hold, which is embedded in the organization's existing patterns of power and authority, may be threatened. For example, executives might delay or directly oppose resilience-building efforts if they think it might threaten their authority or future career opportunities. Executives who have spent years in the fossil fuel industry, for example, can resist their organization's transition to clean renewable sources of energy such as solar and wind because it might call into question the virtue of their entire career, or their current status and power.

As mentioned, resistance to a change in culture can also occur if people experience overwhelming levels of uncertainty, or unpredictability, or when the changes are "too much, too fast" for people to cope. For example, members of an organization might deny that human-induced climate disruption is happening. Then, out of the blue they might find colleagues, family, or themselves harmed by a historically unprecedented tempest such as Superstorm Sandy. The sudden reality of climate disruption can be too much to come to grips with, causing the people to conclude that it was just a freak event and there is no need to prepare for future climate impacts.

In addition, resistance can occur when people have no say in how the initiative is organized, if they fear they will be singled out or their poor performance or other undesirable behaviors will be exposed for others to see, and when low levels of trust exist or members feel resentful toward others due to past events. People might resist an initiative to enhance human resilience, for instance, if the people leading the effort have in the past promoted their own status over the wellbeing of the others.

Resistance to a change in culture can take many forms. Sometimes it is stealthy and occurs below the surface. When it exists for long periods or time, clandestine resistance will usually sink a cultural change initiative. Claims by individuals that they have too much on their plate to participate in resilience-building efforts, the unwillingness to attend meetings, or showing up late and leaving early are frequent signs of surreptitious resistance.

Resistance can also be overt. Direct complains or doubts about the importance of building resilience, proclamations that people already have ample resilience skills, and the unwillingness to commit time, personnel, or financial resources to resilience-building efforts are signs of explicit resistance. Open resistance is typically easier to deal with than covert forms because it can be seen, heard, and talked about.

How does resistance to change occur in your organization?

In the space provided describe the ways in which people overtly and covertly resist change in your organization:

- Examples of overt resistance to change:

  _____

- Examples of covert resistance to change:

  _____

Successful changes in culture result from a coherent theory of change

How can resistance be overcome and the culture of an organization be transformed to make the shift from a trauma-organized to a trauma-informed human resilience-enhancing entity? Although they don't necessarily start their change initiatives with a clear change strategy in mind, the leading organizations learn by doing, and spend considerable time thinking through how they can transform their social systems.

Even though most do not begin with a clear approach, the best human resilience-building efforts tend to view all of the people, units, and processes within their organizations, as well as its many stakeholders, as interconnected elements in their system of success. As seen in the Sandler O'Neill example, they take great care to understand how each step of the change process will interact with the others to form a natural reinforcing loop that leads to long-term transformation.

In contrast, the less successful organizations do not seem to have a theory of change, or if one exists it is based on fundamental misperceptions about the nature of their social systems and the types of cultural change required to become resilience-enhancing entities. Those struggling to improve their capacity to enhance personal and collective resilience, as well as the condition of the environment, tend to view the key factors of success in isolation rather than seeing them as parts of an interconnected whole.

Without a coherent theory of change, organizations often end up pursuing a scattered array of activities that lead to marginal improvements or dead ends. An effective theory of change, in contrast, provides the means to consistently examine proposed activities to determine if they will produce the desired outcomes. It also helps in avoiding actions that may undermine the cultural change effort.

What is your theory of change?

In the space provided describe the theory you currently hold about how you can alter the culture of your organization to become a human-resilience-building entity:

_____

_____

Leverage points for transformation to a resilience-enhancing organization[364]

There is no single "right way" to alter the culture of an organization. However, a good deal of research over the past few decades has identified leverage points that are particularly important and powerful.[365] They include the following:[366]

- **The most powerful leverage point for transforming the culture of an organization is to change the mindset or mental model that initially created or currently controls the thinking and actions of the group.** The greatest leverage for change comes from altering the organization's overall way of seeing, interpreting, and responding to the conditions around them. The stated and unstated ideas held by the majority of group members about the way the world works and their places in it shape everything they do. If you can alter the dominant mental model of the members of an organization, you can change the entire way it functions.

  How do you change the controlling mindset so that it prioritizes building the capacity for Transformational Resilience? By creating and relentlessly repeating a new social narrative about why the organization exists and what it is striving to achieve focused on the imperative and benefits of building the personal and collective resilience of employees, clients, and stakeholders.[367]

- **The second greatest leverage point for shifting the culture of an organization is to rearrange its parts.** Recall that the way the individuals and sub-groups that make up an organization are arranged determines how it functions. If you rearrange the way people are organized—especially the individuals and groups that hold decision-making power—you can alter the way the overall organization functions. Often the composition of the people responsible for deciding how an organization functions remains the same for years on end. Either the same people dominate decision-making, or when new people are included they are chosen because they see and respond to the world in the same way as existing decision-makers. Consequently, every issue is viewed the same way, and "solutions" to problems always seem to mirror actions taken in the past.

  How can this situation be altered? By rearranging the parts of the organization to include new people in decision-making roles. This can occur by forming what I call "Human Resilience Teams," although many other titles can be used. This team should be composed of people representing all of the different levels and units of the organization. The teams should be given the responsibility to move beyond the normal channels of communications by reaching out to different people who operate at different levels of the organization—from those working on the loading dock, to administrative assistants, line workers, low- and mid-level managers, senior executives, and others—and lead the transition from a trauma-informed to a human resilience-enhancing entity. When the decision-making bodies of an organization are rearranged in this way, many new ways of seeing and responding to challenges will typically emerge.[368]

- **The third greatest leverage for changing the culture of an organization is to alter its mission and purpose, vision of success, and guiding ethical principles.**[369] The mission and purpose of an organization directs attention, energy, and interactions among its members in a certain direction. The ethical principles it uses to guide decision-making serve as a screen to decide what is acceptable and unacceptable. If you change what people focus on and discuss on a regular basis along with the values it uses to make decisions, you can change entire way it operates.

How do you change the purpose, vision, and guiding ethical principles of an organization to enhance the capacity for Transformational Resilience? By empowering the "Human Resilience Teams" to use the information they gathered from people at different levels of the organization to reframe the existing mission or craft a new purpose, vision of success, and guiding ethical principles required to build the capacity for Transformational Resilience. When it is finalized, the teams should also be empowered to continually promote the new purpose, vision of success, and decision-making principles within and outside of the organization.

- **The fourth greatest leverage point for changing the culture of an organization is to restructure its rules of engagement.**[370] Over time, individuals and units within most organizations or any size fall into a pattern of interacting with certain other people and groups while having little interaction with others. Chains of command are also established that determine who reports to who and which people and units have more authority. These rules of engagement influence what people do on the job and how they do it.

  How do you change the rules of engagement in an organization so that they promote building the capacity for Transformational Resilience? By working through the "Human Resilience Teams" to developing new partnerships and collaborations among different individuals and units focused on building widespread levels of Transformational Resilience within the organization.

- **The fifth greatest lever of altering culture is to shift the flows of information within the organization.**[371] The information people see and discuss on a regular basis determines how they see and respond to the world around them. When the information people receive changes, their views and behaviors also begin to shift.

  How do you change the information flows within an organization to focus on building the capacity for Transformational Resilience? By empowering the "Human Resilience Team(s)" to continually disseminate and discuss information about the organization's new purpose, vision of success, and ethical guidelines, and the benefits of the new focus. Role modeling by members of the teams is also important. Through the way they talk, manage their emotions, and act they must visibly demonstrate what it means to build capacity for Transformational Resilience.

- **The sixth greatest leverage point for modifying the culture of an organization comes by correcting its feedback mechanisms.**[372] The data people receive related to the outcomes of their activities helps them determine if and how to alter their approach to increase efficiency and effectiveness. When credible new feedback is provided indicating the need for improvement, people can respond appropriately. When this type of information is absent, people are likely to continue to do what they are already doing.

  How do you change the feedback mechanisms of an organization to embrace the imperative of building capacity for Transformational Resilience? By leaving no stone unturned to constantly evaluate the progress being made toward the new purpose and vision of success. This can include internal assessments, rewarding employees that identify problems, and obtaining feedback directly from external clients, customers, and stakeholders. The results should be widely disseminated and continually discussed. People throughout the organization who use the feedback to innovate and find ways to improve the process can also be rewarded.

- **Finally, the seventh most powerful leverage for altering the culture of an organization is to adjust its policies, procedures, and regulations.**[373] This involves aligning employee performance criteria, incentive and reward systems, purchasing, and other policies and procedures that influence the behavior of employees and stakeholders with the new goal of building the capacity for Transformational Resilience.

  Many people believe that the most important leverage point for change in any social system is to enact new policies and regulations. This is a misunderstanding. It is true only if the core elements of the old ways of doing things have been fundamentally altered, including the controlling mental model, along with the composition of decision-makers, mission and purpose, vision of success, information flows, and feedback mechanisms. If these core systems and structures remain unchanged, it will be impossible to generate sufficient support to enact new policies, or when they are adopted they will be substantially watered down and, even then, people will ignore or find ways to work around them. However, when new

FIGURE 10.4   Greatest leverage points and interventions for shifting from a trauma-organized to a trauma-informed resilience-enhancing organization

	Leverage point	Intervention
Greatest leverage for change ↑	1. Change the mindsets that shape the way the community typically views and responds to issues	Create a new narrative of why the entity exists and what it strives to achieve with a new focus on the need and benefits of building human resilience
	2. Rearrange the way planning and decision-making in the community is structured	Organize very inclusive "Human Resilience Teams"
	3. Alter the vision, goals and decision-making criteria of the community	Teams clarify the new mission or purpose, craft an inspiring vision of success, and the guiding principles to be used to achieve it
	4. Restructure the rules of engagement among groups within the community	Develop new collaborations and partnerships to develop new strategies focused on building human resilience
	5. Shift the flows of information within the community	Relentlessly communicate the new mission or purpose, vision, guiding principles and strategies through two-way interaction *and* role modeling
	6. Correct the feedback loops of the community	Constantly evaluate progress, disseminate results, and encourage and reward improvement
Least leverage for change	7. Adjust the policies and regulations of the community	Embed new policies and regulations in systems, structures, and standard operating procedures

policies and regulations follow and build on the previous key leverage points for change, they can embed the goal of building the capacity for Transformational Resilience deep within the organization's culture and standard operating procedures. This is summarized in Figure 10.4.

What leverage points has your change initiative emphasized?

In the space provided describe the leverage points for change you have emphasized in your effort to shift the culture of your organization to embrace building human resilience. Also describe the rationale behind your choices:

- Leverage points you have emphasized so far:

  _____

- Your reasoning:

  _____

The wheel of change toward Transformational Resilience in organizations

I just described the highest leverage points for change and associated interventions in a stepwise linear fashion. In reality, culture change does not occur this way. It usually begins in surprising ways, is messy, and involves numerous starts and stops, forward and backward movement, and ups and downs.

Sometimes the only way to begin a culture change initiative is to start with one of the less impactful levers and then work toward the more powerful ones. For example, it is often not possible to launch an effort to shift from a trauma-organized to resilience-enhancing entity by trying to directly change the mental model held by the majority of group members, which is the most powerful leverage point for change. People might fiercely resist for a number of reasons, such as the belief that things are working just fine, or they don't want to feel that their past actions were wrong. This type of resistance is often, of course, the core of the problem. However, directly challenging people will usually generate significant push back.

Instead, it is likely more effective to begin a culture change initiative by engaging a few mid-level members and leaders in informal discussions to determine how they feel about their job and their work, share your perspective about how trauma and stress might be affecting them and the likelihood that climate disruption will add much more, and solicit their thoughts on the benefits and means of engaging people in the organization in efforts to build their capacity for Transformational Resilience. This can begin to shift the information flows of the social system, which is a version of the fifth most powerful leverage point for change. This type of informal process might capture their interest and slowly, over time, more and more people can be engaged in the discussions.

When a number of key people grasp the issues and feel the need for change, the effort can be expanded. After sufficient support exists, the issue can rise upward and be presented to senior executives who can authorize the establishment of a human resilience team or teams, which is the second greatest leverage point for change. When the team or teams seem ready, discussions can occur about the pros and cons of the current way most people in the organization see and respond to challenges, and if it would be beneficial to be discuss new ways to respond in order to build capacity for Transformational Resilience—which is the most powerful leverage for change.

This underscores that no single leverage point on its own can generate successful culture change. They are interlinked and each affects and is affected by every other intervention. Just as a flat tire of an automobile slows the entire vehicle, any weak interventions can delay the entire change process or bring it to a complete halt. Each intervention must therefore be sufficiently robust for the change process to keep rolling forward.

For example, change leaders might assume that everyone is clear about why the organization exists and what it is striving to achieve. My experience is that this is almost never the case. In most organizations a wide range of perspectives usually exist about its mission or purpose and what success involves. When leaders make this type of miscalculation, the change initiative will often stall because people will not grasp the need or engage in meaningful discussions about how building human resilience differs from current practices. If this type of confusion occurs, change leaders can back up and focus on a less powerful change lever, such as fostering and highlighting a few visible successes of building human resilience—which changes the feedback loops of the organization and represents the fifth most powerful lever of change. This can help people gain clarity about what a new purpose and vision of success looks like and breathe new life into the change initiative.

Good timing and a great deal of flexibility are therefore essential in any effort to shift the culture of an organization to prioritize building the capacity for Transformational Resilience. Human-resilience-building efforts can fail if you move too rapidly to a new phase before sufficient groundwork has been laid in the previous stage, or if you focus too long on a leverage point where little progress is being made and ignore others where success can be achieved. Good leadership is needed to skillfully and wisely guide the process.

FIGURE 10.5   The wheel of change toward resilience

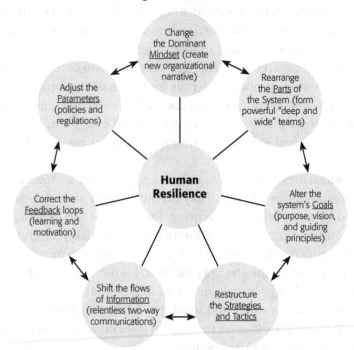

Source: Adapted from Doppelt, B. (2003). *Leading Change Toward Sustainability: A Change Management Guide*. Sheffield, U.K.: Greenleaf Publishing.

The "Wheel of Change" (see Fig. 10.5) toward Transformational Resilience in organizations describes the interconnected nature of highest leverage points for change and associated interventions for shifting the culture and operations of a group or organization.[374]

Because the seven leverage points compose a continuous system of change, many of the organizations that are furthest advanced in building personal and group resilience find that they often need to continually revisit one or more of the elements of the Wheel of Change. For example, when they begin efforts to enact new policies or regulations, change leaders often realize they must reach out and meaningfully engage new people, or generate greater clarity about the initiative's purpose and benefits, or revisit other elements of the Wheel of Change, before they can obtain the level of support needed to adopt meaningful new policies.

Example of how the Wheel of Change can be used by an organization to build the capacity for Transformational Resilience[375]

It just so happens that the U.S. Department of Veterans Affairs, cited earlier in this chapter, has developed a climate adaptation plan. Let's use this example to illustrate how an organization could use the Wheel of Change to build its capacity for Transformational Resilience.

U.S. President Barack Obama issued an Executive Order in November 2013 requiring Federal Departments and Agencies to assess their vulnerabilities to the impacts of climate disruption and include them in Climate Change Adaptation Plans that outline how they will protect Federal programs, assets, and investments.

The Climate Change Adaptation Plan of the U.S. Department of Veterans Affairs (VA), released in June 2014, says that its climate vulnerabilities include possible damage to buildings and built infrastructure from extreme weather events, sea-level rise, and other direct impacts, as well as damage due to indirect factors such as interruptions of its systems from electrical blackouts in storms, water shortages generated by drought, or other sources. In addition, the report says that climate change might have widespread effects on the health of VA staff and on the veterans they serve due to increased demand for emergency care during disasters, greater stress on the staff involved in emergency care, and increased risk of physical health impacts such as heat stress, new diseases, and increased allergen load.

The plan goes on to describe how the VA will respond to the physical threats by relocating and building stronger buildings, and other steps.

In response to the possible negative impacts on its staff and patients, the plan says it is providing VA staff, veterans, and local, state, and federal public health authorities with information about the impacts of climate disruption, and monitoring climate-related public health issues.

The report then lists a number of future actions the Department will take, which mostly emphasize improving and expanding its existing focus.

Conspicuous by its absence

One thing that immediately stands out when reading the VA's Climate Adaptation Plan is the failure to even briefly mention the likelihood of negative personal mental health or psycho-social-spiritual impacts on its patients or employees resulting from climate disruption. The absence of this factor is all the more remarkable given the levels of PTSD and other trauma and toxic stress-related mental health problems often seen among veterans, and the well-known links between psychological and physical health problems.

These omissions, however, should come as no surprise given the fear-based culture that exists within the VA that caused it to become a trauma-organized entity. As noted, when people exist in a defensive, self-protective mode, they have a difficult time grasping what is occurring within and around them. This is a form of organizational dissociation, and it typically leads to the continual reenactment of the behaviors and practices that originally precipitated the problems.

Further, the adaptation plan says nothing about how its operations and energy use might be contributing to climate disruption. In addition, by only identifying the vulnerabilities that were required by the President's Executive Order, the plan says nothing about the VA's existing strengths and resources that can be serve as a platform for building physical as well as personal and psycho-social-spiritual resilience.

Application of the Wheel of Change to enhance organizational capacity for Transformational Resilience

How could the VA utilize the Wheel of Change and the other information presented in this book to begin the transition to a trauma-informed resilience-enhancing organization, and in doing so also develop a more insightful and comprehensive climate adaptation plan?

Step 1: Organize a new and diverse steering team

Their first action could be to organize a diverse Human Resilience Planning (or Steering) Team composed of people from different units and levels of the VA, along with past and current patients and key stakeholders. Their mission could be twofold: a) to analyze and discuss the current status and desired future of the Department, with a major focus on how the ideal vision of success would look and function for staff, patients and stakeholders, and how that would compare with the existing structure and operations; and b) determine how the ideal vision of success might shape the development and implementation of a robust climate adaptation plan that enhances the well-being of its people, patients, *and* the condition of the natural environment.

The planning team would be more effective if it included more than the usual suspects, meaning people from different levels and units within the Department and those with different perspectives that do not normally have planning or decision-making authority. If people would likely be less open and candid when senior executives are involved, it would be best if the team was organized and led by mid-level VA staff.

Taking this step would mean that the initiative begins with the second most powerful leverage point for change in a social system—rearrange the parts of the system.

Step 2: Clarify or alter the VA's purpose and vision of success

One of the first tasks of the team could be to use the checklist provided earlier in this chapter to objectively assess the degree to which the VA is trauma-organized. A discussion could then take place, without accusations or blame, about the implications of the findings for the Department's ability to accomplish its overarching mission which is, "To care for him who shall have borne the battle, and for his widow, and his orphan by serving and honoring the men and women who are America's veterans,"[376] and for its ability to adapt to climate impacts in ways that actually increase human and environmental wellbeing.

If, after sufficient discussion, enough people feel committed to altering the way the Department functions to ensure that it enhances both human wellbeing and the condition of natural environment, the team could make the decision to develop a culture change strategy.

This process might begin by clarifying or rewriting the Department's purpose, goals, core values, and vision of success using the foundational theme of the need and benefits of reorienting itself to simultaneously increase the wellbeing of its staff and patients and the condition of the natural environment. A central element of the dialogue should be the need to explicitly address not only external infrastructure and physical health—as the current climate adaptation plan is limited to—but also the likely personal mental health and psycho-social-spiritual maladies experienced by VA staff and patients, including but not limited to those likely generated by climate disruption. I am not suggesting that the statutory mission of the VA be altered. I'm referring to the specific ways that employees, clients, and stakeholders currently see the Department's purpose, goals, vision of success, and core values.

This step would constitute the third most powerful leverage point for change in a social system—alter the purpose of the system.

Step 3: Understand and shift the dominant agency mindset

At this point the team could initiate a discussion about the basic assumptions, beliefs, and values currently held by a majority of people within the

VA, along with the behaviors and practices they commonly produce. The VA's website declares that its five core values include "Integrity, Commitment, Advocacy, Respect, and Excellence."[377] But the fear-based deceptions and cover-ups that permeate the Department indicate that in practice those are not widely held principles. The goal would be to determine if the mindset that actually dominates the organization is likely to facilitate or impede progress toward the new mission, goals, and vision of success.

At this point (and/or later in the process) the team could learn about the psychobiology of trauma and toxic stress and discuss how fear-based reactions to real or perceived threats might have affected the ability of VA staff to achieve its stated purpose, goals, and core values. If this discussion determines that the mental model the dominates the VA is likely to hamper its transition to a human resilience-enhancing Department, the team could identify the types of assumption, belief, and way of thinking that will be needed to successfully make the change. New social narratives could then be crafted that explain in language that resonates with the Department the benefits of the new way of thinking and acting.

This would begin to address the most powerful leverage point for change in a social system—alter the dominant mindset.

Step 4: Redesign strategies and tactics

As the new social narratives are being developed, the team could actively engage the different units of the Department in identifying strategies and tactics that could effectively and efficiently implement the new approach and achieve the new purpose, and vision of success. In addition to everyday operations, the existing Climate Adaptation Plan would also be updated and improved.

The starting point for the strategies could be to clarify how the Department's existing strengths, skills, and resources can be utilized to help it make the transition to a human resilience-enhancing entity. A core element of the strategies could be to inform staff, patients, and stakeholders about the psychobiology of trauma and stress so they understand how wartime trauma, as well as the traumas and toxic stresses experienced in everyday life—and those generated by climate disruption—might affect not only their physical health but also their mental health and the psycho-social-spiritual health and resilience of the groups they associate with. Individuals might then be taught simple Presencing and Purposing skills to help them learn how to calm their bodies and minds and use adversities as catalysts to learn, grow, and thrive. In addition, the principles and practices of the Sanctuary

Model, or a similar approach, could be adopted to provide everyone, from senior executives to the office secretaries, with a method to alter the way they personally behave and interact with each other so that the Department becomes a safe, emotionally well-regulated, ethical, open, honest, democratic, and nonauthoritarian human resilience-enhancing organization.[378] Strategies and work plans would be developed, and implementation would begin.

This would address the fourth most powerful leverage point for change in a social system—restructure the rules of engagement.

Step 5: Relentlessly communicate the new approach through new social narratives

The process described in step four is certain to take a good deal of time, and as it unfolds it would be essential for information about the updated mission, goals, vision of success, values, and strategies, along with their benefits, to be relentlessly communicated via the new social narratives to employees, patients, and stakeholders. This would require the use of multiple communications venues including social media, training workshops, notices, talks by senior executives, and more. The narratives about new approaches—including how the Department will change to better serve its patients and how it will adapt to growing climate impacts—will need to be continually repeated for a year or more to ensure that they eventually permeate everyone's consciousness. In addition, senior executives and mid-level managers would need to walk-the-talk and role model the new approaches so that everyone realizes they are serious and not merely nice sounding rhetoric.

This step would address the fifth greatest leverage point for change in a social system—shift the flows of information.

Step 6: Continually evaluate progress, learn, and improve

As the new strategies and tactics are being implemented, the teams could devise metrics, tools, and protocols and regularly measure progress toward the new mission, vision, goals, and values. Personnel and funding will need to be allocated to continually measure, analyze, and widely report the progress being made. These metrics would be added to those already used by the VA, including those listed in the Climate Adaptation Plan, for measuring success.

Staff violations of the core values, lack of progress in improving patient services, failures to adapt to climate impacts in ways they benefit people and the natural environment, and any other negative outcomes would serve as vital information indicating that something is amiss and steps would be rapidly taken to improve the situation. Similarly, successes would be highlighted so that people constantly see the types of change that are desired and their benefits for people and the environment.

This addresses the sixth greatest leverage point for change in a social system—correct the feedback mechanisms.

Step 7: Embed the new approach in policies and procedures

After a sufficient amount of time has passed in which the VA has implemented and measured the success of it new approach, the methods and processes should be refined sufficiently enough to allow for new procedures and policies to embed within the organization's standard operating procedures and policies. Although a few small policy changes might be adopted early on, it would likely take one or two years before the details of more substantive policies are understood well enough to codify them.

This would address the seventh greatest leverage point for change in a social system—adjust the parameters.

I have just described the elements of the change strategy in a stepwise fashion. As noted, the process is highly unlikely to unfold that way. It will undoubtedly necessitate moving backwards to make improvements in previously addressed steps, and jumping forward to achieve small successes in other leverage points as a way to illustrate the benefits of making even bigger changes. For example, as new strategies and tactics are implemented and their effectiveness measured, it is possible that the mission, goals, and vision of success will need to be tweaked yet again to better reflect the findings. That's why I call the process the "Wheel of Change." Organization change is not a linear process. To keep the process rolling forward requires constant attention to all of the key leverage points for change.

The end result, however, is certain to be numerous positive changes in the internal culture of VA that produce operational improvements that benefit staff, patients, stakeholders and the natural environment. These changes will allow the Department to develop a much more robust and effective Climate Adaptation Plan that, in addition to addressing infrastructure and physical health, increases the capacity of everyone to use adversity to learn, grow, and thrive in ways that benefits Veterans, taxpayers, and the natural environment.

In the final chapter of the book I offer a few policy recommendations that could stimulate this type of cultural change within organizations.

Describe your strategy for shifting the culture of your organization to embrace building the capacity for Transformational Resilience

Does the information provided in the VA example offer insight into how you might be able to develop a change strategy for your organization? If so, in the spaces below describe the elements of a change strategy to shift the culture of your organization from a trauma-organized to a trauma-informed human resilience-enhancing entity:

- My vision of what a successful cultural change initiative would look and function like includes:

- The initial leverage points for change I will focus on include:

- The subsequent sequence of leverage points for change I will emphasize include:

- I will strive to alter the mental model that dominates my organization by:

- The individuals I will try to initially engage in the Human Resilience Teams include:

- The individuals I will try to engage later in the change program include:

- I will seek to change the purpose, vision of success, and principles that guide decision-making within my organization by:

- I will seek to alter the flows of information within my organization by:

  _____

- I will seek to alter the feedback mechanisms use by my organizations by:

  _____

- I will seek to alter the policies and regulations of my organizations by:

  _____

Senior leadership is important, but most change initiatives are launched and led by mid-level people

The Sandler O'Neill story shows that exemplary leadership is very important for any successful organizational change initiative. Leaders must be good listeners and communicators, savvy politicians with the ability to understand and negotiate agreements among competing interests, and expert motivators. Top-level management skills are also needed.

However, the leadership provided by senior executives at Sandler O'Neill is often an anomaly. Senior executives usually do not initiate or lead most organizational change efforts. To the contrary, the catalysts and leaders are typically thoughtful, energetic, and motivated people who sit in the middle or lower levels of an organization. More often than not, these people see the need for change long before senior executives because they are engaged in daily product or service delivery, while executives are focused on budgets, financing, and the like.

Mid- and lower-level staff therefore often initiate a cultural change initiative by engaging people next to, and slightly above or below them, and then slowly build momentum outward and upward. Eventually enough support exists that senior executives take notice. At that point they might *announce* the initiative and appear to be leading the effort. But in practice, senior leaders usually follow, rather than lead the development of this type of change effort. After they embrace the initiative, however, it is essential that senior executives use their influence and authority to move the process forward.

This means that even if you are not a senior executive, you can catalyze a major change initiative in your organization. Indeed, that is the way most get started.

11
Building Transformational Resilience in communities

For years, Tarpon Springs, a town of 24,000 people on the Gulf Coast of Florida, had experienced high levels of child abuse, domestic violence, substance abuse, crime, and violence.[379] In 2009–10 when she was a commissioner and vice-mayor of Tarpon Springs, Robin Saenger kept asking community leaders, "why is nothing changing?"[380] After speaking with a friend who was a consultant with the National Center for Trauma-Informed Care, she finally understood the problem. The root cause was trauma. Tarpon Springs was trauma-organized.

Social service leaders in The Dalles, Oregon, had a similar experience. Sitting on the edge of the Columbia River 70 miles east of Portland, this town of 15,000 was subject to high levels of child abuse and neglect, poverty, and under-performing schools with excessive truancy rates and office discipline referrals. Many residents seemed hypersensitive to change. Lawsuits against government agencies came out of left field, sometimes associated with widely publicized personal threats. In response, officials often adopted knee-jerk policies that only produced more negative reactions. After investigating the causes, the leaders concluded their town was trauma-organized.

As you will read later in this chapter, both communities decided to address these problems by beginning the transition to trauma-informed human resilience-enhancing communities. Although they were not designed for this purpose or use these terms, both initiatives offer important insights into how communities can build the capacity of their residents for Transformational Resilience to address the adversities generated by climate disruption.

Few communities are incorporating human resilience into their climate plans

Unfortunately, few communities anywhere in the world are incorporating principles or practices similar to the ones used in Tarpon Springs and The Dalles to help their residents respond constructively to any type of trauma, let along those generated by climate disruption. The movement to develop trauma-informed communities is just beginning, and in the U.S. it is mostly focused on addressing Adverse Childhood Experiences (ACEs).

That said, one of the better community-based climate adaptation plans I've seen was developed by the Pacific Institute in partnership with the Oakland Climate Action Coalition for Oakland, California.[381] It begins by analyzing the likely impacts of climate disruption on the city. It then assesses vulnerabilities, with a major focus on "social vulnerabilities" which the plan says are influenced by income, race, health, age, English fluency, and other factors. The plan then describes 50 adaptation strategies focused on ways to adapt to extreme heat, floods, wildfires, rising utility and food costs, poor air quality, and other impacts. All of the proposed adaptations emphasize external physical changes. For instance, early warning systems are proposed to deal with extreme heat events, and constructing green infrastructure, raising the height of existing structures, and preserving/restoring wetlands are recommended to deal with flooding. These are all important. However, nowhere in the plan are the likely negative personal mental health or psycho-social-spiritual impacts of climate disruption mentioned or recommendations offered to address these risks.

In some ways this is surprising because many people of color living in Oakland have for years experienced racism, economic injustice, and other forms of systemic oppression. As a result, many neighborhoods of Oakland appear to be trauma-organized. As noted, the acute traumas and toxic stresses generated by climate disruption amplify ongoing problems such as social injustice and inequality, erode peoples' psychological and social protective supports, and increase the risks of new personal and group maladies. Thus, the impacts of climate disruption are likely to aggravate many of the hardships Oakland residents already experience and run the risk of pushing many more areas of the community further in a trauma-organized direction. Beefing up physical infrastructure and making other external changes will not address these problems.

However, in other ways the focus of the Oakland community-based climate adaptation plan makes total sense. Many residents have been or are currently traumatized and they want to eliminate or diminish the sources of their suffering. This theme could be seen when, early in the development of my organization's Transformational Resilience program, we ran a pilot workshop in Oakland that was attended by about 50 people including staff from the City of Oakland municipal government and residents that were members of the Oakland Climate Action Coalition. We worked with a local planning committee to develop the workshop. During this process we continually received requests to focus on how to bring about social and political changes. It took time to help people understand that building their capacity for Transformational Resilience would not only help safeguard them from the harmful personal and social reactions to climate impacts, it could also provide a platform for addressing many of the activities in the community that traumatize them. This could occur initially by helping the police and other authorities, as well as the populace as a whole, understand the psychobiology of trauma and toxic stress. This information would help authorities and others grasp why they react to people that look, speak, or act differently with fear-based aggressive or neglectful harmful actions. Personal and group skills would then be taught to help people calm their body, emotions, and thoughts when they are frightened and make wise and skillful decisions that would increase personal and collective wellbeing, rather than harming themselves, other people, or the natural environment.

The Oakland pilot workshop turned out to be very successful. In the end 97% of the participants who completed post-workshop surveys strongly agreed or agreed that the skills they learned would be very useful in their lives. Further, the pilot was a train-the-trainer workshop and 87% of the participants said they strongly agreed or agreed that they learned a great deal about how to teach Transformational Resilience skills to others. One participant, a local Reverend, wrote on her post-workshop evaluation, "Don't be afraid to attend this workshop! It may be different than what you are used to; it may not offer everything you believe or need; or, it may change your life!" Another participant who managed a county emergency call line wrote, "I went in feeling I was quite the expert in self-care and realized I was quite the novice starting out. I have felt blessed (truly) and have felt good through every minute of the training."[382]

Oakland is not the only community that has failed to grasp the importance of building the capacity of their residents for Transformational Resilience. In June 2013 *Inside Climate News*[383] reported that the Massachusetts Institute of Technology estimated that in 2011 only about 20% of cities globally have developed climate adaptation strategies. The story also said that the Georgetown Climate Center estimated that only about 100 adaptation plans have been developed by U.S. city, county, and state governments.

The article went on to describe "6 of the World's Most Extensive Climate Adaptation Plans" which included plans developed for New York City, London, Chicago, Rotterdam in the Netherlands, Quito in Ecuador, and Durban in South Africa. Not one of them addresses the impacts of climate disruption on personal mental health or psycho-social-spiritual wellbeing, nor do they focus on how to increase the capacity of individuals and groups for Transformational Resilience.

I will come back to the Oakland plan at the close of the chapter and offer suggestions for how it could incorporate efforts to build human resilience.

Common characteristics of trauma-organized communities

Left unchecked, the failure of communities to proactively build the capacity for Transformational Resilience among their residents for the traumas and toxic stresses generated by climate disruption is certain to end up a mistake of epic proportions. The omission will leave millions of people across the planet at grave risk of self-inflicted, socially generated, or both types of fear-based harmful reaction. A first step toward addressing this problem is to understand the characteristics of trauma-organized communities.

Summarized below are the patterns commonly seen in communities that have come structured to defend themselves from threats but which end up further traumatizing and severely stressing people. The traits are similar to those seen in trauma-organized organizations described in the previous chapter. The primary differences are that in communities the characteristics show up in different ways in different populations, and often interact in ways that produce surprising consequences (Fig. 11.1 describes the traits). Within a community the outcomes can include:

- Lack of clarity about and persistent social narratives describing what wellbeing and resilience requires for community members and the ethical principles used to guide decision-making toward those ends

- Lack of good emotional management among large groups of residents or authority figures, leading to communications and

FIGURE 11.1   Common traits of trauma-organized communities

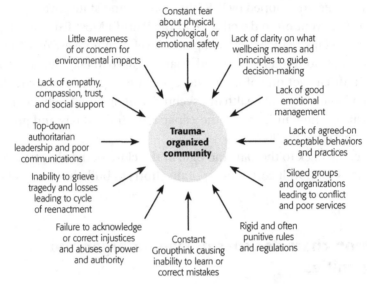

Source: Adapted from Bloom, S. (2013). *Destroying Sanctuary & Restoring Sanctuary*. Oxford: Oxford University Press; Doppelt, B. (2003). *Leading Change Toward Sustainability*. Sheffield, U.K.: Greenleaf Publishing.

behaviors that frighten others as well as high levels of interpersonal aggression, crime, violence and more

- Lack of agreement on what constitutes acceptable behaviors and practices
- Siloed and disconnected social support networks, organizations, and responsibilities leading to gaps, overlaps, and conflicts in services
- Rigid and often punitive policies, laws, and regulations
- Constant quick-fix thinking, Groupthink, and the inability to learn and resolve problems
- Failure to acknowledge or correct injustices, inequities, and abuses of power and authority
- Inability to grieve losses, leading to reenactment of problematic behaviors
- Authoritarian leadership and top-down nonparticipatory decision-making

- Lack of trust, empathy, compassion, and social support

- Little awareness of or concern for the impacts on the natural environment

- Widespread fears over personal safety

An extreme example: Ferguson, Missouri, U.S.A.

Ferguson, Missouri, a suburb of St. Louis, illustrates what can happen when a community experiences relentless adversity and becomes trauma-organized. In 2015, after Mike Brown, an unarmed young black man, was shot to death by police, years of pent-up frustration exploded leading to rioting and looting by community members which caused serious damage to numerous buildings, and economic losses to many businesses. Law enforcement authorities reacted with a military style mobilization that treated the community like a war zone and forced residents to deal with martial law.

The senseless shooting was merely the straw that broke the camel's back for this heavily traumatized community. Numerous studies showed that for years the city had racially segregated neighborhoods with high rates of poverty and unemployment. Student achievement was poor in the overwhelmingly black schools. Racially biased policing occurred regularly with many black people stopped at least once a month by police for little reason other than that they were black. Many homes were abandoned and derelict cars were found scattered throughout the area. Government officials and other authorities in the city refused to reach out and meaningfully engage the black community in planning or decision-making, leaving them feeling powerless.

It seems that the not-too-subtle social narrative of the police and other authorities in Ferguson was that people of color are bad, or inferior, and cannot be trusted. In response, a dominant social narrative among people of color was that police and other higher-ups are oppressive, authoritarian racists. In addition, there seemed to be almost no linking social networks that could connect the bonding and bridging social networks that existed among people of color with higher authorities and possibly help de-escalate the problems. The end result was that people of color, the police, city officials, and other members of the community all operated in a self-protective, survival mode. Rather than offering protection, however, the fear-based behaviors and practices further traumatized everyone. The anger and distress built up and finally exploded when Mike Brown was killed.

The reactions of people in Ferguson are not, as of now, related to the impacts of climate disruption. However, the U.S. National Climate Assessment predicts more frequent and extreme heat waves, increased humidity, more extreme rainfall events, flooding, and declining air and water quality for Missouri. These impacts will reduce public health and negatively affect transportation, agriculture, and the economy.[384] What will happen when these traumas and toxic stresses are added to the racism, economic inequality, and other adversities community members already face?

Without significant preventative efforts, as global temperatures rise by 1.5°C or higher above pre-industrial levels, more and more communities in the U.S., the EU, and around the world will be at risk of experiencing similar problems as those that occurred in Ferguson.

Further, although the high levels of poverty in Ferguson suggest that the community's greenhouse gas emissions are likely low, no one in the city is spending time reducing their emissions. The self-protective survival mode of most residents and authorities turns their focus inward and leaves no room to care about external issues such as their environmental impacts. This illustrates the tremendous difficulties that lie ahead in reducing climate disruption to manageable levels if more communities become trauma-organized.

Does your community exhibit any of these characteristics?

In the spaces below, note any traits that suggest your community is trauma-organized. It might not be nearly as severe as Ferguson, Missouri. But ask yourself if certain groups or a large number of people are unable to effectively manage their emotions? Does confusion exist over what wellbeing and resilience mean for different populations and the community as a whole? List whatever traits seem present in your community here:

- Lack of clarity about and persistent social narratives describing what wellbeing and resilience requires for community members and the ethical principles used to guide decision-making toward those ends:

_____

- Lack of good emotional management among large groups of residents or authority figures:

- Lack of agreed-on accepted behaviors and practices:

- Siloed social support networks and external organizations leading to mistrust, misunderstandings, conflicts, and gaps and deficiencies in services:

- Rigid and often punitive laws, rules, and regulations:

- Constant Groupthink leading to the inability to learn and correct mistakes:

- Failure to acknowledge or correct injustices and abuses of power and authority:

- Inability to grieve tragedy and losses leading to cycle of enactment:

- Top-down authoritarian leadership and poor communications:

- Lack of empathy, compassion, trust and social support:

- Little awareness of or concern for environmental impacts:

New social narratives are needed to build the capacity for Transformational Resilience within communities

It would not be unusual if you identified some, but not all, of the traits listed above. As economic, social, and environmental stresses increase, many communities around the world are slowly sliding into a trauma-organized condition, and the adversities generated by climate disruption will make things substantially worse. As illustrated in Ferguson Missouri, when a community becomes trauma-organized a significant effort is needed to reverse the trend. Post-disaster mental health treatment will *never* be sufficient to address the growing number of communities that become trauma-organized as global average temperatures rise by 1.5°C or more above pre-industrial levels. Only by making significant investments in *prevention* prior to overwhelming adversities can communities hope to avoid this type of downward spiral.

On the other hand, communities that have built widespread capacity for Transformational Resilience among their residents will not only have a much greater likelihood of preventing these patterns from emerging, they will also increase their chances of recovering more quickly when they do occur. In addition, they will be more likely to identify ways to use the difficulties as catalysts to adjust their perspectives, goals, practices, and policies so they increase the wellbeing of people as well as the condition of the natural environment and climate substantially above previous levels. In sum, they will be better able to promote human and other forms of life on Earth rather than degrading it.

A first step in making the transition to a trauma-informed human resilience-enhancing community is to understand the cultural myths that dominant the populace and how those stories influence the thinking, behaviors, and activities of residents. By cultural myths I mean the deep-seated set of socially constructed assumptions and beliefs about the way the world works that shape the way people view external events, think, and act.

Like organizations, communities are composed of people interacting with each other and their external environment. And, just like individuals and organizations, communities develop and maintain powerful cultural myths transmitted by continually repeated social narratives aimed at defining how to deal with adversity and live a proper life. In Western culture, and the U.S. in particular, the dominant cultural myths and associated social narratives emphasize rugged individualism, dog-eat-dog competition, and the belief that anyone can achieve success if they have a positive outlook, rely primarily on themselves, and persevere.[385]

In this cultural myth, the natural psychobiological reactions to Adverse Childhood Experiences that a great many young people experience that hinder their ability to learn and surface in adulthood as mental and physical health problems, and the traumas caused when people experience persistent racism, poverty, economic inequality, and other forms of systemic oppression, are denied or ignored. People who cannot rise above adversity are seen as mentally weak or lazy. Those who fail to achieve success, which is primarily defined by material and financial standards—have no significant cultural role, and instead are often viewed as free-riding outsiders or losers.[386]

Certainly, not every community in the U.S. or other Western nations adheres to these cultural myths. But many do, at least in part, even if the values and norms are understated or never openly acknowledged. This makes it difficult to focus on building human resilience because the dominant belief is that people should be able to cope with adversities such as those generated by climate disruption on their own, without help from others. This might be one reason why there are few operational models for building personal or psycho-social-spiritual resilience within communities, at least in the U.S.[387]

In addition, the cultural myths that dominate many communities in Western nations likely contribute to the fact that the climate preparedness field has focused almost exclusively on hardening physical infrastructure and adapting natural resources, while ignoring the human mental health and psycho-social-spiritual dimensions of the crises. Transportation, energy, water, and other physical systems need to be strengthened, so the thinking goes, but people should be able to take care of their own psychological needs.

It also could be one of the primary reasons why mental health programs in Western societies emphasize psychotherapy, drug therapy, and post-disaster treatment and place very little emphasis on building skills that can help prevent personal psychological or psycho-social-spiritual maladies before they occur. Again, the dominant cultural myths suggest that people should be able to handle adversity on their own.

Another cultural myth that is ubiquitous in Western nations is the righteousness of what can be called cornucopianism. This is the belief that there are few natural limits to growth. Therefore, it is perfectly natural and appropriate for humans to relentlessly dig, mine, chop, frack, and in other ways take minerals, metals, wood, coal, oil, gas and other substances from the Earth with little concern for the damage that results. According to the cornucopian cultural myth, ecosystems and biodiversity have no intrinsic value of their own. Instead, oceans, water bodies, forests, soils, streams, and biodiversity are nothing more than "resources" to be used for human purposes with little concern for the consequences.

Despite their powerful influence on how people see and respond to the world, there are often profound differences between a cultural myth and the way the world actually functions (which is why they are called "myths"). For instance, rather than being benign, the cultural myth of extractivism is one of the root causes of the climate crisis that now threatens the very existence of human civilization. And it is not just the mentally weak who experience psychological or emotional troubles. When any community experiences acute traumas or persistent toxic stresses, such as those generated by climate disruption, much of the population can become dysregulated if they lack good Presencing and Purposing skills. The fear-based reactions that result cause people to retreat into a self-protective survival mode. When they persist, many people will adopt self- or socially destructive coping behaviors. A vicious cycle often results that is difficult to reverse, causing many people to end up further traumatized.

In short, as I have previously stated, to save the planet from uncontrollable climate disruption we must first save ourselves from ourselves. The outdated and scientifically erroneous cultural myth of extractivism is one of the root causes of the climate crisis. Left unaddressed, our flawed cultural myths of rugged individualism, dog-eat-dog competition, and self-reliance will leave millions of people unprepared to deal with the physical damage caused by climate disruption and make it likely that their fear-based destructive reactions will be as harmful as the actual physical impacts.

To minimize this type of maladaptive human reaction, new social narratives are needed that counter the existing faulty cultural myths by establishing a new and better way to interpret external events, think, and act. The new social narratives must offer a compelling new story about the tremendous benefits of learning and utilizing Presencing and Purposing skills. As part of this, the social narratives must help people realize that the most powerful way to find the meaning and purpose in life they are so desperately searching for today is by focusing, in their own unique way, on increasing the wellbeing of other people and the condition of the Earth's natural environment and climate substantially above previous levels.

The power of compelling new social narratives becomes clear if you recall the story I opened the book with about how Father Vien promoted a new narrative that rallied the residents of Village de l'Est in New Orleans to take care of each other and rapidly rebuild their neighborhood after Hurricane Katrina better than it was before.

The importance of social narratives that emphasize building Presencing and Purposing skills

It is important to realize that, even though he did not use these terms, Father Vien included in his social narratives the importance of using Presencing and Purposing. The benefits of promoting these skills and perspectives can be seen in many other successful community recovery and sustainability-building efforts as well.

When people know how to use culturally and age-appropriate methods to calm their bodies, emotions, and thoughts when they are pushed outside of their Resilient Growth Zone, they are more likely to avoid personally or socially harmful behaviors and increase their chances of making wise and skillful decisions. Further, when people know how to gain insight and meaning from traumatic events, clarify the values they want to live by, and adopt a mission greater than themselves such as the residents of Village de l'Est did when they decided to take care of each other and rebuild better than before, they become more inspired to work together to achieve a better future.

The importance of robust bonding, bridging, and linking social support networks

In communities, one of the Presencing skills that is particularly important is the capacity to build strong social support networks. This is another lesson that was learned after Hurricane Katrina devastated New Orleans, and it is relevant worldwide.

Many residents in both Village de l'Est and the Lower 9th Ward had close nurturing relationships among a small group of family, friends, or neighbors—which as you recall from Chapter 5 can be called *bonding* social support networks. Those networks were also connected with other bonding social networks that existed in the neighborhood through what can be called *bridging* social support networks. However, the bonding and bridging social support networks of many people in Village de l'Est also had the capacity to connect to higher up decision-makers and external government and not-for-profit organizations that made it possible for them to block a toxic waste facility that was proposed for their neighborhood and obtain financial and other resources to help their neighborhood. These, as you might remember, can be considered *linking* social support networks.[388] In contrast, members of the Lower 9th Ward did not have these types of link. Researchers determined that their connections to external authorities and resources were one of the reasons why residents of Village de l'Est were able to rebuild more quickly than those in the Lower 9th Ward.[389]

This underscores that, when seeking to build the capacity for Transformational Resilience in communities it is vital to maintain, strengthen, and expand all three types of social support network (also called "social capital networks").[390]

Let's delve a bit more into the complex nature and processes involved with these social support networks. The term "bonding social support networks" refers to the trusting relationships among a close-knit group of family members, friends, and neighbors who provide emotional buffering and support as well as practical assistance when people experience adversity. Bonding social support networks center on the relationships and levels of cooperation that exist between people who are very familiar with each other.[391]

In communities, bridging social support networks are also very important. These are connections between members of a bonding social support network and other similar close-knit bonding social support networks that differ in their geographic location, economic, ethnic, or racial status, or religious affiliations. Maintaining and enhancing the number and strength of bonding social support networks increases the likelihood that critical information and resources can be exchanged throughout a community. It is also extremely important to prevent conflict with people considered to be outsiders, while enhancing the possibility of cross-sectoral problem-solving and other opportunities to build trust and understanding among diverse segments of the community.[392]

Also extremely important when building the capacity for Transformational Resilience within communities are linking social support networks. These are explicit relationships between bonding and bridging social support networks and institutionalized sources of power and authority such as elected officials, the police, and government agencies, as well as not-for-profits, private companies, and others that can offer important resources or services. Low-income neighborhoods often have strong bonding networks composed of family and friends and a few bridging social networks with other tight-knit groups of family and friends. However, because it takes all of their time and effort to care for themselves, low-income groups often have weak or non-existent links to external authorities or organizations.[393]

All three types of social support network, and the ways in which they are combined, will be important when seeking to help community members use the adversities generated by climate disruption to increase their own as well as collective wellbeing, and the condition of the natural environment above previous levels. For example, strong social support networks in communities have been found to play a key role in reducing rates of ethic violence,[394] improving governance,[395] providing important policy feedback to government,[396] and helping people recover from disasters.[397]

One of the reasons these benefits exist is that bonding, bridging, and linking social support networks can establish norms and requirements about compliance that shape the expectations people have about the behavior of others. For example, if every individual and family in a neighborhood is taught that they are expected to participate in neighborhood crime patrols, attend neighborhood watch meetings, and call the police when they see suspicious activity, they are very likely to actively engage in these activities. Research has shown that areas with this type of high social engagement have fewer crimes and murders. In addition, the costs are much higher for people who break from the expected patterns of behavior. Thus, robust social support networks are one of the best ways to combat crime and violence. In contrast, neighborhoods where people believe someone else will be responsible for spotting crime or for calling the police when problems occur are more likely to be less safe.[398]

Bonding, bridging, and linking social networks can also disseminate information and knowledge to their members about local conditions, trends, opportunities, and other issues of importance.[399] The capacity of social support networks to diffuse knowledge and information throughout the community is far greater than anything government can offer. For instance, people usually seek out information from members of their social support network rather than spend time searching newspapers, the web, or government documents. If respected people discount or ignore certain types of information, others in their social support network are likely to do so as well. Conversely, when some members of a social support network see certain types of knowledge and information as credible and important, others in their group are likely to do so as well.

In addition, robust bonding, bridging, and linking social support networks can create trust among their members by transmitting images about the honesty, dependability, and credibility of people.[400] Individuals are much more likely to share resources, engage in the exchange of critical material resources or other types of transaction, and provide assistance to others when those people are deemed to be trustworthy by their social support networks. Building this type of trust is essential to convince people that one of the most potent ways to increase their own wellbeing is by helping other people and improving the condition of the natural environment.

Finally, strong social support networks are extremely important to help people deal constructively with and overcome racism, sexism, economic discrimination, and other types of systemic oppression, as well as the harmful economic and institutional practices associated with extractivism. People can either be resigned to hopelessness and depression when they experience these injustices, or they can increase their power sufficiently to compel social change. This can be achieved in two ways: by enhancing one's own personal power; and by forming groups with allies that together generate more power than any single individual can develop on their own. A good deal of self-discipline is essential to enhance one's person power. This includes a firm commitment to use some type of Presencing and Purposing skill to keep yourself in top-notch psychological and emotional condition, refrain from engaging in personally or socially destructive behaviors, and abide by a clear set of values that enable you to refuse to feel humiliated by the injustices while pressing for social change. Finding people who hold similar views and are willing to commit to similar goals is also very important to create social change because groups often have much more staying power, diversity of ideas, and overall capacity than individuals acting alone. Being a member of a robust bonding social support network can provide the emotional nurturance you need to maintain your self-discipline and persevere in the face of discrimination and injustice. Being connected to other bonding social support networks increases your chances of finding True Allies to partner with to deal with the adversities. And, when your social support networks have links to external authorities and organizations, you and your allies have a much greater chance of bringing about social change.

It is important to remember that social support networks can also have downsides

Although robust social support networks are a key to building human resilience, it is also important to keep in mind that they can have downsides. For example, individuals involved with close bonding and bridging social networks can deny important information to people who are not part of their group, exclude them from decisions that affect them, or deny them financial or other resources that are critical to their health and wellbeing. As noted in Chapter 3, deindividuation can occur when people merge their personal identity with their group allowing them to commit atrocious acts of violence. Groups such as the Ku Klux Klan and the ISIS terrorists achieve internal cohesion by focusing their hatred on outsiders. Without effective skills, people with deeply felt commitments to their group can easily demonize, isolate, or commit violence against those that look, talk, or think differently, or in other ways are considered to be outsiders.

When maintaining and building social support networks it is therefore very important to continually watch for and prepare for these types of negative outcome.

Methods for maintaining and strengthening social support networks

Researchers have examined different ways in which the depth and breadth of social support networks can be enhanced to build human resilience. Some of these strategies include:

Community Mapping

An important first step is to map the nature of the existing bonding, bridging, and linking networks that exist in the community. This can be accomplished by asking individuals to complete the "Circles of Support" exercise described in Chapter 5, and then asking them to share the nature of their social support networks with others. In addition, organizations that work with or represent different populations and sectors in the community can be asked to describe the services they offer as well as their clients, customers, and stakeholders. Using simple tools such as flip charts or Excel spreadsheets, a comprehensive map can be developed of the linkages among groups and organizations in the community. This type of process can identify isolated individuals that lack a bonding social support network. It can also surface important gaps between different bonding social support networks, between those networks and key public, not-for-profit, faith, and private organizations in the community, and linkages and relationship gaps among those organizations themselves. Efforts can then be made to close the gaps and strengthen and expand linkages.

My organization is using this low-tech method to map the many networks that existed in a region in Oregon as part of a community-based Transformational Resilience initiative we are facilitating called Building a Resilient Lane County. The most important aspect of the process is not the actual map itself. It is the dialogue and learning that takes place during the process of developing the map.

High-tech mapping techniques can also be used. The Los Angeles County Public Health Community Disaster Resilience Project, for example, placed a major emphasis on mapping the resources and sectors in different neighborhoods and then developing new partnerships among them to avoid overlap, keep information flowing, and open lines of communication. They used a tool called Sahana developed by the Sahana Software Foundation.[401]

Neighborhood events and facilitated meetings

With or without a mapping process, one way to increase social connections and trust is to organize social events and facilitator-led discussions throughout the community. Parades, block parties, local celebrations, meetings in neighborhoods and at the block level, and similar activities offer opportunities for neighbors to interact, build relationships, and learn from each other. For instance, discussions held in a neighborhood about the psychobiology of trauma, the nature of social justice and inequities, or the likely impacts of climate disruption can increase understanding while also allowing people to get to know each other and increase understanding and trust.

The Los Angeles County Public Health Community Disaster Resilience Project has used this approach to bring neighbors together to develop plans to address potential disasters.[402] The Neighborhood Empowerment Network in San Francisco does something similar. Research in both Nicaragua and South Africa found that regular meetings among neighborhood level groups created higher trust levels, not only in the people that participate but also in their society as a whole.[403]

Time Banking and Community Currency

Time Banking and Community Currency offer another unique approach to building robust social support networks. These are mechanisms for incentivizing volunteerism, and rewarding people who spend time assisting their communities, by giving them some type of currency redeemable at local merchants. They also help to develop relationships between and link different organizations together.

Here is how Time Banking works: When you volunteer for an hour to help someone in your community, such as at a community garden or local school, you earn a Time Bank Hour (also called time credits, service credits, or time dollars). You can use the credit for an hour's worth of childcare, home repair, dental work, or other services provided by other people in the community. As more people volunteer, the benefits begin to spread and a virtuous cycle of people helping people kicks in.[404]

Community Currencies are sometimes called "complementary currencies" that are developed and used within a specific community. Some examples include Bay Bucks, Ithaca Hours, and Berkshares. The idea is to keep local people and businesses connected by continually recirculating the currency within a specific geographic area, or between specific types of business. At the heart of many community currencies is an innovation known as the Mutual Credit System. This system enables its members to create money when it is needed to facilitate transactions. In this system, money is not something scarce that must be hoarded. It is abundant and most beneficial to all when it is freely spent.[405] No matter how it is organized, community currency is designed to meet the needs of a specific group and seeks to create more equal and sustainable conditions.

Both of these community-based, bottom-up exchange systems are aimed at promoting more socially connected, vibrant, equitable, and sustainable communities. One study found that both mental and physical health improved in people who participated in a time banking program.[406] A number of communities impacted by disasters in Japan have adopted community currency or time banking programs, and claim to have seen strong material and mental health benefits.[407]

Community planning and design

The physical layout of a community can enhance or retard the degree of interaction, connection, and trust that exists. When a community is designed to facilitate frequent interactions among residents by, for example, locating coffee houses, bookstores, hair salons, libraries, public squares, grocery stores, and similar facilities close to each other, people are more apt to spend time talking and sharing. Even brief encounters can lead to increased connections and trust. Communities where residents feel connected due to the way their neighborhood is designed and built have been found to have higher levels of social capital and lower crime rates.[408]

Characteristics of a human resilience-enhancing community

With this information as background, below I describe the characteristics of communities that are leading the way in transitioning from a trauma-organized to trauma-informed human resilience-enhancing entities. To develop this list I reviewed a number of non-climate-focused community-based human-resilience-building community efforts under way around the world to identify the key characteristics of success.[409] Although the details differ, the traits of the most successful programs are very similar to those found in organizations that prioritize building the capacity of their members for Transformational Resilience. Below is a summary of the common traits I found (see Fig. 11.2):[410]

- **Common agreement on, and powerful social narratives clarifying the purpose, vision of wellbeing and resilience, and ethical principles that will guide decision-making.** A majority of residents have a basic understanding of and agreement over what is needed to achieve wellbeing and enhance personal mental health and psycho-social-spiritual resilience. They also understand and support a related set of ethical principles focused on social responsibility, equity, and justice that are used to guide decision-making toward those ends.

- **Good emotional regulation.** A majority of community members have a basic understanding of how trauma and toxic stress can affect them and others—that is, they have learned the basics of the psychobiology of trauma and toxic stress and are trauma-informed. In addition, even though they may not use these terms, residents can utilize simple Presencing skills to regulate their "Fear and Alarm Centers" in ways that avoid personally and socially destructive behaviors as well as Purposing skills that enable them to use adversity as catalysts to gain new insights, grow, and increase personal, social, and environmental wellbeing.

- **Widespread agreement over acceptable behaviors and practices.** Because many residents have the capacity to calm their bodies and minds, communities that emphasize building personal and psycho-social-spiritual resilience are undergirded by certain widely agreed-on habits and practices. This includes concurrence about what constitutes social responsibility, equity, justice, environmental protection and restoration, meaningful engagement in decisions, and other issues.

- **Robust social support networks and partnerships among local organizations.** Most people have strong bonding social support networks as well as bridges to other bonding social support networks and linkages to external organizations and authorities. In addition, many organizations within the community know each other and work together in partnerships and collaborations. Organizations thus generate more by working cooperatively together

FIGURE 11.2   Common traits of human resilience-enhancing communities

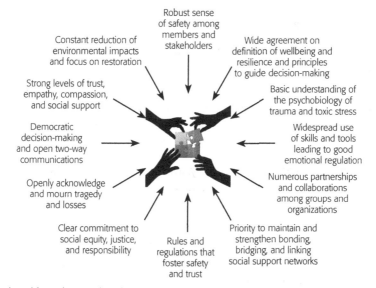

Source: Adapted from Bloom, S. (2013). *Destroying Sanctuary & Restoring Sanctuary*. Oxford: Oxford University Press; Doppelt, B. (2003). *Leading Change Toward Sustainability*. Sheffield, U.K.: Greenleaf Publishing.

than any single entity could do on their own, while avoiding actions that undermine each other.

- **Laws, regulations, and procedures that foster safety and trust.** Most community members understand and support the laws, regulations, and procedures that exist because they believe them to be well-intentioned, reasonable, just, and aimed at protecting overall health, safety, and wellbeing.

- **Openness to challenges and criticism that help promote continual improvement.** Community members are encouraged to respectfully raise concerns, share contrasting information, and challenge mainstream views in order to improve understanding and increase the effectiveness of policies, programs, and practices.

- **Commitment to social responsibility, equity, and social justice.** Inequities, injustices, and abuses of power and authority are seen as totally unacceptable and when they appear, the community quickly acts to correct the problems and make amends to those who have been harmed. Wealthier and powerful groups do not shift the burden of solutions to those who played small or no roles at all in creating the problems.

- **Openly acknowledge and mourn losses.** Public rituals, symbolic gestures, pauses in daily life, and other methods are used to allow people to grieve when injuries, death, or other tragedies occur that affect large segments of the community.

- **Value diversity, participation, and democratic decision-making.** Individuals and groups representing the diversity within the community are actively sought out, encouraged, and given assistance to participate in planning and decision-making. Decisions that affect everyone are thoroughly discussed and vetted through all levels of the community before they are finalized.

- **Strong levels of trust, empathy, and social support.** Many community members have strong social support networks, and those who do not are given assistance to link up with people and organizations that can provide support. Empathy and compassion is strong for people who make mistakes or experience difficulty—though this does not mean that drug or alcohol abuse, crime, violence, or other harmful behaviors are condoned or allowed to go unaddressed.

- **Constant focus on reducing their environmental impacts and ecological restoration.** Public, private, and non-profit organizations as well as individuals constantly seek to identify and phase out materials, substances, practices, and policies that degrade ecosystems and the climate and place a major emphasis on restoring ecological systems.

- **Strong sense of safety and security.** Due to the factors described above, community members feel safe in their homes and around town. Interpersonal aggression, crime, or violence that occur are seen as anomalies and most people are confident that the problems will be dealt with quickly and fairly and safety will be quickly restored.

Which of these traits does your community exhibit?

Even when a community exhibits a number of traits that suggest it might be trauma-organized, many signs of being a human resilience-enhancing entity might also exist. By identifying these positive traits, they can serve as the building blocks to enhance the capacity of your community for Transformational Resilience.

In the space below list any of the characteristics described above that you believe are common within your community:

- Does widespread agreement exist on what is involved with wellness and resilience for different community members, along with ethical principles that will be used to guide decision-making toward those ends?

- Do most individuals and groups understand the psychobiology of trauma and toxic stress and manage their emotions well?

- Is there strong agreement on acceptable behaviors and practices?

- Do numerous robust bonding, bridging, and linking social support networks as well as partnerships exist among organizations leading to improved services?

  _____

- Do laws, regulations, and procedures foster trust, health, and safety?

  _____

- Do most people embrace and utilize criticism and contrasting information to learn and improve?

  _____

- Is there a clear commitment to social responsibility, equity, and social justice?

  _____

- Do people openly acknowledge and mourn tragedy and losses?

  _____

- Does democratic decision-making and open two-way communication exist?

  _____

- Are there strong levels of trust, empathy, compassion, and social support?

  _____

- Do most individuals and organizations constantly search for and reduce their environmental impacts and focus on restoring nature?

  _____

- Do most people feel they are physically, psychologically, and emotionally safe?

  _____

The Dalles, Oregon story[411]

The small rural community of The Dalles seems like an unlikely place for a community-based human resilience initiative to be under way. But it is a very inspiring effort.

In 2008, SAMHSA (the U.S. Federal Substance Abuse Mental Health Services Administration) awarded the community a five-year US$2.7 million Safe Schools/Healthy Students (SSHS) grant. It specified that law enforcement, mental health, juvenile justice, and educational agencies work together to make schools healthier and students safer. The Department of Human Services was added to the group. Trudy Townsend was hired as the project director.

Senior officials from these agencies formed a core team that began to meet once a month. These discussions built a foundation of trust. "It was really amazing to watch them form relationships and build trust," said Townsend.

One of the group's earliest successes involved a social justice issue. An event at the middle school that resulted in police action forced the SSHS Core Team to analyze the number of calls for law enforcement at schools. After some digging, it was discovered that police were being called out for minor disturbances on school campuses almost daily and there was a disproportionate amount of school discipline referrals and subsequent police contact with Hispanic youth. "Outreach meetings were held to discover the perspective of the Hispanic population and establish better methods of communication between these families, schools, and law enforcement officials. Through this process many of the issues were resolved." Townsend told me that, "This exercise was one of the events that helped the team understand that our community was trauma-organized."[412]

As the SSHS Core Team reflected on this experience and many other factors related to community livability and social outcomes, they came to the realization that the dominant problem was trauma. It "was the great equalizer, impacting everyone: individuals, organizations, and the entire community."

With this new awareness, they "went looking for a method to guide our madness," said Townsend. Maggie Bennington Davis, a psychiatrist at Cascadia Behavioral Health Care in Portland, was invited to give a one-day training on trauma-informed care. She spoke to a packed house of over 250 people, including the core team. Participants heard about how trauma and toxic stress affect the human mind and body. They also learned about the Adverse Childhood Experiences study that shows that many children experience traumatic experiences that surface in adulthood as mental and physical health problems.

In addition, participants learned about The Sanctuary Model developed by Dr. Sandra Bloom and the Sanctuary Institute. As previously discussed, it offers a pathway to change by establishing a new social narrative through commitments to principles such as democracy, open communication, good emotional regulation, nonviolence, and more, as well as the S.E.L.F. model for recovery from trauma. When consistently implemented these new ways of thinking and acting fundamentally reshape the culture of a group.

Following the event, the core team decided to learn more about the Sanctuary Model by sending members to a five-day training. "It was a revelation for the (school) superintendent," recalled Townsend. It also had a profound effect on the other participants.

After the core team returned home it adopted a new vision for The Dalles: "Our goal was to re-script the future for our community," she said. "In addition to better outcomes for children, youth, and families, we wanted a more positive outlook and more people taking pride in the community." In other words, they wanted to establish a new social narrative for the community focused on wellbeing and resilience.

Just as they were getting this new phase off the ground, disaster struck. Within a span of two weeks two homicides and a police-involved shooting occurred. People throughout the community were in shock. But rather than reacting as in the past with recrimination and knee-jerk policies, the core team organized "a trauma-informed response." For instance, the shooting happened on Wednesday and by Saturday night they had organized a candlelight vigil. The local newspaper reported how the community had come together. Townsend recalls that, "it marked a first step toward literally re-scripting the future."

Since that time community members have participated in a number of Sanctuary Institute educational and skills training programs. Even after the SAMHSA funding ended in 2013, the core team, expanded to include representatives from a diverse set of organizations in the community, has continued to meet in a "learning circle" on a monthly basis. The numerous individuals and organizations involved in the initiative are, "specifically working on building a shared language, a shared value system, and shared problem-solving tools across the community," said Townsend.[413] New partnerships and collaborations have emerged out of the ongoing dialogues.

As a result, a growing number of community members have developed a basic understanding of how trauma and toxic stress affect humans. They have also learned how a traumatic events and chronic stressors in the community can impact the culture of a place. For example, following up on their focus on social justice, residents learned about the traumas that Native Americans who reside near The Dalles have historically experienced. This ranged from the construction of The Dalles Dam on the Columbia River that in 1957 submerged Celilo Falls, a longtime Native American fishing site, to the suffering they felt during the railroad wars that occurred early in the last century. People also became aware of how the influx of workers into town to build the dam led to the creation of two different school districts representing "different sides of the tracks" that has caused ongoing rifts in the community.

Further, community members learned about more recent traumas, such as the acrimony that occurred when a new state law was passed that banned the use of Native American mascots. Resolving that conflict, "engaged people in discussions about both social justice and community trauma."[414] One result is that relationships are improving, allowing the community to slowly overcome the previous lack of trust and siloed relationships.

Throughout all of this, individuals and organizations continue to be trained in the Sanctuary Principles and trauma-informed practices. This led all major social service organizations in The Dalles to agree to implement the Sanctuary Model, including the school district, the Wasco County Youth Services Department, and others.

The initiative is using a wide range of factors to measure progress, including juvenile crime rates, school attendance, school climate, student mental health and wellbeing, and more. The information helps to alter the feedback mechanisms used within the community to measure the effectiveness of their initiates and its impact on wellbeing.

Some of the early signs of progress include significant changes in the schools. For instance, according to Townsend, in the past during an expulsion hearing for a child with serious behavioral problems, the panel would listen to the teacher tell their story of how terrifying the child was and quickly expel them. Now, the approach has changed from "What's wrong with this kid?" to "What happened to initiate this behavior and what type of help is needed?" If the panel decides that an expulsion is still necessary, a plan is developed to help the child and family. This same shift in perspective also applies in the case of conflict among staff in the school district. This has reduced acrimony and increased equanimity in the organization.

Other measurable signs of success, said Townsend, include a significant drop in juvenile crime rates. In addition, there has been a major change among residents in the attitudes and beliefs about the community. "We are hearing more and more positive references for our community and we are noticing that people are coming here for tourism reasons, which can be accredited largely to a significant effort on the part of our city and chamber of commerce taking a positive approach," said Townsend.[415]

Perhaps the most visible outcome of the progress that has been made in the past seven years is that in 2014 The Dalles was named #1 on a list of the Ten Best Cities to Live in Oregon.[416] No one within or outside of the community would have seen that coming seven years ago!

Because of the outstanding knowledge and leadership Townsend demonstrated throughout the initiative, I contacted her and together we began to co-facilitate Transformational Resilience workshops focused on building community resilience for climate disruption.

The Dalles initiative shows that an explicit focus on climate disruption is not required—but it is helpful

Creating Sanctuary in The Dalles does not explicitly focus on building human resilience for environmental traumas such as those generated by climate disruption. However, the initiative applies to all types of trauma and toxic stress, and it has helped to build the community's capacity to deal with wildfires that often threaten the town during warm dry months. More frequent and intense wildfires are, of course, one of the impacts in forested areas of the world that are aggravated by climate disruption. Thus, The Dalles program is addressing some of the risks posed by warming global temperatures, even if climate disruption is not explicitly discussed.

This raises an important point. Community efforts aimed at enhancing the capacity of residents for Transformational Resilience do not need to solely or specifically focus on climate disruption. Instead, it can emphasize building human resilience for the unique challenges facing the community, be they high levels of adverse childhood experiences, soaring school dropout rates, widespread substance abuse, crime and violence, or other issues. As long as people are taught basic information about how trauma and toxic stress can affect them, along with simple age and culturally appropriate Presencing and Purposing skills, community members will gain the knowledge and tools needed to help them use adversities associated with climate disruption as catalysts to gain insight, grow, and thrive rather than adopting destructive fear-based reactions.

That said, the planet is speeding toward irreversible civilization-altering climate disruption. The more that community-based human-resilience-building initiatives directly address this issue, the greater our chances of reducing the climate crisis to manageable levels.

In The Dalles, for example, community leaders and residents could be informed about what the expected impacts of climate disruption will be, along with how they are likely to affect the mental health of individuals and psycho-social-spiritual wellbeing of groups. As climate disruption worsens, for example, hotter temperatures are expected in the Columbia River Gorge where the town is located. In addition, more extended droughts intermixed with periods of heavier precipitation are likely. The town is surrounded by forest and farming is a key part of the local economy. More frequent and intense forest fires, impacts on agriculture, as well as public health problems can also be expected.[417]

With this information in hand, community members could apply what they have learned about how trauma and toxic stress affect people, and discuss the possible negative human reactions that will occur as temperatures rise. The risks of rising anxiety, depression, PTSD, and suicide, for example, could be debated, along with the likelihood of increased aggression, crime, and violence. Efforts could then begin to build the capacity of individuals and groups to respond skillfully and wisely to the adversities generated by climate disruption, and use them as catalysts to find ways to increase the wellbeing of all community members, including Native Americans, as well as the condition of the natural environment.

Key leverage points for changing the culture of a community

Creating Sanctuary in The Dalles also illustrates that some leverage points for change are more powerful than others when seeking to change the culture of a community. The most potent levers are similar to those used in successful organizational change efforts. Just as in organizations, the most deep-seated changes occur when the assumptions and beliefs that shape the thinking and behavior of the majority of people change—that is, when the overarching cultural myths of the community are altered. Once again, this requires the development and continual repetition of new social narratives that over time alter the mental models held by a majority of residents and decision-makers.

However, building a culture that enhances the capacity for Transformational Resilience within a community is much more difficult than doing so in an organization. As mentioned, at least in Western nations, one of the reasons is the difficulty in overcoming the cultural myths of rugged individualism, dog-eat-dog competition, and self-reliance. In addition, organizations usually have a purpose, goals, and values that members must support in order to be part of the group. In contrast, a community of any size usually includes individuals and groups with different historical backgrounds, goals, values, and norms. Some people might have a history of being discriminated against or experience ongoing abuse, which creates tension and reduces trust for others. In addition, certain actions, words, and images frequently mean different things to people with different cultural backgrounds. This often causes community members to unknowingly talk past one another or to say or do things that offend or anger others. These and other issues make it difficult to get everyone on the same page, let alone moving in the same direction. But it is not an impossible task.

Below is a summary of the most powerful leverage points for changing the culture of a community to embrace building human resilience (represented in Fig. 11.3).

- **The most powerful leverage point for building the capacity for Transformational Resilience within a community is to alter the mental models that shape the way a majority of residents and community leaders see and respond to the world so that it prioritizes enhancing human resilience.**

  How can you alter the controlling mindset so that it emphasizes enhancing the resilience of individuals and groups? By establishing new social narratives in the community describing the need, benefits, and collective responsibility of residents to understand how they are affected by trauma and toxic stress, use simple Presencing and Purposing skills, and care for themselves by caring for other people and the natural environment.

- **The second most powerful leverage point for shifting a community from a trauma-organized to one that builds widespread capacity for Transformational Resilience is to rearrange its**

FIGURE 11.3   Greatest leverage points and interventions for shifting from a trauma-organized to a human resilience-enhancing community

Greatest leverage for change	Leverage point	Intervention
	1. Change the mindsets that shape the way the community typically views and responds to issues.	Educate people about the need and benefits of building human resilience including information on trauma theory and climate disruption.
	2. Rearrange the way planning and decision-making in the community is structured.	Organize deep, wide, and inclusive "Human Resilience Committees."
	3. Alter the vision, goals and decision-making criteria of the community.	Committees clarify the new vision of resilience and wellbeing and the guiding principles to be used to in decision-making to achieve the vision.
	4. Restructure the rules of engagement among groups within the community.	Develop new collaborations and partnerships and develop strategies to ensure comprehensive services in building human resilience.
	5. Shift the flows of information within the community.	Use every means to communicate the new vision, guiding principles, and strategies through two-way interaction *and* role modeling.
	6. Correct the feedback loops of the community.	Constantly evaluate progress, disseminate results, and encourage and reward improvement.
Least leverage for change	7. Adjust the policies and regulations of the community.	Embed new policies and regulations in systems, structures, and standard operating procedures.

parts—especially the groups and networks that make key decisions and control the flow of resources within the community.

How can you rearrange the parts? As in organizations, this can occur by forming a diverse "Human Resilience Committee" (or whatever title makes sense) composed of people representing all of the different populations, sectors, and interests in the community. In large cities committees can be formed at the neighborhood level. The committees should develop a plan to lead the transition from a trauma-organized to a trauma-informed resilience-enhancing community. When greater diversity and representation is established among the individuals and groups that plan, make decisions, and allocate resources in a community, many new ways of seeing and responding to the world are likely to emerge.

- **The third most powerful leverage point for shifting from a trauma-organized to a community that builds the capacity for Transformational Resilience is to change its purpose.**

  How can you alter the purpose of a community to promote enhancing human resilience? By reaching out broadly in the community to gather feedback on what wellbeing and resilience mean to them and then crafting an overall ideal vision of wellbeing and resilience for community, as well as short- and long-term goals for achieving it. Mirroring the decision by the committee that led Creating Sanctuary in The Dalles to "re-script" the future of their community, the vision should emphasis continually increasing the wellbeing of all community members as well as the condition of the natural environment. A fundamental element of the new vision should be the identification of principles such as good emotional regulation, social responsibility, equity, justice, and environmental protection that will be used to guide decision-making toward the new vision and goals—and the benefits of following these principles for all residents. The committees should also be empowered to engage with people of all types at all levels of the community to relentlessly explain the new purpose, vision, and guiding principles.

- **The fourth most powerful leverage point for making the shift to a community that builds the capacity for Transformational Resilience among its residents is to restructure the rules of engagement.**

  How can you alter the rules of engagement in a community so that they promote human resilience? By identifying and mapping the informal and formal groups including not-for-profit, private, and government organizations that exist in the communities, as well as the populations they serve and the services they provide, and then developing robust networks of new partnerships and collaborations among them to close gaps, eliminate overlaps, build mutual support, and enhance the community's capacity to build human resilience.

- **The fifth most powerful lever for transitioning to a human resilience-enhancing entity is to shift the information flows within the community.**

  How can you change the information flows within a community to focus on enhancing human resilience? By using all possible means including social media, TV, radio, presentations to civic groups, and others methods to reach out to community members and continually communicate the new purpose, vision of wellbeing and resilience, guiding ethical principles, and benefits of the new approach to community members. This includes the benefits of learning Presencing and Purposing skills and continually reducing environmental impacts while ensuring social responsibility, equity and justice. Role modeling by members of the "Human Resilience Committees" and other community leaders is also important. People will quickly discount the effort if a number of community leaders repeatedly communicate or behave in ways that undermine rather than enhance human resilience.

- **The sixth most powerful leverage for helping a community build the capacity of its residents for Transformational Resilience is to correct its feedback mechanisms.**

    How can you change the feedback mechanisms to help a community enhance its capacity to build human resilience? By actively engaging a wide variety of community members in continually evaluating and disseminating data about the progress being made toward the community's vision of wellbeing and resilience, and the principles of social responsibility, equity, justice, and environmental protection and restoration being used to transition toward those goals. This data helps people identify ways to continually learn and improve programs, practices and policies.

- **The seventh most powerful lever for transitioning to community that buildings the capacity for Transformational Resilience is to adjust its policies and regulations.**

    Just like in organizations, many people hold the belief that new policies and regulations are the key to change in a community. Again, this is a misperception. If a majority of people have not altered their core assumptions and beliefs, the key decision-makers remain unchanged, and other elements of the old way of doing business remain unaffected, it will be difficult, if not impossible, to get new policies enacted. And, even if new policies are enacted they are likely to be so watered down as to be ineffective and even then many people will find ways to avoid or work around them. In contrast, when new policies follow and build on the previous key leverage points for change, they can make human resilience building a

FIGURE 11.4   The wheel of change toward Transformational Resilience in communities

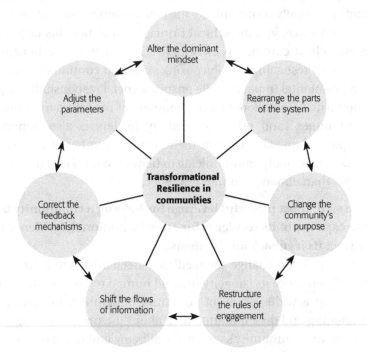

Source: Adapted from Doppelt, B. (2003). *Leading Change Toward Sustainability: A Change Management Guide*. Sheffield, U.K.: Greenleaf Publishing.

core element of the community's standard operating procedures. Within communities, that means amending existing, and establishing new policies, regulations and procedures that influence the behavior of residents with the new purpose, vision of wellbeing and resilience, and ethical principles that will guide decision-making being embraced by the community.

The Wheel of Change toward Transformational Resilience in Communities seen in Figure 11.4 describes the interrelated nature of these leverage points.

What leverage points have you emphasized?

In the space provided, describe the initial leverage points you will emphasize in your effort to transition your community to one that embraces building human resilience. Also describe the rationale behind your choices:

- Leverage points you will emphasize:

  _____

- Your reasoning:

  _____

The Wheel of Change toward Transformational Resilience in a community

As in organizations, building human resilience does not unfold linearly. It can begin with any of the interventions just described and focus on different leverage points at different times. For example, it might begin with conversations among small groups of civic-minded people in the community. When a sufficient number of people grasp the need and benefits and voice support, presentations can be made to key individuals and groups such as local government staff and elected officials, or influential organizations such as the local chamber of commerce or civic and environmental groups. Through the process one of the priorities can be to identify influential people that are willing to champion the effort. After one or two influential champions are on board, the initiative can continue to expand its outreach, eventually leading to the creation of "Human Resilience Committees" (or whatever name the community decides to use). This group can decide when and how to push on the other key levers of building human resilience.

No matter where it begins, you should expect the process of building Transformational Resilience to be messy, with progress occurring in fits and starts. Perseverance will be essential. It is also important to remember that all of the key leverage points must eventually become robust enough to keep the wheel of change rolling forward. Weak leverage points, such as insufficient communications, or the failure to consistently evaluate and discuss progress, can be the kiss of death for human-resilience-building initiatives.

Tarpon Springs, Florida—the first city in the U.S. to declare itself a trauma-informed community

After Tarpon Springs commissioner and vice-mayor Robin Saenger real-ized that her community was trauma-organized, she began to speak with numerous people in the community about trauma and its effects. Eventu-ally she arranged for the Mayor and the board of commissioners to hear a presentation about the consequences of trauma. Saenger said, "I could tell that (the mayor) completely grasped the concept, and as a city leader, was in position to do something about it. He was also director of Citizens Alliance for Progress, a neighborhood family center, and he realized that trauma is the root cause behind many of the challenges faced by neighbor-hood residents."

Following the meeting, she met with the police chief, the city manager, and others to discuss what Tarpon Springs could do to address the high levels of trauma that plagued the community. Everyone was interested and together they put together a list of 30 people they thought might be willing to be engaged in what they called the "Peace4Tarpon" initiative. The group met and formed a broad-based steering committee that Saenger told me is actually a "community forum."[418] It is composed of representatives from local churches, the school district, library, St. Petersburg College, the Juve-nile Welfare Board, the community health center, housing authority, police and sheriffs department, the mayor, city manager, and many community residents and concerned citizens. This was the first time such a diverse group had come together to address the issues, and it led to many new per-spectives and proposed solutions.

As a result of the ongoing discussions that occurred, in early 2011 the local Rotary Club held a "community education day" on the topic of trauma. Six days later, as a result of the steering committee's work, a Memorandum of Understanding was signed by the "Tarpon Springs Community Trauma Informed Community Initiative." One of the primary goals was to "increase awareness of issues facing members of our community who have been trau-matized to promote healing." In short, Tarpon Springs decided to develop a new social narrative about what wellbeing meant and how to bring it about by "becoming the first trauma-informed community in the U.S."

Since that time education and skills building have been important elements of the community initiative. The local housing authority, for instance, trained their entire staff in how to become aware of and deal with people who have experienced trauma. The program was called, "Why Are

You Yelling At Me When I'm Only Trying to Help You?" Peace4Tarpon also co-sponsored "Being a Better Bystander" to educate and train residents in how to safely help someone who is experiencing domestic violence or child abuse. Numerous other educational and training programs have taken place for children and adults throughout the community.

Developing new collaborations and partnerships among organizations has been a priority. Saenger said, "We meet monthly and usually there will be 30–40 people at the table. Often many of the participants will be new— they heard about it from a friend and want to be involved. In addition to education and skills building, the meetings focus on making new or stronger connections between individuals and organizations and networking— not in the way a business group would network, but in finding out what others do and how they or their organization can help to build a trauma-informed community."[419] In other words, social support networks within the community are being strengthened.

By continuing to meet, hold their own or support other education programs, host community events, and develop collaborations and partnerships, the idea of becoming a trauma-informed community has spread. Many people now understand what the community is striving to achieve. "A 'basic understanding' of how trauma affects people exists among much of the population."[420]

Peace4Tarpon is a completely volunteer initiative. There is no budget or funding. Even though she is no longer in office, Saenger continues to coordinate the effort—as a nonpaid volunteer. But five years after it started, interest remains strong and continues to expand.

Although measuring progress has not been easy, primarily due to lack of funding, Saenger told me that one of the signs they use to indicate success is that "People continue to show up *enthusiastically* [emphasis added to connote her words] at meetings—now five years after we started."[421] Other examples of success include the fact that Wells Fargo Bank now sponsors financial literacy programs for people in public housing, which Saenger sees as essential because "financial health is often a reflection of someone's trauma history." And in 2014 Tarpon Springs was selected as a finalist in the 2014 All-American City Award hosted by the National Civic League in large part because of its work on Peace4Tarpon. This type of public recognition has helped to shift the feedback mechanisms of the community by helping people see the results of their efforts.

Peace4Tarpon works through its partner organizations to address social justice and human rights, Saenger told me "One of the churches we partner with has a strong Social Justice committee whom we work with. We also are working within the juvenile justice system. Our goal is to make more sense of current models by making them work for the people they are designed to serve."

Five years after the initiative began, some of the partners in Peace4Tarpon are now beginning to adopt new policies and procedures, "To make them more trauma informed and also focused on building resilience," said Saenger.[422]

The newest Memorandum of Understanding asks for an even deeper level of engagement by partners. The emphasis is on viewing difficult situations through a trauma-informed lens, which means with the "understanding that things just don't happen at random without cause—there are always reasons behind challenging behaviors and following the thread back will lead to trauma of some sort. Even that basic understanding that things don't happen in a vacuum is very helpful for folks to make sense of what appears on the surface to be senseless."[423]

Perhaps most importantly, said Saenger, engagement in Peace4Tarpon has given many community members "a new purpose and mission in life—helping people in their community learn how to reduce and deal with trauma."[424]

How Peace4Tarpon could be expanded to explicitly address climate disruption

As with Creating Sanctuary in The Dalles, Peace4Tarpon is not specifically focused on building the capacity of individuals and groups to constructively deal with the traumas and stresses generated by climate disruption. However, Saenger told me that their focus and approach, "Absolutely applies. We see it as a proactive response to community violence—and climate change will add to the traumas that cause violence."[425]

Even though Peace4Tarpon implicitly helps residents learn how to deal with the impacts of rising temperatures, the initiative could explicitly address the issue by informing community leaders and residents about the expected direct and indirect impacts, along with how they are likely to affect the mental health of individuals and psycho-social-spiritual wellbeing of groups. The city is located 45 minutes north of St. Petersburg along the shore of the Gulf of Mexico. Projected climate impacts for this region include even hotter temperatures, increased intensity of storms such as hurricanes, rising sea levels and larger storm surges, and associated flooding and damage, and more.[426]

Most residents of Tarpon Springs are sure to be at least vaguely familiar with this information. In addition, many people now have at least a basic understanding of how trauma and toxic stress affect humans. With this knowledge as background, discussions could be held within the community about how the projected climate impacts are likely to affect the personal mental health and psycho-social-spiritual wellbeing of the community. For instance, the probability of increased debilitating anxiety, depression, PTSD, and suicides could be discussed. Psycho-social-spiritual maladies such as increased child and spousal abuse, interpersonal aggression, crime, and violence could also be discussed. The preventative skills and methods that are already included in the initiative could then be expanded to help youth and adults alike within the community build their capacity for Transformational Resilience. Organizational executives and community leaders could also use the information as a catalyst to adopt principles and practices such as those included in the Sanctuary model to proactively build their entities capacity for Transformational Resilience.

How Transformational Resilience could be included in the Oakland community-based Climate Adaptation Plan

Using Creating Sanctuary in The Dalles and Peace4Tarpon as illustrations, let's now briefly circle back and explore how Oakland could expand its climate adaptation plan to include a focus on building the capacity of residents for Transformational Resilience.

First, the adaptation plan developed by the Pacific Institute in partnership with the citizen-based Oakland Climate Action Coalition offers a solid platform to use to focus on building the personal mental health and psycho-social-spiritual resilience of residents. As I said, it is one of the few such plans that directly address some of the social impacts of climate disruption, not just physical infrastructure and natural resources. In addition, it is not a top-down plan developed by government. It was developed with the active input and involvement of local citizens and not-for-profit groups. And, a diverse steering committee already exists (or existed in the past) that could be engaged to lead an expanded approach.

These attributes suggest that it would be a natural step to expand the focus of the adaptation plan to address how traumas and toxic stresses directly or indirectly generated by climate disruption might aggravate the social and economic adversities residents already experience, and add many new ones. The process could begin with educational workshops and talks for members of the Oakland Climate Action Coalition, city government staff, and others in the community on the psychobiology of trauma and stress. (This was one of the focuses of the pilot project my organization ran—and a staff member from the City of Oakland did follow up by attending a workshops focused on how to teach this information as well as Presencing and Purposing skills to others.)

After a sufficient number of people have a basic understanding of how trauma and toxic stress might affect them, members of the planning committee, with input from a diverse set of community members, could develop an ideal vision of how Oakland could use the adversities generated by climate disruption as information and catalysts to help residents learn, grow, and thrive. The strengths and resources that exist within the city that could be used to help the community achieve the vision could then be identified, along with ethical principles to guide decision-making, and short and long-term goals. This would shift the focus of the current plan from merely addressing vulnerabilities, to building on strengths to increasing wellbeing.

The coalition could then develop and use every possible means to promote new social narratives describing the need and widespread benefits of the new vision, goals, and ethical principles to individuals and organizations of all types within the community. Promotion of the new social narratives would continue throughout the balance of the initiative.

As people learn about the new approach they would be engaged in strategy development to identify how to achieve those ends. As part of the strategies, train-the-trainer Presencing and Purposing skills training workshops could then be offered to build a cadre of people from different sectors who could teach the skills to others. Educational and skills building programs for adults and youth of all types could then be launched to steadily increase the number of people in the community who understand and can utilize the skills. I'll say more about this option at the end of the chapter.

In addition, a major emphasis could be placed on mapping the social support networks in the community and on helping people maintain, strengthen, and expand their bonding support networks, make connection with other similar bonding networks, as well as developing linkages with external organizations such as public agencies. The later step would be facilitated by the fact that the Oakland Climate Action Coalition is a citizen-based group that already has links to city government and other organizations.

Still another part of the strategy could be to establish an outreach program to inform organizational and community leaders about the means and benefits of using The Sanctuary Model or other similar principles and practices to transition their group to trauma-informed resilience-enhancing entities. Thus, education, training, and cultural change initiatives would occur at the individual, organizational, and community levels simultaneously.

As these efforts unfold, metrics could be developed and implemented to measure progress toward the vision of success, and the results could be widely shared within the community to help people continually learn and grow.

Finally, a year or more after the initiative begins, policies could be identified to embed the new approach into standard operating procedures and local organizations, the City of Oakland, Alameda County, and others.

Through the process just described, the need, benefits, and means of building the personal mental health as well as psycho-social-spiritual resilience of residents would continually grow and expand in Oakland. (It should be noted that some of these steps are already being taken and Oakland is building a more extensive climate adaptation plan through its Resilient Oakland Initiative supported by the Rockefeller Foundation's 100 Resilient Cities program.)

Describe the sequence of key leverage points you will pursue

In the space below describe how you can use the key leverage points to launch an initiative to transition your community to one that builds the capacity for Transformational Resilience among residents. For example, might it be possible to begin by striving to alter the dominant mindset— which is the most powerful leverage point for change—by educating key individuals and groups within the community? If that's not feasible, can you begin by measuring the level of human resilience and widely disseminate your findings—the sixth most powerful lever of change—as a way to catalyze the need to address the issues? Your answers to these questions can form a starting point:

- My vision of what a successful human-resilience-building initiative in my community would look and function like includes:

  _____

- The initial leverage points for change I will focus on include:

  _____

- The subsequent sequence of leverage points for change I will focus on likely include:

  _____

- I will strive to alter the mental model held by the majority of people in the community to emphasize the need to build human resilience by:

  _____

- The group of people I will initially try to engage in the human resilience committee include:

  _____

- I will seek to alter the purpose, vision of success, and principles that guide decision-making within my community to foster human resilience by:

  _____

- I will seek to maintain, strengthen, and expand the social support networks that exist in my community by:

  _____

- I will seek to alter the flows of information within my community to foster human resilience by:

  _____

- I will seek to alter the feedback mechanisms of my community to foster building human resilience by:

  _____

- I will seek to alter the policies and regulations of my organizations to foster building human resilience by:

Helpful approaches and tools

A number of unique tools and approaches might prove helpful to your community's efforts to enhance human resilience. For example:

Train-the-Trainer and Pay-It-Forward programs

One of the most powerful ways to spread Transformational Resilience knowledge and skills in a community is to train a group of people who make a commitment to pass on the skills by teaching others what they have learned. In this way the knowledge and skills can continue to grow exponentially. This is especially important because few communities around the world have a sufficient number of mental health or social service professionals to share the information and teach the skills to a majority of residents and stakeholders. This is true in both wealthier and poorer communities. However, the skills involved with Transformational Resilience are easy to learn and simple to use. They can be taught and passed down to others by almost anyone who has invested time learning them.

One example of a Train-the-Trainer Program is the Community Resilience Model developed by the Trauma Resource Institute. Executive Director Elaine Miller-Karas travels around the world training groups of mental health and social service workers, teachers, and others Tracking, Grounding, Resourcing, and other skills involved with the Community Resilience Model (CRM) described in Chapter 4. These people, in turn, commit to teach the skills to people in their community, and the number of people who learn the skills continually expands. In the town of Cebu in the Philippines, the approach has been so successful that the group of people that were originally trained organized a not-for-profit called "PHILACTS—Philippines-CRM Skills Trainer" which teaches Resourcing, Tracking, Grounding, and other skills to people in their country.[427]

My organization also offers a Pay-It-Forward program focused on the skills included in the *Resilient Growth*™ model described in this book.

Educational and assistance apps

A number of programs use smartphone and computer applications (apps) as well as social media sites such as Twitter, Facebook, and Instagram to educate community members about how trauma and toxic stress affect the human body and mind. Some apps and technologies offer methods to calm the body and mind, and still others offer ways for community members to identify assistance and resources during stressful times. For instance, the Trauma Resource Institute developed the iChill app that is available for smartphones, PCs, and Macs to support a community-oriented for responding to traumatic events and most importantly, how to restore or enhance resiliency.[428] The Mental Health Association of New York City launched a program called iHelp: Sandy Stress Relief that offers people counselors and other resources to help with anxiety, substance abuse, and other issues.[429] In the future it will be important to develop multilingual materials and "signing" language apps for the deaf as well.

Note, however, that social media and informational apps do not always work in the midst of an extreme weather event or other emergencies if the power is cut off or cell phone towers are damaged. In addition, smartphones, PCs, and other electronic technologies require huge amounts of raw materials and fossil-fuel-based energy to manufacture, are composed of numerous toxic materials, require energy to use—which today primarily means energy derived from fossil fuels and thus greenhouse gas emissions—and generate significant amounts of solid and toxic waste when they are discarded. The environmental impacts will be tremendous if the majority of people around the world use these devices given the current way they are produced, powered, and discarded

Measure the capacity for Transformational Resilience

Most nations use Gross Domestic Product (GDP) to measure wellbeing. Many observers have pointed out that this measurement focuses people on the wrong goal. GDP does not, for example, measure psychological wellbeing, economic inequality, the level of racism, sexism, or other forms of systemic oppression, the status of the climate, forests, or other essential ecological systems, the ability of people to use adversity to learn, grow, and thrive, or society's ability to make wise and skillful decisions about those issues. Instead, it lumps the production and consumption of beneficial and harmful goods and services together to paint a picture of how things are going. Despite the very misleading image it presents, this ongoing measurement defines society's goal as being to continually increase GDP. The result is that government responds to a drop in GDP by promoting actions to keep it growing, many of which are destructive such as ramping up economic activities that further degrade nature, generate greenhouse gas emissions, or increase economic inequality.

Our communities would be very different if we adopted new goals and measured different things such as the capacity of residents for Transformational Resilience. Measuring Gross National Happiness (GNH) is an example.[430] This began in the nation of Bhutan and is a reflection of their culture, which is based on Buddhist spiritual values. It includes indicators of psychological wellbeing such as life satisfaction, emotional balance, and spirituality, as well as levels of social support, community relationships, and other factors that contribute to the capacity for Transformational Resilience.

Some of the indicators used in the Bhutan GNH index are fuzzy. Nevertheless, it has stimulated attempts worldwide to develop more effectively ways to measure wellbeing.[431] For example, in 2014 the British government began to measure new indicators of wellbeing. In 2012 Seattle, Washington, in the U.S. launched a happiness index, emphasizing measures similar to the GNH Index.[432] These types of indicator could be improved, and indicators of pre- and post-disaster personal psychological and physical health, such as the number of reported alcoholism and drug abuse cases and hospital visits, as well as indicators of psycho-social-spiritual wellbeing such as family abuse, crime, and violence could be added to serve as gauges of the capacity of community members for Transformational Resilience. The more you measure and highlight the capacity for Transformational Resilience among residents, the more likely it is that people will focus on improving it.

Update your change strategy

Now that you have read about communities that have begun to build human resilience, are there any adjustments you would like to make in the initial change strategy you developed? If so, describe the changes here:

_____

_____

Building the capacity for Transformational Resilience within communities worldwide will be essential to respond skillfully and wisely to the impacts of climate disruption. Good leadership will be needed to catalyze and guide the initiatives. This does not mean residents should wait around for elected officials or other formal leaders to engage. People of all ages and from all walks of life can kindle and lead their community to make the changes needed to help people calm their body, emotions, and thoughts, and find meaning, direction, and hope, even as the adversities generated by climate disruption grow worse.

12
Closing thoughts on building universal capacity for Transformational Resilience

The concept of resilience originated in physics to mean the quality of a material to regain its original shape after being bent, compressed, or stretched. In the mental health field, this notion has been interpreted to denote the capacity to "bounce back" to previous conditions following adversity. In the climate field, in addition to bouncing back, the term resilience is used to describe the ability to adapt to changing climatic conditions by projecting and making adjustments to future impacts in order to maintain relatively stable levels of homeostasis.

Although it will be important to avoid long-term psychological impairment, our response to the rising levels of acute traumas and chronic toxic stresses generated by climate disruption must aim much higher than merely adapting or returning to previous conditions. We must build the capacity of individuals and groups worldwide to *increase* their sense of wellbeing, as well as the health of the natural environment, well above previous conditions, even as climate impacts accelerate. This can only occur if it becomes a top priority worldwide to help people learn simple skills to calm their body and mind, and turn toward and use adversities as catalysts to learn, grow, and find new meaning, purpose, and hope in life. The information and tools provided in this book are intended to provide a framework to guide this type of urgently needed international movement.

Before closing I want to offer a few additional thoughts and recommendations.

Building Transformational Resilience within whole societies

First, you might be wondering if it is possible for entire societies to reorient themselves to prioritize building widespread capacity for Transformational Resilience? I believe the answer is yes. Just as the choices an individual makes determine whether they respond to serious hardships by remaining impaired, bouncing back to pre-crisis conditions, or increasing their well-being beyond previous conditions, the decisions a nation or society makes will determine if it emphasizes building the capacity of its members to learn, grow and thrive in the midst of rising climate traumas and stresses.

Although the magnitude of this type of change might seem too large to imagine, it is important to remember that many societies in the past have made decisions that produced rapid widespread social transformation. For instance, in a matter of months after the attacks on Pearl Harbor in 1941, the entire U.S. economy was reoriented to focus on the war. In 1941 more than 3 million cars were manufactured in the U.S. But during the remaining years of the war only 139 more were produced as, almost overnight, the entire auto industry shifted gears. Factories of all types ran around the clock seven days a week. Making money was no longer the top priority for most people. Individuals and groups quickly adopted a new mission and purpose in life of doing what was required to win the war.[433]

Left unchecked, the physical and ecological damage, combined with the resulting personal mental health and psycho-social-spiritual harms generated by rising global temperatures, will threaten the very existence of human civilization as we know it. This threat demands a wartime-like mobilization focused as much on building widespread capacity for Transformational Resilience as on reducing emissions and hardening infrastructure. Individuals and groups of all types must learn Presencing and Purposing skills that resonate with them. Organizations, communities, and entire societies must adopt principles, practices, and policies that enable them to become human resilience-enhancing entities. In the era of human-caused climate disruption, everyone must learn that the only way for them to find meaning, purpose, and hope in life now is by caring for other people and dramatically improving the condition of the natural environment.

Achieving this will require that programs to address the climate crisis—as well as mental health, emergency response, education, faith, and many other programs around the world—quickly launch Transformational Resilience initiatives.

The Pyramid of Change

The key to building the capacity for Transformational Resilience within whole societies is to remember that people create change, not technologies or policies. The Pyramid of Change explains the process.

Most of the time, our attention is focused on the events we deal with on a daily basis. This is natural. To get through the day, we must attend to pressing tasks, solve immediate problems, and respond to people in the present moment.

However, when we step back a bit and take a wider perspective, we can see that the issues and crises we deal with on a daily basis are often part of a long-term pattern. They tend to appear again and again, often in slightly different forms. That's because they result from the way our social, political, and economic systems are structured. The systemic structures include the policies we adopt, the technologies we employ, the types of practice and behavior that are seen as acceptable, and which groups hold power and authority and which do not.

In my experience, these two issues—the events we deal with on a daily basis and the systemic structures that produce them—are almost always the primary focus of organizational and community change initiatives. They are certainly the dominant focus of most programs that address climate disruption.

If, however, we go even deeper, it becomes possible to see that the policies we adopt, the types of technology we develop, and other elements of the systemic structures we create that produce the daily crises we deal with result from the core assumptions, beliefs, and sense of purpose held by the majority of people. That is, our personal stories, and the social and cultural myths and narratives that influence and continually reinforce them, determine the types of policy, technology, and other elements of the systemic structures we choose to adopt—and those we choose to ignore.

If we take an even broader perspective, we find that the types of experience people have had in the past, and are experiencing today, shape the stories they tell about the world and themselves. These experiences, in turn, shape their mental model—their core assumptions and beliefs and sense of purpose—which determines the types of systemic structure they develop or support, which in turn determines the types of daily crisis they deal with.

Building the capacity for Transformational Resilience within entire societies will therefore require much more than changes at the top two levels of the Pyramid of Change (see Fig. 12.1). All four levels must be addressed,

FIGURE 12.1 The pyramid of change for climate disruption

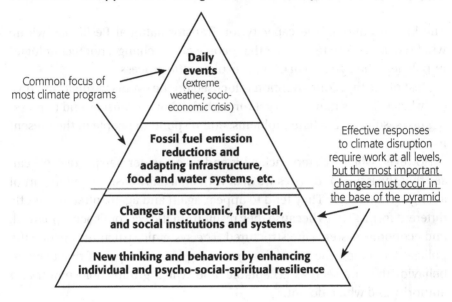

but the *most important* changes much occur in the bottom two—the mental models people hold and the experiences that shape those assumptions, beliefs, and ways of seeing the world.

Once again, the most important question to ask regarding why people, especially in the U.S. and other Western nations, act in ways that harm themselves, other people, and the Earth's climate is, "What happened to them?" not "What's wrong with them?" This way of viewing things does not excuse destructive behaviors or let people who act poorly off the hook. Instead, when we view predicaments in this way it opens the door to new and different ways to initiate and promote the changes needed to respond.

The new perspective might, for example, lead to the realization that rather than focusing only on reducing emissions and preparing infrastructure and natural resources to adapt to climate impacts, a major worldwide initiative should be launched to help individuals and groups understand that, in the era of ever-intensifying human-caused climate disruption, only by assisting other people and improving the condition of the natural environment and climate will it be possible for them to take care of their families and themselves. This will require significant investments in teaching Presencing and Purposing skills to all ages, and engaging organizations and communities everywhere in making the transition to trauma-informed human resilience-enhancing entities.

The public policies that can best promote building the capacity for Transformational Resilience vary based on the culture, demographic make-up, and other factors unique to a society. However, a few priorities and related policies (summarized in Fig. 12.2) will help speed the process including:

- **Establish a National Strategy For Building Transformation Resilience.** The strategy should be an integrated approach that clarifies the roles of the national, state/provincial, county, and municipal governments, as well as civil society such as not-for-profits and the faith community, and grassroots efforts by neighborhood groups, social support networks, families, and individuals in building widespread capacity for Transformational Resilience. Policies, funding, and evaluation mechanisms should be included to support implementation of the national strategy.

- **Prioritize prevention.** The national strategy—and all programs and policies that seek to implement it—should emphasize *prevention*, not just preparing for and responding to disasters. The cultural myths that dominate most Western nations, and the U.S. in particular, make it difficult for governments to prioritize prevention. However, making this shift will be essential.

  New policies establishing prevention of personal mental health and psycho-social-spiritual maladies as a top priority of all levels of government, educational, and other human services agencies and programs could go a long way in kick-starting new national and international efforts to build widespread capacity for Transformational Resilience.

- **Authorize the widespread formation of human resilience committees.** With prevention as the goal, "human resilience committees" (or councils, teams, or whatever other name seems appropriate) should be formed in public, private, and not-for-profit organizations of all types, as well as in communities and as many neighborhoods as possible within large cities. These groups should lead the effort to build widespread levels of Transformational Resilience. The beginning point could be an assessment of the existing knowledge and skills held by members that can launch and support education and training programs for adults and youth.

  To support these efforts, national, provincial/state, and municipal governments can enact policies that authorize the establishment of Human Resilience Committees, and provide funding to support their development and operations. *The long-term goal should be to make building the capacity for Transformational Resilience as common as learning to read and write.*

- **Expand education about the psychobiology of trauma and stress and Transformational Resilience skills to civic, not-for-profit, faith, private, and government executives.** Transformational Resilience education and skills building efforts should reach as many civic, faith, education, not-for-profit, private-sector, and government leaders as possible. These education and skills building programs can be linked with or embedded within many existing educational and training programs. The more that executives as well as influential leaders understand how trauma and stress affect the human mind and body, learn how climate disruption will aggravate most of the stressors people already experience and add many new ones as well, and develop Presencing and Purposing skills, the more likely they are to support and lead efforts to build the capacity for Transformational Resilience within their circles of influence.

  National, provincial/state, and municipal governments could enact policies such as financial incentives to encourage people spend time learning this information and developing the skills.

- **Allocate resources to maintain, strengthen, and expand social support networks.** In addition to personal skills, the capacity for Transformational Resilience depends on individuals having a robust network of family members, friends, and neighbors whom they can count on to support and assist them in the midst of adversity. Close-knit bonding social support networks are more effective when they are connected to other similar bonding networks through bridging networks, and linked to larger organizations, government agencies, and others with political power and economic and financial resources. Helping people develop and expand bonding, bridging, and linking social support networks should therefore become a priority of public policy.

  Policies that can enhance efforts to strengthen and expand social support networks include: funding for Time Banking, and Community Currencies projects; special events that allow neighbors and community members to meet and interact; and planning guidance and regulations that support redesigning neighborhoods to facilitate greater personal interactions.

- **Allocate resources to maintain and expand partnerships and collaborations among local groups and organizations.** The development of deep and wide webs of collaborations and partnerships among organizations and agencies in a community increases the likelihood that people will obtain important information, gain access to critical resources, and develop more robust social support networks. Networks among groups and organizations also helps people know about the provision of different services and closes gaps in critical services. Collaborations and partnerships can also enhance a community's capacity to identify and eliminate ways in which it damages the natural environment and climate.

  Policies that can enhance efforts to strengthen and expand partnerships and collaborations among local organizations include: support for Community Mapping of groups and organizations, and financial and other types of incentive for organizations to work together rather than compete, such as grants for collaborative projects.

- **Identify and teach Transformational Resilience skills to vulnerable populations—but proceed carefully.** Certain individuals and groups, including low-income populations, the unemployed, infirm, minorities, women, children, and the elderly are often at greater risk of being traumatized by climate-enhanced adversities. The level of risk depends on their geographic location, economic status, gender, age and other factors—but even more important are their personal skills and strength of and embeddedness in social support networks. High-risk groups should be identified and their status assessed. Those that lack important attributes that support personal and group resilience should be given assistance to learn Transformational Resilience skills and maintain and expand their social support networks. However, as discussed, not all of the people within any group deemed to be "vulnerable" are necessarily at risk. For example, even when their incomes are low, many people of color in the U.S. are much more resilient than Caucasians with higher incomes because a lifetime of discrimination and hardship have helped them hone their skills. Further, as temperatures rise close to or beyond 1.5°C above pre-industrial levels, *everyone* will be at risk of harmful fight, flee, or freeze reactions. Thus, while it is very important to help vulnerable individuals and groups prepare for the psychological and social impacts of climate disruption, this should not be the sole focus. *Everyone* will benefit by learning this information and skills.

Policies that can support this focus including funding and technical assistance to schools, not-for-profit, faith, and other organizations to assess the location and degree of at-risk populations and inform them about Presencing and Purposing skills.

- **Address the socioeconomic-environmental determinants of personal mental health and psycho-social-spiritual resilience.** Finally, as I will discuss in a moment, the capacity of any individual or group for Transformational Resilience will be enhanced the more that the social, political, and economic factors that influence personal and collective wellbeing are addressed.

  The policies needed to address the physical factors that negatively influence personal mental health and psycho-social-spiritual resilience are beyond the scope of this book. But it is important to remember that it is *essential* to address the socioeconomic determinants of health and wellbeing.

FIGURE 12.2   Core elements of building societal capacity for Transformational Resilience

---

Need major <u>preventative</u> initiatives to <u>build resilience skills</u>, not just treat trauma

- Establish a national strategy for building widespread capacity for Transformational Resilience, along with policies to support it.

- Form "Human Resilience Committees" in <u>communities</u> and <u>organizations</u> to assess levels of personal and psycho-social-spiritual resilience and then <u>support</u> or <u>directly teach</u> preventative human resilience skills to <u>all</u> <u>adults and youth</u>

  <u>Human resilience education should become as common as learning to read and write!</u>

- Teach <u>leaders</u> how to <u>recognize signs of trauma and stress</u> within their <u>organizations and communities</u> and become <u>resilience-enhancing entities</u>

- Strengthen <u>personal social support networks</u> and <u>organizational partnerships</u>

- Identify and prepare the <u>most vulnerable populations</u>—but not to the exclusion of others

- Strengthen <u>mental health elements</u> of emergency services infrastructure

- Address the <u>socioeconomic-environmental factors</u> that influence personal and psycho-social-spiritual resilience

The importance of effective leadership

Exceptional leadership will be required to build widespread capacity for Transformational Resilience. I don't just mean leadership from senior executives of public, private, and not-for-profit organizations and elected officials, although strong support and direction from these people would be extremely helpful. As previously mentioned, most change initiatives begin at the lower or middle levels of an organization, community, and society. And it is lower- and mid-level people who tend to do the hard work required to keep a major change initiative moving forward. Thus, exemplary leadership is needed from many people.

This reinforces the point that good leaders emerge from surprising quarters. Even if you do not think of yourself as a leader or a change agent, you have the potential to stimulate and lead an initiative to build Transformational Resilience within your spheres of influence, whether it is your family, neighborhood group, spiritual or religious organization, workplace, or other community.

One of the keys will be to remember the differences between management and leadership. Management (see Fig. 12.3) is about keeping complicated systems of people and technologies working together to accomplish specific objectives. It involves planning, budgeting, organizing, staffing, supervising, and the like. These can be considered qualities of *control*.

Leadership, on the other hand, is something very different (see Fig. 12.4). It involves a set of processes that help people define and keep moving toward a desired future, despite the many obstacles that arise along the way.

FIGURE 12.3   Management

A set of processes that keeps complicated systems of people and technology running smoothly:

- Planning
- Budgeting
- Organizing
- Staffing
- Supervision
- Problem-solving

These are important qualities of <u>control</u>

FIGURE 12.4   Leadership

A set of processes that helps a human community shape its future and embrace and sustain significant change:

- Helps define what future should look like
- Mobilizes the forces to align people with that vision
- Inspires them to make it happen despite obstacles
- Encourages and role-models good emotional management
- Responds to crisis by motivating people to learn, grow, and keep improving

These are essential qualities of <u>influence</u>

Effective leaders help people define what the future should look like, mobilize and inspire them to work together to achieve that vision, help them exhibit good emotional management, and motivate them to use adversities as catalysts to learn, grow and improve. These can be considered qualities of *influence.*

Good management will be important to build the capacity of individuals and groups for Transformational Resilience. However, my experience is that most organizational and community change initiatives are vastly overmanaged and underled. We cannot manage our way toward Transformational Resilience. Exemplary leadership will be required.

Transformational Resilience within different age groups and cultural settings

I use the concepts, skills, and tools described throughout the book in the Transformational Resilience programs my organization operates. We have worked primarily with adults in the U.S. and the way of thinking about resilience and most of the methods offered here are applicable in these groups. Through our work we have learned that different cultures frame how to use adversity to find new meaning, direction, and hope in life in different ways. Thus, the skills and tools required to enhance the capacity for Transformational Resilience must be tailored to the make-up of the groups you work with.

Many African-Americans in the U.S., for example, emphasize the crucial role of the church and spirituality in building personal and collective resilience due to the sense of connection, spiritual guidance, and coherence these institutions have provided through two centuries of discrimination and suffering.[434] Although there are many differences in their beliefs, many Asian, African, and other ethnic groups around the world also place religion and spirituality at the heart of their culture. Native Americans view spirituality, as well as the extended family and the veneration of age/wisdom/tradition, respect for nature, cooperation, and sharing, as central elements of their culture and thus of what's required for resilience. In addition, in many cultures art, poetry, folktales, oral traditions, music, and group rituals such as singing and dancing hold central roles in defining and transmitting what it means to be individually and collectively resilient.[435]

For this reason, it is important to carefully tailor your efforts to build the capacity for Transformational Resilience to the age group, demographic make-up, and culture in which you are working. This requires dropping any sense that you are the "expert," and closely listening to and working with the people you are engaged with to design programs, teach skills, and share or build tools that make sense within and can be embraced by the culture.

This point applies to working with youth as well. All of the skills and tools describe in the book can be taught to children and adolescents in the U.S. and other western nations. However, the methods for doing so will be different than those described here. There are many strategies to teach different age groups Presencing and Purposing skills. Make sure you do the research needed to understand which approach works best for the age group you are working with.

A primer on teaching and facilitating Transformational Resilience

The importance of adjusting your approach to the culture and demographics of the people you work with underscores that there is no single "right way" to teach Presencing and Purposing skills. As mentioned, each leader and educator must use the knowledge and skills they have and adjust their approach to the age, demographic make-up, and culture of the individuals and groups they are working with. That said, the following guidelines are offered to assist those who want to lead Transformational Resilience programs or teach the skills. They are the principles and practices my organization asks instructors in our Transformational Resilience programs to abide by.[436]

Core themes for leaders and teachers to emphasize to participants

- There is more right with you than wrong. Even though you might often feel inadequate or broken, you are more than your suffering, and have greater skills and capacity than you believe.

- You are the expert regarding the best way to deal with stress and adversity in your life. Building the capacity for Transformational Resilience is about helping you realize your own innate genius to calm your body and mind and find meaning, direction, and hope deal in the midst of adversities including climate disruption.

- Transformation Resilience is not therapy and is not focused on resolving past problems. However, learning the information and skills can be therapeutic.

- Transformational Resilience is not a "technique"—it is a way of being in relationship with yourself and the world.

- Transformational Resilience is not about "improving" yourself or "making you different"—it is an invitation to become more aware of who you already are, noticing what's happening in the present moment, and having compassion for yourself.

- Some skills might be difficult to learn—stay with them, as dealing with experiences we both like and dislike is part of building the capacity for Transformational Resilience. Everything that comes up as you build your capacity for Presencing and Purposing is part of the curriculum of learning how to use adversity as a catalyst to gain new insight, grow, and thrive.

- Building your capacity for Transformational Resilience requires intention, commitment, and practice.

A helpful attitude for leaders and teachers to adopt when leading programs

- You are not here to "fix" others. However, you can help people become more aware of their current relationship with trauma and stress, and offer skills and tools they can employ if they choose to enhance their personal resilience.

- You are engaged in the same process of enhancing your own capacity for Transformational Resilience as the participants are. You are likely to learn as much as participants do from the information, exercises, and skills.

- You do not have "the answers" for someone else. Everyone is human and you are likely be struggling with many of the same issues as the people you work with. We are all "wounded healers." However, as instructors and facilitators you can offer perspectives and skills that might be helpful if people choose to use them.

- Try to not fear or restrain the expression of deep emotions because sometimes learning Presencing and Purposing skills can trigger emotional release. It is OK for people to feel a little "out of sorts" when they learn the information and skills because important issues often come up that need to be mulled over for a while. When someone shares something with deep emotions, trust their capacity to self-regulate.

Some recommendations on teaching methods

- Transformational Resilience is a *self-education* program. Leaders and teachers can offer information and exercises, but you must hope that they spark a fire within the individuals and groups you work with, and that they become inspired to take the insights and run with them.

- As much as possible, it is best to engage people in an experience first, and *then* explain the principles and concepts behind it. Engaging experientially before learning the theory behind it greatly enhances the capacity of people to understand factual information provided later.

- Use "invitational" language that reminds people to look inward for more insight into what they are experiencing, rather than looking to you the leader or instructor for answers. Even when someone asks a pointed question, invite inquiry by asking, "What do you think?" or "What has been your experience with this ...?" Continually use language that invites inquiry. "I invite you to …," "When you are ready …," and "If you are willing …."

- Use humor, laugh and have fun as much as possible. Participants will be put at ease and be more open to self-examination, learning, and growth.

- Use repetition as a teaching tool. Repeating key words, phrases, and concepts helps people more easily grasp their meaning.

- Don't fill up all of the dead space. Allow silence to exist as it gives time to process things and come to their own conclusions.

- Be yourself. Talk like a "normal person" (not a professional therapist, educator, or other specialist), and share yourself with others as an equal.

- Take care not to misrepresent yourself in any way.

- Never give advice. Instead, keep asking questions in ways that invite people to look inside themselves for insights and answers. Trust in the inherent wisdom of the participants to figure out answers on their own, in their own time.

Don't neglect other changes required to reduce climate disruption to manageable levels

Finally, it is very important to remember that Transformational Resilience skills on their own, or their integration into organizations and communities, are by no means the only changes needed to respond to climate disruption. However, building the capacity for Transformational Resilience will be essential to help people stay calm and centered, find meaning, purpose, and hope, and therefore be able to make values-based wise and skillful decisions in the midst of ongoing climate traumas and toxic stresses.

Human-caused climate disruption is a systemic problem. Systemic problems require systemic solutions. Although it is extremely important, climate disruption cannot be reduced to manageable levels merely by switching from fossil fuels to renewable energy as many people have been led to believe. The human demand for materials and energy is already well beyond the Earth's capacity to provide ecological resources and the life-giving services they provide at sustainable rates. Instead, what is called economic growth today is often nothing more than continually drawing down natural capital and degrading ecological processes. It is estimated that if everyone on Earth consumed at the level of U.S. citizens, it would require roughly five earths to support them without seriously degrading ecological systems and resources. If everyone on Earth consumed at the level of Europeans, it would require three earths to support them without depleting ecological systems and the climate.[437] Thus, it is the U.S. and other Western nations that are the primary contributors to climate disruption, and shifting to renewable energy, while essential, will not be enough to counter the ecologically degrading and unsustainable nature of our economic systems and lifestyles.

Stabilizing the Earth's climate and eventually returning it to healthy conditions will therefore require fundamental changes in our economic model, which in its current form requires continued expansion of material consumption and energy use (along with associated waste including greenhouse gasses) to prevent collapse. These changes, in turn, will undoubtedly require deep-seated changes in our lifestyles—a shift to what Molly Hemstreet in Chapter 9 called "sufficiency"—rather than today's emphasis on never-ending maximization. In addition, major changes will certainly be required in the global financial system that today is dominated by Wall Street and the City of London, and which is structured to extract wealth from the majority of people and place it in the hands of a small number of the superrich, rather than creating the type of wealth that benefits the whole of society and restores the natural environment. Reducing the climate crisis to manageable levels will likely also require stabilizing and eventually reducing the world's population.

These changes will not about come easily. The people who benefit from the existing economic and related financial systems will fight tooth and nail to maintain their power and status. And, the shifts I just described will need to come about in the midst of continually rising climate-enhanced traumas and toxic stresses. As I have said throughout the book, unless people have basic knowledge and effective skills, tools, and social support systems, many individuals and groups are certain to react to the distress with fight, flee, or freeze reactions that harm other people, the natural environment, and/or themselves.

If, however, it becomes a top priority across the planet to enhance the capacity for Transformational Resilience, such harmful reactions can be minimized, when they do occur they can be more quickly dealt with. In addition, many people will be able to adopt a new mission and purpose in life focused on assisting others and improving the condition of the natural environment and climate as a way of increasing their own wellbeing.

This approach is certain to be more effective than trying to treat the millions of people who, without these skills, will be traumatized by climate impacts. The benefits will also be more long lasting and, over time, far more effective in helping to reduce the climate crisis to more manageable levels. In fact, individuals and groups with these skills will find ample ways to live fulfilling lives and thrive even as global temperatures rise.

Every group, organization, and society develops a relatively stable set of attitudes toward what is possible. These assumptions and beliefs invariably set ceilings on what people imagine and achieve. But the impossible happens all the time. For generations it was assumed that it was not possible to run a four-minute mile. Then Roger Bannister did it. After he removed that psychological obstacle, others quickly followed. It is our job now to eliminate the barriers that stand in the way of believing is it possible to build widespread capacity for Transformational Resilience and launch an international movement to make it happen.

Notes

Introduction: Climate disruption can be humanity's greatest teacher

1. Wooten, T. (2012). *We Shall Not Be Moved: Rebuilding Home in the Wake of Katrina*. (2012). Boston, MA: Beacon Press. pp. 204-205.
2. Ibid.
3. Chamlee-Wright, E. (2010). *The Cultural and Political Economy of Recovery: Social Learning in a Post-Disaster Environment*. New York, NY: Routledge.
4. Leong, K.J., *et al.* (2007). Resilient history and the rebuilding of a community: The Vietnamese American community in New Orleans East. *Journal of American History*, 94, 770-779.
5. Wooten, T. (2012). *We Shall Not Be Moved: Rebuilding Home in the Wake of Katrina*. Boston, MA: Beacon Press. p. 119.
6. Ibid.
7. This information is derived from a phone interview with Arthur Johnson, CEO of Sustain the Nine: Lower 9th Ward Center for Sustainable Engagement and Development on July 27, 2015. For more information about current status and projects see the website of Sustain the Nine: http://blog.sustainthenine.org.
8. The one exception is the International Transformational Resilience Coalition, which I organized and coordinate: website: http://www.theresourceinnovationgroup.org/transformational-resilience.
9. See for example: Gist, R. (Ed.). (1999). *Response to Disaster: Psychosocial, Community and Ecological Approaches*. Philadelphia, PA: Taylor & Francis; World Health Organization (2008). *Protecting Health from Climate Change*. Geneva: World Health Organization; Roberts, S., & Ashley, W.C. (2008). *Disaster Spiritual Care: Practical Clergy Responses to Community, Regional and National Tragedy*. Woodstock, VT: SkyLight Paths.
10. For example, there was not one mention of the impacts of, or need to address, the psycho-social-spiritual impacts of climate disruption in the April 2015 report issued by the White House Task Force on Climate Preparedness and Resilience found at: https://www.whitehouse.gov/sites/default/files/docs/task_force_report_0.pdf.
11. This is an adaptation of the Sufi teaching story about the Mulla named Nasrudin.
12. Aldwin, C. (2007). *Stress, Coping, and Development; An Integrated Perspective*. New York, NY: The Guilford Press.
13. See, for example, logotherapy, post-traumatic growth, and other similar concepts.

14. Aldwin, C.M., & Levenson, M.R. (2004). Posttraumatic growth: A developmental perspective. *Psychological Inquiry*, 15(1), 9-22.

15. Silver, R., & Updegraff, J. (2013). Searching for and finding meaning following personal and collective traumas. In K.D. Markman, T. Proulx, & M.J. Lindberg (Eds.), *The Psychology of Meaning*. Washington, DC: APA. Retrieved from: https://webfiles. uci.edu/rsilver/Silver%20&%20Updegraff%20Searching%20for%20Meaning%20 2013.pdf.

16. Joseph, S. (2009). Growth following adversity: Positive psychological perspectives on post-traumatic stress. *Psychological Topics*, 19(2), 335-344.

Part 1: The personal mental health and psycho-social-spiritual impacts of climate disruption

Chapter 1: The psychological effects of climate disruption on individuals

17. Dooley, M. (2014). Mental health toll of Superstorm Sandy lingers 2 years later. *The Huffington Post*. Retrieved from: http://www.huffingtonpost.com/2014/10/29/ superstorm-sandy-mental-health_n_6068178.html.

18. Aussie Helpers. (No date). Suicide in Queensland drought stricken farming communities now at all time high. Retrieved from: http://aussiehelpers.org.au/suicide-in-queensland-drought-stricken-farming-communities-now-at-all-time-high.

19. NOAA, National Centers for Environmental Information. (December, 2015). State of the Climate. Retrieved from: https://www.ncdc.noaa.gov/sotc/.

20. Hansen, J., *et al.* (2015). Ice melt, sea level rise and superstorms: Evidence from paleoclimate data, climate modeling, and modern observations that 2°C global warming is highly dangerous. *Atmospheric Chemistry and Physics*. Discussion 15, 20059-20179. DOI: 10.5194/acpd-15-20059-2015. Retrieved from: http://www. atmos-chem-phys-discuss.net/15/20059/2015/acpd-15-20059-2015.html.

21. Rogelj, J., Luderer, G., *et al.* (2015). Energy system transformations for limiting end-of-century warming to below 1.5°C. *Nature Climate Change*, 21.

22. Milman. O. (December 12, 2015). James Hansen, father of climate change awareness, calls Paris a "fraud." *The Guardian*. Retrieved from: http://www.theguardian. com/environment/2015/dec/12/james-hansen-climate-change-paris-talks-fraud.

23. Wenju, C., *et al.* (2015). Extreme La Niña event frequency. *Nature Climate Change*. Retrieved from: http://www.nature.com/nclimate/index.html.

24. Webster, P.J., *et al.* (2005). Changes in tropical cyclone number, duration, and intensity in a warming environment. *ScienceXpress*, 312(5770). DOI: 10.1126/ science.1123560.

25. Holland, G., & Webster, P. (2007). Heightened tropical cyclone activity in the North Atlantic: Natural variability or climate trend? *Philosophical Transactions of the Royal Society of London*. Retrieved from: http://rsta.royalsocietypublishing.org/ content/365/1860/2695.

26. Siegele, L. (2012). Loss and damage: The theme of slow onset impact. Climate Development Knowledge Network. Retrieved from: https://germanwatch.org/en/ download/6674.pdf.

27. Ibid.

28. Dutton, A., *et al.* (2015). Sea-level rise due to polar ice-sheet mass loss during past warm periods. *Science*. 349(6244). DOI: 10.1126/science.aaa4019. Retrieved from: http://www.sciencemag.org/content/349/6244/aaa4019; Jevrejeva, S.J.C.,

et al. (2012). Sea level projections to AD 2500 with a new generation of climate change scenarios. *Global and Planetary Change*, 80-81, 14-20. DOI:10.1016/j.gloplacha.2011.09.006.

29. Taleb, N. (2012). *Antifragile: Things That Gain From Disorder.* New York, NY: Random House Publishing Group.

30. Francis, J. (2015, February). A melting Arctic and weird weather: The plot thickens. *The Conversation.* Retrieved from: https://theconversation.com/a-melting-arctic-and-weird-weather-the-plot-thickens-37314.

31. After they were established my organization spun off the S.E. Florida Regional Climate Compact and the American Academy of Adaptation Professionals to the Institute for Sustainable Communities to allow a staff member who was engaged with both programs to continue working on them.

32. Taleb, N. (2012). *Antifragile: Things That Gain From Disorder.* New York, NY: Random House Publishing Group.

33. See, for example: Llanos, M. (2014). Bad news for Florida: Models of Greenland ice melting could be way off. *NBC News.* Retrieved from: http://www.nbcnews.com/science/environment/bad-news-florida-models-greenland-ice-melting-could-be-way-n268761.

34. See, for example: Chamlee-Wright, E. (2010). *The Cultural and Political Economy of Recovery: Social Learning in a Post-Disaster Economy.* New York, NY: Routledge; Morrow, B. (2000). Stretching the bonds: The families of Andrew. In W. Peacock, B. Morrow, & H. Gladwin (Eds.), *Hurricane Andrew: Ethnicity, Gender, and the Sociology of Disasters* (pp. 141-170). Miami, FL: International Hurricane Center; Eoh, M.S. (1998). *A Comparative Study of Recovery Time Between Counties That Experience Floods Frequently and Infrequently.* PhD Dissertation, Texas A&M University.

35. Yohe, G.W., *et al.* (2007). Perspectives on climate change and sustainability. In M.L. Perry, *et al.* (Eds.), *Climate Change 2007: Impacts, Adaptation and Vulnerability* (pp. 811-841). Contribution of Working Group II to the Fourth Assessment Report of the Intergovernmental Panel on Climate Change. Cambridge, U.K.: Cambridge University Press.

36. Warner, K., *et al.* (2012). Evidence from the frontlines of climate change: Loss and damage to communities despite coping and adaptation. United Nations University, Institute for Environmental and Human Security. Retrieved from: http://unu.edu/publications/policy-briefs/evidence-from-the-frontlines-of-climate-change-loss-and-damage-to-communities-despite-coping-and-adaptation.html.

37. Healy, A., & Malhortra, N. (2009). Myopic voters and natural disaster policy. *American Political Science Review*, 103(3), 387-406.

38. Monat, A., & Lazarus, T. (1991). *Stress and Coping: An Anthology.* New York, NY: Columbia University Press; Weisath, D.S. (1993). Disasters: Psychological and psychiatric aspects. In L. Golberger, & S. Breznitz (Eds.), *Handbook of Stress: Theoretical and Clinical Aspects* (pp. 591-616). New York, NY: Free Press.

39. Ibid.

40. This discussion is adapted from Hobfoll, S.E., *et al.* (2007). Five essential elements of immediate and mid-term mass trauma intervention: Empirical evidence. *Psychiatry* 70(4), 283-315.

41. See for example: Weems, C.F., *et al.* (2007). The psychosocial impact of Hurricane Katrina: Contextual differences in psychological symptoms, social support, and discrimination. *Behaviour Research and Therapy*, 45(10), 2295-2306; Weems, C.F., *et al.* (2007). Pre-disaster trait anxiety and negative affect predict posttraumatic stress in youths after Hurricane Katrina. *Journal of Consulting and Clinical Psychology*, 75(1), 154-159.

42. See for example: Bourque, L.B., *et al.* (2006). Weathering the storm: The impact of hurricanes on physical and mental health. *Annals of the American Academy of Political and Social Science*, 604, 129-150; Kessler, R.C., *et al.* (2008). Trends in mental illness and suicidality after Hurricane Katrina. *Molecular Psychiatry*, 13, 374-384; Keisler, R.H., *et al.* (2006). Mental health and recovery in the Gulf Coast after Hurricanes Katrina and Rita. *Journal of the American Medical Association*, 296, 585-588.

43. Porter, M., & Haslam, N. (2005). Predisplacement and postdisplacement factors associated with mental health of refugees and internally displaced persons: A meta-analysis. *Journal of the American Medical Association*, 294(5), 602-612.

44. Abramson, D., Garfield, R., & Redlener, I. (2007). The recovery divide: Poverty and the widening gap among Mississippi children and families affected by Hurricane Katrina. Columbia University, New York: Mailman School of Public Health. Retrieved from: http://academiccommons.columbia.edu/item/ac:148100.

45. Keenan, H., *et al.* (2004). Increased incidence of inflicted traumatic brain injury in children after a natural disaster. *American Journal of Preventative Medicine*, 26(3), 189-193.

46. Bulbena, A., *et al.* (2006). Psychiatric effects of heat waves. *Psychiatric Services*, 57, 1519.

47. See for example: Anderson, C.A., & Anderson, K.B. (1996). Violent crime rate studies in philosophical context: A destructive testing approach to heat and southern culture of violence effects. *Journal of Personality and Social Psychology*, 70, 740-756; Anderson, C., *et al.* (1997). Hot years and serious and deadly assault: Empirical tests of the heat hypothesis. *Journal of Personality and Social Psychology*, 73(6), 1213-1223.

48. See for example: Gamble, J., & Hess, J. (2012). Temperature and violent crime in Dallas, Texas: Relationships and implications of climate change. *Western Journal of Emergency Medicine*, 13(3), 239-246; Bulbena, A., *et al.* (2006). Psychiatric effects of heat waves. *Psychiatric Services*, 57, 1519; Poumadere, M., *et al.* (2005). The 2003 heat wave in France: Dangerous climate change here and now. *Risk Analysis*, 25, 1483-1494; Anderson, C.A. (2001). Heat and violence. *Current Directions in Psychological Science*, 10(1), 33-38; Rotton, J., & Cohn, E.G. (2003). Global warming and U.S. crime rates: An application of routine activity theory. *Environment and Behavior*, 35(6), 802-825.

49. Jones, B., *et al.* (2015). Future population exposure to U.S. heat extremes. *Nature Climate Change*, 5, 652-655.

50. Gasparrini, A., *et al.* (2015). Climate and health: Mortality attributable to heat and cold. *The Lancet Medical Journal*. Retrieved from: http://www.thelancet.com/journals/lancet/article/PIIS0140-6736(15)60897-2/fulltext.

51. Tarhule, A. (2005). Damaging rainfall and flooding: The other Sahel hazards. *Climatic Change*, 72, 355-377.

52. See for example: Causes of farmer suicides in Maharashtra: An enquiry: Final report submitted to the Mumbia High Court. Retrieved from: http://www.academia.edu/9979507/Causes_of_Farmer_Suicides_in_Maharashtra_AN_ENQUIRY_Final_Report_Submitted_to_the_Mumbai_High_Court; Preti, A., & Miotto, P. (1998). Seasonality in suicides: The influence of suicide method, gender and age on suicide distribution in Italy. *Psychiatry Research*, 81(2), 219-231.

53. See for example: Paranjothy, S., *et al.* (2011). Psychosocial impact of the summer 2007 floods in England. *BMC Public Health*, 11(145). DOI: 10.1186/1471-2458-11-145; Reacher, M., *et al.* (2004). Health impacts of flooding in Lewes: A comparison of reported gastrointestinal and other illness and mental health in flooded and non-flooded households. *Communicable Disease and Public Health*, 7(1), 39-46; Ahern,

M., *et al.* (2005). Global health impacts of floods. *Epidemiologic Reviews*, 27, 36-46; New York Times (1991, October 14). Farmer suicide rate swells in 1980s. *New York Times*. Retrieved from: http://www.nytimes.com/1991/10/14/us/farmer-suicide-rate-swells-in-1980-s-study-says.html; Sartore, G.M., *et al.* (2007). Drought and its effect on mental health—how GPs can help. *Australian Family Physician*, 36(12), 990-993; Goldwert, L. (2011, September 2). Climate change threatens mental health too: Droughts, floods have psychological impact. *The Daily News*. Retrieved from: http://www.nydailynews.com/life-style/health/violent-weather-threatens-mental-health-study-article-1.953454

54. Queensland University of Technology (2015). Flood aftermath linked to post-traumatic stress, study shows. *Science Daily*. Retrieved from: http://www.sciencedaily.com/releases/2015/05/150527103104.htm.

55. See for example: Azad, A.K., *et al.* (2013). Flood-induced vulnerabilities and problems encountered by women in northern Bangladesh. *International Journal of Disaster Risk Science*, 4(4), 190-199. DOI: 10.1007/s13753-013-0020-z; Alston, M., & Whittenbury, K. (Eds.). (2013). *Research, Action and Policy: Addressing the Gendered Impacts of Climate Change.* Dordrecht: Springer.

56. Carroll, N., *et al.* (2009). Quantifying the costs of drought: New evidence from life satisfaction data. *Journal of Population Economics*, 22(2), 445-461.

57. See for example: Sartore, G.M., *et al.* (2008). Control, uncertainty, and expectations for the future: A qualitative study of the impact of drought on a rural Australian community. Retieved from: http://www.rrh.org.au/publishedarticles/article_print_950.pdf; Coêlho, A., *et al.* (2004). Psychological responses to drought in northeastern Brazil. *Revista Interamericana de Psicología*, 38, 95-103; Chand, P.K., & Murthy, P. (2008). Climate change and mental health. *Regional Health Forum*, 12, 43-48.

58. See for example: New York Times (1991, October 14). Farmer suicide rate swells in 1980s. *New York Times*. Retrieved from: http://www.nytimes.com/1991/10/14/us/farmer-suicide-rate-swells-in-1980-s-study-says.html; G.M. Sartore, *et al.* (2007). Drought and its effect on mental health—how GPs can help. *Australian Family Physician*, 36(12), 990-993; Goldwert, L. (2011, September 2). Climate change threatens mental health too: Droughts, floods have psychological impact. *The Daily News*. Retrieved from: http://www.nydailynews.com/life-style/health/violent-weather-threatens-mental-health-study-article-1.953454.

59. Chattopadhyay, P., *et al.* (1995). Air pollution and health hazards in human subjects: Physiological and self-report indices. *Journal of Environmental Psychology*, 15, 327-331.

60. Pedersen, C., *et al.* (2004). Air pollution from traffic and schizophrenia risk. *Schizophrenia Research*, 66, 83-85.

61. Jacobs, S., Evans, G., Catalano, R., & Dooley, D. (1984). Air pollution and depressive symptomatology: Exploratory analyses of intervening psychosocial factors. *Population & Environment: Behavioral & Social Issues*, 7, 260-272.

62. Rotton, J., & Frey, J. (1985). Air pollution, weather, and violent crimes: Concomitant time-series analysis of archival data. *Journal of Personality and Social Psychology*, 49, 1207-1220.

63. See for example: Strazdins, L., *et al.* (2007). What does family-friendly really mean? Wellbeing, time, and the quality of parents' job. *Australian Bulletin of Labour*, 33(2), 202-225; Berry, H.L., *et al.* (2007). Preliminary development and validation of an Australian community participation questionnaire: Types of participation and associations with distress in a coastal community. *Social Science and Medicine*, 64(8), 1719-1737.

64. Katon, W., *et al.* (2007). The prevalence of DSM-IV anxiety and depressive disorders in youth with asthma compared with controls. *Journal of Adolescent Health*, 41, 455-463.

65. Nagao, K., *et al.* (2001). Mental symptoms induced by a massive outbreak of infectious disease in elementary school children: Six cases of delayed and reactivated stress-related disorders, including PTSD. *Japanese Journal of Child and Adolescent Psychiatry*, 42, 315-322.

66. See, for example: Carter, J.A., *et al.* (2005). Persistent neurocognitive impairments associated with Aevere Falciparum malaria in Kenyan children. *Journal of Neurology, Neurosurgery & Psychiatry*, 76, 476-481; Haaland, K.Y., *et al.* (2006). Mental status after West Nile Virus infection. *Emerging Infectious Diseases*, 12, 1260-1262; Olness, K. (2003). Effects on brain development leading to cognitive impairment: A worldwide epidemic. *Journal of Developmental & Behavioral Pediatrics*, 24, 120-130; Pancharoen, C., & Thisyakorn, U. (2001). Neurological manifestations in dengue patients. *Southeast Asian Journal of Tropical Medicine and Public Health*, 32, 341-345.

67. See for example: Fritze, J.G., *et al.* (2008). Hope, despair and transformation: Climate change and the promotion of mental health and wellbeing. *International Journal of Mental Health Systems*, 2(1). DOI: 10.1186/1752-4458-2-13; Berry, H.L., *et al.* (2010). Climate change and mental health: A causal pathways framework. *International Journal of Public Health*, 55, 123-132. DOI: 10.1007/s00038-009-0112-0; Dohrenwend, B.R. (1990). Socioeconomic status (SES) and psychiatric disorders: Are the issues still compelling? *Social Psychiatry Psychiatric Epidemiology*, 25, 41-47.

68. Stern, N. (2007). *The Economics of Climate Change: The Stern Review*. Cambridge, U.K.: Cambridge University Press.

69. Coêlho, A., *et al.* (2004). Psychological responses to drought in northeastern Brazil. *Revista Interamericana de Psicología*, 38, 95-103.

70. Okamoto-Mizuno, K, & Mizuno, K. (2012). Effects of thermal environment on sleep and circadian rhythm. *Journal of Physiological Anthropology*, 31(1). DOI: 10.1186/1880-6805-31-14.

71. See for example: Collingwood, J. (April 2007). The physical effects of long term stress. *PsychCentral*. Retrieved from: http://psychcentral.com/lib/the-physical-effects-of-long-term-stress; Rupa, B. (2014). The impacts of recent heat waves on human health in California. *Insurance NewsNet*. Retrieved from: http://insurancenewsnet.com/oarticle/2014/01/24/the-impact-of-recent-heat-waves-on-human-health-in-california-a-449609.html

72. Fritze, J., *et al.* (2008). Hope, despair and transformation: Climate change and the promotion of mental health and wellbeing. *International Journal of Mental Health Systems*. Retrieved from: http://www.ncbi.nlm.nih.gov/pmc/articles/PMC2556310/pdf/1752-4458-2-13.pdf.

73. Karsten, I., & Moser, K. (2009). Unemployment impairs mental health: A meta-analysis. *Journal of Vocational Behavior*, 74, 264-282.

74. Stern, N. (2007). *The Economics of Climate Change: The Stern Review*. Cambridge, U.K.: Cambridge University Press.

75. See for example: Marmot, M., & Wilkinson, R. (Eds.). (2005). *Social Determinants of Health: The Solid Facts*. Oxford: Oxford University Press; World Health Organization. (2010). *A Conceptual Framework for Action on the Social Determinants of Health*. World Health Organization; Shields, M., & Price, S. (2001). Exploring the economic and social determinants of psychological and psychosocial health. Discussion Paper No. 396. Bonn: Institute for the Study of Labour.

76. Ibid.

77. See for example: Brown, A. (2012, October). With poverty comes depression, more than other illnesses. Retrieved from: http://www.gallup.com/poll/158417/poverty-comes-depression-illness.aspx; Ferrari, A.J., *et al.* (2013). Burden of depressive disorders by county, sex, age and year: Findings of the global burden of disease study 2010. *PLOS Medicine*, 10(11). DOI: 10.1371/journal.pmed.1001547.

78. U.S. EPA (no date). Climate impacts on human health. Retrieved in January 2015 from: http://www.epa.gov/climatechange/impacts-adaptation/health.html.

79. Ibid.

80. See for example: Searle, K., & Gow, K. (2010). Do concerns about climate change lead to distress? *International Journal of Climate Change Strategies and Management*, 2(4), 362-379; Fritze, J., *et al.* (2008). Hope, despair and transformation: Climate change and the promotion of mental health and wellbeing. *International Journal of Mental Health Systems*, 2(1). DOI: 1186/1752-4458-2-13.

81. See for example: Collingwood, J. (April 2007). The physical effects of long term stress. *PsychCentral*. Retrieved from: http://psychcentral.com/lib/the-physical-effects-of-long-term-stress; Rupa, B. (2014). The impacts of recent heat waves on human health in California. *Insurance NewsNet*. Retrieved from: http://insurancenewsnet.com/oarticle/2014/01/24/the-impact-of-recent-heat-waves-on-human-health-in-california-a-449609.html; Carlson, N.R. (2004). *Physiology of Behavior* (8th Ed.). New York, NY: Allyn & Bacon.

82. Bloom, S., & Farragher, B. (1996). *Destroying Sanctuary: The Crisis in Human Service Delivery Systems*. Oxford: Oxford University Press; Bloom, S., & Farragher, B. (2013). *Restoring Sanctuary: A New Operating System for Trauma-Informed Systems of Care*. Oxford: Oxford University Press.

83. Joseph, S. (2011). *What Doesn't Kill Us: The New Psychology of Posttraumatic Growth*. New York, NY: Basic Books. p. 91.

Chapter 2: The psycho-social-spiritual effects of climate disruption on organizations, communities, and societies

84. Story and quote from Furman, P. (2013, October 26). Hurricane Sandy one year later. *New York Daily News*. Retrieved from: http://www.nydailynews.com/new-york/hurricane-sandy/hurricane-sandy-year-business-article-1.1493143.

85. Ibid.

86. Witters, D., & Ander, S. (2014). Depression increases in areas Superstorm Sandy hit hardest: Daily worry and anger also increase in most affected areas. Gallup-Healthways poll. Retrieved from: http://www.gallup.com/poll/159704/depression-increases-areas-superstorm-sandy-hit-hardest.aspx.

87. Healthcare Quality Strategies Inc. reviewed Medicare claims data in the year before and after Sandy.

88. The Daily Herald (2014, October 29). Sandy's mental health impact looms large. *The Daily Herald*. Retrieved from: http://www.dailyherald.com/article/20141029/news/141028083.

89. Insurance Institute for Business and Home Safety. Retrieved from: http://www.disastersafety.org.

90. Scientists say that climate disruption did not directly cause Superstorm Sandy. However, rising sea levels and other effects of human-caused climate disruption significantly aggravated the hurricane. For more information see: Main, D. (2012). Climate change partly to blame for hurricane damage. *Livescience*. Retrieved from: http://www.livescience.com/24566-hurricane-sandy-climate-change.html.

91. Romm, J. (2013). Superstorm Sandy's link to climate change: The "case has been strengthened" says researcher. *Climate Progress*. Retrieved from: http://thinkprogress. org/climate/2013/10/28/2843871/superstorm-sandy-climate-change.

92. Munich Reinsurance Company (2012). Annual report 2012. Retrieved from: http:// www.munichre.com/site/corporate/get/documents/mr/assetpool.shared/ Documents/0_Corporate%20Website/_Publications/302-07807_en.pdf.

93. Securities and Exchange Commission (2010). Release Nos. 33-9106; 34-61469; FR-82. Commission guidance regarding disclosure related to climate change. Retrieved from: http://www.sec.gov/rules/interp/2010/33-9106.pdf.

94. Hubler, M., *et al.* (2008). Costs of climate change: The effects of rising temperatures on health and productivity in Germany. *Ecological Economics*, 68, 381-393.

95. Hsiang, S. (2010). Temperatures and cyclones strongly associated with economic production in the Caribbean and Central America. *Proceedings of the National Academy of Sciences of the United States*, 107(35). Retrieved from: http://www.pnas. org/content/107/35/15367.full.

96. The Risky Business Project (2014). Risky business: The economic risks of climate change in the United States. Retrieved from: http://riskybusiness.org/uploads/ files/RiskyBusiness_Report_WEB_09_08_14.pdf.

97. Four Twenty Seven Climate Solutions and the University of Notre Dame's Global Adaptation Index (2015). 2015 Corporate adaptation report. Retrieved from: http:// gain.org/sites/default/files/2015%20Corporate%20Adaptation%20Survey.pdf.

98. Humanitarian News and Analysis (2012, October). Nigeria: Worst flooding in decades. *Humanitarian News and Analysis*. Retrieved from: http://www.irinnews. org/report/96504/nigeria-worst-flooding-in-decades.

99. See for example, Bloom, S., & Farragher, B. (2011). *Destroying Sanctuary: The Crisis in Human Service Delivery Systems*. Oxford: Oxford University Press; Bloom, S., & Farragher, B. (2013). *Restoring Sanctuary: A New Operating System for Trauma-Informed Systems of Care*. Oxford: Oxford University Press.

100. Ibid.

101. See for example: Doppelt. B. (2003). *Leading Change toward Sustainability: A Change Management Guide for Business, Government, and Civil Society*. Sheffield, U.K.: Greenleaf Publishing; Doppelt, B. (2008). *The Power of Sustainable Thinking*. Earthscan Publishing; Doppelt, B. (2012). *From Me to We: The Five Transformational Commitments Required to Rescue the Planet, Your Organization, and Your Life*. Sheffield, U.K.: Greenleaf Publishing.

102. United Nations Human Settlement Program (UN-Habitat) (2011). Cities and climate change: Global report on human settlements: The impacts of climate change upon urban areas. Retrieved from: http://unhabitat.org/wp-content/uploads/2012/06/ GRHS2011-4.pdf.

103. Ibid.

104. Ibid.

105. U.S. EPA (2013). Climate impacts on human health. Retrieved in January 2015 from: http://www.epa.gov/climatechange/impacts-adaptation/health.html.

106. European Commission Joint Research Centre (2014). The health impacts of climate change in Europe. Retrieved from: https://ec.europa.eu/jrc/sites/default/files/ pesetaii_health_2014_1694__jrc_86970_correcteddp2.pdf.

107. World Health Organization (2008). The impacts of climate change on human health: Statement by the WHO Director-General Dr. Margaret Chen. Retrieved from: http:// www.who.int/mediacentre/news/statements/2008/s05/en.

108. United Nations Human Settlement Program (UN-Habitat) (2011). Cities and climate change: Global report on human settlements: The impacts of climate change upon

urban areas. Retrieved from: http://unhabitat.org/wp-content/uploads/2012/06/GRHS2011-4.pdf.

109. Wang, P.S., *et al.* (2008). Disruption of existing mental health treatments and failure to initiate new treatment after Hurricane Katrina. *American Journal of Psychiatry*, 165(1), 34-41.

110. United Nations Human Settlement Program (UN-Habitat) (2011). Cities and climate change: Global report on human settlements: The impacts of climate change upon urban areas. Retrieved from: http://unhabitat.org/wp-content/uploads/2012/06/GRHS2011-4.pdf.

111. Ibid.

112. Myers, N. (2005). *Environmental Refugees: An Emergent Security Issue* (13th Ed.). Prague: Economic Forum.

113. See for example: Rotton, J., & Cohn, E.G. (2003). Global warming and U.S. crime rates: An application of routine activity theory. *Environment and Behavior*, 35, 802-825; Horrocks, J., & Menclova, K. (2011). The effects of weather on crime. *New Zealand Economics Papers*, 45(3), 231-254; Mishra, A. (2014). Climate and crime. *Global Journal of Science Frontier Research: H Environment & Earth Science*, 14(6). Retrieved from: https://globaljournals.org/GJSFR_Volume14/5-Climate-and-Crime.pdf; Brunsdon, C., *et al.* (2009). The influence of weather on local geographical patterns of police calls for service. *Environment and Planning Design*, 36(5), 906-926; Bushman, B., *et al.* (2005). Is the curve relating temperature to aggression linear or curvilinear? *Journal of Personality and Social Psychology*, 89(1), 62-66; Cohn, E., & Rotton, J. (2000). Weather, seasonal trends, and property crimes in Minneapolis, 1987–1988: A moderator-variable time-series analysis of routine activities. *Journal of Environmental Psychology*, 20(3), 257-272; Cohn, E. (1990). Weather and crime. *British Journal of Criminology*, 30(1), 51-64.

114. Bushman, B. (2013). Global warming can also increase aggression and violence: Hot temperatures can lead to hot tempers. *Psychology Today*. Retrieved from: https://www.psychologytoday.com/blog/get-psyched/201307/global-warming-can-also-increase-aggression-and-violence.

115. Hipp, J., *et al.* (2004). Crimes of opportunity or crimes of emotion? Testing two explanations of seasonal change in crime. *Social Forces*, 82(4), 1333-1372. Retrieved from: http://www.unc.edu/~curran/pdfs/Hipp,Bauer,Curran,Bollen(2004).pdf.

116. Ranson, M. (2014). Crime, weather, and climate change. *Journal of Environmental Economics and Management.* 67, 274-302.

117. Hipp, J., *et al.* (2004). Crimes of opportunity or crimes of emotion? Testing two explanations of seasonal change in crime. *Social Forces*, 82(4), 1333-1372.

118. Simister, J. (2008). Links between violence and high temperatures. *Development Ideas and Practices Working Paper*. DIP-08-05. Retrieved from: https://www.academia.edu/443678/Links_Between_Violence_and_High_Temperatures.

119. Bulbena, A., *et al.* (2006). Psychiatric effects of heat waves. *Psychiatric Services*, 57(10), 1519; The Independent (2011, August). Climate change threatens mental health too: Study. *The Independent*. Retrieved from: http://www.independent.co.uk/life-style/health-and-families/climate-change-threatens-mental-healthtoo-study-2346415.html.

120. Bloom. S. (2006). Human service systems and organizational stress: Thinking & feeling our way out of existing organizational dilemmas. Report for the Trauma Task Force. p. 25. Retrieved from: http://www.sanctuaryweb.com/Portals/0/Bloom%20Pubs/2006%20Bloom%20Human%20Service%20Systems%20and%20Organizational%20Stress.pdf.

121. Ibid.

122. Bergen, P. (2012). *The Homegrown Threat: Right- and Left-Wing Terrorism Since 9/11*. New American Foundation and Syracuse University's Maxwell School of Public Policy.

123. Postmes, T., & Spears, R. (1998). Deindividuation and antinormative behavior: A meta-analysis. *Psychological Bulletin*. 123(3), 238-259.

124. World Health Organization (2002). World report on violence and health. Geneva: World Health Organization.

125. For more information: Centers for Disease Control and Prevention. Climate Effects on Health. Retrieved from: http://www.cdc.gov/climateandhealth/effects/default. htm.

126. Hansen, A., *et al.* (2008). The effect of heat waves on mental health in a temperate Australian city. *Environmental Health Perspectives*, 116(10), 1369-1375.

127. Stern, N. (2007). *The Economics of Climate Change: The Stern Review*. Cambridge, U.K.: Cambridge University Press.

128. The DARA Group and Climate Vulnerability Forum (2012). Climate vulnerability monitor: A guide to the cold calculus of a hot planet. Retrieved from: http://daraint. org/wp-content/uploads/2012/09/CVM2ndEd-FrontMatter.pdf.

129. Interagency Working Group on Social Cost of Carbon, United States Government (2010). Technical support document: Social cost of carbon for regulatory impact analysis—under executive order 12866. Retrieved from: http://www.whitehouse. gov/sites/default/files/omb/inforeg/for-agencies/Social-Cost-of-Carbon-for-RIA. pdf.

130. Moore, F., & Diaz, D. (2015). Temperature impacts on economic growth warrant stringent mitigation policy. *Nature Climate Change*. Retrieved from: http://www. eenews.net/assets/2015/01/13/document_cw_01.pdf.

131. See for example: Lee, Y., Lee, M.K., Chun, K.H., Lee, Y.K., & Yoon, S.J. (2001). Trauma experience of North Korean refugees in China. *American Journal of Preventive Medicine*, 20, 225-229; Yu, S., & Hannum, E. (2007). Food for thought: Poverty, family nutritional environment, and children's educational performance in rural China. *Sociological Perspectives*, 50, 53-77.

132. See for example: Chilton, M., & Booth, S. (2007). Hunger of the body and hunger of the mind: African American women's perceptions of food insecurity, health and violence. *Journal of Nutrition Education and Behavior*, 39, 116-125; Lee, Y., Lee, M.K., Chun, K.H., Lee, Y.K., & Yoon, S.J. (2001). Trauma experience of North Korean refugees in China. *American Journal of Preventive Medicine*, 20, 225-229.

133. See for example: Tanner, E.M., & Finn-Stevenson, M. (2002). Nutrition and brain development: Social policy implications. *American Journal of Orthopsychiatry*, 72, 182-193; Wachs, T.D. (2000). Nutritional deficits and behavioral development. *International Journal of Behavioral Development*, 24, 435-441.

134. Bohle, H.G., *et al.* (1994). Climate change and social vulnerability: Toward a sociology and geography of food insecurity. *Global Environmental Change*, 4, 37-48.

135. Abbott, C. (2008). *An Uncertain Future: Law Enforcement, National Security, and Climate Change*. London: Oxford Research Group.

136. Laczko, F., & Aghazarm, C. (Eds.). (2009). Migration, environment and climate change: Assessing the evidence. International Organization for Migration. Retrieved from: http://publications.iom.int/bookstore/free/migration_and_environment. pdf.

137. Hsiang, S.M., *et al.* (2013). Quantifying the influence of climate on human conflict. *Science*, 341. DOI: 10.1126/science.1235367.

138. Ibid.

139. Ibid.

140. Institute for Security Studies (2014, May). Links between climate change, conflict and governance in Africa, No 234. Retrieved from: http://www.issafrica.org/uploads/Paper_234.pdf.

141. Adorni, T., *et al.* (1993). *The Authoritarian Personality (Studies in Prejudice)*. New York, NY: W.W. Norton Company.

142. King, D., *et al.* (2015). Climate change: A risk assessment. Retrieved from: http://www.csap.cam.ac.uk/projects/climate-change-risk-assessment.

143. Darby, M. (2015). Global warming raises tensions in Boko Haram region. Retrieved from: http://www.rtcc.org/2015/01/16/global-warming-raises-tensions-in-boko-haram-region/#sthash.7BBuqRaF.dpuf.

144. See for example: Doherty, M., & Clayton, S. (2011). The psychological impacts of global climate change. *American Psychologist*. Retrieved from: http://www.apa.org/pubs/journals/releases/amp-66-4-265.pdf; Van Sustern, L., & Coyle, K. (2012). The psychological effects of global warming in the United States: And why the mental health system is not adequately prepared. Reston, VA: National Wildlife Federation Climate Education Program; U.S. Department of Defense (2014). Climate change adaptation road map. U.S. Department of Defense. Retrieved from: http://www.defense.gov/News/News-Releases/News-Release-View/Article/605221; Ranson, M. (2014). Crime, weather, and climate change. *Journal of Environmental Economics and Management*, 67, 274-302.

145. Taylor, C. (2012). *Meaning, Morals, and Modernity*. Malden, MA: Blackwell Publishers.

146. Solnit, R. (2010). *A Paradise Built in Hell: The Extraordinary Communities That Arise in Disaster*. London: Penguin Books.

147. See for example: Shrady, N. (2008). *The Last Day: Wrath, Ruin, and Reason in the Great Lisbon Earthquake of 1755*. New York, NY: Viking; Brinkley, D. (2007). *The Great Deluge: Hurricane Katrina, New Orleans, and the Mississippi Gulf Coast*. New York, NY: Harper, as cited in Aldrich, D. (2012). *Building Resilience: Social Capital in Post-Disaster Recovery*. Chicago, IL: University of Chicago Press.

148. See for example: Sweet, S. (1998). The effect of a natural disaster in social cohesion: A longitudinal study. *International Journal of Mass Emergencies and Disasters*, 16(3), 321-331; Tatuski, S. (2010). The effects of empowered social capital during the disaster recovery period. Paper presented at the annual meeting of the Association for Asian Studies as cited in: Aldrich, D. (2012). *Building Resilience: Social Capital in Post-Disaster Recovery*. Chicago, IL: University of Chicago Press.

149. My longtime friend and colleague Ernie Niemi, Principal with Natural Resource Economics inc. and one of the top natural resource economists in the U.S., came up with the idea of creating a three-legged stool to describe the need to include building Transformational Resilience to the responses to climate disruption.

Chapter 3: The imperative of building widespread capacity for Transformational Resilience

150. Frankl, V.E. (2014). *The Will to Meaning: Foundations and Applications of Logotherapy* (first published in 1970, expanded edition 2014). New York: Plume, p. 26.

151. Ryff, C.D., & Singer, B. (1996). Psychological well-being: Meaning, measurement, and implications for psychotherapy research. *Psychotherapy and Psychosomatics*, 65, 14-23.

152. World Health Organization (2014). Mental health: A state of well-being. Retrieved from: http://www.who.int/features/factfiles/mental_health/en.

153. Ruini, C. (2014). The use of wellbeing therapy in clinical settings. *The Journal of Happiness and Well-being*, 2(1), 75-84.

154. See for example: Ryan, R., & Deci, E. (2001). On happiness and human potentials: A review of research on hedonic and eudaimonic well-being. *Annual Psychological Review*, 52, 141-166; Waterman, A. (2007). On the importance of distinguishing hedonia and eudaimonia when contemplating the hedonic treadmill. *American Psychologist*, 62(6), 612-613; Ryff, C., & Singer, B. (2006). Know thyself and become what you are: A eudaimonic approach to psychological well-being. *Journal of Happiness Studies*, 9, 13-39.

155. Bonanno, G.A. (2004). Loss, trauma and human resilience: Have we underestimated the human capacity to thrive after extremely adverse events? *American Psychologist*, 59(1), 135-138.

156. Ibid.

157. American Psychological Association (2010). *The Road to Resilience*. Washington D.C.: American Psychological Association. Retrieved from: http://www.apa.org/helpcenter/road-resilience.aspx.

158. This is not in any way a criticism of the book *Bouncing Back* by Linda Graham, which I highly recommend. I'm speaking of the general notion that resilience means bouncing back to previous conditions after adversity.

159. Feeding America (No date). *Hunger in America*. Retrieved from: http://www.feedingamerica.org/hunger-in-america/impact-of-hunger/child-hunger/child-hunger-fact-sheet.html.

160. World Health Organization (2009, May). Addressing adverse childhood experiences to improve public health: Expert consultation, 4–5 May 2009. Geneva: World Health Organization. Retrieved from: http://www.who.int/violence_injury_prevention/violence/activities/adverse_childhood_experiences/global_research_network_may_2009.pdf.

161. Keck, M., & Sakdapolrak, P. (2013). What is social resilience? Lessons learned and ways forward. *Erdkunde*, 67(1), 5-19.

162. Ibid.

163. Ibid.

164. Aldwin, C.M., & Levenson, M.R. (2004). Posttraumatic growth: A developmental perspective. *Psychological Inquiry*, 15(1), 9-22.

165. Crum, J.A., *et al.* (2013). Rethinking stress: The role of mindsets in determining the stress response. *Journal of Personality and Social Psychology*, 104(4), 716-733. Retrieved from: https://mbl.stanford.edu/sites/default/files/crum_rethinkingstress_jpsp_2013_0.pdf.

166. Davidson, R., & Begley, S. (2012). *The Emotional Life of Your Brain*. London: Penguin Group.

167. Found in the "Maxims and Arrows" section of his book *Twilight of the Idols* (1888).

168. Keck, M., & Sakdapolrak, P. (2013). What is social resilience? Lessons learned and ways forward. *Erdkunde*, 67(1), 5-19.

169. See for example: Silver, R., & Updegraff, J. (2013). Searching for and finding meaning following personal and collective traumas. In K.D. Markman, T. Proulx, & M.J. Lindberg (Eds.), *The Psychology of Meaning* (pp. 237-255). Washington, D.C.: American Psychological Association; Keck, M., & Sakdapolrak, P. (2013). What is social resilience? lessons learned and ways forward. *Erdkunde*, 67(1), 5-19.

170. This is the definition I developed in 2013 when my organization launched the Transformational Resilience program. I share it with groups in workshops and webinars so they understand the goals and intended outcomes of the program.

171. Calhoun, L., & Tedeschi, R. (1999). *Facilitating Post Traumatic Growth: A Clinicians Guide*. New York, NY: Routledge, Taylor and Francis Group.

172. This term is a variation on the Resilience Zone used by my friend and colleague Elaine Miller-Karas from the Trauma Resource Institute. Elaine has developed with Community-Resilience Model (CRM) and other leading approaches to trauma and stress. For more information see the TRI website: http://traumaresourceinstitute.com.

173. Ibid.

174. See for example: Schwarzer, R., & Knoll, N. (2003). Positive Coping: Mastering demands and searching for meaning. In S.J. Lopez & C.R. Snyder (Eds.), *Positive Psychological Assessment: A Handbook of Models and Measures* (pp. 393-409). Washington, D.C.: American Psychological Association; Janoff-Bulman, R. (1992). *Shattered Assumptions: Toward A New Psychology of Trauma*. New York, NY: The Free Press; Janoff-Bulman, R. (2006). Schema-change perspectives on post-traumatic growth. In L.G. Calhoun & R.G. Tedeschi (Eds.), *Handbook of Post-Traumatic Growth: Research and Practice*. Mahwah, NJ: Lawrence Erlbaum Associated.

175. Frankl, V.E. (1962 [1946]). *Man's Search for Meaning*. Boston: Beacon Press.

176. See for example: Janoff-Bulman, R. (1992). *Shattered Assumptions: Toward A New Psychology of Trauma*. New York, NY: The Free Press; Janoff-Bulman, R. (2006). Schema-change perspectives on post-traumatic growth. (2006). In L.G. Calhoun & R.G. Tedeschi (Eds.), *Handbook of Post-Traumatic Growth: Research and Practice*. Mahwah, NJ: Lawrence Erlbaum Associated.

177. Ibid.

178. Calhoun, L.G., & Tedeschi, R. (2006). Foundations of post-traumatic growth. In L.G. Calhoun & R. Tedeschi (Eds.), *Handbook of Post-Traumatic Growth: Research and Practice* (pp. 1-23). Mahwah, NJ: Lawrence Erlbaum.

179. Silver, R., & Updegraff, J. (2013). Searching for and finding meaning following personal and collective traumas. In K.D. Markman, T. Proulx, & M.J. Lindberg (Eds.), *The Psychology of Meaning* (pp. 237-255). Washington, D.C.: American Psychological Association.

180. Ibid.

181. My organization offers a variety of Transformational Workshops for individuals and organizations throughout the U.S. and Europe. We ask participants to complete pre- and post-workshop as well as six-month follow up questionnaires to determine the effectiveness of the workshops. 97% of participants who completed post-workshop surveys either strongly agree or agree that what they learned would be very useful in their own lives. 87% of participants strongly agree or agree that they learned new skills and improved existing capacity to teach others resilience skills.

182. Siegel, D. (No date). About interpersonal neurobiology. Retrieved from: http://www.drdansiegel.com/about/interpersonal_neurobiology.

183. Herman, J. (1992). *Trauma and Recovery*. New York, NY: Basic Books.

184. Janoff-Bulman R. (1992). *Shattered Assumptions: Toward a New Psychology of Trauma*. New York, NY: The Free Press.

185. Briere, J., & Scott, C. (2006). *Principles of Trauma Therapy: A Guide To Symptoms, Evaluation And Treatment*. Thousand Oaks, CA: Sage.

186. van der Kolk, B. (2014). *Trauma, Attachment & Neuroscience with Bessel van der Kolk, M.D.: Brain, Mind & Body in the Healing of Trauma*. Eau Claire, WS: PESI Publishing & Media.

187. Joseph, S. (2011). *What Doesn't Kill Us: The New Psychology of Posttraumatic Growth*. New York, NY: Basic Books.

188. Tedeschi, R.G., & Calhoun, L.G. (1995). *Trauma and Transformation: Growing in the Aftermath of Suffering.* Thousand Oaks, CA: Sage.

189. Herman, J. (1992). *Trauma and Recovery.* New York, NY: Basic Books.

190. Lazarus, R., & Folkman, S. (1984). *Stress, Appraisal, and Coping.* New York, NY: Springer Publishing.

191. Murray, M., *et al.* (2009). Using the constructive narrative perspective to understand physical activity reasoning schema in sedentary adults. *Journal of Health Psychology,* 14, 1174-1183.

192. Monk, G., *et al.* (1997). *Narrative Therapy in Practice: The Archaeology of Hope.* San Francisco: John Wiley and Sons.

193. See for example: Kabat-Zinn, J. (1990). *Full Catastrophe Living: Using the Wisdom of Your Body and Mind to Face Stress, Pain and Illness.* New York, NY: Delacorte; Kabat-Zinn, J. (2003). Mindfulness based intervention in context: Past, present, and future. *Clinical Psychology: Science and Practice,* 10, 144-156.

194. See for example: Fava, G.A., & Ruini, C. (2013). Well-being therapy: Theoretical background, clinical implications, and future directions. In I. Boniwell, S.A. David, & A. Conley Ayers (Eds.), *Oxford Handbook of Happiness.* DOI: 10.1093/oxfordhb/9780199557257.013.0077.

195. Hayes, S., & Strosahl, K. (2004). *A Practical Guide to Acceptance and Commitment Therapy.* New York, NY: Springer Publishing.

196. The Linehan Institute (No date). What is DBT? Retrieved from: http://behavioraltech.org/resources/whatisdbt.cfm.

197. More information about the shift from the belief in independence to embracing interdependence can be found in my book *From Me to We: The Five Transformational Commitments Required to Rescue the Planet, Your Organization, and Your Life.* (2012). Sheffield, U.K.: Greenleaf Publishing.

Part 2: Presencing—the first building block of Transformational Resilience

Chapter 4: Ground and center yourself by stabilizing your nervous system

198. As the Pages Turn (2011, December 12). Interview with Whitney Stewart. Retrieved from: https://asthepagesturn.wordpress.com/tag/hurricane-katrina-suvivor.

199. See for example: Glendinning, C. (1995). Technology, trauma, and the wild. In T. Roszak, M.E. Gomes, & A.D. Kanner (Eds.), *Ecopsychology: Restoring the Earth, healing the mind* (pp. 41-54). San Francisco, CA: Sierra Club Books; Goleman, D. (2009). *Ecological Intelligence: How Knowing the Hidden Impacts of What We Buy Can Change Everything.* New York, NY: Doubleday; Clinebell, H.J. (1996). *Ecotherapy: Healing Ourselves, Healing the Earth.* New York, NY: Haworth Press.

200. Joseph, S. (2011). *What Doesn't Kill Us: The New Psychology of Posttraumatic Growth.* New York, NY: Basic Books. p. 167.

201. See for example: Kostanski, M., & Craig, H. (2008). Mindfulness as a concept and a process. *Australian Psychologist,* 43(1), 15-21; Manna, A., *et al.* (2010). Neural correlates of focused attention and cognitive monitoring in meditation. *Brain Research Bulletin,* 82(1-2), 46-56; Siegel, D. (2010). *Mindsight.* New York, NY: Random House.

202. The following description is adopted from the Community Resilience Model Handbook by the Trauma Resource Institute, which is a partner in my organization's

Transformational Resilience Program. Note that the CRM model focuses on "Resourcing" first, not Grounding. This means identifying internal images and strengths as well as external people and activities that can help calm the body and mind. In the *Resilient Growth*™ model, which is a preventative, not trauma-treatment approach, Resourcing is included in the next step, which I call Remembering your personal strengths, skills, resources, and social support network. However, it is very important to note that Elaine Miller-Karas, Executive Director of TRI, says that when people are already significantly dysregulated it is important to begin with Resourcing to avoid triggering additional adverse reactions.

203. For more information see: http://traumaresourceinstitute.com/community-resiliency-model-crm.
204. The following description is adopted from the Community Resilience Model Handbook by the Trauma Resource Institute, which is a partner in my organization's Transformational Resilience Program.
205. Ibid.
206. The Trauma Resource Institute. (No date). The Philippines-January 2014, April 2014 and November 2014. Retrieved from: http://traumaresourceinstitute.com/philippines.
207. Joseph, C.N. (2005). Slow breathing improves arterial baroreflex sensitivity and decreases blood pressure in essential hypertension. *Hypertension*, 46, 714-718.
208. Schmidt, S., & Walach, H. (Eds.). (2014). *Meditation: Neuroscientific Approaches and Philosophical Implications*. New York, NY: Springer International Publishing.
209. Siegel, D. (2015). The science of mindfulness. *Mindful: Taking Time for What Matters*. Retrieved from: http://www.mindful.org/the-science/medicine/the-science-of-mindfulness.
210. I developed the Reset Button as part of my organization's Transformational Resilience Program.
211. This event occurred in 2014, although Janice is not the real name of the person who told me the story.
212. Note that there are other techniques that can be used to stabilize your nervous system when you are disregulated, such as Eye Movement Desensitization and Reprocessing (EMDR). However, EMDR and other approaches are not easily self-administered and usually initially require the assistance of a therapist. I therefore have not included them in this list.
213. For more information go to: http://www.mbsrtraining.com/body-scan-benefits.
214. For more information: http://www.mbsrtraining.com/walking-meditation-guided-audio.
215. For more information: http://www.mbsrtraining.com/audio-laying-yoga.
216. For more information: http://www.yogajournal.com/article/beginners/yoga-questions-answered.
217. See for example: Gallup, A. (2007). Yawning as a brain cooling mechanism: Nasal breathing and forehead cooling diminish the incidence of contagious yawning. *Evolutionary Psychology* 5(1), 92-101; for a lay summary, see: Science Daily (2007, June 21). Psychologists attribute yawning to the need to cool the brain and pay attention. Retrieved from: http://www.sciencedaily.com/releases/2007/06/070621161826.htm.
218. The following description is adopted from the Community Resilience Model Handbook by the Trauma Resource Institute, which is a core partner in my organization's Transformational Resilience Program.
219. Borgman, D. (1998). *The Importance of Dance in Africa*. S. Hamilton, MA: Center for Youth Studies.

220. Gerbarg, P., & Brown, R. (2005, October). Yoga: A breath of relief for Hurricane Katrina refugees. *Current Psychiatry*, 4(10), 55-67.

Chapter 5: Remember your personal strengths, skills, resources, and social support network

221. This story was retrieved from Caporima, A., & O'Connell, C. (2015). The rescuers in Tom's river. Inspiring stories: The heroes of Hurricane Sandy. *Readers Digest*. Retrieved from: http://www.rd.com/true-stories/inspiring/inspiring-stories-the-heroes-of-hurricane-sandy.
222. Bandura, A. (1997). *Self-Efficacy: The Exercise Of Control*. New York, NY: W.H. Freeman.
223. Research on important protective factors and processes in resilience has been completed by: Kumpfer, K.L. (1999). Factors and processes contributing to resilience: The Resilience Framework. In M.D. Glantz & J.L. Johnson (Eds.), *Resilience and Development: Positive Life Adaptations* (pp. 179-224). Norwell, MA: Kluwer Academic/Plenum Publishers; Gunnestad, A. (2006). Resilience in a cross-cultural perspective: How resilience is generated in different cultures. *Journal of Intercultural Communication*, 11, 1; Masten, A. (2001). *Ordinary Magic: Resilience in Development*. New York, NY: The Guilford Press; Aldrich, D. (2012). *Building Resilience: Social Capital in Post-Disaster Recover*. Chicago, IL: University of Chicago Press.
224. See for example: Helgeson, V.S. (2003). Social support and quality of life. *Quality of Life Research*, 12 (Suppl. 1), 25-31; Helgeson, V.S., & Cohen, S. (1996). Social support and adjustment to cancer: Reconciling descriptive, correlational, and intervention research. *Health Psychology*, 15, 135-148; Luthar, S.S. (2006). Resilience in development: A synthesis of research across five decades. In D. Cicchetti & D.J. Cohen (Eds.), *Developmental Psychopathology: Risk, Disorder, and Adaptation: Vol 3* (2nd ed.) (pp. 739-795). New York, NY: Wiley; Okun, M.A., & Lockwood, C.M. (2003). Does level of assessment moderate the relation between social support and social negativity?: A meta-analysis. *Basic and Applied Social Psychology*, 25, 15-35; Aldrich, D.P. (2012). *Building Resilience: Social Capital in Post-Disaster Recovery*. Chicago, IL: University of Chicago Press.
225. Miller-Karas, E., & Leitch, L. (2013). *Community Resilience Model Workbook*. Trauma Resource Institute, p. 17.
226. This exercise builds on the research on important protective factors and processes in resilience by: Kumpfer, K.L. (1999). Factors and processes contributing to resilience: The Resilience Framework. In M.D. Glantz & J.L. Johnson (Eds.), *Resilience and Development: Positive Life Adaptations* (pp. 179-224). Norwell, MA: Kluwer Academic/Plenum Publishers; Gunnestad, A. (2006). Resilience in a cross-cultural perspective: How resilience is generated in different cultures. *Journal of Intercultural Communication*, 11, 1404-1634; Masten, A. (2001). *Ordinary Magic: Resilience in Development*. New York, NY: The Guilford Press; Aldrich, D. (2012). *Building Resilience: Social Capital in Post-Disaster Recover*. Chicago, IL: University of Chicago Press.
227. Aldrich, D. (2012). *Building Resilience: Social Capital in Post-Disaster Recovery*. Chicago, IL: University of Chicago Press.
228. This step is an adaptation of the Resource Intensification technique developed by Elaine Miller-Karas and Laurie Leitch than can be found in the Community Resilience Model Handbook by the Trauma Resource Institute.

229. Siegel, D. (2010). *Mindsight: The New Science of Personal Transformation*. London: Random House.

230. Dooley, E. (2014, October 27). Poll: Neighbors key to coping with disasters. Associated Press. Retrieved from: http://www.apnorc.org/news-media/Pages/News+Media/poll-Neighbors-key-to-coping-with-disasters.aspx.

231. Aldrich, D. (2012). *Building Resilience: Social Capital in Post-Disaster Recovery*. Chicago, IL: University of Chicago Press.

232. Ibid.

233. World Meteorological Organization. (2014). Record greenhouse gas levels impact atmosphere and oceans. Retrieved from: https://www.wmo.int/pages/mediacentre/press_releases/pr_1002_en.html.

234. See for example: Brewin, C.R., *et al.* (2000). Meta-analysis of risk factors for posttraumatic stress disorder in trauma-exposed adults. *Journal of Consulting and Clinical Psychology*, 68, 748-766; Ozer, E.J., *et al.* (2008). Predictors of posttraumatic stress disorder and symptoms in adults: A meta-analysis. *Psychological Trauma: Theory, Research, Practice and Policy*, 1 (Supplement 1), 3-36.

235. Moak, Z.B., & Agrawal, A. (2010). The association between perceived interpersonal social support and physical and mental health: Results from the national epidemiological survey on alcohol and related conditions. *Journal of Public Health*, 32, 191-201.

236. Ibid.

237. Hogan, B.E., *et al.* (2002). Social support interventions: Do they work? *Clinical Psychology Reviews*, 22, 383-442.

238. Uchino B., Capioppo, J., & Keicolt-Glaser, J. (1996). The relationship between social support and physiological processes: A review with emphasis on underlying mechanisms and implications for health. *Psychological Bulletin*, 119(3), 488-531.

239. Joseph, S. (2011). *What Doesn't Kill Us: The New Psychology of Post Traumatic Growth*. New York, NY: Basic Books.

240. See for example: Ozbay, F., *et al.* (2007). Social support and resilience to stress: From neurology to clinical practice. *Psychiatry*, 4(5), 35-40; Dougall, A.L. (2006). Optimism and traumatic stress: The importance of social support and coping. *Journal of Applied Social Psychology*. DOI: 10.1111/j.1559-1816.2001.tb00195.x; Scrignara, M., *et al.* (2010). The combined contribution of social support and coping strategies in predicting post-traumatic growth: A longitudinal study of cancer patients. *Psycho-Oncology*, 20, 823-831.

241. Brown, L., *et al.* (2003). Providing social support might be more beneficial than receiving it: Results from a prospective study of mortality. *Psychological Science*, 14, 320-327.

242. Southwick, S., & Charney, D. (2012). *Resilience: The Science of Mastering Life's Greatest Challenges*. Cambridge: Cambridge University Press, p. 110.

243. Maddi, S.R., & Khoshaba, D.M. (2005). *Resilience at Work: How to Succeed No Matter What Life Throws at You*. New York, NY: AMACOM.

244. This story was told to me in 2015, though Pete's name has been changed.

245. Adapted from the version described in Graham, L. (2013). *Bouncing Back: Rewiring Your Brain for Maximum Resilience and Wellbeing*. Novato, CA: New World Library.

Chapter 6: Observe your reactions to and thoughts about the situation nonjudgmentally with self-compassion

246. This story was shared in 2014, though Sam's name has been changed.

247. The cognitive-behavioral approach to change is based on the work of Aaron Beck and Albert Ellis in the 1960s. My friend and colleague Dr. Glenn Schiraldi of Resilience Training International has adapted this work to provide a simple easy to use model. See: Schiraldi, G.R. (2011). *The Complete Guide to Resilience: Why It Matters; How to Build and Maintain It.* Ashburn, VA: Resilience Training International.

248. Ibid.

249. This step is an adaptation of the Resource Intensification technique developed by Elaine Miller-Karas and Laurie Leitch than can be found in the Community Resilience Model Handbook by the Trauma Resource Institute.

250. Hoelting. K. (No date). Walking the tightrope between joy and fear. Kurt Hoelting Inside Passages. Retrieved from: http://insidepassages.com/walking-the-tightrope-between-joy-and-fear.

251. Despite numerous attempts I could not find who originally authored this saying.

252. This exercise is adapted from Paul Gilbert's Compassionate Mind Training program. Retrieved from: http://www.compassionatemind.co.uk/downloads/training_materials/1.%20Workbook_2010.pdf.

253. The first workshop took place in 2014 and the follow up workshop occurred in early 2015, though Betty's name has been changed.

254. Ullrich, P., & Lutgendorf, S. (2002). Journaling about stressful events: Effects of cognitive processing and emotional expression. *Annals of Behavioral Medicine*, 24(3), 244-250.

Part 3: Purposing—the second building block of Transformational Resilience

255. Neitzsche, F. (1898) *Twilight of the Idols, or How to Philosophize with a Hammer.*

256. Joseph. S. (2011). *What Doesn't Kill Us: The New Psychology of Posttraumatic Growth.* New York, NY: Basic Books, p. 12.

257. A good meta-analysis of these findings was produced by Helgeson, V.S., *et al.* (2006). A meta-analytic review of benefit finding and growth. *Journal of Consulting and Clinical Psychology*, 74, 797-816.

258. Peterson, C., *et al.* (2008). Strengths of character and posttraumatic growth. *Journal of Traumatic Stress*, 21, 214-217.

Chapter 7: Watch for new insight and meaning in life as a result of climate-enhanced hardships

259. From Wooden, T. (2012). *We Shall Not Be Moved: Rebuilding Home in the Wake of Katrina.* Boston, MA: Beacon Press, pp. 81-82.

260. Joseph, S. (2011). *What Doesn't Kill Us: The New Psychology of Posttraumatic Growth.* New York, NY: Basic Books.

261. Affleck, G., & Tennen, H. (1996). Construing benefits from adversity: Adaptational significance and dispositional underpinnings. *Journal of Personality*, 64(4), 899-922.

262. Antoni, M.H., *et al.* (2001). Cognitive-behavioral stress management intervention decreases the prevalence of depression and enhances benefit finding among women under treatment for early-stage breast cancer. *Health Psychology*, 20(1), 20-32.

263. These terms can be found in numerous publications and are summarized on the Growth Initiative website hosted by Wake Forest University, the University of Pennsylvania found at: http://growthinitiative.org.

264. Mandela, N. (1995). *Long Walk to Freedom: The Autobiography of Nelson Mandela*. London: Little, Brown, and Company.

265. This event took place during a Transformational Resilience workshop in 2014, although Carole is not the participant's real name.

266. This tool is adapted from the diaries and self-monitoring mechanisms used in "well-being therapy" described by Fava, G.A., & Ruini, C. (2003). Development and characteristics of a well-being enhancing psychotherapeutic strategy. *Journal of Behavioral Therapy and Experimental Psychiatry*, 34(1), 45-63.

267. Joseph S. (2011). *What Doesn't Kill Us: The New Psychology of Posttraumatic Growth*. New York, NY: Basic Books. p. 114.

268. Ibid.

269. This exercise is adapted from Calhoun L., & Tedeschi, R. (2013). *Posttraumatic Growth in Clinical Settings*. London: Routledge. pp. 103-104.

270. Frankl, V. (1996). *Man's Search for Meaning*. New York, NY: Buccaneer Books.

271. The information that follows and much of this chapter is adapted from Viktor Frankl's work (Frankl, V. (1996). *Man's Search for Meaning*. New York, NY: Buccaneer Books) as it is used in Meaning-Centered Psychotherapy. Specifically, the following is adapted from Breitbart, W., & Poppito, S. (2014). *Meaning-Centered Group Psychotherapy for Patients with Advanced Cancer: A Treatment Manual*. Oxford: Oxford University Press.

272. Wong, P., *et al.* (2006) A resource-congruence model of coping and the development of the Coping Schema Inventory. In P.T.P. Wong, & L.C.J. Wong (Eds.), *Handbook of Multicultural Perspectives on Stress and Coping* (pp. 223-283). New York, NY: Springer.

273. Ibid.

274. O'Hanlon, B., & Beadle, S. (1999). *A Guide to Possibility Land: Fifty-one Methods for Doing Brief, Respectful Therapy*. New York, NY: Norton.

275. Much of the discussion that follows is adapted from Ramos, C., & Leal, I. (2013). Posttraumatic growth in the aftermath of trauma: A literature review about related factors and application contexts. *Psychology, Community and Health*, 2(1), 43-54. I have also included citations for specific points for people that want to know more.

276. See for example: Tedeschi, R.G., & Calhoun, L.G. (2004). Posttraumatic growth: Conceptual foundations and empirical evidence. *Psychological Inquiry*, 15, 1-18; Calhoun, L.G., *et al.* (2010). The posttraumatic growth model: Sociocultural considerations. In T. Weiss & R. Berger (Eds.), *Posttraumatic Growth and Culturally Competent Practice* (pp. 1-14). Hoboken, NJ: Wiley & Sons; Janoff-Bulman, R. (1992). *Shattered Assumptions*. New York, NY: Free Press; Janoff-Bulman, R. (2006). Schema-change perspectives on posttraumatic growth. In L.G. Calhoun & R.G. Tedeschi (Eds.), *Handbook of Posttraumatic Growth* (pp. 81-99). Mahwah, NJ: Erlbaum; Updegraff, J.A., & Taylor, S.E. (2000). From vulnerability to growth: Positive and negative effects of stressful life events. In J. Harvey & E. Miller (Eds.), *Loss and Trauma: General and Close Relationship Perspectives* (pp. 3-28). Philadelphia, PA: Brunner-Routledge.

277. Ibid.

278. Ibid.

279. Ibid.

280. Ibid.

281. Ibid.

282. Morrow-Howell, N., *et al.* (2006). Older adults in service to society. Center for Social Development, CSD Research Report 06-05. Retrieved from: http://csd.wustl.edu/Publications/Documents/RP06-05.pdf.

283. See for example: Isen, A.M., & Daubman, K.A. (1984). The influence of affect on categorization. *Journal of Personality and Social Psychology*, 47, 1206-1217; Isen, A., Daubman, K., & Nowicki, G. (1987). Positive affect facilitates creative problem solving. *Journal of Personality and Social Psychology*, 52(6), 1122-1131.

284. For more information see my book, Doppelt, B. (2012). *From Me to We: The Five Transformational Commitments Required to Rescue the Planet, Your Organization, and Your Life*. Sheffield, U.K.: Greenleaf Publishing.

285. Jacobson. G.R., Ritter, D.P., & Mueller, L. (1977). Purpose in life and personal values among adult alcoholics. *Journal of Clinical Psychology*, 33(1), 314-316; Wong, P. (1998). Meaning-centered counseling. In P.T.P. Wong, & P. Fry (Eds.), *The Human Quest For Meaning: A Handbook of Psychological Research and Clinical Applications*. Mahwah, NJ: Lawrence Erlbaum Associates.

286. Musick, M.A., & Wilson, J. (2003). Volunteering and depression: The role of psychological and social resources in different age groups. *Social Science and Medicine*, 56, 259-269.

287. Janoff-Bulman, R. (1992). *Shattered Assumptions: Toward a New Psychology of Trauma*. New York, NY: The Free Press, pp. 6-12.

288. Van der Kolk, B.A. (1989). The compulsion to repeat the trauma: Re-enactment, revictimization, and masochism. *Psychiatric Clinics of North America*, 12(2), 389-411.

289. This scenario is a slight adaptation of the situation many people experienced in New Orleans before, during, and after Hurricane Katrina.

290. This event occurred in 2014 although Jenny's name has been changed.

291. This section is adapted from Stephen Joseph's work. Joseph, S. (2011). *What Doesn't Kill Us: The New Psychology of Posttraumatic Growth*. New York, NY: Basic Books, pp. 155-156. The American Psychological Association has also described the value of using metaphors for people dealing with serious trauma: http://www.apa.org/monitor/dec06/ethics.aspx.

292. This information is from The Mayo Clinic. (No date). *Stress Relief from Laughter? It's No Joke*. Retrieved from: http://www.mayoclinic.org/healthy-living/stress-management/in-depth/stress-relief/art-20044456.

293. Strack, F., *et al.* (1998). Inhibiting and facilitating conditions of the human smile: A non-obtrusive test of the facial feedback hypothesis. *Journal of Personality and Social Psychology*. 54(5), 768-777.

294. Knowles, R., *et al.* (2010). Family resilience and resiliency following Hurricane Katrina. In R.P. Kilmer, V. Gil-Rivas, R.G. Tedeschi, & L.G. Calhoun (Eds.), *Meeting the Needs of Children, Families, and Communities Post-Disaster: Lessons Learned from Hurricane Katrina and Its Aftermath* (pp. 97-115). Washington, D.C.: American Psychological Association.

Chapter 8: Tap into the core values you want to live by in the midst of adversity

295. This event occurred in 2015, though Shana's name has been changed.

296. Adapted from Harris, R. (2012). *The Reality Slap: Finding Peace and Fulfillment When Life Hurts*. Oakland, CA: New Harbinger Publications, p. 108.

297. More information on how to use a Paired Comparison Analysis can be found here: https://www.mindtools.com/pages/article/newTED_02.htm.

298. Adapted from Harris, R. (2012). *The Reality Slap: Finding Peace and Fulfillment When Life Hurts*. Oakland, CA: New Harbinger Publications, p. 108.

299. Southwick, S.M., & Charney, D.S. (2012). *Resilience: The Science of Mastering Life's Greatest Challenges*. Cambridge, U.K.: Cambridge University Press, p. 76.

300. Southwick, S.M., & Charney, D.S. (2012). *Resilience: The Science of Mastering Life's Greatest Challenges*. Cambridge, U.K.: Cambridge University Press, p. 79.

301. This event occurred in 2014, but Fred's name has been changed.

302. Wood, A.M., *et al.* (2010). Gratitude and well-being: A review and theoretical integration. *Clinical Psychology Review*, 30(7), 890-905; Emmons, R.A., & McCullough, M.E. (2003). Counting blessings versus burdens: An experimental investigation of gratitude and subjective well-being in daily life. *Journal of Personality and Social Psychology*, 84(2), 377-389.

303. Wood, A.M., *et al.* (2007). Coping style as a psychological resource of grateful people. *Journal of Social and Clinical Psychology*, 26, 1076-1093.

304. Williams, L. (2014). The science of saying thanks. *Emotion News*. Retrieved from: http://emotionnews.org/gratitude.

305. Emmons. R. (2007). *Thanks!: How the New Science of Gratitude Can Make You Happier*. Boston, MA: Houghton Mifflin.

306. Ibid.

307. The video can be found here: http://www.mindfulness.ie/resources/video/selma-baraz-mother-of-author-james-baraz-discusses-her-son.

308. For information about the James Baraz Awakening Joy course go to: https://www.awakeningjoy.info.

309. Baraz, J., & Alexander, S. (2010). *Awakening Joy: 10 Steps to Happiness*. New York, NY: Bantam Books.

310. Politico Magazine. (No date). 19: Tom Steyer. Retrieved from: http://www.politico.com/magazine/politico50/2014/tom-steyer-19.html#.VdYo-ixVhBc.

Chapter 9: Harvest hope for new possibilities by making choices that increase personal, social, and environmental wellbeing

311. The information included in this story was obtained from: Hemstreet, M. (2015, August 11). Telephone interview; information on the Opportunity Threads website: http://opportunitythreads.com, and an article about Opportunity Threads in *YES Magazine*: Garza, C. (2015, July). A North Carolina textile co-op gives immigrant workers a stake in the business. *YES Magazine*. Retrieved from: http://www.yesmagazine.org/new-economy/north-carolina-textile-co-op-immigrant-workers-opportunity-threads-morganton.

312. Garza, C. (2015, July). A North Carolina textile co-op gives immigrant workers a stake in the business. *YES Magazine*. Retrieved from: http://www.yesmagazine.org/new-economy/north-carolina-textile-co-op-immigrant-workers-opportunity-threads-morganton.

313. The term Harvest Hope is adapted from Stephen Joseph's book, Joseph, S. (2011). *What Doesn't Kill Us: The New Psychology of Posttraumatic Growth*. New York, NY: Basic Books, p. 175.

314. Hi, S., *et al.* (2011). The roles of hope and optimism on posttraumatic growth in oral cavity cancer patients. *Oral Oncology*, 47(2), 121-124.

315. See for example: Conversano, C., *et al.* (2010). Optimism and its impact on mental and physical well-being. *Clinical Practice & Epidemiology Mental Health*, 6, 25-29; Fredrickson, B.L., *et al.* (2000). The undoing effect of positive emotions. *Motivation and Emotion*, 24(4), 237-258.

316. Joseph, S. (2011). *What Doesn't Kill Us: The New Psychology of Posttraumatic Growth*. New York, NY: Basic Books.
317. Snyder, C.R., *et al.* (2002). Hope theory: A member of the positive psychology family. In C.R. Snyder, & S.J. Lopez (Eds.), *The Handbook of Positive Psychology* (pp. 257-276). New York, NY: Oxford University Press.
318. U.S. Environmental Protection Agency (2010, June 25). *EcoLogical Blog*. Retrieved on December 2014 from: http://blog.epa.gov/blog/category/studentsforclimateaction.
319. May, R. (1979). *Love and Will*. New York, NY: Norton; May, R. (1967). *Psychology and the Human Dilemma*. New York, NY: D. Van Nostrand.
320. Snyder, C. (2002). Hope theory: Rainbows in the mind. *Psychological Inquiry*. 13(4), 249-275.
321. Ibid.
322. This section is adapted from Khoshaba, D.M., & Maddi, S.R. (2001). *HardiTraining*. Irvine, CA: Hardiness Institute.
323. The Miracle Question is a tool developed for Solutions Focused Brief Therapy in the 1980s by Steve de Shazer and Insoo Kim Berg. One of the best books on the subject was published by Haworth Press: De Shazer, S., & Dolan, Y. (2007). *More than Miracles: the State of the Art of Solution-Focused Brief Therapy*. New York, NY: Haworth Press.
324. Sahakian, W.S. (1985). Viktor Frankl's meaning for psychology. *International Forum for Logotherapy*, 8(1), 11-16.
325. This event occurred in 2015, though Mary's name has been changed.
326. For further information, see: http://www.1millionwomen.com.au.
327. Earth911. (2009). How kids are saving the planet. Retrieved from: http://earth911.com/news/2010/04/19/how-kids-are-saving-the-planet.
328. The conference was held in Vienna, Austria, in November 2012.

Part 4: Building Transformational Resilience in organizations and communities

Chapter 10: Building Transformational Resilience in organizations

329. This is a true story. However, the name of the superintendent and school district has been changed to avoid embarrassing members of the district.
330. Lorenz, D. (2013). The diversity of resilience: Contributions from the social science perspective. *Natural Hazards*, 67(1), 7-24. DOI: 10.1007/s11069-010-9654-y.
331. Blanding, M. (2015, January 26). Workplace stress responsible for up to $190b in annual U.S. healthcare costs. *Forbes*. Retrieved from: http://www.forbes.com/sites/hbsworkingknowledge/2015/01/26/workplace-stress-responsible-for-up-to-190-billion-in-annual-u-s-heathcare-costs.
332. Towers Watson (2012). Global workforce study. Engagement at risk: driving strong performance in a volatile global environment. Retrieved from: https://www.towerswatson.com/Insights/IC-Types/Survey-Research-Results/2012/07/2012-Towers-Watson-Global-Workforce-Study.
333. Spangler, N.W., *et al.* (2012). Employer perceptions of stress and resilience intervention. *Journal of Occupational Environmental Medicine*, 54(11), 1421-1429.
334. Lee, D. (2008). Why you will need a resilient workforce in today's economy. Human-Nature@Work. Retrieved from: http://humannatureatwork.com/wp-content/uploads/2014/06/Why-You-Need-to-Have-a-Resilient-Workforce.pdf.

335. Ernst & Young (2010). Action amid uncertainty: The business response to climate change. Retrieved from: http://www.ey.com/Publication/vwLUAssets/Action_amid_uncertainty_-_The_business_response_to_climate_change/$FILE/EY_Action_amid_uncertainty_-_The_business_response_to_climate_change.pdf.

336. Carbon Disclosure Project (2012, March). Insights into climate change adaptation by UK companies. Retrieved from: https://www.cdp.net/CDPResults/insights-into-climate-change-adaptation-by-uk-companies.pdf.

337. Center for Climate and Energy Solutions (2013). Weathering the storm: Building business resilience to climate change. Retrieved from: http://www.c2es.org/publications/weathering-storm-building-business-resilience-climate-change.

338. The Carbon Trust (2015, June). Titans or titanics: Understanding the business response to climate change and resource scarcity. Retrieved from: https://www.carbontrust.com/media/661891/titans-or-titanics-business-response-climate-change-resource-scarcity.pdf.

339. The Institute for Business & Home Safety (2005). Open for business: A disaster planning toolkit for the small to mid-sized business owner. Retrieved from: http://www.ready.gov/sites/default/files/documents/files/Open%20for%20Business%20-%20small%20to%20meduim%20size%20busineses.pdf.

340. The Hartford (2013). Extreme weather and your business. Retrieved from: http://www.thehartford.com/smallcommercial/dashboard.html.

341. Ibid.

342. Congressional Research Service (2015, February). Climate change adaptation by federal agencies: An analysis of plans and issues for congress. Retrieved from: https://www.fas.org/sgp/crs/misc/R43915.pdf.

343. U.K. Government (No date). Climate change adaptation. Retrieved from: https://www.gov.uk/government/policies/climate-change-adaptation.

344. In Transformational Resilience workshops offered by my program we use the term "Safe Haven" to describe organizations and communities that prioritize building personal and psycho-social-spiritual resilience.

345. Kantor, J., & Streotfeld, D. (2015, August 15). Inside Amazon: Wrestling big ideas in a bruising workplace. *The New York Times, Business Day*. Retrieved from: http://www.nytimes.com/2015/08/16/technology/inside-amazon-wrestling-big-ideas-in-a-bruising-workplace.html.

346. Green, J. (2015, August 22). ACLU reaches out to Amazon employees. *The Register Guard*.

347. Greenpeace. (2014, April). *Clicking Clean: How Companies Are Creating the Green Internet*. Retrieved from: http://www.greenpeace.org/usa/wp-content/uploads/legacy/Global/usa/planet3/PDFs/clickingclean.pdf.

348. Fahrenthold, D. (2014, May 30). Breaking points: When government falls apart. *The Washington Post*. Retrieved from: http://www.washingtonpost.com/sf/national/2014/05/30/how-the-va-developed-its-culture-of-coverups.

349. U.S. House Committee on Veterans Affairs. Witness testimony of Mr. William Schoenhard, Hearing on 3/14/2013. Waiting for Care: Examining Patient Wait Time at VA. Retrieved from: https://veterans.house.gov/witness-testimony/mr-william-schoenhard-fache.

350. Livingston, S. (June, 2015). Employers turn to resilience building to cut worker stress. *Business Insurance*. Retrieved from: http://www.businessinsurance.com/article/20150607/NEWS03/306079981/employers-turn-to-resilience-building-programs-to-cut-worker-stress.

351. Information provided in this example was obtained from the work of: Freeman, S., *et al.* (2003). *Organizational Resilience and Moral Purpose: Sandler O'Neill &*

Partners, L.P. In the Aftermath of the September 11, 2001 World Trade Center Attack. Madison: Academy of Management; and a video made about the company's experience shown on the TV show 60 minutes: Gorsuch, J. (2011). Sandler O'Neill 9/11 60 Minutes September 2002. Retrieved from: https://www.youtube.com/watch?v=QpCzszOnYwI.

352. Ibid.

353. Ibid.

354. Ibid.

355. Ibid.

356. Ibid.

357. Ibid.

358. Ibid.

359. The following discussion is adapted from Part 3 in my book on organizational change: Doppelt, B. (2003). *Leading Change toward Sustainability.* Sheffield, U.K.: Greenleaf Publishing.

360. This section is adapted from Part 2 in my book on organizational change: Doppelt, B. (2003). *Leading Change toward Sustainability.* Sheffield, U.K.: Greenleaf Publishing.

361. Adapted from Kim, D. (1999). *Introduction to Systems Thinking.* Waltham, MA: Pegasus Communications; Anderson, V., & Johnson, L. (1997). *Systems Thinking Basics: From Concepts to Casual Loops.* Waltham, MA: Pegasus Communications.

362. Ackoff, R. (1999). *Recreating the Corporation: A Design of Organizations for the 21st Century.* Oxford: Oxford University Press, p. 33.

363. Wilkins, A., & Ouchi, W. (1983). Efficient cultures: Exploring the relationships between culture and organizational performance. *Administrative Science Quarterly,* 28, 468-481.

364. This is a variation of the "Wheel of Change Toward Sustainability" that I developed more than 15 years ago out of my work on organizational transformation. It was first published in Doppelt, B. (2003). *Leading Change Toward Sustainability.* Sheffield, U.K.: Greenleaf Publishing.

365. See, for example, the work of Donnella Meadows, Russell Ackoff, Marshall Goldsmith, John Kotter, Peter Senge, Roger Conners and Tom Smith, and many others.

366. These leverage points are adapted from my earlier work that resulted from a long-term assessment of approaches to organizational change. See Doppelt, B. (2003), *Leading Change toward Resilience: A Change Management Guide for Business, Government, and Civil Society.* Sheffield, U.K.: Greenleaf Publishing.

367. This leverage point was extremely well described by Donnella Meadows in her article in Whole Earth and other writings. It is also a key tenant of John Kotter's work on leadership and change.

368. Meadows stated that the second greatest leverage point for change is to change the goals of a system. I find, however, that it is not possible to make a permanent and meaningful shift in goals unless new people with fresh ideas and all of the key power brokers are involved in the decision-making process. For this reason, I believe that the second greatest lever for change is to involve the right people—i.e., rearranging the parts of the system.

369. Ibid.

370. Meadows stated that the fourth greatest leverage point for change is to change the rules of the system. By this, she meant the incentives, punishments, constraints, etc. However, because the issue is so new, a good deal of time and experience is needed before an organization can identify thinking and behaviors that are consistent . with good sustainability practices. Therefore, I find that it is not possible to change

policies and procedures at this stage. Instead, at this stage the rules that govern how the parts of an organization interact to achieve their goals must be changed.

371. Information in this context focuses on communication and should not be confused with the information generated through improved feedback systems.

372. Meadows said positive and negative feedback loops are key levers of change. In the organizational context, I find that improving feedback systems can generate both types of feedback.

373. Meadows talks about changing the numbers (by which she means subsidies, taxes, standards) as the last of the greatest leverage points for change. In the organizational context related to sustainability, changing the numbers and changing the rules are very similar and usually occur only after each of the other interventions have been implemented.

374. This is a variation of the "Wheel of Change Toward Sustainability" that I developed out of my work on organizational transformation first published in Doppelt, B. (2003). *Leading Change toward Sustainability*. Sheffield, UK.: Greenleaf Publishing.

375. This case study uses information found in: U.S. Department of Veterans Affairs (2014, June). Climate change adaptation plan. Retrieved from: http://www.green. va.gov/docs/2014VAccap.pdf.

376. U.S. Department of Veterans Affairs (No date). VA mission, vision, core values and goals. Retrieved from: http://www.va.gov/about_va/mission.asp.

377. Ibid.

378. For more information on the Sanctuary Model, see: http://sanctuaryweb.com/ TheSanctuaryModel.aspx.

Chapter 11: Building Transformational Resilience in communities

379. Much of the details in this case study and some of the quotes were obtained from the Philadelphia Health Federation Community Resilience Cookbook found at: http://www.healthfederation.org/portfolio/community-resilience-cookbook.

380. Personal communication, August 10, 2015.

381. The Pacific Institute and Oakland Climate Action Coalition (2012). *Community-Based Climate Adaptation Planning: Case Study of Oakland, California*. Retrieved from: http://pacinst.org/publication/community-based-climate-adaptation -planning-oakland-case-study.

382. These quotes were received in the post-workshop evaluations. The names of the individuals are omitted to maintain their privacy.

383. Inside Climate News (2013, June). 6 of the world's most extensive climate adaptation plans. Retrieved from: http://insideclimatenews.org/news/20130620/6-worlds -most-extensive-climate-adaptation-plans.

384. The White House. (2014, May 6). Fact sheet: What climate change means for Missouri and the Midwest. Retrieved from: https://www.whitehouse.gov/sites/default/ files/microsites/ostp/MISSOURI_NCA_2014.pdf.

385. Janoff-Bulman, R. (1992). *Shattered Assumptions: Toward a New Psychology of Trauma*. New York, NY: The Free Press, pp. 153-154.

386. Ibid.

387. Schoch-Spana, M., *et al.* (2008). Community resilience roundtable on the implementation of Homeland Security Presidential Directive 21 (HSPD-21). *Biosecurity and Bioterrorism*, 6, 269-278.

388. The terms bonding, bridging, and linking social support networks are borrowed from Aldrich, D. (2012). *Building Resilience: Social Capital in Post-Disaster Recovery.* Chicago, IL: University of Chicago Press.

389. Aldrich, D. (2012). *Building Resilience: Social Capital in Post-Disaster Recovery.* Chicago, IL: University of Chicago Press, p. 131.

390. Aldrich, D. (2012). *Building Resilience: Social Capital in Post-Disaster Recovery.* Chicago, IL: University of Chicago Press.

391. Aldrich, D. (2012). *Building Resilience: Social Capital in Post-Disaster Recovery.* Chicago, IL: University of Chicago Press, p. 31.

392. Aldrich, D. (2012). *Building Resilience: Social Capital in Post-Disaster Recovery.* Chicago, IL: University of Chicago Press, p. 32.

393. Aldrich, D. (2012). *Building Resilience: Social Capital in Post-Disaster Recovery.* Chicago, IL: University of Chicago Press, p. 33.

394. Varshney, A. (2001). Ethnic conflict and civil society: India and beyond. *World Politics*, 53(3), 362-398.

395. Putnam, R. (1993). *Making Democracy Work: Civic Traditions in Modern Italy.* Princeton, NJ: Princeton University Press.

396. Aldrich, D. (2008). *Site Fights: Divisive Facilities and Civil Society in Japan and the West.* Ithaca, NY: Cornell University Press.

397. Aldrich, D. (2012). *Building Resilience: Social Capital in Post-Disaster Recovery.* Chicago, IL: University of Chicago Press.

398. See, for example: Boix, C., & Poster, D. (1998). Social capital: Explaining its origins and effects on government performance. *British Journal of Political Science*, 28(4), 686-693; Coleman, J. (1998). Social capital in the creation of human capital. *American Journal of Sociology*, 94(Supplement), 95-120; Winship, C., & Rosen, S. (1988). *Organizations and Institutions: Sociological and Economic Approaches to the Analysis of Social Structure.* Chicago, IL: University of Chicago Press; Lee, M., & Bartkowski, J. (2004). Love thy neighbor? Moral communities, civic engagement, and juvenile homicide in rural areas. *Social Forces*, 27, 741-766.

399. Aldrich, D. (2012). *Building Resilience: Social Capital in Post-Disaster Recovery.* Chicago, IL: University of Chicago Press, p. 38.

400. Aldrich, D. (2012). *Building Resilience: Social Capital in Post-Disaster Recovery.* Chicago, IL: University of Chicago Press, pp. 38-39.

401. Eisenman, D., *et al.* (2014). The Los Angeles County community disaster resilience project—A community-level, public health initiative to build community disaster resilience. *International Journal of Environmental Research and Public Health*, 11, 8475-8490.

402. Eisenman, D., *et al.* (2014). The Los Angeles County community disaster resilience project—A community-level, public health initiative to build community disaster resilience. *International Journal of Environmental Research and Public Health*, 11, 8475-8490.

403. Brune, N.E., & Bossert, T. (2009). Building social capital in post-conflict communities: Evidence from Nicaragua. *Social Science and Medicine*, 68, 885-893; Pronyk, P.M., *et al.* (2008). Can social capital be intentionally generated? A randomized trial from rural South Africa. *Social Science and Medicine*, 67, 1559-1570; as described in Aldrich, D.P., & Meyer, M. (2014). Social capital and social resilience. *American Behavioral Scientist.* DOI: 10.1177/0002764214550299.

404. See, for example: http://timebanks.org/what-is-timebanking.

405. The Center for the New American Dream. (2013). *What are community currencies and how do they work?* Retrieved from: https://www.newdream.org/blog/community-currencies.

406. Lasker, J. *et al.* (2011). Time banking and health: The role of community currency organization in enhancing well-being. *Health Promotion Practice*, 12, 102-115, as described in Aldrich, D.P., & Meyer, M. (2014). Social capital and social resilience. *American Behavioral Scientist*. DOI: 10.1177/0002764214550299.

407. Aldrich, D.P., & Meyer, M. (2014). Social capital and social resilience. *American Behavioral Scientist*. DOI: 10.1177/0002764214550299.

408. Aldrich, D.P., & Meyer, M. (2014). Social capital and social resilience. *American Behavioral Scientist*. DOI: 10.1177/0002764214550299.

409. The models I examined include: Carnegie UK Trust & Fiery Spirits Community of Practice. (2011). *Exploring Community Resilience in Times of Rapid Change*. Retrieved from: http://www.carnegieuktrust.org.uk/getattachment/75a9e0c4-8d75-4acb-afac-6b1cbd6f2c1e/Exploring-Community-Resilience.aspx; Los Angeles County Department of Public Health's Community Disaster Resilience Project (LACCDRP) as described in Eisenman, D., *et al.* (2014). The Los Angeles County Community Disaster Resilience Project: A community-level, public health initiative to build community disaster resilience. *International Journal of Environmental Research and Public Health*, 11, 8475-8490; Silove, D. (2013) The ADAPT model: a conceptual framework for mental health and psychosocial programming in post conflict settings. *Intervention: The Journal of Mental Health and Psychosocial Support in Conflict Affected Areas*, 11(3), 237-248. Retrieved from: http://journals.lww.com/interventionjnl/Fulltext/2013/11000/The_ADAPT_model___a_conceptual_framework_for.2.aspx; Transitions U.S. (2013, July). Overview of community resilience models. (July 2013). Retrieved from: http://thrivingresilience.org/wp-content/uploads/2012/08/Overview-of-Community-Resilience-Models-and-Toolkits.pdf; Kirmayer, M.D., *et al.* (2009). Community resilience: Models, metaphors and measures. (2009). *Journal de la santé autochtone*, November, 62-117; Resilience Research Centre (no date). *A Multidimensional Model of Resilience*. Retrieved from: http://resilienceresearch.org/about-the-rrc/our-approach/16-a-multidimensional-model-of-resilience.

410. This list is an adaptation of the principles of trauma-informed communities developed by Dr. Sandra Bloom and the Sanctuary Institute focused on trauma-informed systems of care. For more information see: http://www.thesanctuaryinstitute.org/about-us/the-sanctuary-model.

411. This case study was complied from information provided to me by Trudy Townsend, former coordinator of The Dalles initiative, direct quotes provided by Townsend in emails and phone conversations, and from information obtained about The Dalles efforts found on the Philadelphia Health Federation Community Resilience Cookbook found at: http://www.healthfederation.org/portfolio/community-resilience-cookbook.

412. Personal communication, August 11, 2015.

413. Ibid.

414. Ibid.

415. Ibid.

416. Lake, R. (2014, September 1). Study: Best cities to live in Oregon. CreditDonkey. Retrieved from: https://www.creditdonkey.com/live-oregon.html.

417. Oregon Climate Change Research Institute (No date). Climate of Oregon. Retrieved from: http://occri.net/climate-science/the-climate-of-the-pacific-northwest/climate-of-oregon.

418. Ibid.

419. Ibid.

420. Ibid.

421. Ibid.

422. Personal communication, August 11, 2015.

423. Personal communication, August 11, 2015.

424. Personal communication, August 10, 2015.

425. Ibid.

426. U.S. Environmental Protection Agency (2003). Integrated assessment of the climate change impacts on the Gulf Coast region. Retrieved from: http://downloads.globalchange.gov/nca/nca1/gulfcoast-complete.pdf.

427. The information was obtained through personal communications with Elaine Miller-Karas, who is a partner in my organization's Transformational Resilience Program and can be found on The Trauma Resource Institute website: http://traumaresourceinstitute.com. Elaine is also a founding sponsor of the International Transformational Resilience Coalition (ITRC).

428. Trauma Resource Institute. (No date). iChill. Retrieved from: http://traumaresourceinstitute.com/ichill-3.

429. The Mental Health Association of New York City. (No date). *iHelp: Sandy Stress Relief.* Retrieved from: http://ihelpcbt.com.

430. Sabina, U., *et al.* (2012). *A Short Guide to Gross National Happiness Index.* The Centre for Bhutan Studies. Retrieved from: http://www.grossnationalhappiness.com/wp-content/uploads/2012/04/Short-GNH-Index-edited.pdf.

431. Office of National Statistics. *Measuring What Matters.* Retrieved from: http://www.ons.gov.uk/ons/guide-method/user-guidance/well-being/index.html.

432. The Happiness Alliance. Retrieved from: http://www.happycounts.org/about.html.

Chapter 12: Closing thoughts on building universal capacity for Transformational Resilience

433. WETA Public Broadcasting. (2007). War production. Retrieved from: https://www.pbs.org/thewar/at_home_war_production.htm.

434. White, J.L., & Cones, J.J. III. (1999). *Black Man Emerging: Facing the Past and Seizing the Future in America.* New York, NY, Freeman.

435. Gunnestad, A. (2006). *Resilience in a Cross-Cultural Perspective: How Resilience is Generated in Different Cultures.* Journal of Intercultural Communication, 11.

436. Many of the points described below were adapted from the teaching methods described by the Mindfulness-Based Stress Reduction program developed by the University of Massachusetts Medical School, where I learned the skills and became an MBSR instructor. Through my work with different groups I have amended some of the key MBSR points and added new ones.

437. For more information on global overshoot see the Global Footprint Network. Website: http://www.footprintnetwork.org/en/index.php/GFN/page/earth_overshoot_day.

About the author

Bob Doppelt is Executive Director of The Resource Innovation Group (TRIG), a sustainability and global climate change education, research, and technical assistance organization affiliated with the Center for Sustainable Communities at Willamette University, U.S.A. He is also an adjunct professor in the Department of Planning, Public Policy, and Management at the University of Oregon. Trained as both a counseling psychologist and environmental scientist, Bob

has combined the two fields throughout his career. For over 30 years he has also practiced socially engaged Buddhism. He leads TRIG's Transformational Resilience Program and coordinates the International Transformational Resilience Coalition (ITRC). In 2015 he was named one of the world's "50 Most Talented Social Innovators" by the World CRS Congress.

Bob is the author of *From Me to We: The Transformative Five Commitments Required to Rescue the Planet, Your Organization, and Your Life* (Greenleaf Publishing, 2012); *The Power of Sustainable Thinking: How to Create a Positive Future for the Climate, the Planet and Your Life* (Earthscan Publishing, 2008), which in the summer of 2010 was deemed by *Audubon Magazine* to be one of the "eleven most important books on climate change"; and *Leading Change toward Sustainability: A Change Management Guide for Business, Government and Civil Society* (Greenleaf Publishing, 2003, 2010), which just six months after its release was deemed one of the "ten most important publications in sustainability" by a GlobeScan survey of international sustainability experts.

Index

Printed in the United States
by Baker & Taylor Publisher Services